D0074850

The Philosophy of Karl Popper

Karl Popper is one of the greatest and most influential philosophers of the twentieth century. Perhaps his greatest book, *The Logic of Scientific Discovery*, sets out his epistemology of critical rationalism, while his most famous book, *The Open Society and Its Enemies*, applies the principles of critical rationalism to social philosophy.

Herbert Keuth's book (first published in German in 2000) is a systematic exposition of Popper's philosophy covering, in Part I, the philosophy of science; in Part II, the social philosophy; and in Part III, the later metaphysics, in particular the theses proposed by Popper to solve the indeterminism/determinism and mind/body problems, and the famous idea of a third world of objective thought contents.

This book is more comprehensive than any current introduction to Popper. Owing to its perspicuous structure and lucid exposition, it could be used in courses in both the philosophy of science and the philosophy of social science.

Herbert Keuth is Professor of Philosophy of Science at Eberhard Karls Universität, Tübingen.

The Philosophy of Karl Popper

HERBERT KEUTH

Eberhard Karls Universität, Tübingen

PUBLISHED BY THE PRESS SYNDICATE OF THE UNIVERSITY OF CAMBRIDGE
The Pitt Building, Trumpington Street, Cambridge, United Kingdom

CAMBRIDGE UNIVERSITY PRESS
The Edinburgh Building, Cambridge CB2 2RU, UK
40 West 20th Street, New York, NY 10011-4211, USA
477 Williamstown Road, Port Melbourne, VIC 3207, Australia
Ruiz de Alarcón 13, 28014 Madrid, Spain
Dock House, The Waterfront, Cape Town 8001, South Africa

http://www.cambridge.org

Die Philosophie Karl Poppers © J.C.B. Mohr (Paul Siebeck) 2000
English translation © Herbert Keuth 2005

This book is in copyright. Subject to statutory exception
and to the provisions of relevant collective licensing agreements,
no reproduction of any part may take place without
the written permission of Cambridge University Press.

First published in German in 2000
English edition first published 2005

Printed in the United States of America

Typeface ITC New Baskerville 10/13 pt.   *System* LaTeX 2$_\varepsilon$ [TB]

A catalog record for this book is available from the British Library.

Library of Congress Cataloging in Publication data
Keuth, Herbert, 1940–
[Philosophie Karl Poppers. English]
The philosophy of Karl Popper / Herbert Keuth.
p.   cm.
Includes bibliographical references and indexes.
ISBN 0-521-83946-7 – ISBN 0-521-54830-6 (pbk.)
1. Popper, Karl Raimund, Sir, 1902–1994   I. Title.
B1649.P64K4813   2004
192 – dc22   2004045179

ISBN 0 521 83946 7 hardback
ISBN 0 521 54830 6 paperback

B1649
.P64
K4813
2005

0 54503549

To Marianne

Contents

Abbreviations

BJPS   *The British Journal for the Philosophy of Science*
CP   Peirce, *Collected Papers*
CPR   Kant, *Critique of Pure Reason*
EHU   Hume, *An Enquiry Concerning Human Understanding*
EPW   *Enzyklopädie Philosophie und Wissenschaftstheorie*
HWP   *Historisches Wörterbuch der Philosophie*
PI   Wittgenstein, *Philosophical Investigations*
PKP   Schilpp, *The Philosophy of Karl Popper*
Proleg.   Kant, *Prolegomena to Any Future Metaphysics That Will Be Able to Present Itself as a Science*

Works of Karl Popper

A   *Intellectual Autobiography*
CR   *Conjectures and Refutations*
EH   *Das Elend des Historizismus*
GPE   *Die beiden Grundprobleme der Erkenntnistheorie*
KBMP   *Knowledge and the Body-Mind Problem*
LdF   *Logik der Forschung*
LP   *Alles Leben ist Problemlösen*
LSD   *The Logic of Scientific Discovery*
OG   *Die offene Gesellschaft und ihre Feinde*
OK   *Objective Knowledge*
OS   *The Open Society and Its Enemies*
OU   *The Open Universe*
PH   *The Poverty of Historicism*

QTSP *Quantum Theory and the Schism in Physics*
RAS *Realism and the Aim of Science*
WP *A World of Propensities*

Preface

In 2000, the German version of the present book, *Die Philosophie Karl Poppers*, was published by Mohr Siebeck in Tübingen. I have tried to provide a translation that is as close to the original as possible. A few minor errors, mostly bibliographical, have been corrected, and summaries have been omitted.

In Chapter 7, "Verisimilitude," the original section 7.24, on attempts to rehabilitate Popper's comparative definition of verisimilitude, has been reduced to a single paragraph at the end of section 7.23, because in the meantime the concept of "relevant consequence," which was central in section 7.24, has been refined by its authors. In section 15.32, four paragraphs on Carnap's methodological solipsism have been reduced to a very short paragraph, both because they are not essential to my argument and because it proved too difficult to provide an adequate translation of certain (more or less) phenomenalistic statements into English. The bibliography now includes more English and fewer German titles.

Many of the texts from which I quoted in the German original have been translated into English. Wherever possible, I now quote from the English editions. Unfortunately, a number of texts, even Popper's *Die beiden Grundprobleme der Erkenntnistheorie*, are not (yet) available in English. Moreover, some of the translations were inaccessible to me. Thus I have had to provide some translations myself. Wherever I have considered the slightest misunderstanding possible, I have added "m.t." for "my translation." Where emphasis has been supplied, I have added "i.a." for "italic added."

I thank Mr. Thomas Piecha, who carefully looked through my translation and prepared the files for the diagrams.

Introduction

Karl Raimund Popper was born on 28 July 1902 in Vienna. He died on 17 September 1994 in London. His father, Simon Siegmund Carl Popper, a lawyer, was interested in philosophy and actively involved in social reform. When World War I ended in 1918, Karl left school and, as a guest student, began studying history, literature, psychology, philosophy, mathematics, and physics. He joined a leftist youth group and even considered himself a communist for a few months during the spring of 1919, but he soon took this to be an aberration. It was in part his criticism of Marxism that put Popper on the path to his masterpiece, *The Logic of Scientific Discovery*, and that early aroused his interest in the *methods of the social sciences*. (The biographical data are taken from Popper's *Intellectual Autobiography* [1974a] and from Victor Kraft's *The Vienna Circle* [1950/1953]. More details can be found in Malachi Hacohen's *Karl Popper – The Formative Years, 1902–1945* [2000].)

In 1922, Popper passed, as an external candidate, the exam called the Matura. Now he could enroll as a regular student at the University of Vienna. At the same time, he attended a teachers college. He also became a carpenter's apprentice and, for a year, studied church music at the conservatory of Vienna. In 1924, he passed his apprentices' final examination as a carpenter and graduated as a primary school teacher. Then he worked as a tutor in a county council care centre for socially endangered and disadvantaged children. From 1925 to 1927, he was a student at the Paedagogical Institute of Vienna and advocated school reform. In 1928, he completed his doctoral dissertation, "Zur Methodenfrage der Denkpsychologie" (On the Problem of Method in the Psychology

1

of Thinking), and passed his oral exams in philosophy (under Moritz Schlick) and psychology (under Karl Bühler).

I

Now Popper turned to more general questions of *methodology* and *epistemology*. Such questions are at the core of his philosophy, which he calls "*'critical rationalism'*" (OS, 229, i.a.), and they are the subject of Part I: The Philosophy of Science of the present book.

In the term "critical rationalism," the word "rationalism" is used in a broad sense; it is the opposite of "irrationalism," not of "empiricism." This kind of rationalism comprises empiricism and classical rationalism – as, for example, that of Descartes, which Popper calls "'intellectualism'" (OS II, 224ff.). Uncritical or comprehensive rationalism follows the principle "that any assumption which cannot be supported either by argument or by experience is to be discarded"; but this principle is inconsistent, "for since it cannot, in its turn, be supported by argument or by experience, it implies that it should itself be discarded" (230). Therefore, Popper replaces comprehensive rationalism with critical rationalism, which "recognizes the fact that the fundamental rationalist attitude results from an (at least tentative) act of faith – from faith in reason" (231). As the rationalist demand for the justification of all assumptions is untenable, Popper takes "rational discussion" to be "critical discussion in search of mistakes with the serious purpose of eliminating as many of these mistakes as we can, in order to get nearer to the truth" (CR, 229).

Acquainted with leading members of the Vienna Circle through his family, Popper critically examined theses that were being defended in the Vienna Circle and its milieu, in particular by Ludwig Wittgenstein. The Vienna Circle was a group of scientists which at that time played the leading part in "logical empiricism" or "neopositivism" (cf. Kraft 1950/1953).

At first, Popper wrote notes but did not publish them. Finally, when Herbert Feigl urged him to publish his ideas in the form of a book, a manuscript evolved, called "Die beiden Grundprobleme der Erkenntnistheorie" (The Two Fundamental Problems of Epistemology). He means the problems of induction and demarcation. Early in 1932, Popper completed the part that he intended to publish as the first volume. Several members of the Vienna Circle read the manuscript. In 1933, Moritz Schlick and Philipp Frank accepted it for publication in the series Schriften zur wissenschaftlichen Weltauffassung (Writings on the Scientific Conception of the World). But the publishing house Julius Springer in Vienna limited the size of the book to 240 pages. Therefore, Popper prepared another manuscript containing excerpts, this time from both volumes. As it was still too voluminous, Popper's uncle Walter Schiff condensed it to about half its size. This last excerpt appeared in December 1934 as *Logik der Forschung. Zur Erkenntnistheorie der modernen Naturwissenschaft* (literally: The Logic of Research: On the Epistemology of Modern Natural Science). The year of publication indicated in the book was 1935. The subtitle was omitted in all later editions. (For the sake of brevity, I will refer to the – first – English edition, which he called *The Logic of Scientific Discovery*, in the text as "*Logic*" and will cite it as "LSD." Accordingly, the abbreviations for the – second – German edition will be "*Logik*" and "LdF.") The manuscript of the first volume of the *Grundprobleme* still exists; the manuscript of a major part of the second volume has been lost. What was left was published only in 1979 by Troels Eggers Hansen. (Hacohen voices scepticism as to the existence of a second volume; 2000, 195ff.)

In a letter to the editor of the journal *Erkenntnis*, Popper sketched his basic ideas. The letter was published under the title "A Criterion of the Empirical Character of Theoretical Systems" and was reprinted as Appendix *I of the *Logic*. Here Popper weighs the two fundamental problems. "*Hume's problem of induction* – the question of the validity of natural laws" is but a preliminary question (LSD, 312; cf. section 1.1 of this book). As opposed to this, "the *problem of demarcation* (Kant's problem of the limits of scientific knowledge)" is the main problem (313; cf. section 1.2). Popper defines this as "the problem of finding a criterion by which we can distinguish between assertions (statements, systems of statements) which belong to the empirical sciences, and assertions which may be described as 'metaphysical'" (313).

Already in 1935 Rudolf Carnap counted Popper's *Logik* among the most important works in the field of the logic of science. Above all, he valued Popper's contribution to the debate on "protocol sentences," or the problem of the "empirical basis of science" (section 4.1, this volume). According to Popper's proposal, the observation statements that are used to test theories must be tested in their turn, and though they are accepted or rejected on the basis of sense perceptions, they do not refer to sense perceptions but to physical objects or events. There are connections between the problem of the empirical basis, on the one hand, and the problems of induction and demarcation, on the other hand, for in the last analysis all three problems concern the confrontation of statements with reality.

Today, Popper's *Logik* is counted among the most important works of the twentieth century in the philosophy of science. It contains the basic ideas of critical rationalism, which explain why all our "knowledge" of facts is fallible and why we learn, not from expectations that are fulfilled, but from expectations that fail: The progress of knowledge results from trial and the elimination of error. His reader *Conjectures and Refutations: The Growth of Scientific Knowledge* (1963) is a collection of articles elaborating these ideas.

In the thirties, conditions were not favourable for the *Logik* to have influence on a wide audience. True, Popper reports in his autobiography on its surprising success: "There were more reviews, in more languages, than there were twenty-five years later of *The Logic of Scientific Discovery*, and fuller reviews even in English" (A, 85). And Gilbert Ryle reports in his review of Popper's *The Open Society and Its Enemies* that "Popper was previously known as the author of an original work on the method of natural science, the 'Logik der Forschung'" (Ryle, 1947, 167). But in 1960, Warnock welcomes the translation of the *Logik* "for that influential book has been, in the twenty-five years since its publication in Vienna, often misrepresented and *too seldom read*" (99, i.a.). Popper himself states that until the publication of the English edition, "philosophers in England and America (with only a few exceptions, such as J. R. Weinberg) seem to have taken [him] for a logical positivist" (A, 69). And in 1959, when *The Logic of Scientific Discovery* was published, an anonymous reviewer in *The Times Literary Supplement* "described it as a 'remarkable book' and declared: 'One cannot help feeling that if it had been translated as soon as it was originally published philosophy in this country might have been saved some detours'" (Miller 1995, 121).

When *Logik der Forschung* appeared in December 1934, the (second) Vienna Circle, whose philosophy the *Logik* comments on, had already got into great difficulties. The Dollfuß government had (in February 1934) ordered the dissolution of the Verein Ernst Mach (Ernst Mach Society). This ended the political and enlightening activities of the Vienna Circle. But its influence on an international, philosophically interested public had only just begun.

II

Influenced by the developments of the thirties, Popper's political commitment again came to the fore. Now he increasingly turned to problems of social philosophy and political theory, the subject of Part II: The Social Philosophy of this book. In 1936, Popper read a paper on "The Poverty of Historicism" in a seminar led by the liberal economist Friedrich August von Hayek at the London School of Economics (PH, iv). Toward the end of 1936, he was offered a lectureship at Canterbury University College in Christchurch, New Zealand. Popper and his wife thereupon gave up their teaching positions. In January 1937 they left Vienna, and in March they reached New Zealand. In Christchurch, Popper planned to elaborate the paper, showing "how 'historicism' inspired both *Marxism* and *fascism*" (A, 90, i.a.).

Then the manuscript proliferated. Later it developed into the book *The Poverty of Historicism* (see Chapter 10). But as Colin Simkin reports, he considered this manuscript "too abstract for wide appreciation" (Simkin 1993, 185). Thus he began "a companion article to be called 'Marginal Notes on the History of Historicism'" (ibid.). He considered the two works his "war effort" (A, 91). The latter work – which, in a more advanced stage, he intended to call "'False Prophets: Plato – Hegel – Marx'" (A, 90) – later developed into the book *The Open Society and Its Enemies* (see Chapter 11). The book was completed in February 1943, but it proved difficult to find a publisher; it appeared only in 1945, in two volumes, in London. *The Poverty of Historicism* first appeared in 1944–45 as an article in three parts in the journal *Economica*, and only in 1957 did it appear in London and Boston in book form. The journal *Mind* had rejected the manuscript (A, 94). While *The Poverty of Historicism* primarily addresses theoretical and methodological concerns, the emphasis in *The Open Society* is on political and historical considerations – in particular, on the history of philosophy. *The Open Society* became Popper's best-known work by far.

In both works, Popper transferred the basic ideas of critical rationalism to political philosophy: "[O]ne of the best senses of '*reason*,'" he argues, is "*openness to criticism.*" Not only statements are criticizable, but also demands and value judgements. Therefore, Popper suggests "that the demand that we extend the critical attitude as far as possible might be called '*critical rationalism*'" (A, 92, i.a.).

According to critical rationalism, all "knowledge" of facts is fallible, and ethical knowledge is impossible. Hence, as we cannot know what we ought to do, we must decide what we want to do and take responsibility for our decisions (Chapter 9). As opposed to this, the *Critical Theory of Society*, which is based on Marx's political economics, claims to obtain ethical knowledge from the philosophy of history. In the sixties, the confrontation between these two positions led to the "positivist dispute in German sociology" (Chapter 12).

III

The sobre methodology of the *Logik* (1935) and the social philosophical engagement of *The Open Society* (1945) were followed by studies addressing mainly metaphysical problems, the subject of Part III: Metaphysics of this book. Though *epistemology* remains a central topic of Popper's work, the emphasis shifts from *methodological* to *ontological* considerations. While in the *Logik* he took objectivity to be *intersubjective testability*, he now takes the logical contents of theories to be objective in the sense of their *real existence* in what he calls a third world. For Popper, "'objectively true'" is a "third-world predicate" (OK, 158).

When, a quarter of a century after *Logik der Forschung*, the English edition *The Logic of Scientific Discovery* appears (1959), it contains twelve new appendices, mostly on the theory of probability. The subject of Appendix *x, "Universals, Dispositions and Natural or Physical Necessity," is epistemology. Under the head words "universals" and "dispositions," Popper elaborates ideas that he had already formulated in the first edition of the *Logik*. On the other hand, his statements on *natural necessity* are new (see Chapter 13).

His work on classical metaphysical problems begins with his article "Language and the Body-Mind Problem" (1953) and ends only with his book *Knowledge and the Body-Mind Problem* (1994). Beginning in 1966, he publishes on a *theory of three worlds* (see Chapter 15), which adds to the first, physical world not only – as is traditional in philosophy – a second, mental world but also a third world of objective thought contents. In connection with his theory of world 3, he sketches a *theory of evolution* (section 15.3) and critically examines the *determinism-indeterminism problem* (Chapter 14).

In order to save the ideas of freedom of will, responsibility, and creativity, Popper defends an ontological (metaphysical) indeterminism (Chapter 14), which may be necessary for this purpose but is not at all sufficient (section 14.7). Therefore, he also postulates the "openness" of the first, physical world toward the second, mental world and, in the end, toward the third world of objective thought contents.

PART I

THE PHILOSOPHY OF SCIENCE

1

The Two Fundamental Problems in the
Theory of Knowledge

In 1979, Karl Popper's book *Die beiden Grundprobleme der Erkenntnistheorie* (GPE) (The Two Fundamental Problems in the Theory of Knowledge) was published. It contains a collection of drafts and preliminary work dating from 1930 to 1933 to his masterpiece, *Logik der Forschung* (LdF), which appeared late in 1934. *Logik der Forschung* was published in English in 1959 as *The Logic of Scientific Discovery* (LSD). The title *Die beiden Grundprobleme der Erkenntnistheorie* alludes to *Die beiden Grundprobleme der Ethik* (The Two Fundamental Problems of Ethics) by Schopenhauer (1788–1860), who had written two prize essays, "On the Freedom of Will" and "On the Foundation of Morals," and whom Popper took as an example because of the clarity of his style.

According to Popper, the two fundamental problems in the theory of knowledge are the problem of induction and the problem of demarcation. The *problem of induction* is the "question whether the universal statements of the empirical sciences can be valid or can be justified" (GPE, 3), or, more precisely, the "question whether inductive inferences are justified, or under what conditions" (LSD, 28). The *problem of demarcation* is the question, "How can we decide in case of doubt whether a statement is scientific or 'only' metaphysical?" (GPE, 4), or, more precisely, the "problem of finding a criterion which would enable us to distinguish between the *empirical sciences* on the one hand, and *mathematics and logic* as well as '*metaphysical*' *systems* on the other" (LSD, 34, i.a.). Following Kant (1724–1804), Popper calls the problem of induction "Hume's problem," and he considers calling the problem of demarcation "Kant's problem" (34).

At first glance, the problem of induction does seem to be epistemologically important. After all, it is not insignificant which universal statements of the empirical sciences are accepted on the basis of particular experiences and whether they are rightly accepted. On the other hand, the problem of demarcation seems to be only a terminological question. Why should it be so important whether a certain statement is called "scientific"?

Popper reports that he already had "(in the winter of 1919–20) formulated and solved the problem of demarcation between science and non-science... [but] did not think it worth publishing" (OK, 1 n1). After he had also found (what he thought was) the solution to the problem of induction (around 1927), he discovered a connection between the two problems. This led him to think that the problem of demarcation is of utmost importance "for research work in the less highly developed sciences" (GPE, 4), and even that "the problems of both the classical and the modern theory of knowledge (from Hume via Kant to Russell and Whitehead) can be traced back to the problem of demarcation, that is, to the problem of finding the criterion of the empirical character of science" (LSD, 55 n3). But why is the problem of demarcation more fundamental than the problem of induction (LSD, 34)?

Since the time of Francis Bacon (1561–1626), the "problem of *drawing a line of demarcation*" between the statements of empirical science, on the one hand, and "pseudoscientific" and "metaphysical" statements or statements of pure logic or pure mathematics, on the other, has become increasingly important: "The most widely accepted view was that science was characterized by its *observational basis*, or by its *inductive method*, while pseudo-sciences and metaphysics were characterized by their *speculative method* or, as Bacon said, by the fact that they operated with '*mental anticipations*' – something very similar to hypotheses" (CR, 255).

David Hume (1711–1776) also considered it an empirical fact that universal hypotheses are, in everyday life and in science, formed on the basis of repeated observations of singular events, that is, that they are *found* by inductive generalization. On the other hand, he showed – as Sextus Empiricus had shown before him – why no inductive method can secure the truth of universal hypotheses. Induction does not *justify* hypotheses.

Popper agrees to the latter proposition but emphatically contradicts the former. He claims to have discovered that instead of a *method of generalization*, we use a "*method of trial and the elimination of error*": First we make conjectures, then we test them by sense experience and try to replace them by better conjectures. Thus the "place of the *problem of induction* is usurped by the *problem of the comparative goodness or badness of the rival conjectures* or theories that have been proposed" (PKP, 1016, i.a.). As opposed to this, the *problem of demarcation* remains, and in order to solve it, Popper first makes strict empirical *falsifiabilty*, later "practical" falsifiability or *testability* of a statement, the criterion of its *scientific character*.

1.1. THE PROBLEM OF INDUCTION

Our word "induction" is derived from the Latin word *inductio*. This is Cicero's (106–43) translation of the Greek word *epagoge* (*Topics*, X, 42), "induction," as *Aristotle* (384–322) called the "progress from particulars to universals" (*Topica*, I, XII, 105 a 13). Science takes this path in order to *prove* its statements. In order to avoid an infinite regress, it has to start from *unprovable* principles, the *archai*, which are at once true, unmediated, and prior to the conclusion. Knowledge of the *archai* is based on *epagoge*: "Sense-perception gives rise to memory,... and repeated memories... give rise to experience," which "is the universal when established as a whole" (*Posterior Analytics*, II, XIX, 100 a 6). Aristotle believed that the universal was really contained in the things and that *epagoge* was therefore immediately *evident* insight into the one in addition to the many. This seems both to *explain* the *formation* of (the most) universal statements and to *justify* their *acceptance* as true (cf. OK, 3).

But the sceptic *Sextus Empiricus* (ca. 200–250) criticized the idea of a reliable "progress from particulars to universals." Until today, his argument has not needed any essential improvement. It says: "[W]hen they propose to establish the universal from the particulars by means of induction, they will effect this by a review either of all or of some of the particular instances. But if they review some, the induction will be insecure, since some of the particulars omitted in the induction may contravene the universal; while if they are to review all, they will be toiling at the impossible, since the particulars are infinite and indefinite" (*Outlines of Pyrrhonism*, II, xv, 204). Hence induction *cannot justify* the acceptance of universal statements as true.

For this reason, *Hume* distinguishes between the *genesis* of an expectation or hypothesis and its *validity*. In the context of his discussion of causality (the "Idea of necessary Connexion"), he distinguishes between a logical and an empirical problem. Popper proceeds from this distinction. In Popper's words, Hume's *logical problem* is:

H_L: Are we justified in reasoning from (repeated) instances of which we have experience to other instances (conclusions) of which we have no experience? (OK, 4)

Hume answers: "No, however great the number of repetitions." And Hume's *psychological* (empirical) *problem* is:

H_P: Why, nevertheless, do all reasonable people expect, and *believe*, that instances of which they have no experience will conform to those of which they have experience? (OK, 4)

Hume answers: "Because of 'custom or habit,'" that is, because we are conditioned by repetition and the association of ideas. Without this mechanism, he says, we could hardly survive. As opposed to this, *Popper* believes that assumptions about future events, let alone universal hypotheses, *cannot even be found inductively*. He writes: "Induction simply does not exist, and the opposite view is a straightforward mistake" (PKP, 1015; cf. OK, 7).

1.11. Hume's Logical Problem

We subdivide "Hume's logical problem" into the problem of logical inference (1.111) and a methodological problem (1.112) to which there is a logical answer. And instead of talking about the inference to *future instances*, we speak, as Popper does (OK, 9), of the inference to *universal laws*:

H_{L_1}: Can universal laws be *proved* on the basis of true observation statements? In other words: Can a principle of induction be an *analytic* statement? (cf. LSD, 28)

H_{L_2}: Can universal laws be judged true on the basis of true observation statements in a way that *excludes errors with certainty* (even though not on logical but) *on factual grounds*? In other words: Can we *know for certain* that there is a *true synthetic principle of induction*?

Both are aspects of the problem of whether *certain knowledge* represented in universal statements (or in the principles of induction justifying them) is possible.

1.111. We found the correct answer to the question H_{L_1} – "Can universal laws be proved on the basis of true observation statements?" – already in Sextus. He also explained correctly why the answer must be no. Let us now apply his answer to a well-known example: Suppose we want to infer from the observation of *some* white swans that *all* swans are white. As long as we have not examined all swans, the truth of the universal statement is uncertain, because there may still be swans that are not white. But it is impossible to examine all of them, because the search for them could never end either in space or in time. Is there anything more to say?

Now, Sextus does not content himself with such examples; rather, like Aristotle, he speaks of "the universal" and "the particulars." Doesn't this imply that "*the universal*" and "*the particulars*" exist? In order to avoid such ontological assumptions, logical empiricists prefer to speak of *universal statements* and *particular statements*. Rather than the "material mode of speech," they choose the "formal mode of speech." Popper also replaces "Hume's '*instances of which we have experience*' by '*test statements*'" (OK, 7, i.a.).

Accordingly, question H_{L_1} has been worded in the formal mode of speech; and consequently, the answer must read: "It would be possible to *prove* universal laws on the basis of true observation statements, if, and only if, the laws could be *derived* from the observation statements" (cf. OK, 8f.). For logical derivation, and that alone, provides the "transfer of truth" from the premises to the conclusions. But no finite number of singular statements – for example, "Antony is a swan and he is *white*" [$Sa \wedge Wa$], "Bertha is a swan and she is white" [$Sb \wedge Wb$], and so on – *implies* a universal statement such as "All swans are white" [$(x)(Sx \rightarrow Wx)$]. Hence the *proof* we are looking for is *impossible*. This is uncontested, and with that the question H_{L_1} is answered. *The problem of logical inference from singular observation statements to universal laws is unsolvable.*

Why does the *universal statement* "All swans are white" not follow even from an arbitrary though finite number of singular statements such as "Antony is a swan and he is white"? The universal statement says more than all of the singular statements together; it has a greater logical content, for it refers to an *open* class of instances. Popper therefore calls it " '*strictly universal*' " (LSD, 62). This universal statement implies as well that all swans that have *not yet been observed* are white. As opposed to this, a *singular observation statement* says only that a particular swan is white; and hence the *conjunction* of all observation statements that have up to a given time been formulated asserts only that all swans *that have up to this time been observed* are white. But their number is always *limited*. Therefore, Popper calls the statement "All swans that have up to now been observed are white" " '*numerically universal*' " (62). As there are *no content-increasing inferences* in logic or mathematics – for instance, from numerically universal to strictly universal statements – *a principle of induction cannot be an analytic statement but must be a synthetic statement* (LSD, 28).

In the introduction to his *Critique of Pure Reason,* Kant had written: "Experience never gives its judgments true or strict but only assumed and *comparative universality* (through induction), so properly it must be said: as far as we have yet perceived, there is no exception to this or that rule" (CPR, B 3f., i.a.). But he considers "*strict universality,*" to which "no exception at all is allowed to be possible," a property only of those statements that are "valid absolutely *a priori*" (B 4, i.a.). He does not distinguish between the logical content (strictly universal) and the validity (a priori) of a statement.

As the *logical problem of induction H_L* is so important to epistemology, we add some formal considerations by way of explanation. These are preceded by an asterisk (*) and followed by a double asterisk (**). Readers who are pressed for time or who are versed in logic may omit them. But they help to draw more precise distinctions, first between the logical problem H_L and the psychological, hence empirical problem H_P, as well as between the problem of logical inference H_{L1} and the methodological problem H_{L2}; and later between the logical problem H_L and the *problem of the confirmation of hypotheses,* for even in the context of confirmation some authors speak of a "*logical view of induction*" (cf. Schurz 1998, 31ff.; section 5.61, this volume). Finally, they show that the logical problem of induction H_L is a special case of a more general problem.

* Let us return to the wording of the problem of logical inference H_{L1}. Why is the question "Can universal laws (or hypotheses) be *proved* on the basis of true observation statements?" equivalent to the question "Can a *principle of induction* be an *analytic* statement?"? We proceed step by step, examining first of all the inference from statements about the past to statements about the future.

Let *Fa, Fb,* and so on be statements that on the basis of past or present observations attribute the property *F* to the objects *a, b, . . . , m*; but let us assume that *n* has not yet been tested for the property *F*. Now the following holds:

If, and only if, the statement "If *Fa* and *Fb* and . . . and *Fm,* then *Fn*" [$Fa \wedge Fb \wedge \ldots \wedge Fm \to Fn$] is *analytic,* that is, true for purely logical reasons, there is a *valid inference* from the statements *Fa, Fb, . . . , Fm* to the statement *Fn* [does $Fa \wedge Fb \wedge \ldots \wedge Fm \Rightarrow Fn$ hold].

For, if $Fa \wedge Fb \wedge \ldots \wedge Fm \to Fn$ were *analytic,* then *Fn* could not be false, should the statements *Fa, Fb, . . . , Fm* all be true. Therefore, a logical *inference* from $Fa \wedge Fb \wedge \ldots \wedge Fm$ to Fn would also provide this "transfer of truth," and this inference would furnish the *proof* we are looking for.

But even if the statements $Fa, Fb, \ldots, Fm$ should all be true, Fn may still be false, and in this case the if-then statement $Fa \wedge Fb \wedge \ldots \wedge Fm \rightarrow Fn$ would also be false. Hence it is *not analytic*, because *counterexamples are conceivable*. (In finite model languages we may even test by means of truth tables whether it is a *tautology*, and the – negative – result may be transferred to the infinite natural languages.) Hence *there is no logical inference from past experiences to future experiences*.

The same holds correspondingly for the statement "If Fa and Fb and ... and Fm, then *all* things are F" $[Fa \wedge Fb \wedge \ldots \wedge Fm \rightarrow (x)Fx]$. Therefore, even a very specific "*principle of induction*" such as "If the swans a, $b, \ldots$, m are white, then all swans are white" $[Sa \wedge Wa \wedge Sb \wedge Wb \wedge \ldots \wedge Sm \wedge Wm \rightarrow (x)(Sx \rightarrow Wx)]$ would *not* be *analytic*. Hence *there is no logical inference from past experiences to universal laws*.

We would expect a principle of induction to permit inferences not only to one specific universal hypothesis but to all such hypotheses, or at least to all hypotheses of a specific kind. In this case, what we said about the *hypothesis* "All swans are white" holds for *all* (of those) hypotheses. Consequently, what we said about the very specific *principle of induction* "If the swans a, $b, \ldots$, m are white, then all swans are white" holds as well of *any* more general principle of induction. **

It is a characteristic of all deductive logics that *the conclusion of a valid inference cannot have a greater logical content than the conjunction of its premises*. This holds equally for arguments involving only *declarative* sentences and for arguments involving (also) *prescriptive* or *evaluative* sentences. Hence it also relates to *ethics*. "Hume's Law" states that no "ought" can be deduced from an "is." The reason for this is quite simple: Declarative sentences imply neither prescriptive sentences nor value judgements, because the latter express something that the former do not express. The attempt to deduce an "ought" from an "is" is called the "naturalistic fallacy." Natural law theories are based on this fallacy. The same holds, correspondingly, for the more modern "cognitive" ethics that have been proposed by language philosophers. (A "cognitive" ethics not only *proposes* moral norms or value judgements but also claims that they can be *known* to be true or right. Some authors prefer to call their postulates "reasonable" rather than "right." Nevertheless, they claim that their postulates do not merely express their personal opinions but are universally binding.) We shall return to the "dualism of facts and standards" (cf. Chapters 9 and 12).

1.112. It is more difficult to answer the question H_{L2}, "Can we know for certain that there is a true *synthetic* principle of induction?" Therefore, we divide H_{L2} into two parts: "Can we know this *a priori?*" (1.112.1) and "Can we know this *a posteriori?*" (1.112.2)

        1.112.1. Empiricism rules out synthetic statements a priori (statements whose truth can be known for certain and independently of experience). But transcendental philosophers object that empiricists thus abandon a path to knowledge that Kant had opened up. It is true that Kant rejects the inference "from something to everything" (*Logik*, A 195n), but according to Popper, he took "the principle of induction (which he formulated as the 'principle of universal causation') to be '*a priori* valid'" (LSD, 29; cf. section 1.121). In order to test Kant's thesis, let us perform a thought experiment. Let the transcendental philosopher propose a *synthetic principle of induction* that – being a statement a priori – is "thought along with its *necessity*" (CPR, B 3, i.a.). The result of our thought experiment will be decisive not only for the problem of induction but also for the significance of any transcendental argument for empirical science.

    Against the transcendental philosopher's proposal, the empiricist will raise the following objection: If the principle of induction implies the truth of an empirical hypothesis, and if this hypothesis fails later on because a prediction is not fulfilled, then for logical reasons the principle itself fails. Though it had been considered a priori ("*absolutely* independently of all experience," CPR, B3; or as "pure knowledge by reason," Proleg. § 5) *true*, it turned out a posteriori ("drawn from experience," Proleg. § 5) to be *false*. In other words: A statement cannot be known a priori to be (necessarily) true, if it could be refuted a posteriori. Hence *there can be no a priori synthetic principle of induction* that can prove empirical hypotheses. All statements proved by an a priori principle would have to be a priori true and not, like empirical hypotheses, at best a posteriori true. (If we take into account that induction involves not only a principle of induction but also observation statements, the failure of an induced hypothesis refutes the principle only if the observation statements are true. But this makes no fundamental difference.)

    The empiricist can also formulate his objection in a different way. The assumption that a hypothesis about the empirical world could be judged a priori true is untenable. For how could we *know* independently of experience, *by pure reasoning, that something conceivable* (the world is not as the hypothesis says) *is not the case, or is even impossible, for reasons that do not depend on reasoning* alone? Even according to Kant, appearances (things as they appear to us) are affected by things-in-themselves. Obviously, the idea that knowledge has such a capacity is contradictory.

The same holds, correspondingly, if the statements a priori are not about appearances but about our capacity to know them, or even if they are about both. After all, Kant declares the synthetic statements a priori of pure natural science to be conditions of scientific experience as well as of its objects.

In order to illustrate this, we let the transcendental philosopher assert that his *principle of induction* is one of those sentences that state the *necessary conditions of the possibility of experience*, and that consequently there can be no experience that could refute it. To this, the empiricist will object: "If there can be no experience contradicting the statements proved by (means of) the principle, then these statements are not empirical but *metaphysical.* Hence the principle cannot prove *empirical* hypotheses. It must also be *metaphysical* itself and thus can only serve as a *heuristic.* Anyway, being metaphysical is a logically *necessary* condition for a synthetic statement to be a priori true, and there is no way to find out which are the *sufficient* conditions." So there is no reason why the empiricist should share Kant's view that metaphysics is the helper of scientific enquiry that puts the light on (*Monadologie, Vorbemerkungen* [preliminary remarks]). Rather, the empiricist will ask whether the transcendental philosopher's reflection, which makes him assume that his principle of induction is both synthetic and *a priori necessarily true*, really is *infallible.* The empiricist will ask the same question with regard to any other statement that is supposed to be synthetic a priori.

1.112.2. Obviously, the principle of induction can only be a synthetic statement a posteriori. It has to rest on experience. However, being a principle, it cannot, unlike a singular statement, be directly tested by observation. Hence to "justify it, we should have to employ inductive inferences; and to justify these we should have to assume an inductive principle of a higher order; and so on" (LSD, 29). The matter does not change if the principle is to prove (the truth of) *probability hypotheses* instead of (that of) universal hypotheses, or if it is to prove (not the truth of but) the *probability of universal or probabilistic hypotheses* (29).

So according to Popper, "like every other form of inductive logic, the logic of probable inference, or 'probability logic', leads either to an *infinite regress* [i.a.; if one resorts to further and further principles of induction], or to the doctrine of *apriorism* [if one considers a principle of induction a priori valid]" (LSD, 30). In fact, the logical problem of induction is a special case of the more general *problem of justification. Any attempt to give reasons sufficient to justify* a statement, a value judgement, or a demand leads us for logical reasons into a trilemma that Sextus Empiricus had already described and that Hans Albert (b. 1921) called the "*Münchhausen-Trilemma*" (Albert 1968/1985, 16ff.). In the present case, we get involved in either an *infinite regress* or a *logical circle* (if we resort to a principle of induction that has been "justified" directly or indirectly by another principle that it is to justify in its turn), or we *dogmatically break off* the justification (if we resort to a "last" principle of induction that is not justified in its turn).

Our considerations demonstrate why we cannot prove universal synthetic statements. Hence we never know for certain whether they are true. All assumptions expressed in *universal* statements are *fallible*. Thus "we must regard *all laws or theories as hypothetical or conjectural;* that is, as guesses" (OK, 9). As we shall see, this holds for *all* statements, even for *observation statements.* Accordingly, there is *no certain knowledge* at all, except perhaps in the pure sciences, logic, and mathematics. This is true even of the "hardest" empirical sciences, physics and astronomy. Therefore, the critical rationalist is a *fallibilist.*

1.12. Hume's Empirical Problem

Hume is a *sceptic,* insofar as he thinks that we are not justified in reasoning from instances of which we have experience to other instances of which we have no experience. He holds that only "custom or habit" explains why, nevertheless, all reasonable people expect, and *believe,* that instances of which they have no experience will conform to those of which they have experience. However, he considers it *irrational* to hold beliefs that have been formed by "custom or habit" but cannot be justified. Therefore, Popper called him "a believer in an *irrationalist epistemology*" (OK, 4, i.a.).

1.121.   Section VII of Hume's *Enquiry Concerning Human Understanding* is on the "Idea of necessary Connexion." So he seems to be concerned only with *causality.* He writes: "There are no ideas, which occur in metaphysics, more obscure and uncertain, than those of *power, force, energy* or *necessary connexion*" (EHU, 61f.). How can they be explained? As an empiricist, he answers: "To be fully acquainted, therefore, with the idea of power or necessary connexion, let us examine *its impression;* and in order to find the impression with greater certainty, let us search for it in all the *sources,* from which it may possibly be derived" (63, i.a.).

But what is the result of the search?

When we look about us towards external objects, and consider the operation of causes, we are never able, in a single instance, to discover any power or necessary connexion; any quality, which binds the effect to the cause, and renders the one an infallible consequence of the other. *We only find, that the one does actually, in fact, follow the other* [i.a.]. The impulse of one billiard-ball [the "cause"] is attended with motion in the second [the "effect"]. This is the whole that appears to the *outward* senses. (EHU, 63)

So far, his result is uncontested. It may also be transposed: "But were the power or energy of any cause discoverable by the *mind*, we could foresee the effect, even without experience; and might, at first, pronounce with certainty concerning it, by mere dint of thought and reasoning" (63, i.a.). And as in this case we would not need *experience, induction* could be dispensed with as well. But obviously the mind's abilities are more modest.

At first, according to Hume, the "mind feels no sentiment or *inward* impression from this succession of objects: Consequently, there is not, in any single, particular instance of cause and effect, any thing which can suggest the idea of power or necessary connexion" (EHU, 63). But here disagreement begins. Like Hume, Kant did not believe that the mind had *receptive* impressions of causes and effects, but Kant thought that the mind *ordered* the world, as it appears to us, from the aspect of cause and effect, by means of the category of causality.

Though the "generality of mankind" have neither outward nor inward impressions of connexions between causes and effects, they "never find any difficulty in accounting for the more common and familiar operations of nature – such as the descent of heavy bodies, the growth of plants, the generation of animals, or the nourishment of bodies by food." For they "acquire, *by long habit,* such a turn of mind, that, upon the appearance of the cause, they immediately *expect with assurance* its usual attendant, and hardly conceive it possible that any other event could result from it" (EHU, 69, i.a.).

To the *expectation* that a certain event (the cause) will always be followed by another event (its usual attendant) corresponds a universal *hypothesis*, which asserts at least the *association* of the events, but in most cases their *connexion* as well. Even Popper assumes that "true universal laws of nature" are in a certain sense "'principles of necessity' or 'principles of impossibility'" (LSD, 428), and he proposes a modal operator to express this "*natural necessity*" (432ff.; cf. section 13.2). As the assumption of a connexion cannot be based on impressions of the outward senses, Hume gives it a basis in inward impressions. Long habit produces the *impression of a connexion*:

[W]hen many uniform instances appear, and the same object is always followed by the same event; we then begin to entertain the notion of cause and connexion. We then *feel* a new sentiment or impression, to wit, a customary connexion in the thought or imagination between one object and its usual attendant; and this sentiment is the original of that idea [of power, force, energy or necessary connexion] which we seek for. (EHU, 78)

This may be put in more philosophical words: There is some sort of necessary connexion, but it is not in the objects; rather, it is in the mind; its necessity is not "objective" but "subjective" (Kant, Proleg., A 8). This wording may help us to understand why Hume's consideration inter-rupted Kant's "dogmatic slumber" (Proleg., A 13) – into which, however, Kant immediately fell back when he developed his transcendental phi-losophy. Though this philosophy is called "critical" because of the titles *Critique of Pure Reason*, *Critique of Practical Reason*, and *Critique of Judge-ment* and because of the criticism directed in these books against older metaphysics, it is metaphysical itself; it is dogmatic – especially as Kant claims synthetic statements a priori are necessarily true; hence it is a step backward into pre-Humean dogmatism.

How then do we form explanatory universal hypotheses? Do we add to the *association* of events the *impression of a connexion* only on the ba-sis of repeated observations, because of "custom or habit," as Hume asserts; or are "connections between things...thought *a priori* by the understanding... [by means of] the *concept of the connection* of cause and effect," as Kant claims (Proleg. A 13, 14, i.a.); or are observations always preceded by hypotheses (or implicit expectations), as Popper assumes?

1.122. What is *irrational* about Hume's solution to the empirical prob-lem of induction? His explanation of how we actually form hypotheses may be *false*, but being false does not mean being irrational, and find-ing out whether it is in fact false is the task of empirical science, not of philosophy.

Popper himself draws a "distiction between the *psychology of knowledge* which deals with empirical facts, and the *logic of knowledge* which is con-cerned only with logical relations" (LSD, 30). So he insists that it is not "the business of epistemology to produce what has been called a '*rational reconstruction*' of the steps that have led the scientist to a discovery" (31).

Rather, "the processes involved in the stimulation and release of an inspiration" are "the concern of empirical psychology," while "*subsequent tests* whereby the inspiration may be discovered to be a discovery, or become known to be knowledge" are the concern of epistemology (31).

He even claims to prove that Hume's explanation of the formation of hypotheses is *untenable for logical reasons,* but this is not his reason for calling the explanation "irrational." Rather, he argues that Hume's "result that repetition has no power whatever as an argument, although it dominates our cognitive life or our 'understanding', led him to the conclusion that argument or reason plays only a minor role in our understanding. Our 'knowledge' is unmasked as being not only of the nature of belief, but of rationally indefensible belief – of *an irrational faith*" (OK, 4f.).

Popper quotes Bertrand Russell (1872–1970), who argues even more drastically: that "Hume's philosophy [Popper omits: whether *true* or false] represents the *bankruptcy of eighteenth-century reasonableness*" (Russell 1945, 672, i.a.; OK, 5). It is Hume's *scepticism* that leads reasonableness to go bankrupt, and according to Russell it

rests entirely upon his *rejection of the principle of induction.* [Russell's] principle of induction, as applied to causation, says that, if *A* has been found very often accompanied or followed by *B*, and no instance is known of *A* not being accompanied or followed by *B*, then it is *probable* that on the next occasion on which *A* is observed it will be accompanied or followed by *B*. (Russell 1945, 673, i.a.)

If this principle is correct, then "the causal inferences which Hume rejects are valid, not indeed as giving certainty, but as giving a sufficient probability for practical purposes" (673f.). If, however, "induction (or the principle of induction) is rejected, 'every attempt *to arrive at* general scientific laws from particular observations is fallacious, and Hume's scepticism is inescapable for an empiricist'" (OK, 5, i.a.; Russell 1945, 674).

Now, Hume does not doubt *that* we arrive at universal laws. Rather, his thesis – that we acquire, by long habit, new turns of mind – is intended to explain *how* we arrive at them. His scepticism concerns the *reliability* of the customary connexion in thought. He is, however, criticized not on account of his fallibilism, but because his explanation does not give *reason* a role in the *formation of hypotheses*. This means that he is also sceptical with respect to the capabilities of reason. Yet, according to Russell, his arguments show "that *induction is an independent logical principle,* incapable of being inferred either from experience or from other logical principles, and that without this principle science is impossible"

(Russell 1945, 674, i.a.). Had Hume realized this, he would have had no reason to be sceptical about the capabilities of reason. However, as opposed to Russell, Popper wants to show that it is *logically impossible* even *to arrive at hypotheses by generalization* (i.e., to practice factual, empirical induction). Therefore, Popper must not rely on Russell as a witness of Hume's irrationality.

But is it *irrational to believe a universal hypothesis to be true* if "repetition has no power whatever as an argument"? We shall return to this question in the context of the *corroboration* of hypotheses (sections 5.52, 5.62). Here, to begin, we examine Hume's *explanation of the formation of hypotheses* that Popper so harshly criticizes ("the development of the *expectations* underlying our hypotheses" would be more correct than "the formation of hypotheses").

Let us sum up Hume's argument: We see that the second billiard ball starts moving (event of type *B*) when it is hit by the first ball (event of type *A*). If this occurs repeatedly, we recognize that in the observed cases *A is always followed by B*. But with our outward senses we do not perceive anything *connecting* each *A* with some *B* and thus *causing* their succession. When observing an *A* followed by a *B*, our mind at first "feels no sentiment or *inward* impression from this succession" (EHU, 63). Only "by long habit" (69) does there arise the "new sentiment or *impression*," the "customary *connexion* in the thought" (78, i.a.) that makes us expect that each *A* we see will be followed by a *B*.

Popper does not criticize Hume's idea of a "new *impression*"; rather, he attacks Hume's thesis that this connexion is *customary*. Actually, Hume's explanation of its emergence invites criticism: "For as this idea arises from a number of *similar* instances, and not from any single instance, *it must arise from that circumstance, in which the number of instances differ from every individual instance*. But this customary *connexion* or transition of the imagination is the only circumstance in which they differ. In every other particular they are alike" (EHU, 78, i.a.).

Obviously, there is something wrong here. The new impression is said to arise from a number of similar instances. In order to explain this, Hume asserts that it must *arise* from that circumstance in which the number of instances differ from every individual instance. But that circumstance, he says, *is* the customary connexion itself. Hence Hume's explanation is *circular*. Of course, this implies neither that no such impression arises nor that we in fact do not generalize singular experiences and thus arrive at universal hypotheses. But Popper thinks there is another way to show that such factual generalizations are *logically impossible*.

Popper himself "observed the immensely powerful *need for regularity* – the need which makes [people] seek for regularities; which makes them sometimes experience regularities even where there are none; which makes them cling to their expectations dogmatically" (OK, 23). On the other hand, he admits: "When Kant said that our intellect imposes its laws upon nature, he was right." But he continues: "except that he did not notice how often our intellect fails in the attempt." For the same reason, Kant's transcendental philosophy fails: "[T]he regularities which we try to impose are *psychologically a priori*, but there is not the slightest reason to assume that they are *a priori valid*, as Kant thought." But what is the origin of the need for regularity? Is the need itself acquired as well? Popper thinks that "[t]he need to try to impose such regularities upon our environment is, clearly, *inborn*, and based on drives, or instincts" (24, i.a.). But this statement of fact need not be taken for granted; rather, it has to be empirically tested.

Speaking of drives and instincts may no longer be fashionable, but our central nervous system provides procedures for structuring sense impressions. One example is contrast enhancement at edges, which facilitates making distinctions, forming shapes (*Gestalten*) and separating them from others. (So the *need* to "impose" regularities upon nature might, as Popper suggests, be innate; on the other hand, certain *capabilities* to do so obviously are innate, even though some of them develop only in interaction with sense experience.) For the individual, they are *physiologically a priori*; for the human species, they are the result of a long evolution. In the course of maturation and experience the innate capabilities develop and new expectations are formed. Thus in the course of time recurring shapes evolve from the flux of impressions, and finally the idea of the existence of concrete things with permanent properties emerges. Such expectations might be called *psychologically a priori*, but because they are physiologically represented, there is no sharp boundary between the physiological and the psychological a priori. After extended training, we may recognize our expectations as such and give them the form of explicit hypotheses. Then we may even ask how the formation of hypotheses is possible.

One possible answer is: by induction. Popper writes: "The fundamental doctrine which underlies all theories of induction is *the doctrine of the primacy of repetitions*" (LSD, 420). There are two variants of this doctrine. According to "the doctrine of the logical primacy of repetitions . . . repeated instances furnish a kind of *justification* for the acceptance of a universal law" (420). (There would be no point in still mentioning this variant, if

Popper did not believe that he could refute it in a hitherto unknown way.) As opposed to this, Hume's "doctrine of the temporal (and psychological) primacy of repetitions" implies that repetitions "induce and *arouse* these expectations and beliefs in us," beliefs that are connected to the "acceptance of universal laws." However, both variants "are untenable. This may be shown with the help of two entirely different arguments" (420). We examine the first of these arguments now; the second, on the "transcendence inherent in any description," will be examined later in the context of the "problem of the empirical basis" (cf. section 4.5).

Popper's first argument is the following: "All the repetitions which we experience are *approximate repetitions*; and by saying that a repetition is approximate I mean that the repetititon *B* of an event *A* is not identical with *A*, or indistinguishable from *A*, but only *more or less similar* to *A*" (LSD, 420). This is obviously true, but which conclusion does he draw from it? If "repetition is thus based upon mere similarity, it must share one of the main characteristics of similarity; that is, its relativity. Two things which are similar are always similar *in certain respects*" (420f.). Figure 1.1 will illustrate his point. In this diagram, some of the figures are similar with respect to shape, being circles, triangles, squares, or rectangles. Others are similar with respect to size, and others with respect to shading or its absence. The diagram could be extended – for example, by adding figures of quite different shapes or by adding colours. Obviously, there is an unlimited number of similarities. Things "may be similar *in different respects*," and arbitrary things "which are from one point of view similar may be dissimilar from another point of view" (421).

Popper now resumes his argument: "Generally, similarity, and with it repetition, always presuppose the adoption of *a point of view*: some similarities or repetitions will strike us if we are interested in one problem, and others if we are interested in another problem" (LSD, 421f.). Then

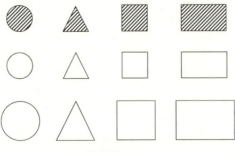

FIGURE 1.1

he draws his conclusion: "[I]f similarity and repetition presuppose the adoption of a point of view, or an interest, or an expectation, it is logically necessary that points of view, or interests, or expectations, are logically prior, as well as temporally (or causally or psychologically) prior, to repetition" (421). Obviously, this is true, for we cannot speak of a repetition if there is no point of view from which to consider something a repetition, and nothing can be perceived as a repetition or judged to be a repetition before there exists such a point of view. But now Popper goes on: "[T]his result destroys both the doctrines of the *logical* [repetitions *justify* the acceptance of universal laws] and of the *temporal* [repetitions *induce* expectations and beliefs] primacy of repetitions" (422, i.a.). Is this true as well?

First, Popper is mistaken when he claims that he can prove in *this way* that the *inference* from a finite number of observation statements to a universal hypothesis is not valid (logical primacy). In fact, even the *observation* of a series of similar cases presupposes a *point of view* from which they are similar. If you like, the repeated observation of white swans even presupposes two points of view – that is, the predicates "is white" and "is a swan." But the fact that such points of view are presuppositions of any observation implies nothing as to the possibility of *inferring* universal hypotheses from *statements* that describe observations.

On the other hand, Popper is right in asserting "that Hume's inductive theory of the formation of beliefs [temporal primacy] could not possibly be true, *for logical reasons*" (OK, 24), for Hume gives a circular explanation of the formation of beliefs. But Popper's objection is different: "[*R*]epetition presupposes *similarity*, and similarity presupposes a *point of view* – a theory, or an expectation" (24, i.a.). This is obviously true. If *B* is to be a repetition of *A*, then *A* and *B* must have at least one property in common. In this respect they are similar, and from the point of view of this similarity the repetition is assessed. According to Popper, this point of view is "a *theory*, or an *expectation*." This is true as well, but not in the sense obviously intended by Popper.

Let us return to the repeated observation of white swans. The appearance (*B*) of the white swan Bertha is a repetition of the appearance (*A*) of the white swan Antony. The two events have at least one property in common, for both involve an entity with the properties "white" and "swan." In this respect the events are similar. In other respects – for example, with respect to place and time – they may differ; with respect to the sex of the birds, they obviously do differ. The points of view relative to which the events are similar also contain *theories* or *expectations*, for each of the *predicates* "is white" and "is a swan" attributes *lawlike* properties to the subjects Antony and Bertha. However, the universal *hypothesis* "All swans are white" is not one of the points of view that are needed in order to assess this repetition. Hence Popper's analysis has so far not shown that *this* hypothesis must precede repeated observations of white swans logically or temporally, and that *it* therefore cannot be formed by generalization on the basis of such repetitions.

Let us now examine the next step in Popper's argument. His "logical analysis" (OK, 24) causes him to strengthen one of his theses. The fact that there "is the general need for a world that conforms to our expectations" leads him "first to the conclusion that expectations may arise without, or before, any repetition" (24). We need not comment on this "conclusion," as there are *physiological* reasons to assume that we have expectations before any repetition. However, according to Popper, his "logical analysis" also shows "that they could *not* arise *otherwise* because repetition presupposes ... an expectation" (24, i.a.). But could a logical analysis possibly show that *no* hypothesis can be formed on the basis of repetitions?

If repeated experience is not sufficient, what makes the formation of hypotheses possible? According to our (logical) considerations, at least one of the *points of view* relative to which we assess similarity for the first time in our life must be *innate*. But what can we learn as long as we can discover only "now (event) *A*" or "now *not-A*"? Obviously, we need at least one additional point of view that permits us to discover *B*. Only then can we *form new expectations* – which may be given the form "If *A*, then always *B*," or "If *A*, then always *not-B*," or "The probability of *B*, given *A*, is *r*" – and *learn from the experiences we make with them.*

But when do we associate *A* and *B*? This question cannot be answered on the basis of the points of view *A* and *B* alone. When further points of view *C, D, E,...,* are taken into account, the deliberation gets even more complicated. Why do we associate *B*, rather than *C, D, E,...,* with *A*? In order to answer this question, we need additional, more general points of view. To Hume, "there appear to be only three principles of connexion among ideas, namely, *Resemblance, Contiguity* in time or place, and *Cause* or *Effect*" (EHU, 24). Though Kantians may rely on the "category of causality," empiricists must – on pain of circularity – renounce Hume's principle of "cause or effect." But we might find *B closer* – in time or place – to *A* than to *C, D, E,* and so on. Or *A* and *B* might be *more similar* to each other, as the points of view relative to which we identify an event as an *A* or a *B, C, D, E,* ... overlap only in the case of *A* and *B*, but not in the case of *A* and *C, A* and *D*, and so on.

If one billiard ball hits another (event *A*) and the latter starts to move (event *B*), then these two courses of events have more in common than either of them has with the colour of the balls (state of affairs C) or the comment of a spectator (event *D*). Obviously, the principles of resemblance and of contiguity cannot themselves be induced on the basis of repetition, as they are considered presuppositions of any perception of a repetition. But this is a problem only for Locke's *tabula rasa* empiricism.

However, starting the avalanche of lifelong learning obviously presupposes a greater number of points of view. Some are "built into" our sense organs, especially into the eye and the ear. So we have many perceptions, whether we like it or not. We simply cannot avoid them. Our senses mature and can be trained. The ear is trained, for example, in music classes. So there is no lack of points of view, whose many possible combinations permit us to form a great number of implicit expectations and eventually also to form explicit hypotheses.

Popper seems to share this opinion: "[T]hose 'strong pragmatic beliefs' which we all hold, such as the belief that there will be a tomorrow, ... are partly inborn, partly modifications of inborn beliefs resulting from the method of trial and error-elimination" (OK, 27). But does this imply that new hypotheses are *always speculatively proposed*, as Popper assumes, or is it possible to *induce some* hypotheses by means of innate points of view on the basis of repeated observations? This at least cannot be *logically* excluded.

Discovering the *empirical* conditions for forming and testing expectations is the task not of philosophy – not even of a "logic of scientific discovery" – but of the empirical sciences, such as neurophysiology and the psychology of perception. Though these disciplines are still far from explaining the formation of concrete hypotheses, they already make Popper's thesis seem questionable. For in simple organisms such as the sea snail *Aplysia*, the specific neurons are already known whose activity weakens a specific reaction to a certain stimulus if that stimulus is repeated within a short period of time, and whose activity causes the reaction to recover if the stimulus fails to arrive for a certain period of time. Thus we may say that *Aplysia* can – owing to its neurophysiological equipment – *detect repetitions* of certain stimuli and adapt its reactions to them. Now, this is a particular stimulus, not an association of two arbitrary stimuli, and no new connexion is formed. But why should our much more complex physiology be in principle unable to *detect repetitions of combinations* of such well-known properties as "swan" and "white," even before we have speculatively formed hypotheses such as "All swans are white" or "The probability that a swan is white is 0.8"?

On the other hand, *logical* analysis may even go one step further. As Henri Poincaré (1853–1912) has pointed out, hypotheses containing *theoretical concepts* cannot immediately be induced on the basis of observations. Hence *not all* universal hypotheses can be empirically induced. But neither is it *impossible* to induce *any* hypothesis. Hence Popper cannot have "solved the problem of induction" or, with "a little generosity," the "*problem of human knowledge*" (PKP, 1014).

1.13. Popper's "Restatement and Solution" of the Logical Problem

According to Popper, Hume's distinction between a logical and a psychological problem of induction is extremely important, and although our exposition of Hume's logical problem (section 1.11) does not originate with Popper, he would nevertheless accept it as a logician. However, he believes that his restatement of the *logical problem of induction* paves the way to a *positive solution*. He approaches the solution step by step.

First, Popper *restates* Hume's *logical* problem of induction as follows:

P_{L_1}: Can the claim that an explanatory universal theory is *true* be *justified* by "empirical reasons"? (OK, 7, i.a.)

Of course, Popper's answer to P_{L_1} is "No, [it] cannot." This may sound "negative," but it "should be interpreted as meaning that we must regard *all laws or theories as hypothetical or conjectural*; that is, as guesses" (9). With that, Popper in fact draws the right conclusion from the negative answer to H_L and P_{L_1}. It says: "If laws cannot be justified, they are mere hypotheses." But does his thesis of conjectural knowledge really solve Hume's logical problem of induction?

Then Popper tries to *generalize* P_{L_1} "by replacing the words 'is true' by the words 'is true or that it is false'" (OK, 7). Thus he obtains his *second restatement*:

P_{L_2}: Can the claim that an explanatory universal theory is *true* or that it is *false* be *justified* by "empirical reasons"? (7, i.a.)

To this question, Popper answers: "Yes, *the assumption of the truth of test statements sometimes allows us to justify the claim that an explanatory universal theory is false*" (7).

This answer he calls "positive"; and it is "positive," insofar as it begins with "yes." But is it really an answer to Hume's question H_L? After all, because of the problem of the empirical basis (cf. Chapter 4), the assumption that a theory is *false* can no more be *justified* than the assumption that a theory is *true*. One of the components of the problem of the empirical basis, the transcendence inherent in any description (cf. section 4.5.), is even analogous to the problem of induction.

Hence Popper's answer to P_{L2} would be false if it referred not only to the *logical* aspect of the falsification of a theory – the deduction of its negation from basic statements and background knowledge – but also to its *empirical* aspect – the "verification" of falsifying basic statements. On the other hand, his statement that P_{L2} "is merely a generalization of" P_{L1} is obviously false (OK, 12). For as a result of the substitution of "is true or that it is false" (in P_{L2}) for "is true" (in P_{L1}), the logical content of P_{L2} is not greater but less than that of P_{L1}.

Finally, Popper asserts that his reply to P_{L2} "becomes very important if we reflect on . . . a situation in which we are faced with *several explanatory theories* which compete" (OK, 7). This "suggests a *third reformulation* [i.a.] of the problem of induction":

P_{L3}: Can a *preference*, with respect to truth or falsity, for some competing universal theories over others ever be justified by such "empirical reasons"? (8)

His answer is: "Yes; sometimes it can, if we are lucky. For it may happen that our test statements may refute some – but not all – of the competing theories; and since we are searching for a *true* theory, we shall prefer those whose falsity has not been established" (OK, 8, i.a.). This answer is "positive" also insofar as it *prefers* one theory to another.

According to Popper, this third reformulation P_{L3} "is merely an alternative formulation of" P_{L2} (OK, 12). This is not entirely correct, but if we have empirical reasons to assume that theory t_1 has been refuted while t_2 has not, then we have reasons to prefer t_2 to t_1. And when Popper asserts that his "answer to $[P_{L2}]$ is in agreement with the following somewhat weak form of *the principle of empiricism: Only 'experience' can help us to make up our minds about the truth or falsity of factual statements*" (12), then he can only mean that his answer is compatible with this principle.

Unfortunately, Popper wants to transfer his "solution" to the logical problem of induction, H_L, to the psychological (empirical) problem, H_P, "on the basis of the following *principle of transference*: what is true in logic is true in psychology" (OK, 6). This is intended to show that if "there is no such thing as induction by repetition in *logic*," then "there cannot be

any such thing in *psychology* (or in scientific method...)" (6). But then
the "principle of transference" must be false, for the logical problem
relates to the justification of hypotheses, while the empirical problem
relates to their development; and why should a hypothesis not arise in a
way in which it cannot be justified? After all, the distinction between the
formation and the validity of statements was an important step forward
in epistemology.

Hence *Popper did not restate and then solve the logical problem of induction;
rather, he drew the right conclusions from its insolubility.* In the context of his
"solution" to the problem of induction by means of his thesis of "hypothetical knowledge," Popper now discusses our "*preference* for theories,"
in particular, their *corroboration*. We shall return to this (cf. Chapter 5).

1.2. THE PROBLEM OF DEMARCATION

In his autobiography, Popper reports that he first developed ideas "about
the *demarcation between scientific theories* (like Einstein's) *and pseudoscientific
theories* (like Marx's, Freud's and Adler's)" (A, 31). As early as 1919 – he
then turned seventeen, and Wittgenstein's *Tractatus Logico-Philosophicus*
was not published until 1921 – he demanded that whoever proposed a
scientific theory should answer the question: "'Under what conditions
would I admit that my theory is untenable?'" (32). His idea was that "*the
more a theory forbids, the more it tells us*" (31).

At this time he was not yet interested in the *demarcation between science and metaphysics*. Things changed, however, when Moritz Schlick
(1882–1936) and Friedrich Waismann (1896–1959) introduced Ludwig
Wittgenstein's (1889–1951) ideas on the role of language in science and
philosophy to the Vienna Circle. In his *Logic*, Popper calls the "problem
of finding a criterion which would enable us to distinguish between the
empirical sciences on the one hand, and mathematics and logic as well
as 'metaphysical' systems on the other" the "*problem of demarcation*" (LSD,
34). As Kant made it the "central problem of the theory of knowledge,"
we might call it "'Kant's problem'" (34).

The first part of the solution to this problem, the *demarcation between
the empirical sciences on the one hand, and mathematics and logic on the other,*
seems to be simple, for the sentences of logic and mathematics are judged
to be true or false on the basis of their *form* alone, while the statements
of the empirical sciences must be tested by *experience*. Beyond all doubt,
logic and mathematics are sciences, however; they are not empirical but
rather pure or formal sciences.

But the second, more important part of the solution, the *demarcation between the empirical sciences on the one hand, and metaphysics and pseudoscience on the other*, requires a new approach. For, as already noted, the inductive method was for many years considered the most important characteristic of empirical science (cf. Chapter 1). This idea even left its traces in linguistic usage. For example, Ernst Mach (1838–1916) in Vienna held the chair in "philosophy, in particular history and theory of the inductive sciences" (Haller 1993, 32). But if, as Schlick writes, " 'The problem of induction consists in asking for a logical justification of *universal statements* about reality' " (LSD, 37), then it proves to be unsolvable, and hence the "*inductivist criterion of demarcation*" fails (37, i.a.).

1.21. Falsifiabilty as a Criterion of Demarcation

Popper's new solution to the problem of demarcation is based on a simple logical consideration: *Universal statements are not verifiable.* For example, no finite number of observations of white swans can guarantee the truth of the statement "All swans are white," unless the observations cover the whole population of swans, but we cannot be certain that the whole population is covered unless we define it as spatiotemporally limited. On the other hand, *every universal statement is falsifiable* if we can presuppose the truth of at least one falsifying basic statement (i.e., an observation statement that contradicts the universal statement). If, for example, the singular statement "Antony is a black swan" is true, then for logical reasons the universal statement "All swans are white" must be false. There is "an *asymmetry* between verifiability and falsifiability," insofar as we can *deductively* infer the *falsity* of universal statements but *not* their *truth* from the truth of singular statements (LSD, 41).

For that reason, Popper proposes a *criterion of demarcation between empirical science and metaphysics,* according to which *those, and only those, synthetic statements are considered to be empirically scientific that are empirically falsifiable,* for "*it must be possible for an empirical scientific system to be refuted by experience*" (LSD, 41). According to this criterion, all those statements are considered to be *metaphysical* that are neither analytic (and hence possibly belonging to the pure sciences), nor contradictory, nor empirically falsifiable (and hence possibly belonging to the empirical sciences). (The qualification "possibly" indicates that normally empirical statements such as "It is raining" are not considered statements of the empirical sciences, and analytic statements such as "It is raining or it is not raining" are not considered statements of the pure sciences.) Hence "*metaphysics*" is a *residual category* and not the name of a philosophical discipline, let alone of a fundamental "first philosophy."

Popper replaces the "criterion of demarcation inherent in *in*ductive logic" by a "criterion of demarcation inherent in *de*ductive logic," for falsification involves a deductive relation between the falsifying and the falsified statements (LSD, 40ff., i.a.). And while positivists "usually interpret the problem of demarcation in a *naturalistic* way... as if it were a problem of natural science" (35), Popper's criterion of demarcation has "to be regarded as a *proposal for an agreement or convention*" (37). He can see "only *one* way... of arguing rationally in support of [his] proposals. This is to analyse their logical consequences: to point out their fertility – their power to elucidate the problems of the theory of knowledge" (38).

* Popper's criterion of demarcation is very simple indeed. Nevertheless, it makes sense to relate this convention to logical and philosophical terminology. (The following explication may be skipped on first reading, as indicated by the asterisk [*] at the beginning of this paragraph and the double asterisk [**] at the end of the explication.)

Table 1.1 classifies all *declarative statements*. This table requires some comment. The "L-concepts" (Carnap 1961, 60ff.) and "F-concepts" (140ff.) as well as the outlines of the table (142) are Carnap's (1891–1970). I have inserted Popper's demarcation between empirical and metaphysical statements into Carnap's scheme. Because logic is a far more precise frame of reference than methodology, this procedure seems advisable.

A statement is *L-true* (*l*ogically true) if, and only if, its truth can be determined by *logical* ("It is raining or it is not raining") or *semantic* analysis ("A bachelor is an unmarried man") alone. Statements of the first kind are called *tautological*, statements of both kinds are called *analytic*. (Kant uses the term "analytic" in a more restricted way: The judgment "All bodies are extended" is analytic, because it says "nothing in the predicate ["extended"] that was not already really thought in the concept of the subject ["body"]" [Proleg., § 2 (a)].) Analytic statements hold "*a priori*" (Proleg., § 2 [b]), that is, "independently of all experience" (CPR, B 2, 3); on this, Kant and the empiricists agree.

In the same purely logical or semantic way, the falsity of an *L-false* statement may be determined. Hence both L-true and L-false statements are *L-determinate* (*l*ogically determinate). Still, L-false statements are in general not called "a priori false" but "*contradictory*," as they imply logical contradictions, or "*inconsistent*." The negation of an analytic statement is

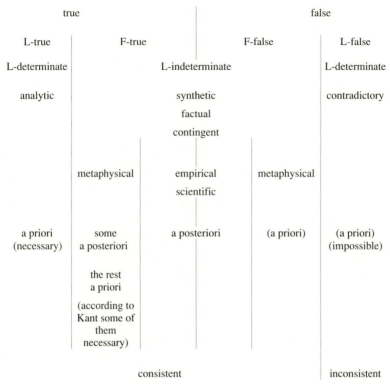

true		false	
L-true	F-true	F-false	L-false
L-determinate	L-indeterminate		L-determinate
analytic	synthetic factual contingent		contradictory
metaphysical	empirical scientific	metaphysical	
a priori (necessary)	some a posteriori	a posteriori	(a priori)	(a priori) (impossible)
	the rest a priori			
	(according to Kant some of them necessary)			
consistent		inconsistent	

Table 1.1

contradictory, and vice versa. Hence the negation of an L-determinate statement is itself L-determinate.

A statement is *F-true* (*factually true*) or *F-false* if, and only if, its truth value *cannot* be determined by logical or semantic analysis alone, that is, if it is *L-indeterminate* or *synthetic*. Consequently, it must be assessed in a different way. Empiricists consider only sense experience an adequate basis of such judgments, while rationalists and criticists rely as well on reason or intellectual intuition. Any statement that is in principle *refutable by sense experience* is "*empirical*" in the sense of Popper's criterion of demarcation.

If the truth or falsity of a statement can only be judged "*a posteriori*, i.e., through experience" (CPR, B 3), then the statement itself is called a "synthetic proposition[ ] *a posteriori*" by Kant (Proleg., § 5). However, not all synthetic statements a posteriori are empirical in the sense of the criterion of demarcation. The observation of a black swan empirically "*verifies*" the existential statement "There is a black swan," but *strictly existential statements* such as this are *not falsifiable* and hence are *not empirical.* Rather, they are *metaphysical* because of their syntactical *form* (being existential statements) and because they contain only universal *concepts* (the interpretation of their nonlogical signs does not imply any spatiotemporal limitation). Hence there are *metaphysical statements a posteriori.*

But most metaphysical statements cannot be assessed by experience, hence they are not a posteriori. The statement "The absolute is sleepy" is empirically neither verifiable nor falsifiable. It is true that it is a simple subject-predicate statement, but its subject term, "the absolute," is not empirically interpreted. Hence it is *metaphysical* according to Popper's criterion of demarcation. Its truth value could only be assessed independently of experience, that is, a priori. All metaphysical statements that are not empirically verifiable are a priori in the sense of having to be assessed independently of experience. (By definition, there are no empirically falsifiable metaphysical statements.)

But when Kant writes that "metaphysics . . . consists of purely synthetic *a priori* propositions" (CPR, B 18), he takes "metaphysics" to be a fundamental philosophical discipline, and he claims that its statements are *necessarily true.* Therefore, he does not consider *false synthetic statements a priori* at all, though for each true statement there is its false negation, and the negation of a statement a priori cannot be a posteriori, because otherwise a statement that is supposed to be independent of experience would depend on experience by its negation.

While Kant believes that "[w]hen . . . strict universality belongs to a judgment essentially, this points to a special source of cognition for it, namely a faculty of *a priori* cognition" (CPR, B4), empiricism might, according to Schlick, be defined as the view that there is no synthetic a priori (Carnap 1966, 180).

Kant's speculations even venture into the domain of physics:

Natural science (*Physica*) contains within itself synthetic *a priori* judgments as principles. I will adduce only a couple of propositions as examples, such as the proposition that in all alterations of the corporeal world the quantity of matter remains unaltered, or that in all communication of motion effect and countereffect must always be equal. In both of these not only the necessity, thus their *a priori* origin, but also that they are synthetic propositions is clear. (CPR, B 17, 18)

However, Kant's principle of the conservation of mass contradicts Einstein's relativistic principle of the conservation of energy. According to Einstein's special relativity theory, mass m and energy E are equivalent and may be transformed into each other in microphysical processes according to the equation $E = mc^2$. If, for the time being, we take special relativity theory to be true, because it is well corroborated, then a statement (the principle of the conservation of mass) known (by Kant) a priori to be *necessarily true* has turned out a posteriori to be *factually false*.

Those *consistent* statements, which are L-indeterminate or synthetic, are also called "*contingent*." Beginning with Kant, "contingent" is often paraphrased by the word "accidental," but then "accidental" expresses the absence of logical necessity or impossibility, not randomness. **

1.22. The Problem of Meaning

The usefulness of Popper's *falsifiability criterion of demarcation* is most easily recognized when it is compared to the *positivist criterion of meaningfulness*. Undoubtedly, we can only assess whether a statement is true if we know what it means. But do we really know what it means only if we can assess whether it is true, as the positivist criterion of meaningfulness implies?

According to Popper, the view that metaphysics is meaningless goes back to Hobbes (1588–1679), Berkeley (1684–1753), and Hume (CR, 258 n12). In order to avoid the idea of a material connexion between cause and effect, David Hume had formulated a *criterion of meaning*: "[A]s we can have no idea of any thing which never appeared to our outward sense or inward sentiment, the necessary conclusion *seems* [Hume's italics] to be that we have no idea of connexion or power at all, and that *these words are absolutely without any meaning*, when employed either in philosophical reasonings or common life" (EHU, 74, i.a.). Accordingly, *words are without any meaning if* – like the word "connexion" – *they seem to refer to something of which we have no idea*, and we can have ideas only of entities of which we had impressions before.

Charles Sanders Peirce (1839–1914) gave this idea its pragmatic form. He repeatedly formulated what he called the *Maxim of Pragmatism* (CP, 5.18) or the *Pragmatic Maxim* (CP, 5.394ff.). In his article "How to Make Our Ideas Clear," it reads as follows: "Consider what effects, that might conceivably have practical bearings, we conceive the object of our conception to have. Then, our conception of these effects is the whole of our conception of the object" (CP, 5.402). Accordingly, *a conception is empty, without any meaning, if we do not conceive the effects of its object to have practical bearings*.

To give an example, Peirce applies the maxim to the concept "hard." But "concept" seems to be too narrow a translation of his word "conception," for in the same section he states more generally that "what a *thing* means is simply what habits it involves" (CP, 5.400, i.a.). And in a footnote he explains that his terms "conceivably," "conceive," and "conception" are intended to be derivative of the Latin word *concipere* (CP, 5.402 n3). So the maxim seems to hold as well for other *products of thought* – for example, for theories. At any rate, Quine traces the *verification theory of meaning*, according to which "the meaning of a statement is the method of empirically confirming or infirming it," back to Peirce (Quine 1961a, 37).

More often, Wittgenstein is considered its author. In his *Tractatus*, he writes: "4.113. Philosophy limits the disputable sphere of natural science." This implies a *demarcation of empirical science*, and its principle is radical: "4.114. It [philosophy] should *limit the thinkable* and thereby the unthinkable" (i.a.). As the unthinkable cannot be meaningful, a *criterion of demarcation* announces itself, which is also a *criterion of meaningfulness*. And his thesis "4.11. The totality of true propositions is the total natural science" implies that all true statements conform to the requirements of the empirical sciences.

But what about the statements of philosophy? "4.111. Philosophy is not one of the natural sciences." Does this mean that philosophy does not produce true statements? According to Wittgenstein, this is not the task of philosophy: "4.112. [Rather the] object of philosophy is the logical clarification of thoughts. [For philosophy] is not a theory but an activity.... [And the] result of philosophy is not a number of 'philosophical propositions', but to make propositions clear. *Philosophy should make clear and delimit sharply the thoughts which otherwise are, as it were, opaque and blurred*" (i.a.).

While Hume deals with the meaning of *words* and Peirce with the meaning of *concepts* and other constructs, Wittgenstein is interested in the meaning of *statements*. He writes: "But to be able to say that a point is black or white, I must first know under what conditions a point is called white or black; in order to be able to say '*p*' is true (or false) I must have determined under what conditions I call '*p*' true, and thereby I determine the sense of the proposition" (4.063, i.a.). Even today, the idea that the *meaning* of a statement is determined by indicating the *conditions of its truth* hardly seems open to attack.

This does not hold for the *verification criterion of meaning* (or meaningfulness). Its best-known wording, by Waismann, seems to be due to Wittgenstein. It reads as follows: "'*If it can in no way be indicated when a statement is true, then this statement does not have any meaning at all; for the meaning of a statement is the method of its verification.... A statement which cannot be definitely verified is not verifiable at all; it just lacks any meaning'"* (Waismann 1930–31, 229, m.t., i.a.).

The first phrase ["If...at all"] may be given the same interpretation as statement 4.063 of the *Tractatus*, and it is equally unproblematic. The second phrase ["for...verification"] may be considered an unfortunate metaphor. But the third phrase ["A statement...meaning"] is not acceptable, for, as we have seen, even a simple universal statement such as "All ravens are black" is for logical reasons not verifiable. Accordingly, it would lack any meaning. But we constantly use such statements. Do we thus constantly talk nonsense?

1.221. Various authors have made quite different proposals to invalidate this reproach. Some of them – for example, Moritz Schlick – believe that it is "'essential to a genuine statement that in principle it can ultimately be verified or falsified'. *If* there are at all '[strictly] general propositions about reality', this holds of them as well" (GPE, 42; Schlick 1979, 196f.).

This is to say that *any genuine statement must be verifiable, if it is true, and falsifiable, if it is false.* Popper calls the view that there are strictly universal statements of facts the "*normal statement view*" (this is not Schlick's view; see below). There are several variants of this view, all of which consider universal statements to be normal statements that are verifiable, at least in principle. If we want to avoid the trilemma into which any attempt at justification leads, the normal-statement view admits of only *two* interpretations of universal statements.

Both of them can already be found in Kant. In the introduction to his *Critique of Pure Reason*, he writes: "Experience never gives its judgments true or strict but only assumed and *comparative universality* (through *induction*), so properly it must be said: as far as we have *yet* perceived, there is no exception to this or that rule" (B 3–4, i.a.). Empiricists may take seemingly universal (though not strictly universal; see below) statements to be synoptic reports. Popper calls this view "*strict positivism*"; other authors call it the "*immanence view*," since it invites us to remain "completely within the scope of the immediately given, of what can be immediately experienced." (GPE, 43, 45). Kant goes on: "Thus if a judgment is thought in *strict universality*, i.e., in such a way that no exception at all is allowed to be possible, then it is not derived from experience, but is rather *valid absolutely a priori*" (B 4, i.a.). For obvious reasons, Popper calls this view "*apriorism.*" In his *Logic of Scientific Discovery*, he replaces Kant's term "*comparative* universality" with "*numerical* universality," while he adopts "*strict* universality" (LSD, 62). (In the German edition he had used the term "*specific* universality" instead of "*strict* universality" [LdF, 34]).

Both "strict positivism" and "apriorism" are untenable if taken literally. This is obvious in the case of *apriorism,* for the fact that we "think a statement of facts in strict universality" would entail its a priori validity only if our thoughts were infallible. It is slightly more difficult to refute *strict positivism.* Here we indicate Popper's argument only briefly, for we shall return to it in the context of the problem of the empirical basis (cf. section 4.5.). He writes: "Each statement, *each description,* in particular each scientific statement *transcends* the immediately given, is more than a meticulously precise description of pure impressions" (GPE, 45). Strictly universal statements transcend the given as well by their "*transcendence of generalization,*" which entails the problem of induction (47, i.a.). But as even observation statements "*transcend any description,*" they are not verifiable either (LSD, 94). Hence the *normal-statement view* is not tenable, for according to this view there would be *no genuine statements at all,* as no (synthetic) statement is definitely verifiable.

1.222. There is another group of attempts to make sense of using strictly universal statements, which Popper calls "*probability views.*" They try to replace the "truth" or "falsity" of a statement with its "probability." According to Reichenbach, "'it is not given to science to reach either truth or falsity . . . but scientific statements can only attain continuous degrees of probability whose unattainable upper and lower limits are truth and falsity'" (LSD, 29f.). Popper objects that it is "untenable to take the 'probability' of a statement to be an objective value of its validity between the values 'true' and 'false'" (GPE, 138).

This "crucial point" of his argument is correct (GPE, 144), but perhaps Schlick, whom he repeatedly quotes (in GPE), need not be interpreted to have meant exactly this. For Schlick writes: "When I say '*A* probably is *B*' (for example, chemical forces are probably electrical in nature), . . . [then I mean that] the proposition '*A* is *B*' represents an *hypothesis*" (Schlick 1925/1985, 389).

Still, Schlick's view remains open to criticism. It is true that he seems to formulate only a theorem of probability theory when he writes: "That the number of sixes among n throws deviates the less from $n/6$ the greater the number n cannot be asserted with *certainty* for a finite n. It is only *probable*" (1985, 392, i.a.). But from the finite probability $(5/6)^n$ of the event "that a six will *not turn up at all* among the throws" (392), he infers: "Regardless of how one twists or turns, it is impossible to specify in this manner the *exact meaning* that a probabilistic [literally: probable (!); 1979, 436] statement has for reality" (392, i.a.). Does he intend to say after all that probability statements do not have an exact meaning, because they do not have a truth value but only a probability?

Why is the "crucial point" of Popper's objection correct? He argues "the fact that a statement *holds* with probability can only be expressed by a statement on this statement" (GPE, 143). A meta-statement such as this says something about the confirmation or corroboration of the object statement. But any degree of confirmation is *relative to a particular time* and hence cannot be a substitute for a *timeless* truth value.

Popper's criticism may still be complemented, for in the object language there is no equivalent to the meta-statement "The statement 'All swans are white' holds with probability 0.95," whereas the meta-statement "The statement 'All swans are white' is true" is logically equivalent to the statement "All swans are white" in the object language (cf. sections 6.2, 6.4). If, on the other hand, the probability views took "The statement 'All swans are white' holds with probability 0.95" to mean "The probability that a swan is white is 0.95," they would not substitute the probability of a statement as an objective value of its validity for its truth or falsity. Rather, they would substitute probability hypotheses for universal statements. For the reasons given, *the probability views fail*, even if not all of Popper's objections are necessarily sound.

1.223. Epistemologically more interesting are the "*pseudostatement views*." Their representatives (e.g., Schlick) insist "that 'it is essential to a genuine statement that in principle it can ultimately be verified or falsified'" (GPE, 160; Schlick 1931/1979, 196). And from the failure of the normal-statement view they draw the conclusion "that natural laws, the so called 'general propositions about reality' are *not* at all *genuine statements*" (GPE, 159) but merely *pseudostatements*, which do not have truth values and thus cannot be verifiable. According to the pseudostatement views, only singular (particular) statements are genuine statements that can be true or false. But what exactly is a pseudostatement?

Schlick believes "that 'a law of nature does not even have the logical character of an "assertion" but represents, rather, a "*prescription for the making of assertions*"'" (GPE, 161; Schlick 1979, 188, i.a.). He attributes this idea to Wittgenstein. In order to explain what kind of directive is meant, he refers to the use we make of natural laws. For instance, we need a natural law to predict a future event from our knowledge of a present event. According to Schlick, the descriptions of both events are verifiable in principle – that is, they are genuine statements – while the natural law is but a directive (comparable to a logical rule) concerning how to infer the description of the future event from that of the present event. He adds: "'Such a directive is not true or false, but good or bad, useful or idle'" (GPE, 164; Schlick 1979, 196). So the natural laws are denied a value of their validity such as "true" or "false." They are supposed to be only of practical value: "The natural law is *useful* for the derivation of the prediction, if the prediction is *true*; *useless*, if the prediction turns out to be *false*" (GPE, 165).

However, the pseudostatement view entails logical oddities. For instance, the statement "All swans are white" is not verifiable, thus it is considered a meaningless pseudostatement; but its negation, "Not all swans are white," is in principle verifiable – it would be sufficient to present a black swan – and is therefore considered a genuine statement. This consequence alone would be too high a price to pay for the verification criterion of meaning. Moreover, we cannot even prove the truth of singular observation statements (cf. section 1.221). Accordingly, they are pseudostatements as well. Hence *there are only pseudostatements according to the pseudostatement view*. Like "strict positivism," the pseudostatement view fails, because it wrongly presupposes that observation statements are verifiable.

All attempts to save the *verifiability criterion of scientific character* have failed. This holds all the more for the *verifiability criterion of meaning*, according to which a statement that is not verifiable does not have any meaning. Thus Popper's *falsifiability criterion of scientific character* is undoubtedly the superior alternative. Owing above all to Popper's criticism, the verifiability criterion was soon given up. But it left its traces, even in the later philosophy of Wittgenstein. For example, Wittgenstein's argument for the impossibility of any private language has presuppositions that amount to a verifiability criterion of truth, if not of meaning (cf. Keuth 1993, 58–62).

1.23. Are Metaphysical Statements Open to Criticism?

Metaphysical statements are not *empirically* refutable. Does this imply that they are immune to *any* criticism? Not at all. To give an example, let us apply Popper's criterion of demarcation to theological statements. The statement

God is almighty

certainly does have a linguistic meaning. But according to Wittgenstein's *verifiability criterion* it is *meaningless*, because it is not empirically verifiable. By contrast, Popper's *falsifiability criterion* implies nothing as to its meaning but classifies it as *not empirical* (or *not scientific*), because it is not falsifiable. (For the sake of our argument we disregard the fact that "God is almighty" seems contradictory, if we ask the old question "Can God create a stone that is so heavy that He cannot lift it?") The same holds for the statement

God is benevolent.

Does this mean that these statements cannot occur in scientific arguments? An example will show that they can. Theodicy is the justification of God in the face of the evil in the world. As our argument shows, it remains problematic:

(1) If God is almighty, He can prevent suffering.
(2) If God is benevolent, He wants to prevent suffering.
(3) But there is suffering (He has not prevented it).

---

(4) God is not both almighty and benevolent.

This is a logical argument, and, as such, it is scientific. In order to avoid its conclusion, "God is not both almighty and benevolent" (Philo's conclusion in Hume's *Dialogues Concerning Natural Religion*, Part 10), we have to discard at least one of its premises. It is true that the argument does not show which premise has to be discarded, but there is no reason to exempt from criticism the two metaphysical premises on God's almightiness (1) and benevolence (2). Hence even metaphysical theses are *open to criticism*.

But are they *refutable* as well? Being metaphysical, they cannot be logically refuted one by one – otherwise they would be contradictory – nor can they be refuted by sense experience – otherwise they would be empirical. This does not imply that they are true, for even two statements contradicting each other, one of which must be false, can both be irrefutable. But there is no *test procedure* that we can apply to metaphysical statements to find out which of them is true and which is false. Thus in the present case *criticism* may confine itself to the (logical) remark that the metaphysical premises on God's almightiness (1) and benevolence (2) *cannot both be true, if* the empirical premise that there is suffering (3) is true. However, criticism may go one step further and assert that at least one of the metaphysical premises *must be false, as* the empirical premise is true. Unlike single metaphysical statements, *a system of metaphysical*

statements may be empirically refutable, if it contradicts an empirical statement or a conjunction of empirical statements that have been severely
tested and accepted as true. The system may be *inconsistent* as well.

In fact, some philosophers and theologians have modified or replaced
one or the other of the two metaphysical premises (cf. Hume, EHU,
section XI). For instance, the assumption that we live in the best of all
possible worlds qualifies the thesis (2) of God's almightiness. It is impossible for Him to create a better world. And in order to defend God's
benevolence, it is sometimes claimed that He lets us suffer only for good
purposes.

1.24. Objections to the Criterion of Demarcation

As we have seen, Popper's criterion of demarcation is in various respects
superior to the neopositivist criterion of meaning. But this alone does
not mean that it serves its purpose. In fact, it is often criticized. Some
authors object that the criterion of demarcation is *too narrow,* insofar as
it *excludes statements that are obviously scientific* (cf. sections 1.242, 1.243).
They mostly refer to certain strictly existential statements and to probability statements. Others object that the criterion is *too wide,* as it *does not
exclude obviously metaphysical statements* (cf. section 1.244). More basic is
the objection that *theories are not refutable in isolation* (the Duhem–Quine
thesis; cf. section 3.6) and hence *cannot be classified as scientific in isolation.*
However, the most severe objection has been raised by Thomas Samuel
Kuhn (cf. section 1.241). According to him, there is *no falsification in
normal science,* and even *in scientific revolutions theories are not refuted by experience* but are superseded by other theories. (This is what Kuhn calls a
"paradigm change.") So the criterion of demarcation seems to be irrelevant to science.

1.241. Kuhn (1922–1996) first raises his objection in his book *The Structure of Scientific Revolutions* (1962), and he repeats it in a milder form in
his article "Logic of Discovery or Psychology of Research?" (1970), where
he writes:

Finally, and this is for now my main point, a careful look at the scientific enterprise
suggests that it is *normal science,* in which Sir Karl's sort of *testing does not occur,* rather
than extraordinary science which most nearly distinguishes science from other
enterprises. If a *demarcation criterion* exists (we must not, I think, seek a sharp or
decisive one), it may lie just in that part of science which Sir Karl ignores." (Kuhn
1970, 6, i.a.)

And even then it is not the *criterion "testing"* but the *criterion "puzzle-solving"* that, according to Kuhn, "is at once the less equivocal and the more fundamental" (7, i.a.).

But Popper's falsifiability – or testability – criterion does not presuppose that a *definite* distinction between testable and nontestable statements is possible, for the test procedures depend on hypotheses and their technical applications. These hypotheses are fallible as well and may be superseded by others. Accordingly, technology changes. Thus *a hypothesis that first was untestable may become testable later on*. Take, for example, the hypothesis that there are craters on the reverse side of the moon. Of course, there are theoretical reasons to assume that it is true, for we could not explain why there should be craters only on the side of the moon that we see from the Earth. But only advanced rocket technology made its empirical testing possible. Thus like the word "corroborated" (cf. section 5.1), the predicates *"testable"* and hence *"scientific"* are *relative to a particular time*.

However, Kuhn even doubts *"that scientific theories can without decisive change be cast in a form which permits the purely syntactic judgments* which this version of Sir Karl's criterion requires" (Kuhn 1970, 15, i.a.). He refers to judgments based on some logical contradiction between a theory and observation statements. But if no such *contradiction* can be found, even when other premises are added, then no observation statement at all can be *deduced* from a set of premises containing this theory. Hence the theory cannot be used for *predictions* or for technological *applications*. Accordingly, there could be no reason for any *"articulations"* (72, i.a.) of the theory (as a result of its failure to solve puzzles). This objection to Popper's criterion of demarcation obviously contradicts Kuhn's own theses on normal science. And there are other contradictions in his book. That he did not seek a sharp or decisive criterion of demarcation made his work popular in the "soft sciences."

1.242. William Kneale (1906–1990) thinks that "it is unwise to be dogmatic about the *logical form* of *scientific theories*, e.g., by saying that they are all unverifiable propositions of unrestricted universality" (Kneale 1974, 217, i.a.). As a counterexample, he mentions Anderson's announcement of the existence of positrons. Obviously, the strictly existential statement "There are positrons" is well corroborated, but Popper's criterion of demarcation classifies it as "metaphysical." For this reason, Kneale thinks that it is *too narrow* and that it has to be replaced by a different criterion.

However, Popper had already examined in his *Logic* a comparable case, the prediction of the existence of hafnium, the element with the atomic number 72. The mere assumption of its *existence* was not sufficient for scientists to find it. Rather, "all attempts to find it were in vain until Bohr succeeded in predicting several of its *properties* by deducing them from his theory. But Bohr's theory and those of its conclusions which were relevant to this element and which helped to bring about its discovery are far from being isolated purely existential statements. They are strictly universal statements" (LSD, 69f., i.a.). Thus, according to Popper, the mere thesis of the existence of hafnium need not be called "scientific," but it may be considered a *metaphysical statement stimulating science.*

But what would have happened if, in spite of every endeavour, an element with those properties had not been found? In this case, the *existential statement* would no doubt have been rejected – that is, it would have been treated as *indirectly empirically testable.* In order to account for this, Popper's criterion of demarcation would have to be more complex. For example, it could as a first step classify the *system* of those statements that were involved in the discovery of hafnium as scientific, because their conjunction is falsifiable, and then derive from this classification a judgment on the scientific character of the *single* statements. But this would not make the application of the criterion easier. Therefore, the advantage of simplicity seems to outweigh the disadvantage of the exclusion of all strictly existential statements from the set of scientific statements.

1.243. Grover Maxwell (b. 1918) believes that the criterion of demarcation is crucial "only for the letter and not for the spirit" of Popper's philosophy of science (Maxwell 1974, 292). The spirit "is concerned with *critical scrutiny* (of knowledge claims) in general and does not limit itself merely to attempts to falsify them" (ibid.). Later on, Popper himself declared the idea of *criticism*, not the idea of falsification, to be a regulative idea. The remainder of Maxwell's argument resembles that of Kneale: Many, perhaps most, scientific theories are not falsifiable, and since the criterion of demarcation classifies only falsifiable statements as scientific, it is much *too narrow* and therefore has to be rejected (ibid.).

Many important statements containing both universal and existential quantifiers are *not falsifiable.* Maxwell's first example is the statement "All men [Mx] are mortal [Ox]" [$(x)(Mx \rightarrow Ox)$], for it says that for each man x there is a particular time at which he dies [Dx,t] [$(x)(Mx \rightarrow (Et)Dx,t)$]. (This is also Russell's interpretation; cf. Russell 1919, Chapter 15.) It does not matter how long a person lives, it is always possible that he will eventually die. So there can be no counterexample. Nevertheless, we consider the statement "All men are mortal" well corroborated, for "although it has no falsifiable instances, *it has verifiable ones*, e.g., 'Jones dies on October 5, 1969' verifies 'Jones is mortal' and such instances that are actually verified are commonly regarded as confirmatory" (1974, 294).

But Maxwell goes even further. According to him, this is but one of many cases in science and everyday life, "where [even] a 'negative outcome' of an experiment or observation not only would fail to falsify the theory or hypothesis . . . , but would . . . disconfirm it only very slightly, while a *'positive outcome' would be highly confirmatory*" (1974, 294). And this poses, he thinks, "an extremely serious difficulty for Popper's *falsificationism, deductivism,* and *criterion of demarcation*" (294). Even according to Popper's concept of corroboration, a nonfalsifiable statement such as "All men are mortal" can be highly corroborated on the basis of observed instances of death. This is literally "*corroboration without demarcation,*" as the title of Maxwell's article reads (294).

As Maxwell suggests, a defender of the falsifiability criterion might counter that the statement "All men are mortal" is *metaphysical* (1974, 294). But whoever makes this statement normally does have an idea of human life expectancy. So it seems more plausible to take the statement to mean approximately "All men die 150 (or even 150,000) years after their birth at the latest." The statement "All men are mortal" would then be falsifiable, and the use of its predicate "mortal" would be a sign of negligent formulation. And up to now, the logically stronger statement "All men die 150 years after their birth at the latest" has been corroborated in every case in which the logically weaker statement "All men are mortal" has been corroborated. Biblical reports of even higher ages need hardly be considered empirical refutations.

According to Maxwell, *falsifiability* may be an important, though usually unattainable, *regulative ideal,* but it cannot "serve as a basis for sharply distinguishing the scientific from the unscientific, nor can attempts at *falsification* serve as the only means for testing theories by experiment and observation" (1974, 295).

In order to illustrate this, he gives an example. Many *theories* and *principles* are so firmly established "that they are taken for granted and virtually never stated explicitly. Among these is 'Every solid has a melting point' or, more explicitly, 'For every solid, at a given external pressure, there is a temperature above which it becomes liquid (or gaseous)'" (1974, 295). This statement is *not falsifiable,* "since we cannot subject any solid to the entire range of temperatures up to infinity [sic!] degrees" (295). But it

is corroborable, as we may find out that different solids become liquid at
different temperatures.

Maxwell considers the objection that this statement should be replaced by the stronger statement "Every solid has '*exactly one* melting
point'" – that is, both at least one and at most one (1974, 295). The
stronger statement would be falsified if a body with two or more melting
points were found. But if "melting point" simply means "'temperature
at which liquefaction begins,'" and if we take into account that there
are "'metastable states,'" then the thesis that there is *at most* one melting point is false (296). Therefore "melting point" must be defined as
"'*equilibrium* liquefaction (or solidification) point.'" But because of the
theoretical character of the predicate "*at equilibrium*," the statement is then
no longer empirically falsifiable; and since *equilibrium is a condition of all tests
of traditional thermodynamics, none of its theories are falsifiable* (296).

This result is of serious consequence, but is it really cogent? Actually, we
do not expect solids to melt only at extremely high temperatures ("infinity degrees"). Rather, we think of temperatures well below 10,000 Kelvin,
and if we leave astrophysics out of account, we do not even consider extremely high pressures. Therefore, it seems more plausible to read the
statement "Every solid has a melting point" as saying something like "At at-
mospheric pressure, every solid has a melting point below 10,000 Kelvin."
In this case, it would be falsifiable, and here the theoretical assumption
of equilibrium would not even be essential. Should the statement be falsified, the limit below which we expect the melting could be raised at will –
say, to 10,000,000 Kelvin – without any change in the logical relations.
We could as well choose a different pressure or a finite range of pressures. Therefore, the existential quantifier in the symbolized version of
the statement "Every solid has a melting point" is not inevitable; rather,
this statement is actually a negligent phrasing of what we really mean.

The result described two paragraphs earlier calls Maxwell's attention
to an even more important point: "In order to derive statements that are
inconsistent with the relevant observational 'basic statements', in most
cases it is necessary, even in the physical sciences, to use as premises not
only the theory in question plus auxiliary theories, but also *singular statements expressing initial conditions involving unobservables*, e.g. '*This system is
at equilibrium*'" (1974, 296, i.a.). So *virtually no scientific theory is falsifiable.*
Falsifiable is at best the conjunction of theory, auxiliary hypotheses (background knowledge), and singular statements about unobservables. With
these remarks, Maxwell seems merely to elaborate the Duhem–Quine
thesis (cf. section 3.6).

However, his argument takes a different turn. Though the theory cannot be falsified, it "can always be 'saved' by conjecturing that some unobservable 'foul up' of initial conditions produced the observed result" (1974, 296). Popper had proposed to exclude such conjectures by methodological convention (cf. section 3.4). But Maxwell argues that they are not always ad hoc, for they may be *corroborated* even though they are neither verifiable nor independently falsifiable (296).

Maxwell's arguments seem weighty. Still, they do not make Popper's criterion of demarcation fail. The reason for this is the same one we gave when discussing Kuhn's objections. If a theory really cannot be refuted by *any* experience, then it is useless for any prediction or for any technological application. However, Maxwell's arguments show that tests of scientific theories depend on more assumptions than we might suppose when we look at simple examples. And these assumptions cannot be tested at the same time as the theory in question. But when he calls them "theoretical," this is of no basic significance, for any statement is theoretical, because of the "transcendence inherent in any description" (cf. section 4.5). No "transcendence of generalization" is necessary for an assumption to be theoretical. On the other hand, the irrefutable "theories and principles" on which Maxwell reports need not be statements at all. Rather, they may be *schemata of theories* or *heuristic principles*, which suggest the formation of groups of empirical hypotheses related to each other. This is plausible, in particular, when the "theories and principles" are "taken for granted and virtually never stated explicitly."

1.244. Donald Gillies (b. 1944) argues that the falsifiability criterion fails "to exclude obvious metaphysical statements . . . because of a result known as the '*tacking paradox*'" (Gillies 1993, 210, i.a.). Take an arbitrary falsifiable theory T – for example, Kepler's first law, "All planets move about the sun in elliptical orbits, having the sun as one of its foci" – and tack on an arbitrary metaphysical statement M – for example, "'The Absolute is sleepy.'" Then any observation statement O that falsifies T, falsifies their conjunction $T \wedge M$ as well. Hence $T \wedge M$ is scientific. In order to avoid this result, Gillies proposes to supplement the criterion of demarcation by "considerations of *simplicity*" and to consider a theory T scientific "if it is falsifiable and of adequate simplicity" (211).

But why should $T \wedge M$ be obviously metaphysical? Gillies seems to assume tacitly that, according to Popper's criterion of demarcation, scientific statements must *not* have *any metaphysical content*. Actually, the criterion excludes only statements that do *not* have *any empirical content*.

1.25. From Falsifiability to Testability

According to the wording of the falsifiability criterion, *probability statements* are not scientific, for they are *not strictly falsifiable*, as they cannot "be contradicted by a conjunction of any finite number of basic statements; and accordingly not by any finite number of observations either" (LSD, 190). But considering probability statements to be unscientific seems unacceptable, because they are unrenouncable in science – for example, in statistical thermodynamics or in quantum theory. So Popper considers a probability hypothesis that fails a statistical test to be "'practically falsified.'" This "'*practical falsification*'" can be obtained "through a methodological decision to regard highly improbable events as ruled out – as prohibited" (191). This is exactly what happens when a "region of rejection" is defined for the statistical test of a hypothesis. This modification turns the falsifiability criterion into a *testability criterion*.

This modification is inevitable for still another reason, one already mentioned. We *cannot prove the truth of falsifying basic statements*, because they state lawlike properties of their objects and hence assert more than could ever be observed ("*transcendence inherent in any description*"; cf. section 4.5) and because expectations or dispositions affect perception ("*transcendence inherent in any perception*"; cf. section 4.2). Consequently, the *universal statements*, which are contradicted by the basic statements, *are not strictly refutable*. Like singular statements and probability statements, they are empirically testable, but their tests do not have certain, definite results, do not result in strict verification or falsification but only in temporary acceptance or rejection. There is no certain knowledge of facts. *Critical rationalism is a kind of fallibilism.*

In his book *Quantum Theory and the Schism in Physics*, Popper defends the indeterminist conception of the world (cf. Chapter 14) and the propensity interpretation of physics (cf. section 8.5). The book ends with a *metaphysical epilogue*, in which he states that indeterminism and the propensity interpretation are not empirically testable theories but pictures or ways of looking at things that guide scientific discovery and "help us to decide whether a scientific hypothesis is to be taken seriously; whether it is a potential discovery, and how its acceptance would affect the problem situation in science, and perhaps even the [indeterminist] picture [of the world] itself" (QTSP, 211). Here we might even find "a criterion of demarcation *within metaphysics*, between rationally worthless metaphysical systems, and metaphysical systems that are worth discussing." Worth considering is a conception of the world that provokes rational criticism and inspires "attempts to supersede it by something better" (211).

1.26. What Is Demarcation For?

Does this modified criterion of demarcation accomplish "the first task of the logic of knowledge to put forward a *concept of empirical science*, in order to make linguistic usage, now somewhat uncertain, as definite as possible, and in order to draw a clear line of demarcation between science and metaphysical ideas – even though these ideas may have furthered the advance of science throughout its history"? (LSD, 38f.) Or is it possible that the task itself is a questionable one?

Barbosa de Oliveira's critique is more fundamental. He primarily attacks not Popper's solution to the problem of demarcation, but the problem itself. In his article "Against Demarcation," he writes: "[T]he problem [!] of demarcation itself ... must be dismissed, since ... it is a manifestation of a scientistic attitude" (1988, 22). According to him, scientists assume that "any discipline, any form of human enquiry, is not good, if it is not a science" (42), and scientism "fills with propaganda an intellectual space that could and should be occupied by rational debate" (47). This author is not just worried about the damage that demarcation could do to the reputations of those disciplines that make lesser demands on their results than the empirical and the pure sciences. He also fears that research programmes might be "intrinsically dangerous" or "go against some ethical principles we hold" (45). But he misses the fact that philosophies can be much more dangerous than scientific theories, as Marxism showed. The same is true of religions. We need only remember the crusades and the Inquisition.

Paul Karl Feyerabend (1924–1993) also goes beyond Kuhn's criticism of the criterion of demarcation. He postulates a pluralist methodology according to which the "separation between the history of a science, its philosophy and the science itself dissolves into thin air and so does the separation between science and non-science" (Feyerabend 1975, 47f.). According to him, we even "should regard the world-views of the Bible, the Gilgamesh epic, the Iliad, the Edda, as fully fledged *alternative cosmologies* which can be used to modify, and even to replace, the 'scientific' cosmologies of a given period" (47 n1).

Because of this far-reaching pluralism, Feyerabend was suspected of not being serious, for his own example shows why it can be useful to maintain a separation between science and nonscience. In the trial of Galilei, the church defended its traditional worldview, but today the church no longer claims to have been right to do so, or to do so in this way. *Perhaps the most important function of the demarcation between science and nonscience is to refuse political and religious authorities the right to pass binding judgments on the truth of certain statements of fact.*

2

The Role of Theories

At the beginning of his *Logic of Scientific Discovery*, Popper quotes Novalis: "Theories [in 1992: Hypotheses] are nets: only he who casts will catch." In its third chapter, "Theories," he adds: "Theories are nets cast to catch what we call 'the world': to rationalize, to explain, and to master it. We endeavour to make the mesh ever finer and finer" (LSD, 59). The "aim of theoretical science ... is to find *explanatory theories* (if possible, *true* explanatory theories); that is to say, theories which describe certain structural properties of the world, and which permit us to deduce, with the help of initial conditions, the effects to be explained" (61 n1). Hence Popper is a realist – that is, he interprets theories as statements about the world, and he criticizes the "instrumentalists" Mach, Wittgenstein, and Schlick, who consider theories to be mere tools for prediction (59 n*1; cf. section 1.223).

But theories do not just *describe* and *explain* the world. As they enable us to *predict* events, they also help us to control nature. The idea that man can and should control nature is age-old. It can be found in religions (Genesis 1:28) as well as in philosophies; in the empiricist Bacon (1561–1626) as well as in the rationalist Descartes (1596–1650). Popper also stresses the economic importance of science: "Science may be regarded as a means of production – as the last word in 'roundabout production'" (LSD, 100). (The expression "roundabout production" ["*Produktionsumweg*"] was proposed by the economist Böhm-Bawerk.)

In his *Logic*, Popper still considers all explanation to be "causal": "I should say here more explicitly that the decision to search for *causal* explanation is that by which the theoretician adopts his aim – or the aim of theoretical science" (LSD, 61 n1, i.a.). Later, he professes to be an indeterminist (cf. Chapter 14). So causal explanation (using universal, deterministic hypotheses) can no longer be the aim. An explanation is causal if it states a (causal) connection between the event or state of affairs to be explained (the effect) and another event or state of affairs (the cause). Hume called the idea of causation the "cement of the universe."

* According to Aristotle, a full explanation of anything must consider the material, the formal, the efficient, and the final cause – the purpose for which the thing exists or was produced. With the rise of modern science, mechanistic explanations of natural phenomena, which appeal only to *efficient* causes, became standard. Some authors still maintain that the explanation of biological processes, of the structure, function, and organization of organisms, requires some kind of teleology. Others, however, reject the idea of a "final cause": "[W]hat accounts for the present changes of a self-regulating system *s* is not the 'future event' of *s* being in *R* [the respect in which *s* is self-regulating], but rather the *present disposition* of *s* to return to *R*" (Hempel 1965, 325). Hospers even considers calling a natural law on which an explanation relies the "formal cause" of the event explained, while he calls (the event described by) the initial condition its "efficient cause" (Hospers 1946, 344). **

To express the idea of (efficient) *causation*, we use not only the verb "to cause" but also such verbs as "make," "produce," "determine," and so on. Other transitive verbs such as "move," "break," and "kill" implicitly assert causal connections. Even the verb "perceive" involves the idea that an observed object causes an experience in the observer. Descartes writes: "Of course, [we experience in ourselves that] whatever we feel undoubtedly comes to us from something different from our mind. For it is not in our power to cause ourselves to feel one sensation rather than another; on the contrary, this plainly *depends on whatever is influencing our senses*" (1983, 39, i.a.).

2.1. THE PRINCIPLE OF CAUSALITY AND THE "REGULARITY THEORY" OF CAUSATION

The idea of "*universal causation*" has been known from ancient times. Aristotle writes: "[E]verything which is generated is generated by something and from something and becomes something" (*Metaphysics*, VII 7, 1032 a 13). Later, Kant asserts: "Everything that happens (begins to be) presupposes something which it follows in accordance with a rule" (CPR, A 189), or rather, "All alterations occur in accordance with the law of the connection of cause and effect" (B 232). Modern formulations of this idea are: "Every event has a cause"; "Nothing happens without a cause"; and "All events are subject to universal laws." Popper calls this the "*principle of causality*' (or 'principle of universal causation')" (LSD, 60); Bertrand Russell (1872–1970) speaks of the *law of causality*, which he believes to be a relic of a bygone age; and John Stuart Mill (1806–1873) refers to the *law of causation* (Russell 1913, 193, 196).

According to David Hume, "[*T*]*he constant conjunction of objects* [alone] *determines their causation*" (1978, 173). But this "constant conjunction" is only spatiotemporal association without exception (cf. section 1.121.). Hume rejects the ontological idea that in addition to this "conjunction" there exists a relation of cause and effect, a "necessary connexion," because this idea is not empirical. Accordingly, he proposes: "[W]e may define a cause to be *an object, followed by another, and where all the objects similar to the first are followed by objects similar to the second*" (EHU, 76).

This "*regularity theory of causation*" is, however, soon criticized. John Stuart Mill objects: "Whenever the factory whistle in Manchester wails, workers in London leave their factories, but the whistle in Manchester does not cause what happens in London." In fact, any statistician is confronted with the problem of which of the empirically found correlations are "genuine" and which are "spurious" correlations. Obviously, there is a similar problem associated with universal (determinist) hypotheses.

In order to make possible a selection from the many empirically found "constant conjunctions," Hume specifies eight rules by which we can determine whether certain types of objects or events really can be called "causes or effects to each other" (1978, 173). The first four rules are the most simple and the most important:

1.   The cause and effect must be *contiguous in space and time.*

This eliminates Mill's objection before it is even raised. The wailing of the factory whistle in Manchester and the behaviour of the workers in London are contiguous in time but not in space.

2.   The cause must be *prior* to the effect.

For most kinds of events, this idea is still accepted today. If event *A* is to influence event *B*, at least a signal originating from *A* must reach *B*, and – according to Einstein's special theory of relativity – no signal can travel faster than light.

According to Isaac Newton (1643–1727), gravitation is an instantaneous long-range interaction. But when two bodies move around a

common centre of gravity, we do not say that the movement of the first
causes the movement of the second, because at all times they mutually
influence each other. If their interaction consists in the exchange of gravitons, it is not instantaneous, because the gravitons are exchanged at the
velocity of light. If two gravitons switch positions, the change of place of
the first does not cause the change of place of the second, either. On the
other hand, the exchange of gravitons may cause the movement of the
two bodies.

Hence Hume's second rule is still well adapted to the present level of
research. Nevertheless, it is useful only if the direction of time can be
ascertained independently of the direction of causation; otherwise, it is
circular.

3.   There must be a *constant* union betwixt the cause and effect. 'Tis chiefly
     this quality, that constitutes the relation [of cause and effect].

This rule excludes causal explanations relying on occasional associations – which are not without exception. The following rule serves the
same purpose in a different respect:

4.   *The same cause always produces the same effect,* and the same effect never
     arises but from the same cause. (1978, 173, i.a.)

However, according to Russell, this rule would make science barren. For
"[a]s soon as the antecedents [causes] have been given sufficiently fully
to enable the consequent [effect] to be calculated with some exactitude,
the antecedents have become so complicated that it is very unlikely they
will ever recur" (Russell 1913, 198). For example, the free fall of physical
bodies depends not only on the medium through which they are falling
(water, air, vacuum, etc.) but also on their altitude and terrestrial latitude.
Theoretically – according to Newton's theory of gravitation – the positions
of the sun and the moon and ultimately those of all other bodies, and
not just celestial bodies, are a factor.

Russell considers the *law of causality* ("Given any event e_1, there is an
event e_2 and a time-interval τ such that, whenever e_1 occurs, e_2 follows
after an interval τ" or simply "Every event [e_2] has a cause [e_1]") to be a
relic from days long past (1913, 195), and Popper shares this view. But
Russell also claims that *physics has given up looking for causes,* because in
fact there are no causes. According to him, the laws of physics are not of
the type "One event A is always followed by another event B"; rather, they
express *functional relations* between certain events at certain times – the

"'*determinants*' " – and other events at earlier or later times or at the same time (205).

We may assent to Russell's thesis on the form of physical laws, but is it of fundamental importance for methodological reasons? Would the determinants themselves – until their description is sufficiently complete to enable the computation of the other events with adequate precision – not "have become so complicated that it is very unlikely they will ever recur"? Obviously, the *number* of factors influencing an event cannot depend on the logical *form* of physical laws, whether they are universal if-then statements or equations. Nonetheless, it is still useful to examine the logical relations between theories and observation statements by the – most simple – example of universal if-then statements.

At the same time, Hume was well aware of the limits of his rules: "All the rules of this nature are very easy in their invention, but extremely difficult in their application" (1978, 175). This applies correspondingly to Popper's methodological rules, and he also knows how little can be achieved by introducing general rules.

Neoempiricists too adhere to Hume's *regularity theory of causality*. According to *Schlick*, the concept of causality expresses the idea that "a process A 'determines' another process, B" (Schlick 1979, 178), and science expresses this dependence by a *law*; "thus *causality* is just another word for the *existence of a law*" (177, i.a.). Hence "it is all one" whether we formulate the "thesis of *determinism*," that "*every* event is a member of a causal relation," or assert the "causal *principle*," that "*everything* in the world takes place according to law" (177). But how do we find out *whether* something happens according to a law? The "true criterion of regularity, the essential mark of causality, is the *fulfilment of predictions*" (185). Referring to Hume, Schlick even postulates that "'A determines B' can mean nothing else whatever but 'B can be *calculated* from A'" (201).

Popper writes in his *Logic*: "The 'principle of causality' is the assertion that any event whatsoever *can* be causally explained – that it *can* be deductively predicted" (LSD, 61). But even if the "*principle of causality*" is not *analytic*, it is not falsifiable, because it asserts that for every event x there is an explanation or a *cause* y [$(x)(Ey)yCx$] without, however, indicating how the explanation or the cause can be found. Therefore, Popper excludes this principle, "as '*metaphysical*' [,] from the sphere of science" (ibid., i.a.).

In its stead, he proposes – at the suggestion of Heinrich Gomperz (1873–1942) – "a *methodological rule* which corresponds so closely to the 'principle of causality' that the latter might be regarded as its metaphysical version. It is the simple *rule that we are not to abandon the search for universal laws and for a coherent theoretical system, nor ever give up our attempts to explain causally any kind of event we can describe.* This rule guides the scientific investigator in his work" (LSD, 61, i.a.). Accordingly, the investigator proceeds *as if* every event had a cause and as if it were his task to find it. In other words, the *assumption that every event is determined* serves as a *regulative principle.* Hermann Helmholtz (1821–1894) had already stated: "The law of sufficient basis [rather: "law of sufficient reason": "*Gesetz vom zureichenden Grunde*"] amounts simply to the requirement of wishing to understand everything" (1867/1962, 34). Popper does not accept the view "that the latest developments in physics demand the renunciation of this rule, or that physics has now established that within one field at least it is pointless to seek any longer for [universal or determinist] laws" (LSD, 61f.). Though he rejects *metaphysical determinism,* he still advocates *methodological determinism.* Later, in his *Postscript to the Logic of Scientific Discovery,* he turns out to be a convinced *metaphysical indeterminist* (cf. Chapter 14, this volume). However, this change of mind is due not to developments in physics but to his desire to defend the ideas of free will and creativity.

Some authors – rightly – doubt that the regularity theory of causality succeeds in distinguishing between genuine and apparent causes. Perhaps Hume already had his doubts. This might explain why – immediately following the definition just quoted – he declares "a cause to be *an object, followed by another, . . . where, if the first object had not been, the second never had existed,"* though he takes the two definitions to be equivalent (EHU, 76).

David Lewis, however, thinks that Hume's second definition is no mere restatement of the first (Lewis, 1973). While Hume's first definition is the foundation for the *regularity theory of causality,* the second definition proposes, according to Lewis, a "*counterfactual analysis of causation*" (557, i.a.). This analysis explains *causal* dependence as *counterfactual* dependence. Correspondingly, "If *A*, then always *B*" (regularity theory) is replaced by "If *A* were the case, then *B* would also be the case" (counterfactual analysis). This counterfactual conditional expresses *B*'s counterfactual dependence on *A*. In order to interpret this and to symbolize it, Lewis introduces the operation $\square \rightarrow$, which is defined by a rule of truth, as follows: "A counterfactual is nonvacuously true iff [if, and only if] it takes less of a departure from actuality to make the consequent true along with the antecedent than it does to make the antecedent true without the consequent" (560).

Do his results justify this expenditure? After all, any universal law implies such counterfactual conditionals, and Lewis himself admits: "Often, perhaps always, *counterfactual* dependences may be ... explained [by *nomic* dependences]" (1973, 564, i.a.). What, then, is the essential difference between the two analyses of causation? Lewis hopes to solve the problems that Hume's rules are intended to solve by rejecting those counterfactual conditionals that do not provide genuine explanations (566). But this implies rejecting the corresponding universal law. And his proposal amounts to rejecting the law if, and only if, a (possible) world, in which the law does not hold, resembles our actual world more than a world in which it does hold (559, 565). However, we answer the question what our actual world is like according to the corroboration of our universal hypotheses. If there are two rival hypotheses, we assume that our world is as the well-corroborated hypothesis says and not as the little-corroborated hypothesis says. Hence we would argue in a circle if we accepted hypotheses as means of genuine explanation, according to Lewis's criterion.

Statisticians are faced with the problem of which of the empirically found *correlations* are "genuine" and which are "*spurious*." In a certain region of East Prussia, a strong positive correlation was found between the frequent occurrence of storks and a high birthrate. Does this correlation explain why the birthrate was high? Why do we think that this is not the case? Because we rely on a *more general and better corroborated biological hypothesis*, which excludes any influence of storks on the production of children. This gives rise to the question of how the correlation itself can be explained. The answer may be: "Where the soil is heavy, there are many frogs and therefore many storks; at the same time, the farmers are well off, as the harvests are rich, and the better off they are, the more children they have." Accordingly, the correlated events (frequent occurrence of storks, a high birthrate) have a common "cause" (heavy soil).

The question of how to distinguish between "genuine" and "spurious" correlations has its counterpart in universal (determinist) hypotheses. As we have seen, we cannot decide by methodological rules alone – without the biological hypothesis – whether the empirical correlation between the frequent occurrence of storks and a high birthrate is "spurious" or not. Just as little could we find out by counterfactual analysis of causation alone that a well-corroborated hypothesis H_1 only *seems to state a cause-effect relation*. Rather, we need a better-corroborated hypothesis H_2, which replaces H_1. In addition, H_2 (or a further hypothesis H_3) should explain how the association stated by H_1 comes about, and thus why H_1 (only) seems to state a genuine cause-effect relation.

When would a counterfactual analysis of causation be superior to the regularity theory? Only when it succeeded better in extracting *restrictive conditions for the acceptance of hypotheses* from *fundamental physical laws*. In one passage, Lewis seems to have something similar in mind. He discards the "stipulation that a cause must always precede its effect," because it "rejects a priori certain legitimate physical hypotheses that posit backward or simultaneous causation" (1973, 566). The corroboration of such hypotheses could be a reason to restrict Hume's second rule in some appropriate manner, but Lewis's vague reference to "certain hypotheses" is surely no sufficient reason to abandon this rule.

2.2. CAUSAL EXPLANATION

What is a causal explanation? Popper writes: "To give a *causal explanation* of an event means to deduce a statement which describes it, using as premises of the deduction one or more *universal laws*, together with certain singular statements, the *initial conditions*" (LSD, 59). Obviously, this is a methodological version of Hume's regularity theory of causality. Since Hempel and Oppenheim worked it out in detail, it has been known as the "deductive-nomological" (D-N) or "hypothetico-deductive" (H-D) model of explanation (cf. Hempel 1965, Chapter 12). Later, Popper will assert that natural laws are "naturally or physically *necessary*," and he will thus return to a pre-Humean position (LSD, 433, i.a.; cf. Chapter 13, this volume).

2.21. Formal Requirements of Adequate Explanation

Popper gives a simple example of a causal explanation. He begins: "[W]e have given a causal explanation of the breaking of a certain piece of thread if we have found that the thread has a tensile strength of 1 *lb.* and that a weight of 2 *lbs.* was put on it" (LSD, 59f.). However, this is only a partial outline. A complete *causal explanation* is a *deductive argument*. It has two kinds of *premises*: "(1) *universal statements, i.e.* hypotheses of the character of natural laws, and (2) *singular statements*, which apply to the specific event in question" and which Popper calls "'initial conditions'" (60). In his example, the singular statement "This thread breaks" is the *conclusion*. [Actually, he writes "'This thread will break,'" and he calls this

statement "a specific or singular *prediction*" (60)]. Hence the scheme of the causal explanation is as follows (60 n*1):
Universal laws:

(1) For every thread of a given structure S (determined by its material, thickness, etc.) there is a characteristic weight w, such that the thread will break if any weight exceeding w is suspended from it.

(2) For every thread of the structure S_1, the characteristic weight w_1 equals 1 *lb.*

Initial conditions:

(3) This is a thread of structure S_1.

(4) The weight [to be] put on this thread is equal to 2 *lbs.*

Singular prediction:

(5) This thread breaks [will break].

Nowadays, premises (1)–(4) are called the *explanans,* and the conclusion (5) is called the *explanandum* (more exactly: the explanandum *statement,* for what is actually to be explained [the "explanandum"] is the explanandum *event* that the explanandum statement describes).

The terms "explanans" and "explanandum" go back to Hempel and Oppenheim (cf. Hempel 1965, 247ff.). Popper's term "*prediction*" for the conclusion of an explanation has not been widely accepted. What he calls "*initial conditions*" are called "*statements of antecedent conditions*" by Hempel and Oppenheim (Hempel 1965, 249). According to Popper, "The initial conditions describe what is usually called the '*cause*' of the event in question.... And the prediction describes what is usually called the '*effect*'" (LSD, 60). Popper will avoid the terms "cause" and "effect" (60), and the term "initial condition" is, like the term "explanandum," used ambiguously: Often it refers not to statements but to the states of affairs they state.

There is still *another form of deductive-nomological explanation.* Some hypotheses can be arranged according to their content – in particular, according to their generality. Then, for example, the less general hypotheses can be deduced from the more general, and the "'deductive inferences from the higher to the lower level' are, of course, *explanations*...; thus the hypotheses on the higher level are *explanatory* with respect to those on the lower level" (LSD, 277 n *1).

Some deductive arguments involve *probability statements* (QTSP, 70). Their conclusions, however, assign probabilities not to singular events but to *types of events* (cf. section 8.51). In an analogy to deductive-nomological explanations of *singular events*, inductive-statistical explanations have been proposed, but their results are epistemically ambiguous – that is, if different subsets of the set of all accepted scientific statements are used as premises in statistical explanations, they may confer high probabilities on logically contradictory results (Hempel, 1965, 394ff.). As Popper did not comment on statistical explanations, we do not consider this problem in detail.

2.22. Material Requirements of Adequate Explanation

Not every deductive argument that meets the formal requirements is, however, an adequate explanation. Rather, empirical explanations must also fulfil *material requirements*. Above all, their premises must be *empirically testable*. In principle, they must also be *true* (cf. Hospers 1946, 345), for only true premises secure the truth of their conclusions, and only a true natural law "expresses a *structural property of our world*" (LSD, 432). But as we cannot know for certain whether a – singular or universal – synthetic statement is true, well-*corroborated* premises will have to suffice.

But does this affect the *definition* of "explanation"? After all, Popper asserts in his *Logic* that it is possible to avoid using the concept "true" (cf. section 6.1), and in his *Postscript* he voices doubts about calling a statement "true" (cf. section 5.52). Even if we do not share his doubts, a comparison will be useful: If, *by definition*, an explanation is adequate only if all of its premises are *true*, we never *know* whether a formally adequate explanatory argument is also a materially adequate explanation. If, on the other hand, a formally adequate explanatory argument whose premises are well *corroborated* is, *by definition*, a materially adequate explanation, then the concept *"explanation"* is – like the concept "corroboration"– *relative to a particular time* (cf. section 5.1).

What does this mean? If a hypothesis, when it is corroborated, is used to explain a certain state of affairs, then the explanation is materially adequate; but if it is used in the same way when it is not corroborated, then the explanation is not materially adequate. Thus one and the same deductive argument may be an adequate explanation at one time but not an adequate explanation at another time. Hence we cannot say "This explanation is adequate," but only "This explanation is adequate at that time."

Now, there is no certain knowledge at all except in the pure sciences. Hence just as we do not know for certain whether a hypothesis is true, we do not know for certain whether it is corroborated at a certain time, that is, whether the statement that it is corroborated at this time is true. But if, for this reason, we tried to replace "This hypothesis is corroborated at that time" with "The assumption 'This hypothesis is corroborated at that time' is corroborated at a certain point in time," we would get into an infinite regress. For a similar reason, William James's (1842–1910) pragmatist definition of truth failed (cf. Keuth 1989, 132). We may easily avoid the regress if we are prepared to consider at least singular statements true – for example, a report on the previous success of a theory. But this move is rather arbitrary, as singular statements too are hypothetical. This suggests making the *truth* of its premises a definitional criterion of an adequate explanation but being content with their *corroboration*, which can be considered an *indicator* of their truth.

According to some authors, an explanation is *complete* only if the states of affairs expressed by its premises are explained in their turn (cf. Hospers 1946, 348ff.; Musgrave 1998, 95ff.). But no explanation can be complete in this sense, for we get into an infinite regress if we keep asking for the *cause of a cause* or the *regularity underlying some regularity*. The regress of the causes is a well-known problem of determinism (cf. section 14.62). Hume mentions it in his *Dialogues Concerning Natural Religion* (part 11), and Kant tries to avoid it by postulating "*Causalität aus Freiheit*" (causality out of freedom). But most people do not believe in transcendental philosophy. They must either be content with explanations that are "incomplete" – this seems admissible when the premises need not be explained in the given context – or give up any attempt at an explanation.

2.3. PREDICTION

In everyday life, a *prediction* is a *statement* asserting a *future* event; in methodology, it is (primarily) a *deductive argument* resulting in such a statement. According to the "*thesis of the structural identity* (or of the symmetry) *of explanation and prediction*," a predictive argument has the same logical form as an explanatory argument (Hempel 1965, 367). The two arguments differ only in pragmatic respects. Above all, the event to be explained must be known at the time that it is explained – that is, it must have occurred in the past or it must be occurring in the present – whereas the event to be predicted must be unknown when the prediction is made, whether it will occur in future or has already occurred (though we still have no knowledge of it).

If we rule out the possibility that future or present events can change the past, the initial conditions (the events, not the statements asserting them) must have occurred – or must at the latest occur – by the time the event to be explained or predicted occurs. The initial conditions must have occurred earlier, provided we assume that they act on the events to be explained or predicted at most by the velocity of light.

Hence we may illustrate a *prediction* (a predictive argument) by adding time indices to the sketch of an explanation given earlier (cf. section 2.21). We exclude instantaneous action and assume instead that the thread will break one second after a weight exceeding its characteristic weight has been suspended from it. If we now assume:

(4′) A weight of 2 lbs. will be put on this thread on the first of January 2050 at 14.28.26 GMT

we obtain the *singular prediction*:

(5′) This thread will break on the first of January 2050 at 14.28.27 GMT.

If, on the other hand, we assume:

(3′) From this semifinished good a thread of the structure S_1 will have been made tomorrow at 11.23 GMT

we obtain the *conditional prediction*:

(5″) If a weight of 2 lbs. will be put on this thread at some time after its completion tomorrow at 11.23 GMT, it will break one second later.

As explanation and prediction are very similar, Popper does not hesitate to call the conclusion of an explanation "a specific or singular *prediction*" (LSD, 60). He adds a note: "The term 'prediction', as used here, comprises statements about the past ('retrodictions'), or even 'given' statements which we wish to explain ('*explicanda*')" (60 n*2).

The *thesis of the structural identity of explanation and prediction* may be considered the conjunction of two subtheses, namely, (i) "*every adequate explanation is potentially a prediction*" and (ii) "*every adequate prediction is potentially an explanation*" (Hempel 1965, 367). It is uncontested, insofar as it asserts only what our examples illustrate.

But there actually are nontrivial *differences* between explanation and prediction. This becomes apparent when these arguments fail. Some (singular) predictions come true, some do not. Astronomical predictions are mostly – within certain limits of error – successful. If, however, they fail (as, e.g., the prediction of the Leonids, a meteor stream, in November 1998), we do not say that there was no prediction; rather, we say the *prediction* was *false* or *inadequate*. Of course, the singular conclusion of the predictive argument is false; the argument itself may also be false (if the astronomer miscalculated) or it may be inadequate (if some of its premises are false). The premises comprise the astronomical theory (e.g., Newton's theory of gravitation) and assumptions about the earlier positions of the celestial bodies concerned, but they also include assumptions about the properties of the instruments used – for example, the precision of the clock.

If, however, we "explain an event" and find out afterward that the supposed event did not occur, we do not say that the explanation was false; rather, we say that there was *no explanation* at all, as the presumably explained entity did not exist. On the other hand, an explanation is *false* if the deductive argument is not valid, and it is *inadequate* if some of its premises are false. Thus we could say there is a structural difference (or an asymmetry) between explanation and prediction: The conclusion of an explanation must be true, that of a prediction may be false.

Most predictions we learn of in news reports are not predictions in the sense intended here. Though economic predictions are deductive arguments, they are not nomological, as they cannot rely on universal hypotheses; rather, they extrapolate trends. And most political predictions are not even deductive arguments, as political trends cannot be definitely ascertained, but are prophecies. However, the prophet may – like the oracle of Apollo at Delphi – be quite wise.

2.4. STRICT AND NUMERICAL UNIVERSALITY

The idea of a causal relation between events of type A, the causes, and events of type B, the effects, presupposes an association without exception of the events A with the events B. *Only universal* hypotheses, but *not all* universal hypotheses, state such associations. Consider two hypotheses. The first is:

(1) "All material systems can absorb or give off electromagnetic radiation only in quanta E, and these are proportional to the frequency v of that radiation $E = hv$." (The constant of proportionality h is called Planck's constant.)

This statement, taken from Planck's quantum theory of absorption and emission of radiation, claims to be true for any place and at any time. Hence it refers to an *open class* of cases and admits of no exception.

Popper calls universal synthetic statements of this kind "*strictly universal statements*" or "*all-statement[s]*" (LSD, 62f.). The second hypothesis is:

(2) "Of all human beings now living on the earth it is true that their height never exceeds ... 8 ft." (LSD, 62).

This statement refers only to a finite spatiotemporal region and, as the objects of physics are finitely extended, only to a *finite number* of objects. Hence it can in principle be replaced by a finite conjunction of singular statements. [If we give (2) the form $(x)(Mx \rightarrow h(x) \leq 8)$, where "$Mx$" means "$x$ is a man" and "$h(x)$" means "the height of x in feet," it can be replaced by the conjunction of the singular statements $Ma \rightarrow h(a) \leq 8$, $Mb \rightarrow h(b) \leq 8, \ldots, Mn \rightarrow h(n) \leq 8$.] Therefore Popper calls statements such as (2) "*'numerically universal'*" (62, i.a.) and counts them among the "*'specific'* or '*singular*' statements" that "relate only to certain finite regions of space and time" (63, i.a.). If we demand that natural laws describe causal relations as well as possible, it is useful "to regard natural laws as synthetic and strictly universal statements ('all-statements')" (63). This is a methodological decision that cannot be considered true nor false but only useful or useless.

2.5. UNIVERSAL CONCEPTS AND INDIVIDUAL CONCEPTS

Statements aren't *strictly* universal by their logical *form* alone. Rather, their nonlogical signs – in our example, the predicate "Mx" and the functor "$h(x)$" – must also be *interpreted* in an appropriate way. In order to show which requirements the interpretation has to meet, Popper distinguishes between universal and individual concepts or names (LSD, 64ff.). We might try to characterize individual concepts by saying that their interpretation somehow refers to individuals. This is true, for example, of the predicate "is on the Earth," which delimits a space. In this case, universal concepts may be characterized by saying that they in no way refer to individuals. But this would merely be an illustration, not a useful definition, for in natural languages there are other ways of expressing spatiotemporal limitations – for example, by adverbs of place such as "here," "now," "there," and "then" or by the demonstrative pronouns "this" and "that." However, we may define: "*Universal concepts* do not, on account of their meaning alone, apply only to finite classes of individuals; all other concepts are *individual concepts*."

2.6. STRICTLY UNIVERSAL AND EXISTENTIAL STATEMENTS

Popper calls statements in which only logical constants and universal concepts occur "'strict' or 'pure'" (LSD, 68). If strict statements are also universal, then they are "*strictly universal* statements" or "*all-statements*"; if they are existential statements such as "There are black ravens," then they are "*strictly or purely existential statements* (or '*there-is*' *statements*)" (68). But a strictly universal statement is equivalent to the negation of a strictly existential statement, and vice versa. Therefore, natural laws may be considered "'prohibitions'": "They do not *assert* that something exists or is the case; they *deny* it" (69, i.a.).

The universal hypothesis "All *r*avens are *b*lack" $[(x)(Rx \rightarrow Bx)]$, for example, does not assert that there are black ravens; rather, it asserts that there are no ravens that are not black, for it is equivalent to the negated existential statement "There are no nonblack ravens" $[\neg(Ex)(Rx \wedge \neg Bx)]$. If there is a nonblack raven – that is, if the prohibited state of affairs is a fact – then the hypothesis is refuted. A less trivial example is the first law of thermodynamics, also called the law of conservation of energy, which states that the total energy E of a mechanical system – that is, the sum of its kinetic energy K and its potential energy U – is always constant ($E = K + U =$ const.). This law rules out the existence of a perpetual motion device that delivers more energy from a falling or turning body than is required to restore it to its original state.

3

On the Problem of a Theory of Scientific Method

According to Popper's proposal, "epistemology, or the logic of scientific discovery, should be identified with the *theory of scientific method*" (LSD, 49, i.a.). On the one hand, epistemology analyzes the *logical relations* between scientific statements; on the other hand, it is "concerned with *the choice of methods* – with decisions about the way in which scientific statements are to be dealt with" (49). These decisions depend on the *aims* chosen, and they lay down suitable rules for the "*'empirical method'*" (49, i.a.), which are to complement Popper's *criterion of demarcation* (54). Consequently, he proposes "to adopt such rules as will ensure the *testability* of scientific statements; which is to say, their *falsifiability*" (49, i.a.).

To ensure the testability of scientific statements is the most general aim of the theory of scientific method: Its rules are intended to help us separate the chaff from the wheat among our assumptions. As *empirical statements* are fallible, scientific method must take their "*susceptibility to revision*" into account, and it has to "analyse the characteristic *ability of science to advance,* and the characteristic manner in which a *choice* is made, in crucial cases, *between conflicting systems of theories*" (LSD, 49f., i.a.).

3.1. WHY METHODOLOGICAL DECISIONS
ARE INDISPENSABLE

Members of the Vienna Circle thought that the statements of a theory of method, if they are not to be unscientific or even meaningless, must be either logical or empirical (LSD, 51 n*1). However, being directives, methodological rules cannot be empirical or logical statements. Popper therefore defends his theory of method against positivist criticism to this effect. Then – in a kind of "Copernican turn" – he reverses the usual way of looking at things: He proposes "that empirical science should be characterized by its *methods*: by our manner of dealing with scientific systems," and he tries "to establish the rules, or if you will the norms, by which the scientist is guided when he is engaged in research or in discovery, *in the sense here understood*" (50, i.a.).

A scientist is "engaged in research or in discovery," in Popper's sense, if he proposes bold hypotheses and then tries, as best he can, to refute them. Thus Popper does not describe methodological customs but proposes new ones. *His theory of methods is not empirical; rather, it determines what is to be considered empirical.* He *defines* "*empirical science* with the help of the criterion of falsifiability" and the methodological rules supplementing it (LSD, 54, i.a.). Correspondingly, he does not study historically the "ability of science to advance"; rather, he proposes methodological rules that are intended to further this ability.

3.2. THE "NATURALISTIC" APPROACH TO THE THEORY OF METHOD

This explains why Popper defends "a genuine theory of knowledge, an epistemology or a methodology" against positivist criticism (LSD, 51). For "the main problem of philosophy is the critical analysis of the appeal to the authority of 'experience' – precisely that 'experience' which every latest discoverer of positivism is, as ever, artlessly taking for granted" (51f.). It is true that positivists also study experience, but they do so using the methods of empirical psychology. Popper, on the other hand, "attempts to analyse '*experience*'[,] which [he] interpret[s] *as the method of empirical science*" (52, i.a.). But how does he do that, if not with the methods of logic or empirical science?

According to the "'*naturalistic*'" view, methodology is "a branch of some empirical science – the science, say, of the behaviour of scientists at work" (LSD, 52). Popper knew the – subject to some limitations empirical – methodological inquiries of Pierre Duhem (1906) and Hugo Dingler (1921). Nowadays, Thomas Samuel Kuhn's *The Structure of Scientific Revolutions* (1962) is far better known. Though Popper admits that "[a] naturalistic methodology . . . has its value, no doubt," he thinks that "'methodology' should not be taken for an empirical science," because he does not believe "that it is possible to decide, by using the methods of an empirical science, such controversial questions as whether science actually uses a principle of induction or not" (52).

But how does Popper answer this question? He proposes to "consider and compare two different systems of methodological rules; one *with*, and one *without*, a principle of induction" (LSD, 52, i.a.). Accordingly, we compare alternatives and then choose one of them. In order to make this choice, we "examine whether such a principle, once introduced, can be applied without giving rise to inconsistencies; whether it helps us; and whether we really need it" (52). Then we choose the system of methodological rules that is more useful – not the system actually used in science, as "naturalists" would do – and this leads us "to dispense with the principle of induction: not because such a principle is as a matter of fact never used in science, but because [we] think that it is not needed; that it does not help us; and that it even gives rise to inconsistencies" (52f.).

Accordingly, Popper compares an *inductivist* methodology to his *falsificationist* methodology. However, this example is not well chosen, for at the very beginning of his *Logic* he asks – approximately – the decisive questions, "Can a principle of induction be an analytic statement?" and "Can we know for certain that there is a true synthetic principle of induction?" His answer to the first question is – again approximately – "No, for there are no content-increasing logical inferences," and his answer to the second question is "No, for the attempt to prove such a principle would lead to the trilemma of justification." Both answers rely on *logical* considerations, and they show that the idea of a principle of induction justifying universal hypotheses is untenable. Hence we need not *compare* falsificationist methodology to inductivist methodology in order to decide which one serves our purposes best. Rather, we need a tenable alternative to inductivist methodology, and Popper's falsificationism provides it.

3.3. METHODOLOGICAL RULES AS CONVENTIONS

Popper regards *methodological rules* as conventions. They do not, however, resemble the rules of logic; rather, they *define "the game of empirical science,"* just as the rules of chess define the game of chess (LSD, 53, i.a.). And the "inquiry into the rules of the game of science – that is, of scientific discovery – [might] be entitled '*The Logic of Scientific Discovery*'" (53, i.a.). Many articles and books deal with Popper's methodological rules, and almost all of his rules have now been criticized (cf., e.g., Maxwell 1972; Johansson 1975). Here we can discuss only some of them; a detailed description and criticism can be found in Johansson. We begin our discussion with two simple rules that are barely vulnerable to criticism.

Popper introduces them in order to show that an inquiry into method can hardly be placed "on the same level as a purely logical inquiry" (LSD, 53). The first rule says

(R₁) The game of science is, in principle, without end. He who decides one day that scientific statements do not call for any further test, and that they can be regarded as finally verified, retires from the game. (53)

What speaks in its favour? All of our "knowledge" is fallible. The reasons for this are partly logical ("transcendence of generalization"; cf. sections 1.11, 1.221; "transcendence inherent in any description"; cf. section 4.5) and partly factual (transcendence of perception, illusions; cf. section 4.2). Hence every synthetic statement that we take to be true, may be false. None of them is strictly verifiable. Thus, if it is important not to take false statements erroneously to be true – at least not for a longer time than is inevitable – then statements may *only provisionally but never definitely be considered true.* According to this *logical* argument, rule (R₁) is an adequate *means* to protect us against the consequences of avoidable errors. If we accept (R₁) for this reason, then we act (means-end) *rationally.* The second rule is

(R₂) Once a hypothesis has been proposed and tested, and has proved its mettle, it may not be allowed to drop out without "good reason." A "good reason" may be, for instance: replacement of the hypothesis by another which is better testable; or the falsification of one of the consequences of the hypothesis. (53f.)

Why is this rule suitable? Well-corroborated hypotheses help us to find our way in the world and help guide our actions. Hypotheses that are "better testable" may be better corroborated (cf. section 5.1). If we give up a well-corroborated hypothesis without having a better alternative or having reasons to suspect that – in spite of its previous corroboration – it is false, we abandon without "good reason" what is presumably a suitable way to reach our aims. This logical argument as well proposes a *rational* decision.

Popper now lays down a "supreme rule...which serves as a kind of norm for deciding upon the remaining rules, and which is thus a rule of a *higher type.*" This rule says that

[MR] the other rules of scientific procedure must be designed in such a way that they do not protect any statement in science against falsification. (LSD, 54, i.a.)

This *meta-*rule is meant to ensure that the (other) rules proposed improve the applicability of the *criterion of demarcation.* Thus they are closely connected both with each other and with the criterion of demarcation. Though this connection is not logical, it is systematic, and therefore Popper speaks of a "*theory* of method" (54). Again, it is a simple *means-end consideration* that motivates us to accept the meta-rule (MR). Accordingly, the theory of method is not very impressive. Popper admits that "the pronouncements of this theory are, as our examples show, for the most part conventions of a fairly obvious kind. Profound truths are not to be expected of methodology." He continues, "Nevertheless it may help us in many cases to clarify the *logical* situation, and even to solve some far-reaching problems which have hitherto proved intractable" (54, i.a.).

Popper defines empirical science by means of the criterion of demarcation and his methodological rules (LSD, 54). His definition is *useful*, as it enables us "to detect inconsistencies and inadequacies in older theories of knowledge, and to trace these back to the fundamental assumptions and conventions from which they spring" (55). This "*method of detecting and resolving contradictions*" – Popper also calls it "the *critical* – or, if you will, the '*dialectical*' – *method*" (55 n3, i.a.) – is applied in science as well, but it is a characteristic trait of the *theory of knowledge* (55, i.a.) – of *epistemology*, which he identifies with the *theory of scientific method* (49).

The application of this method also shows "that the majority of the *problems of theoretical philosophy*, and the most interesting ones, can be *reinterpreted* in this way *as problems of method*" (LSD, 56, i.a.). Popper gives two examples, the "principle of causality" and the problem of objectivity. The requirement of *objectivity* can be understood as the methodological rule

(R_3) that only such statements may be introduced in science as are inter-subjectively testable. (56)

And the *principle of causality*, the thesis that "the world is governed by strict laws" (61), can be replaced by the methodological rule

(R_4) that we are not to abandon the search for universal laws and for a coherent theoretical system, nor ever give up our attempts to explain causally any kind of event we can describe. (61)

Rule R_4 guides the scientist's work. These first five rules do not invite any serious criticism. At most, one might object that they are rather trivial. However, this holds as well for the rules of formal logic, and even the simplest among them can be very helpful in complicated arguments. Less trivial seems a rule that he later introduced – "that after having produced some criticism of a *rival* theory, we should always make a serious attempt to apply this or a similar criticism to our *own* theory" (85 n*1, i.a.).

It is more difficult to comment on some of the other rules. Already in the opening chapter of his *Logic*, Popper proposed a first methodological rule. It refers to the selection of those consequences of a new theory that are to be tested, and it says:

(R_5) With the help of other statements, previously accepted, certain singular statements – which we may call "predictions" – are deduced from the theory; especially predictions that are [i] easily testable or applicable. From among these statements, those are selected which are [ii] not derivable from the current theory, and more especially those [iii] which the current theory contradicts. (LSD, 33, i.a.)

(i) It is economical to test consequences that are *easily testable*. The proposal to do so may seem trivial, but it is not unproblematic. For if certain consequences are – not only in the beginning, but also in the long run – spared testing because their testing would be difficult, we risk holding on to a theory even though it would have been refuted had we tried harder. (ii) For two different reasons, it seems advisable to choose for testing those consequences that are *not derivable from the current theory*. Should we, after having severely tested these consequences, consider them true, we have learnt something new. On the other hand, we expect that these consequences, just because they are not derivable from the current theory, run a higher risk of being falsified. If the new hypothesis is false, we can sooner refute it in this way. (iii) This holds a fortiori for those of its consequences that *contradict the current theory* (cf. section 5.2).

Though methodological rules such as (R_5) are plausible, they are not precise directives that could be followed exactly, like the rule to stop in front of a red traffic signal. Rather, they make us consider certain things and admonish us to weigh the pros and cons of alternative courses of action. But they do not permit us to evaluate the alternatives in such a way that the choice of a certain alternative is determined.

3.4. METHODOLOGICAL RULES AGAINST CONVENTIONALIST STRATAGEMS

Popper quotes from Joseph Black's *Lectures on the Elements of Chemistry* (1803, 193): "'A nice adaptation of conditions will make almost any hypothesis agree with the phenomena. This will please the imagination but does not advance our knowledge'" (LSD, 82). From this, he draws the conclusion: "The only way to avoid conventionalism is by taking a *decision*: the decision not to apply its methods."

[R$_6$] We decide that, in the case of a threat to our system [of hypotheses], we will not save it by any kind of *conventionalist stratagem*. Thus we shall [not try to attain] "for any chosen … system what is called its 'correspondence with reality.'" (82)

This rule is universal, but is it also precise? When do we try to attain "for any chosen system" its correspondence with reality, and when do we actually apply "conventionalist stratagems"?

Popper enumerates the four main *conventionalist stratagems*: (i) we may introduce ad hoc hypotheses (which make refuting evidence seem irrelevant); (ii) we may modify the so-called ostensive definitions (so as to alter the content of a hypothesis and thus possibly its truth value); (iii) we may doubt the reliability of the experimenter (and declare his observations that threaten the tested theory to be irrelevant); (iv) we may doubt the acumen of the theoretician (who does not produce ideas that can save the tested theory) (LSD, 81). In order to counter such stratagems, Popper complements rule (R$_6$) by rule

(R$_7$) We … decide that, whenever we find that a system has been rescued by a conventionalist stratagem, we shall test it afresh, and reject it, as circumstances may require. (82)

The purpose of this rule is obvious, and it is a rule that actually can serve as a directive.

To begin with, let us examine the *first* conventionalist stratagem. Popper uses the concepts "*ad hoc hypothesis*" and "*auxiliary hypothesis*" synonymously. Auxiliary hypotheses are introduced in order to save a theory that seems to be refuted. As they are accepted primarily for this purpose and not because of their corroboration, it is necessary to prevent their being misused in a conventionalist way. To this end, Popper proposes rule

(R$_8$) that only those [*auxiliary hypotheses*] are acceptable whose introduction does not diminish the degree of falsifiability or testability of the system in question, but, on the contrary, increases it. (LSD, 83)

But how can an auxiliary hypothesis save a theory that seems to be refuted, and how can the degree of falsifiability of a theory be assessed?

Suppose we make the astronomical prediction that some comet will at a certain time be in a certain position, but when the time arrives, we do not see it there. Then the *observation statement* asserting that the comet was not in that position at that time logically contradicts the conjunction of (i) our *theory* about its orbit and (ii) another observation statement asserting that the comet was in another position at a certain earlier time. This means the conjunction of the two observation statements is a *falsifying basic statement* relative to our theory. But before we decide to accept this basic statement and thus to reject the theory, we once again check our instruments and find out that our clock was wrong. Then the statement that our clock was wrong may serve as an *auxiliary hypothesis*. But it is not conjunctively added to the system (containing our theory and the two observation statements), for in that way the contradiction between the theory and the basic statement could not be eliminated. Rather, the auxiliary hypothesis explains why the first observation statement and hence the basic statement is false. Thus it saves the theory by eliminating an observation statement from the system. But does the introduction of the auxiliary hypothesis increase the "degree of falsifiability" of the system in question? Popper seems to assume this is the case, if the auxiliary hypothesis itself has "falsifiable consequences," that is, if it is independently testable (LSD, 83).

Let us now examine the *second* conventionalist stratagem. If a hypothesis has apparently failed, we may try to save it by changing the meaning of one or more of its nonlogical signs. Suppose the hypothesis "All swans are white" fails, because the first black swan is found. We may then alter the meaning of the predicate "is a swan" or even of the predicate "is white." But if, by our new definition of "is a swan," only white birds are considered swans, then the false empirical hypothesis "All swans are white" is turned into a true analytic statement. Popper rules out this move, for it would turn hypotheses into mere conventions. But would it be suitable to rule out *any* modification of meanings?

If a hypothesis is modified at all, it should become better testable than it used to be. But it is difficult to compare the testability of different hypotheses or of different versions of the same hypothesis (cf. section 5.3). This seems to be the reason why Popper lays down a rather unspecific rule about undefined concepts:

(R_9) We shall forbid *surreptitious* alterations of usage. (LSD, 84, i.a.)

If this rule forbids only *clandestine* or *accidental* alterations, it demands only the obvious. On the other hand, it must *not* rule out *any* alteration, for otherwise theories could be improved only by *modifying their structure* or by *exchanging their nonlogical signs*. Taken as a strict prohibition, this rule would considerably *impair scientific progress*. But as long as it has not been decided *which* alterations the rule is to forbid as "surreptitious," it is *not applicable*. It would also be difficult to make these decisions, for we would hardly want to rule out alterations that would further scientific progress. In order to make the right decision, we would have to know in advance which alterations would further progress.

3.5. ON POPPER'S "NEGATIVE METHODOLOGY"

According to Quine, the keynote of Popper's theory of scientific method is his "*negative doctrine of evidence*" (Quine 1974, 218, i.a.). What does it assert? While the hypothesis (or law) "'All ravens are black'" is *refuted* by one single case to the contrary – one nonblack raven – "such laws admit no *supporting* evidence as conclusive as the refuting evidence." Of course, it speaks in favour of a hypothesis that it is not refuted by a test. However, this is "*negative support*: the mere absence of refutation" (218, i.a.). Thus "[*a*]*dverse evidence is the primary kind of evidence*," at least if we consider universal if-then statements such as "All ravens are black" (218, i.a.).

The primacy of refutation is reflected in *Hempel's paradox*. Suppose that the existence of a black raven, or the truth of an observation statement such as

(1) $Ra \wedge Ba$: Antony [a] is a raven [R] and he is black [B].

counts as *partial support* of the hypothesis

(2) $(x)(Rx \rightarrow Bx)$: All ravens are black.

Then, accordingly, the existence of any nonblack object that is not a raven, or the truth of an observation statement such as

(3) $\neg Bb \wedge \neg Rb$: Bertha [b] is not black and she is not a raven.

should count as *partial support* of the hypothesis

(4) $(x)(\neg Bx \rightarrow \neg Rx)$: All things that are not black are not ravens.

But, because of the tautology

(5) $(p \rightarrow q) \leftrightarrow (\neg q \rightarrow \neg p)$,

hypotheses (2) and (4) are logically equivalent. Hence both (1) and (3) support hypothesis (2). More generally: *every nonblack object that is not a raven* (e.g., a white mouse) *supports the hypothesis "All ravens are black."* This "seems odd, and is therefore a paradox"; it also "suggests a certain instability in the notion of evidence *for* laws of the form 'All ravens are black'" (Quine 1974, 218).

* There are, however, other instances of the *paradox of confirmation* that appear even more paradoxical. For example, hypothesis (2) implies the *instantial statement*

(6) $Rc \rightarrow Bc$: If Caesar [c] is a raven, then he is black.

and if the state of affairs expressed by the instantial statement (6) counts as partial support of hypothesis (2), then not only black ravens [as in (1)] and nonblack nonravens [as in (3)] but also black nonravens (e.g., a black horse), as in

(7) $\neg Rd \wedge Bd$: Dora [d] is not a raven and she is black.

support hypothesis (2). Only nonblack ravens, as in

(8) $Re \wedge \neg Be$: Emil [e] is a raven and he is not black.

refute (2). This follows immediately from the truth table of the subjunction. Stated more generally: *If any (state of affairs expressed by an) instantial statement counts as partial support of the hypothesis from which it follows, then every hypothesis is supported by anything that does not contradict it.* **

Popper *avoids* the paradox by insisting that we look not for supporting but for refuting evidence. As opposed to this, Quine tries to *dissolve* the paradox. Though he considers black ravens to be a partial support of hypothesis (2) "All ravens are black," he does not consider nonblack nonravens to be a partial support even of hypothesis (4) "All things that are not black are not ravens." Why doesn't he? His reason is "that 'raven' and 'black' are projectible predicates, as Goodman [1955] would say, while 'unblack' and 'non-raven' are not" (Quine 1974, 219). He equates "projectibility of predicates to the naturalness of kinds," explains "our native primitive intuition of natural kinds by Darwinian natural selection," and thinks that the "intuitively natural groupings [that] favor successful inductions . . . have survival value in the evolution of the species" (219).

However, hypothesis (4) "All things that are not black are not ravens" also contains only the projectible predicates "is a raven" and "is black," as the symbolic notation unequivocally shows. Of course, it also contains *negation signs* indicating that *complements* of the "intuitively natural groupings" are formed. But what is wrong with that? Obviously, these complements are heterogeneous, insofar as they contain several "natural kinds" already known to us. For example, the set of all nonblack objects contains not only white and grey but also coloured objects.

It is quite plausible that the formation of homogeneous sets – for example, the set of all black objects – favours generalizations. But doing without any *negation signs* would undoubtedly impair the formation of hypotheses. If, however, negations cannot be dispensed with, how can we then decide in a general way, independently of concrete examples, where they are admissible and where not? Also, *ceteris paribus* clauses form rather inhomogeneous collections. But neither in economics nor even in "hard" sciences such as astronomy and physics can they be dispensed with. For if a heavy object should come close to our solar system, then the orbits of the planets and – to a lesser degree – the gravitational acceleration on the planets would change.

Thus *Quine can hardly claim to have dissolved the paradox of confirmation, but Popper's "negative methodology" shows us how to avoid it.* Also, there is no "instability" in the notion of evidence *against* laws, for any nonblack raven speaks as well against hypothesis (2) "All ravens are black" as against hypothesis (4) "All things that are not black are not ravens." This is not at all paradoxical, for the refuting basic statement (8) "Emil is a raven and he is not black" implies both the negation of hypothesis (2) "Not all ravens are black" and the negation of hypothesis (4) "Not all things that are not black are not ravens." This *logical connection* excludes any *paradox of refutation*. There is no comparable connection between a supporting observation statement and the supported hypothesis. Also, Popper's "negative methodology" is not at all revolutionary. Duhem already quoted Claude Bernard's (1865) demand "'that we must never do experiments in order to *confirm* our ideas but merely to *check* them'" (Duhem 1962, 181, i.a.).

3.6. THE DUHEM–QUINE THESIS

Henri Poincaré (1854–1912) asks: "If we construct a theory based upon multiple hypotheses, and if experiment condemns it, which of the premises must be changed?" He answers, "It is impossible to tell" (1902/1952, 151f.). Accordingly, though all hypotheses are *fallible, isolated* hypotheses are *not falsifiable*. Is this the end of the fundamental idea of Popper's methodology: "Science progresses by proposing bold hypotheses and testing them ruthlessly with the intention of refuting them"? This objection is often raised, but it is seldom based on Poincaré; more often it is adapted from Duhem and Quine. In his *Logic*, Popper himself briefly mentions that "we falsify *the whole system*" [of premises of a prediction that did not come true] (LSD, 76). Obviously, he did not consider this a serious problem. Duhem elaborated Poincaré's idea, and Quine sharpened it, asserting that it was impossible to distinguish strictly between analytic and synthetic statements.

3.61. Duhem's Holism

In his book *The Aim and Structure of Physical Theory* (1906/1962), Pierre Duhem (1861–1916) examines *experimental tests* of physical laws. He describes the situation: "A physicist disputes a certain law; he calls into doubt a certain theoretical point." He asks, "How will he justify these doubts? How will he demonstrate the inaccuracy of the law?" And he answers, "From the proposition under indictment he will derive the prediction of an experimental fact; he will bring into existence the conditions under which this fact should be produced; if the predicted fact is not produced, the proposition which served as the basis of the prediction will be irremediably condemned" (Duhem 1962, 184). Popper gives the same answer, which, however, entails a lot of problems. Thus Duhem entitles the second paragraph of his Chapter 6, "Physical Theory and Experiment": "*An experiment in physics can never condemn an isolated hypothesis but only a whole theoretical group*" (183). This statement already contains the *kernel* of the so-called *Duhem–Quine thesis.*

Accordingly, the refutation of a theory is more difficult than it appears at first sight. For

in order to deduce from this proposition the prediction of a phenomenon and institute the experiment which is to show whether this phenomenon is or is not produced, in order to interpret the results of this experiment and establish that the predicted phenomenon is not produced, [the physicist] does not confine himself to making use of the proposition in question; he makes use also of a whole group of theories accepted by him as beyond dispute. The prediction of the phenomenon, whose nonproduction is to cut off debate, does not derive from the proposition challenged if taken by itself, but from the proposition at issue joined to that whole group of theories; if the predicted phenomenon is not produced, not only is *the proposition questioned* at fault, but so is *the whole theoretical scaffolding* used by the physicist. The only thing the experiment teaches us is that among the propositions used to predict the phenomenon and to establish whether it would be produced, there is *at least one* error; but *where* this error lies is just what it does not tell us. The physicist may declare that this error is contained in exactly the proposition he wishes to refute, but is he sure it is not in another proposition? If he is, he accepts implicitly the accuracy of all the other propositions he has used, and the validity of his conclusion is as great as the validity of his confidence. (Duhem 1962, 185, i.a.)

As Duhem knew, the contemporary view of experimental method is not as discriminating: "People generally think that each one of the hypotheses employed in physics can be taken *in isolation*, checked by experiment,..." (Duhem 1962, 187, i.a.). (Andersson calls this view "*Isolationism*" [1988, 9, i.a.].) In contrast to this, Duhem emphasizes:

"Physical science is a system that must be taken as a whole" (187). (This view is called "*Holism*" [ibid., i.a.].) But he goes on: "[Physical science] is an organism in which one part cannot be made to function except when the parts that are most remote from it are called into play, some more so than others, but all to some degree" (187f.). This is exaggerated, and if it were true, the consequences would be disastrous. For only he who mastered all physical theories could perform the simplest experiment. And who masters them all? But if we disregard this exaggeration, Duhem is certainly right.

This seems to be a serious problem for Popper's methodology. Lakatos (1922–1974) describes it succinctly: "The naive falsificationist [he means Popper] insists that if we have an inconsistent set of scientific statements, we first must select from among them (1) a theory under test (to serve as a *nut*); then we must select (2) an accepted basic statement (to serve as a *hammer*) and the rest will be uncontested background knowledge (to provide an *anvil*)" (1970, 186). The naive falsificationist believes that in this way he can test and falsify isolated hypotheses. Accordingly, falsifications depend on conventional decisions to consider certain basic statements and a certain background knowledge unproblematic (Andersson 1988, 59). Hence we do not know, but we *decide where* the error lies.

Some decision of this kind is unavoidable, but does it have to be arbitrary? If we follow Popper, we decide according to our research programme which hypothesis is to be tested, and we decide according to the results of (previous) research which statements are to be accepted (as basic statements or as background knowledge) for the purpose of testing the present hypothesis. These statements are not called into question while we test the present hypothesis, but this does not mean that, in spite of their fallibility, they are definitely accepted. Hence not only must we always carefully weigh all of the possible decisions – only a well-corroborated hypothesis may be considered unproblematic background knowledge – but any such decision may also be revised. Why should it be "naive" in such circumstances to consider a theory – for the present – refuted?

Duhem, on the other hand, defends the fallibilist who does not "assimilate experimental contradiction to reduction to absurdity" (Duhem 1962, 188). Some empiricists and empirical scientists believe that the method of "reduction to absurdity" – a method that Euclid (ca. 450–370) used in geometry – permits them to know for certain which of several competing hypotheses is true. Duhem describes their view as follows: "Do you wish to obtain from a group of phenomena a theoretically certain and indisputable explanation? Enumerate all the hypotheses that can be made to account for this group of phenomena; then, by experimental contradiction eliminate all except one; the latter will no longer be a hypothesis, but will become a *certainty*" (188, i.a.).

Francis Bacon (1561–1626) proposed a *crucial experiment* for the special case of two rival hypotheses. Later, a decision between the corpuscular theory and the wave theory of light was sought in this way. Dominique Arago (1786–1853) formulates the alternatives: "Does light move more quickly in water than in air? 'Light is a body. If the contrary is the case, then light is a wave'" (Duhem 1962, 190). However, Léon Foucault's (1819–1868) experiment involves a decision "not between two hypotheses, the emission and wave hypotheses, [...] it decides rather between two sets of theories each of which has to be taken as a whole, i.e., between two entire systems, Newton's optics and Huygens's [1629–1695] optics" (189). Hence it refutes at best one of the *systems*, not one of the *hypotheses*.

3.62. Quine's Criticism of the "Dogmas of Empiricism"

In his article "Two Dogmas of Empiricism" (1961a), Willard Van Orman Quine (1908–2000) asserts that modern empiricism has been formed in large part by two dogmas. One is the idea that there is a fundamental difference between *analytic* and *synthetic* statements. This is also Popper's belief. According to this idea, analytic statements are "true by virtue of *meanings* and independently of fact," while the truth of synthetic statements is "grounded in *fact*" (20f., i.a.).

The other dogma is *reductionism*, that is, "the belief that each meaningful statement is equivalent to some logical construct upon terms which refer to immediate experience" (Quine 1961a, 20). This aims at theses in Carnap's book *Der logische Aufbau der Welt* (1928; *The Logical Structure of the World*, 1967), but it doesn't hit Popper, who had – in the original edition of his *Logik der Forschung* (1935) – drawn attention to the "'transcendence inherent in any description'" (LSD, 94; cf. section 4.5) and had – in the first English edition (1959) – stated that "*all* universals are dispositional" and that there is hence no fundamental difference, but only a gradual difference, between theoretical statements and observation statements (LSD, 424).

According to Quine, both dogmas are ill founded. If they are abandoned, then, on the one hand, the "boundary between *speculative metaphysics* and *natural science*" is blurred – which deals a fatal blow to Popper's criterion of demarcation and, in the last analysis, to his entire philosophy of science – and, on the other hand, there is a "shift toward pragmatism" (1961a, 20, i.a.). But is Quine's criticism of the presumptive dogmas justified?

Is there really no fundamental difference between analytic and synthetic statements? Is the assumption that "there is such a distinction to be drawn at all... [even] an unempirical dogma of empiricists, a metaphysical article of faith" (Quine 1961a, 37)? Quine's argument starts from the contemporary formulation "A statement is analytic if, and only if, it is true by virtue of meanings alone and independently of fact." He asks what a *meaning* is. Since there is still no well-corroborated theory of meaning and reference, it is not at all surprising that he considers meanings to be obscure entities that may well be abandoned. Nevertheless, it remains the task of a theory of meaning to explain the *synonymy of linguistic forms* and the *analyticity of statements* (22).

Quine's examples show the connection between synonymy and analyticity (1961a, 22f.). First he formulates the *logically true* statement

(1) No unmarried man is married.

This statement "remains true under all reinterpretations of its components other than the logical particles" (23). Then he formulates the statement

(2) No bachelor is married

which is also *analytic* but not logically true. If, however, in (2) the expression "bachelor" is replaced by the synonymous expression "unmarried man," the logically true statement (1) results. Thus (in this case) *analyticity* is – by *synonymy* – reduced to *logical truth*.

But how do we know that the two expressions actually are synonymous? We might reduce their *synonymy* to *definition*, that is, assume that "*bachelor*" is defined as "*unmarried man*" (1961a, 24). Which kind of definition is this? A lexicographer's definition is an empirical hypothesis stating a *factual* synonymy. As a hypothesis, it is fallible, and even if it is true, it only states the synonymy but does not create it. And a Carnapian *explication* (of concepts) only "improve[s] upon the definiendum by refining or supplementing its meaning" (25). Thus both the lexicographer's definition and the Carnapian explication rest "on *other* pre-existing synonymies" (25). Therefore, it is not surprising that Quine considers "the *explicitly conventional* introduction of novel notations for purposes of sheer abbreviation" to be the only "transparent case[s] of synonymy created by definition" (26, i.a.).

Can we, where there is no such convention, at least ascertain empirically whether two expressions are synonymous? In order to do this, we must, according to Frege (1848–1925), examine the *statements* in which the expressions occur. According to Quine, however, this is not sufficient, because the "unit of empirical significance is [not a single statement but] *the whole of science*" (1961a, 42, i.a.). How could we then empirically find out whether a single scientific statement is empirical or analytic? Does this explain why the belief in some fundamental cleavage between analytic and synthetic statements is but a dogma of modern empiricism?

But how does Quine know about the "*unit of empirical significance*"? After all, there is no empirical theory of meaning for him to rely on. Obviously, he states a *dogma of the philosophy of language.* In view of this dogma, the distinction between analytic and synthetic statements may seem dogmatic, but this is not necessarily so, for if some system of logic is at least *hypothetically* presupposed, *some* statements can be proved *logically true* and hence analytic. Moreover, anyone can declare *some* of his statements to be *definitions* – or, more generally, linguistic rules – and *others* to be synthetic statements – for example, empirical hypotheses. Then we know how the person wants to be understood, and when discussing his statements, we can distinguish between those that may be factually true or false and those that – being true by convention – may be considered only useful or useless.

Under such conditions, the modern empiricist will argue, the distinction between analytic and synthetic statements is not only *possible* but also *appropriate.* After all, it is no peculiarity of the predicates "analytic" and "synthetic" that we do not know of *every* object to which they might be attributed whether they would be rightly attributed. Rather, there are "blurred edges" in the use of any predicate. If this were a reason to stop using them, we couldn't even form subject-predicate statements.

But Quine even adds to the preconditions for a distinction between analytic and synthetic statements: As "a statement *S* is said to be *analytic for* a language *L*, ... the problem is to make sense of this relation [between *S* and *L*] *generally* [i.a.], that is, for variable '*S*' and '*L*'" (1961a, 33). But why should we in every language do without the distinction between analytic and synthetic statements just because we cannot give the word "analytic" a precise meaning in all languages? Normally, we don't dispense with a predicate just because it doesn't have an exact counterpart in every language. Would it not be sufficient to give the word "analytic" an exact meaning specifically for that *part of a language* to which those statements whose truth value we are considering belong?

Does the *verifiability theory of meaning*, which Popper rejected, play a part in the context of the analytic-synthetic dichotomy? Is statement synonymy "likeness of method of empirical confirmation" (1961a, 38)? What then is "the nature of the relation between a statement and the experiences" that confirm or disconfirm it? The most naive answer says that it is a relation "of direct report." Quine takes this to be "*radical reductionism*," for it implies that every "meaningful statement is . . . translatable into a statement . . . about immediate experience" (38). He thinks that the "dogma of reductionism survives in the supposition that each statement, taken in isolation," can be confirmed or disconfirmed (41). As long as we speak of the confirmation of a single statement, it makes sense "to speak also of a limiting kind of statement which is vacuously confirmed," that is, of an analytic statement. In fact, he considers the two dogmas "at root identical" (41).

Like Duhem, Quine thinks that "our statements about the external world face the tribunal of sense experience not individually but only as a *corporate body*" (1961a, 41, i.a.). But while Duhem includes "only" the totality of the statements of *one science* (e.g., of physics) into that corporate body, Quine includes not only those of *all empirical sciences* but also those of *logic* and *mathematics*. He writes:

> the totality of our so called knowledge or beliefs, from the most casual matters of geography and history to the profoundest laws of atomic physics or even of pure mathematics and logic, is a man-made *fabric* which impinges on experience only along the edges. Or, to change the figure, total science is like a *field of force* whose boundary conditions are experience. A conflict with experience at the periphery occasions readjustments in the interior of the field. Truth values have to be redistributed over some of our statements. Reëvaluation of some statements entails reëvaluation of others, because of their logical interconnections – the logical laws being in turn simply certain further statements of the system, certain further elements of the field. Having reëvaluated one statement we must reëvaluate some others, which may be statements logically connected with the first or may be the statements of logical connections themselves. But the total field is so underdetermined by its boundary conditions, experience, that there is much latitude of choice as to what statements to reëvaluate in the light of any single contrary experience. No particular experiences are linked with any particular statements in the interior of the field, except indirectly through considerations of equilibrium affecting the field as a whole. (1961a, 42f., i.a.)

Thus Quine's holism is comprehensive. From the point of view of holism, he now attacks another idea that plays a vital part in Popper's methodology (cf. section 5.4.): "If this view is right, it is misleading to speak of the *empirical content of an individual statement* – especially if it is a statement at all remote from the experiential periphery of the field" (1961a, 43, i.a.).

Quine now resumes his criticism of the "first dogma" of empiricism:

Furthermore it becomes folly to seek a boundary between synthetic statements, which hold contingently on experience, and analytic statements, which hold come what may. Any statement can be held true come what may, if we make drastic enough adjustments elsewhere in the system. Even a statement very close to the periphery can be held true in the face of recalcitrant experience by pleading hallucination or by amending certain statements of the kind called logical laws. Conversely, by the same token, no statement is immune to revision. Revision even of the logical law of the excluded middle has been proposed as a means of simplifying quantum mechanics; and what difference is there in principle between such a shift and the shift whereby Kepler superseded Ptolemy, or Einstein Newton, or Darwin Aristotle? (1961a, 43)

How shall we answer his question? As the history of logic and mathematics shows, calculi can be designed in the armchair – no observation is required. Given the axioms and rules of a calculus, we can – within certain limits – decide whether certain other sentences are derivable (i.e., theorems) or whether the assertion that one sentence follows from another is true. The peculiarities of these disciplines may be formulated more concisely: "A formula of logic or mathematics is universally valid if, and only if, every interpretation of it in every non-empty domain of individuals is true" or "The sentences of logic and mathematics are true or false according to their form alone."

Only if a formula is to be *applied* to an empirical problem must it somehow be connected with *empirical* statements. To this end, either the syntax of a calculus is made the grammar of the empirical statements, or a representation theorem is proved, which shows that certain formal operations and relations are experimentally realizable. If the physical system later turns out to have properties to which there is no counterpart in the formal system, it may be useful to replace the old formal system with a new one. However, the old system has then *not* proved to be *false*, but only (now) to be *inappropriate*. On the other hand, only a few physicists considered one of the proposed quantum logics an appropriate substitute for classical logic.

The distinction between "false" and "inappropriate" is by no means a nicety of modern empiricists. It already played an important part in the trial of Galilei (1564–1642). Cardinal Bellarmino (1542–1621) would have tolerated the thesis that the Earth moves around the sun if Galilei had given it not a realist interpretation – as the heliocentric conception of the world – but an *instrumentalist* interpretation – as a new and superior method of calculating the positions of celestial bodies. In fact, the sentences of logic and mathematics are open to revision, and experience may provide reasons to revise them, but this doesn't turn them into empirical statements, nor does it make them indistinguishable from empirical statements.

4

The Problem of the Empirical Basis

According to Carnap, the *test of observation statements against reality* "constitutes the core problem of the logic of science, that is of the theory of knowledge" (1987, 457). As opposed to this, Popper considers the problems of *induction* and *demarcation* to be the two fundamental problems of epistemology. At the same time, his criterion of demarcation appears to reduce "the question of the empirical character of *theories* to the question of the empirical character of *singular statements*" (LSD, 43, i.a.). He calls any statement "which can serve as a premise in an empirical falsification" a "*'basic statement'*" (i.a.), and he says that "[*p*]*roblems of the empirical basis*" are "problems concerning the empirical character of singular statements" (43). Hence there is a *connection* between the *problem of demarcation* and the *problems of the empirical basis*.

In order to uncover the problems of the empirical basis and to solve them, if possible, we must examine "the relation between *perceptual experiences* and *basic statements*" (LSD, 43). Popper wants to show that perceptual experiences cannot "*justify* or establish the truth of *any* statement" (98, i.a.), because any statement far surpasses the content of our perceptual experiences in the situation(s) to which it refers (Carnap 1935, 290). The idea that we cannot doubt immediate experiences and that statements that render such experiences are exempt from criticism founders "on the problems of induction and universals," or, more exactly, on the problem of the "'transcendence inherent in any description'" (LSD, 94). Hence there is also a *connection* between the *problem of induction* and the *problems of the empirical basis*. No wonder Carnap writes: "The discussion of the problems of the empirical basis counts among the most important parts of the *Logic*" (1935, 290, m.t.). *The problem of demarcation, the problem of induction, and the problems of the empirical basis refer to different aspects of the problem of the relation between our statements and reality.*

4.1. PSYCHOLOGISM AND THE DEBATE
ON PROTOCOL SENTENCES

To begin with, Popper takes up considerations originally introduced by Jakob Friedrich Fries (1773–1843). In his book *Neue oder anthropologische Kritik der Vernunft* (New or Anthropological Critique of Reason, 1807), Fries analyzes the problem of the *basis of experience* and encounters the trilemma of justification, which we met earlier when discussing induction (cf. section 1.112). Popper resumes Fries's considerations as follows:

If the statements of science are not to be [1] accepted *dogmatically*, we must be able to *justify* them. If we demand justification by reasoned argument, in the logical sense, then we are committed to the view that *statements can be justified only by statements*. The demand that *all* statements are to be logically justified (described by Fries as a "predilection for proofs") is therefore bound to lead to an [2] *infinite regress*. Now, if we wish to avoid the danger of dogmatism as well as an infinite regress, then it seems as if we could only have recourse to [3] *psychologism, i.e.* the doctrine that statements can be justified not only by statements but also by perceptual experience. (LSD, 93f.)

Hence the third branch of Fries's trilemma is not the logical circle but "psychologism."

Popper's aversion to "psychologism" is quite understandable if we remember the *debate on protocol sentences* (or protocol statements). Its most important arguments are contained in a series of three articles that begins with Carnap's "Die physikalische Sprache als Universalsprache der Wissenschaft" (Physics as a Universal Science) (1932b/1934), continues with Neurath's reply, "Protokollsätze" (Protocol Sentences) (1932/1959), and ends with Carnap's rejoinder, "Über Protokollsätze" (On Protocol Sentences) (1932c/1987). At the end of this last piece, Carnap resumes:

In all theories of knowledge up until now there has remained a certain *absolutism*: in the realistic ones an absolutism of the object, in the idealistic ones (including phenomenology) an absolutism of the "given," of "experience," of the "immediate phenomena." There is also a residue of this idealistic absolutism in positivism; in the logical positivism of our circle – in the writings on the logic of science (theory of knowledge) of Wittgenstein, Schlick, Carnap published up to now – it takes the refined form of an absolutism of the ur-sentence ("elementary sentence," "atomic sentence"). (1987, 469, i.a.)

Popper criticizes this absolutism. But what are "elementary sentences"?

Schlick, on the one hand, considers universal hypotheses to be not genuine statements but directives for forming statements (cf. 1.223.); on the other hand, he ascribes particular properties to "*'confirmations'*" ("*Konstatierungen*") such as "Here now so and so" (Schlick 1933/1959, 221, 224). If we direct our attention to what the words "now" and "here" refer to, we understand the meaning of the "confirmation," and at the same time we recognize whether or not it is true. This idea is adopted from *Wittgenstein.* As is normally the case only with analytic statements, "determining the meaning" and "determining the truth . . . coincide" in the case of "'confirmations'" (225). They "are the only synthetic statements that are not *hypotheses*" (227). As they are "*'absolutely certain'*" *and* "*final*" (223), they "bring verification (or also falsification) to completion" (222). However, "confirmations" are only *subjective,* and their function lies only "in the *immediate present*" (222, i.a.). Accordingly, they cannot be written down in the form of statements such as "*NN* perceived at time *t* in place *p* this and that." Hence there is also no *logical* relation between "confirmations" and the hypotheses to be tested. Rather, "confirmations" play only a *pragmatic* part in the evaluation of hypotheses.

Carnap comments in a more complicated and cautious way. According to the idea of unified science, there is – in the material mode of speech – only *one* kind of objects and only one kind of states of affairs. Accordingly, there is – in the formal mode of speech – only one universal and intersubjective language, namely, the language of physics (1932b/1995, 67ff.). The statements of this *system language* are tested by means of protocol statements – that is, the simplest statements of the *protocol language.* *Protocol statements* are – in the formal mode of speech – "statements *needing no justification* and serving as foundation for all the remaining statements of science" (45, i.a.). They refer – in the material mode of speech – "to the given, and describe directly given experience or phenomena, i.e. the simplest states of which knowledge can be had" (45).

But "[w]hat kinds of word occur in protocol statements" (1932b/1995, 45)? Carnap describes three different answers. According to the first answer, protocol sentences have, for example, the form "'Here, now, blue; there, red'" (1932b/1995, 46). This is the view of atomistic positivism, which Carnap ascribes – not altogether rightly – to Ernst *Mach.* According to the second answer, which *Carnap* in those days accepted, protocol sentences have the form "'Red circle, now'" (46); and according to the third, which he obviously ascribes to *Neurath,* they have the form "'A red cube is on the table'" (47). In this last case, things are the elements of the "given."

Neurath emphasizes in his reply: "*There is no way of taking conclusively established pure protocol sentences as the starting point of the sciences*" (1959, 201). In this respect, protocol sentences are like the other statements of science. However, they contain the name of a person drafting the protocol, an indication of place and time, and a perception term. "A complete protocol sentence might, for instance, read: 'Otto's protocol at 3:17 o'clock: [At 3:16 o'clock Otto said to himself: (at 3:15 there was a table in the room perceived by Otto)]'" (202). Such protocol sentences too are "subject to verification" (205). If necessary, they can be *changed* (203) or even *discarded* (204). Thus Neurath rejects the absolutism of the original sentences: "The fact that men generally retain their own protocol sentences more obstinately than they do those of other people is a historical accident which is of no real significance for our purposes" (206).

In his rejoinder, *Carnap* asserts that Neurath's conception of protocol sentences doesn't contradict his own; rather, these are "*two different methods for structuring* [rather: constructing] *the language of science both of which are possible and legitimate*" (1987, 457). Carnap had (in 1932b) proposed "the first language form: protocol sentences outside the system [language]" (1987, 458ff.), while Neurath proposed "the second form of language: protocol sentences inside the system language" (463ff.). On the other hand, Carnap rejects Neurath's proposal to admit only protocol sentences of a certain *form* (see above); rather, he accepts Popper's proposal: "*Every* concrete sentence of the physicalistic system language can serve under certain circumstances as a protocol sentence" (465, i.a.). Accordingly, "there are *no absolute initial sentences* for the structure [rather: construction] of science" (466, i.a.). In Popper's "testing procedure there is *no last sentence*; his system describes therefore the most radical elimination of absolutism" (469, i.a.). Now Carnap himself replaces the phenomenal language (of appearances) that he had proposed in his *Aufbau* (1928/1967) with an intersubjective, physicalistic language (thing language) (467).

Popper also comments in his *Logik* (1935) on Neurath's reply: "Neurath's view that protocol sentences are not inviolable represents, in my opinion, a notable advance.... It is a step in the right direction; but it leads nowhere if it is not followed up by another step: we need a set of rules to limit the arbitrariness of 'deleting' (or else 'accepting') a protocol sentence" (LSD, 97). And he reports that "Reininger describes a method of testing ... 'elementary' statements [recording experiences], in cases of doubt, by means of other statements – it is the *method of deducing and testing conclusions*" (96f., i.a.).

4.2. PHYSIOLOGY AND EPISTEMOLOGY

Phenomenalism, which for some time prevailed in the Vienna Circle, was – at least in part – a step backwards to a state of epistemology that Hermann Helmholtz (1821–1894) had already surpassed in his *Handbuch der physiologischen Optik* (1867; *Treatise on Physiological Optics*, 1962). In the program leaflet "Wissenschaftliche Weltauffassung: Der Wiener Kreis" (The Scientific Conception of the World: The Vienna Circle) of the Verein Ernst Mach (Ernst Mach Society) (1929/1973, 6), Helmholtz is counted among the philosophical precursors of the Vienna Circle, but neither in Carnap's *Aufbau* (1928), nor in Popper's *Logik* (1935), nor in Victor Kraft's *Der Wiener Kreis* (1950) is he mentioned at all. Clearly his distinction between pure geometry and physical geometry, and perhaps also his thesis that we can in principle visualize non-Euclidean spaces, were considered important (15f.). But especially in the section "Von den Wahrnehmungen im allgemeinen" (Concerning the Perceptions in General) of his *Handbuch*, Helmholtz obtains – based on physiological and psychological considerations – results at which also Popper arrives – based on linguistic considerations – in his *Logik*, above all in Chapter 5, "The Problem of the Empirical Basis," and in Appendix *X, "Universals, Dispositions, and Natural or Physical Necessity." Popper presents them in the formal mode of speech – as statements not about properties but about disposition predicates – and he thinks that he thus overcomes neopositivism. Helmholtz also offers a better alternative to Popper's unfortunate conventionalism (cf. section 4.6).

Helmholtz follows Kant insofar as Kant

derived all real *content* of knowledge from *experience*. But he made a distinction between this and whatever in the *form* of our apperceptions and ideas was conditioned by the peculiar ability of our *mind*. . . . According to this view *perception* is recognized as an *effect* produced on our sensitive faculty by the object perceived; this effect . . . being just as dependent on what causes the effect as on the nature of that on which the effect is produced. (Helmholtz 1962, 35f., i.a.)

On the other hand, he criticizes Kant, who had "briefly represented space and time as given [transcendental] forms of all apperception" (36).

Helmholtz's *inference theory of perception* says: "The psychic activities that lead us to infer that there in front of us at a certain place there is a certain object of a certain character" are in their result "equivalent to [an unconscious] *conclusion*, to the extent that the observed action on our senses enables us to form an idea as to the possible cause of this action; although, as a matter of fact, it is invariably simply the nervous stimulations that are perceived directly, that is, the actions, but never the external objects themselves" (1962, 4).

It would have been more accurate to say: We *explain* our sensations by assuming that they are common effects of external objects and of our nature, but we do not immediately perceive the objects, or our nature, or the circumstance that the objects have an effect on our nature. The premises of this explanation have a metaphysical kernel – the assumption of an external world acting on us – and it is this metaphysics that phenomenalism tries to avoid. But Helmholtz's wording already shows why even *daily assumptions* about properties of external objects are *highly theoretical*. Hence the results even of the most careful observations are *uncertain*.

But doesn't Helmholtz present himself as a naive realist when he speaks of external objects as existing in certain places? This suspicion is baseless, for he indicates that we can change some, but not all, of our sensations. Where we cannot change them, we assume an *external cause of our sensations*, and this cause is "recognized as an *object existing independently of our perception*" (1962, 32, i.a.). In addition, he holds an empiricist theory of the "intuition of space," and he considers non-Euclidean spaces not only possible but also visualizable (cf. 1870). And what we said about single *objects* is true as well of the *external world* as a whole: Only by "*inferring from the changing sensation that external objects are the causes of this change*" do we get from "*the world of our sensations to the apperception of an external world*" (32, i.a.).

But to what extent, if at all, do our *ideas correspond to their objects* (1962, 18)? "Things as they appear to us" are not even *pictures* of "things in themselves." Rather, as Helmholtz emphasizes in his rector's speech "Die Tatsachen in der Wahrnehmung" (The Facts in Perception, 1878): "Insofar as the quality of our sensation informs us about the peculiarity of the external impact by which it is produced, it may be considered a *sign* of the impact, but not its *image*. . . . But a sign need in no way be similar to that of which it is a sign" (Helmholtz 1998, 153, m.t.). However, "we must be on our guard against saying that all our ideas of things are . . . *false*, because they are not *equal* to the things themselves, and that hence we are not able to know anything as to the *true nature* of things," as Kant assumed (1962, 24).

Hence our "ideas of things" are "signs for things," and having "learned correctly how to read those symbols, we are enabled by their help to adjust our actions so as to bring about the desired result; that is, so that the expected new sensations will arise" (1962, 19). The "result" is not meant to be merely pragmatic, for "the idea of a thing is *correct* for him who knows how to determine correctly from it in advance what sense-impressions he will get from the thing when he places himself in definite external relations to it" (23, i.a.).

Not only is there *in reality* no other comparison at all between ideas and things – all the schools agreed about this – but any other mode of comparison is entirely *unthinkable* and has no sense whatever. ... Idea and the thing conceived evidently belong to two entirely different worlds, which no more admit of being compared with each other than colours and musical tones. (19f.)

All properties that we assign to objects of the external world "may be said to be simply *effects* exerted by them either on our senses or on other natural objects" (1962, 20). Therefore, all properties of the objects of nature are discovered only if we arrange their interaction with other objects or with our sense organs (21). As "we see invariably the peculiar sort of interaction occurring, we attribute to the objects a permanent capacity for such effects which is always ready to become effective. This permanent capacity is ... called ... [a] *property*" (21).

Accordingly, properties are dispositions to lawlike behaviour. There-fore, the predicates that we use to ascribe such properties to objects must be *dispositional predicates*. As we do not perceive the dispositions them-selves but only what we take to be their effects, statements that ascribe properties to the objects must transcend any experience.

Like Berkeley and Hume, Helmholtz rejects Locke's (1632–1704) dis-tinction between *primary* and *secondary* qualities: In actual fact, the "*prop-erties* of natural objects, in spite of this name, do not denote something that is peculiar to the individual object by itself, but invariably imply some relation to a second object (including our organs of sense)" (1962, 21). When we speak of properties that become apparent when an object of the external world acts upon another object, we do not doubt that the kind of effect must depend both on the acting body and on the body acted upon. That's exactly what we forget when we are concerned with the ef-fect that an object of the external world has on our sense organs; hence we forget "that colour, smell, and taste, and feeling of warmth or cold are also effects quite essentially depending on the nature of the organ that is affected" (21). Thus "the red colour of vermilion exists merely in so far as there are eyes which are constructed like those of most people. Persons who are red-blind have just as much right to consider that a characteristic property of vermilion is that of being black" (22).

However, there seems to be an exception: "*the chronological order of the events*" (1867, 445, m.t., i.a.), for the

> only respect in which there can be a real *agreement between our perceptions and the reality* is the time-sequence of the events.... Simultaneity, sequence, the regular recurrence of simultaneity or sequence, may occur likewise in the sensations as well as in the events. The external events, like their perceptions, proceed in time; and so the temporal relations of the latter may be the faithful reproduction of the temporal relations of the former. (1962, 22, i.a.)

But do external events and perceptions occur in the same absolute time? We in fact no longer believe in Newton's absolute time. On the other hand, the chronological ordering of the external events is of the same kind as that of our perceptions. This does not, however, imply that the events and their perceptions are ordered in the same way. According to Helmholtz,

> the time-sequence of the sensations is not quite a faithful reproduction of the time-sequence of the external events, inasmuch as the transmission from the organs of sense to the brain takes time, and in fact a different time for different organs. Moreover, in case of the eye and the ear, the time has to be added that it takes light and sound to reach the organ. (1962, 22)

Lightning and thunder show how much the times may differ even when the distance is the same. We may also refer to Einstein's idea of the relative time of external events. Two events – say, two flashes of lightning – may affect observers in different orders depending on their spatial positions relative to them (i.e., depending on whether an observer is closer to one event or to the other). Hence the same events can cause different observers to have different sequences of perceptions and therefore different ideas about the succession of these events.

As a sensation is no true image of reality, this holds even less of a statement. Hence a *statement* cannot be *true* insofar as it correctly reproduces reality, but only insofar as it *assigns the correct sign to a part of reality, i.e., the sign that is usually associated with that part*. Also, a statement can be "based on sensations" only insofar as (1) the sensations are reliably associated with parts of reality and (2) the statement is reliably associated with the sensations. Is this the end of "psychologism"?

To begin with, let us consider the first association; we shall return to the second later on (cf. section 4.5). In fact, trying to imagine reality or Kant's "'thing in itself' having positive attributes" is contradictory. "We can, however, know the lawful *order* in the realm of reality, even though our knowledge is represented only in the system of the signs of our sensations" (Helmholtz 1878/1998, 170, m.t., i.a.). Ideally, the ordering of our sensations would be *isomorphic* to the ordering in the realm of reality. According to Helmholtz, there is only a rather weak relation between a sign and that of which it is a sign: "The same object acting upon us in the same circumstances evokes the same sign, so that different signs are always evoked by different impacts" (153).

The fact that we can orient ourselves by our senses does not imply that the two orderings really are isomorphic. For, on the one hand, there is reason to suppose that the orderings of our sensations are much coarser than the orderings in the realm of reality – for example, our eyes perceive only a small part of the electromagnetic spectrum – and, on the other hand, like qualities of objects may give rise to different sensations ("red" or "black" vermilion), and different constellations of objects may give rise to the same sensations (in the case of geometric illusions). But somewhere there must be some approximation to the ideal case. The development of this approximation may be considered a result of the evolution of our sense organs.

Geometric illusions, for one thing, presuppose that different constellations of objects may give rise to the same sensations. In order to "perceive" the constellations, we must in addition "infer" them from the sensations. To this end, we use *implicit assumptions* about the properties and spatial relations of objects. Helmholtz speaks of "*inductive conclusions* leading to the formation of our sense-perceptions" (1962, 26f., i.a.). In both cases (implicit assumptions, inductive inferences), the perceptions transcend the sensations. The expression "*transcendence inherent in any perception*" is to my knowledge due to Hans Albert (1987, 56).

We choose from among the relevant assumptions, and our choice may be more or less fortunate. Quite generally, an *illusion of the senses* is, according to Helmholtz, "rather simply an illusion in the *judgment* of the material presented to the senses, resulting in a false idea of it" (1962, 4, i.a.). Does this "judgment" – like Popper's "free decision" (LSD, 109; cf. section 4.6) – presuppose some kind of free will? This is not necessarily so, for, according to Helmholtz, we "might say that *all apparition* originates in *premature, unmediated inductions*" (28, i.a.). In order to explain illusions, we need not even speak of inductions. Rather, it suffices to assume an accidental or determined deviation from the way of processing sensations that in comparable cases usually leads to predictive success and is therefore taken as a standard for detecting errors. We are not going to speculate epistemologically. We want to show only that Helmholtz's naturalist thesis is by no means more problematic than Popper's conventionalist thesis that scientists *rationally decide* on the acceptance or rejection of basic statements.

4.3. FORMAL PROPERTIES OF BASIC STATEMENTS

But what exactly is a *basic statement*? Popper uses the term "basic statement" in more than one sense. (i) In its widest sense, "basic statement" means "statement of an observed event" (LSD, 69), "*observation statement*" (101 n*1, i.a.), or "falsifiable singular statement" (78). In this broad sense, the simple subject-predicate statement

(1) Wa : Antony [a] is white [W]

is a basic statement. (ii) More important is the narrower sense in which a single basic statement may serve as the sole premise of an empirical falsification (43). A "*falsifying basic statement*" such as this "consists of the conjunction of the initial conditions with the negation of the derived prediction" (127, i.a.; 101 n*1, 102). For example, the universal hypothesis

(2) $(x)(Rx \rightarrow Bx)$: All ravens [R] are black [B]

is refuted by the falsifying basic statement

(3) $Ra \wedge \neg Ba$: Antony is a raven and he is not black.

(Here "Ra" is the "initial condition" and "$\neg Ba$" is the "negation of the derived prediction.") Hypothesis (2) immediately implies the "*instantial statement*" (101 n*1)

(4) $Ra \rightarrow Ba$: If Antony is a raven, then he is black.

But (4) is equivalent to the negation of (3), as

(5) $(p \rightarrow q) \leftrightarrow \neg(p \wedge \neg q)$

is a tautology of propositional logic. Thus, if the falsifying basic statement (3) is true, then the instantial statement (4) and hence hypothesis (2) are false.

However, Popper pays most attention to (iii) a special kind of falsifying basic statement. In fact his "official definition" says: "[*B*]*asic statements have the form of singular existential statements*" (LSD, 102). Accordingly, the singular statement (3) is replaced by the logically weaker singular existential statement

(6) $(Ex)(Rx \wedge Px,d,e,f,t \wedge \neg Bx)$: There is at least one raven that is at time t in place d,e,f [P] and is not black.

Why does Popper propose this definition? On the one hand, *singular existential* statements imply *strictly existential* statements – thus (6) implies the statement

(7) $(Ex)(Rx \wedge \neg Bx)$: There is at least one raven that is not black,

where it suffices to omit the references to the space-time regions (LSD, 102). On the other hand, *strictly existential* statements [such as (7)] are equivalent to *negations* of *strictly universal* statements [such as (2)], as the logical equivalences

(8) $(Ex)(Rx \wedge \neg Bx) \leftrightarrow \neg(x)\neg(Rx \wedge \neg Bx) \leftrightarrow \neg(x)(Rx \rightarrow Bx)$

show. Thus strictly existential statements may seem to be the ideal "*falsifiers*" of strictly universal statements.

Conversely, strictly universal statements are equivalent to negations of strictly existential statements, as the logical equivalences

(9) $(x)(Rx \rightarrow Bx) \leftrightarrow \neg(Ex)\neg(Rx \rightarrow Bx) \leftrightarrow \neg(Ex)(Rx \wedge \neg Bx)$

show. Hence there is a *logical symmetry between strictly universal statements and strictly existential statements.* According to (9), a strictly universal statement may be considered a "prohibition" [LSD, 69; e.g., (2) "forbids" the existence of nonblack ravens); and, according to (8), a strictly existential statement asserting that this "prohibition" is violated – if it is true – falsifies the corresponding strictly universal statement (cf. section 2.6).

However, the *strictly existential statement* (7) is *no adequate premise for an empirical falsification* of hypothesis (2), for (7) is *not empirical* in the sense of the criterion of demarcation (cf. section 4.4). It is true that (7) is *verified* if a nonblack raven is found [for (7) logically follows from singular basic statements such as (3) and from singular existential basic statements such as (6)]. But (7) is *not falsifiable,* as we cannot search the whole universe at all times in order to rule out the possibility that somewhere at some time there is a nonblack raven. For the same reason, the *strictly universal statement* (2) [which is equivalent to the negation of (7); cf. (9)] is *not verifiable* (LSD, 70). On the other hand, the strictly universal statement (2) is falsified if a nonblack raven is found [and therefore a basic statement such as (3) or (6) is accepted].

But as *singular existential statements* such as (6) refer to *limited* space-time regions that may in principle be completely searched, they appear to be not only verifiable but also falsifiable, hence *empirical*, so that they may be considered *basic statements*. This, together with the fact that they imply strictly existential statements, and along with the logical symmetry between strictly existential statements and strictly universal statements, explains Popper's "official definition."

However, singular existential statements are falsifiable only if they are judged directly by *observations*, for there is *no basic statement logically contradicting them*, as the negations of singular existential statements such as (6) are equivalent to numerically universal statements such as

(10) $(x)(Rx \wedge Px,d,e,f,t \rightarrow Bx)$.

For that reason, Andersson criticizes Popper's definition: Basic statements cannot be singular existential statements either, "as in this case they cannot be falsified by other basic statements" (1998, 150, m.t.). Accordingly, only statements of type (i) [such as (1)] and type (ii) [such as (3)] can rightly be called "basic statements," and only statements of type (ii) can be called "falsifying basic statements."

4.4. MATERIAL PROPERTIES OF BASIC STATEMENTS

In addition to those formal requirements, basic statements have to meet material requirements: The events on which they report must be " '*observable*' "; that is, "basic statements must be testable, inter-subjectively, by 'observation' " (LSD, 102). By putting "observation" in quotation marks, Popper tries to set himself off against "psychologism." It is true that he too defends the fundamental thesis of realism, according to which there is an exterior world independent of our thought, and the fundamental thesis of empiricism, according to which all statements are to be judged in the end by sense experience. But he criticizes Fries's view that in *sense experience* "we have '*immediate knowledge*': [and that] by this immediate knowledge, we may *justify* our '*mediate knowledge*' – knowledge expressed in the symbolism of some language. And this mediate knowledge includes, of course, the *statements* of science" (LSD, 94, i.a.).

In order "to save the term 'observable' . . . from the stigma of psychologism," Popper asserts that "the concept of an *observable event* . . . might just as well be replaced by "an event involving position and movement of

macroscopic physical bodies'" (LSD, 103). "Basic statements are therefore – in the material mode of speech – statements asserting that an
observable event is occurring in a certain individual region of space and
time" (103). He does not try to define the term "*observable*"; rather, he introduces it "as an *undefined term* which becomes sufficiently precise in use:
as a *primitive concept* whose use the epistemologist has to learn" (103, i.a.).

Being a neoempiricist, he hardly can reject the thesis that "perceptual
experience must be the sole 'source of knowledge' of all the empirical
sciences," for even the boldest theories must in the end be tested by
sense impressions (LSD, 94). But this does not imply, as sensationalism
and positivism assume, that "[a]ll we know about the world of facts must
therefore be expressible in the form of statements *about our experiences*"
(94).

4.5. THE TRANSCENDENCE INHERENT IN ANY DESCRIPTION

The *theoretical character of all assumptions* has linguistic consequences: What
a statement asserts transcends any experience on which it relies; for this
reason alone, no experience can establish the truth of a statement; rather,
any statement is a fallible hypothesis. Popper states this idea in Chapter 5,
"The Problem of the Empirical Basis," of his *Logic*; in Appendix *X, "Universals, Dispositions, and Natural or Physical Necessity," he elaborates it
in detail.

Universal laws transcend experience, insofar as they refer to an open,
possibly infinite class of cases "and thus transcend any finite number of
their observable instances" (LSD, 425). This entails the *problem of induction*. Even *singular statements* transcend experience, "because the *universal
terms* which normally occur in them entail dispositions to behave in a
law-like manner, so that they entail *universal laws* (of some lower order
of universality, as a rule)" (425, i.a.). Popper gives an example: "The
statement 'Here is a glass of water' cannot be verified" (95), because the
universals (cf. section 2.5) "is glass" and "is water" express *lawlike behaviour,
dispositions*, and each of these laws transcends experience (424).

But could we not avoid the transcendence inherent in our descriptions by making statements having less content that only express what
we actually are perceiving? We shall now approach this aim step by step
in a series of thought experiments, and we shall see why we can never
attain it.

(1) To begin with, we examine what we assert when we say only "This is
water" (cf. Keuth 1989, 3.211). Water has lawlike properties. Each sample

displays them, either continually or when certain conditions are met. For example, water is liquid at a certain pressure in a certain range of temperatures. It looses this property if it is heated beyond its boiling point or cooled down below its freezing point. Instead of being liquid, it takes on other properties; it becomes gaseous or solid. Hence it is impossible to observe all of its properties at the same time, and normally we have not even observed all of them successively when we assert that there is water in some vessel. In these cases, we base our statement on perceptions that point to only *some* of the lawlike properties of water. Perhaps we notice that the content is liquid, clear, and odourless.

Above all, we can, if we look now, at best observe that some of these properties are present *here and now*. But for our sample of a liquid to be water, it must *always* be liquid *wherever* the same pressures and temperatures prevail, even if we *do not perceive* it. Moreover, it would have to be liquid on the surface of the sun a minute from now, if it could get there that fast and if the same pressures and temperatures prevailed there; both of which are *not the case*. (For the relation between lawlike hypotheses and irreal conditionals, see Chapter 13.)

Furthermore, a property like that of being *liquid* is rather *theoretical*. It is true that we can see some of its effects – for example, waves on the surface of a sample – and that we can have certain sensations of touch and warmth that we expect when dealing with liquids. Again, however, we thus apprehend only *some* of the properties of liquids.

(2) *Colours* seem to be less theoretical properties, as we are physiologically equipped to perceive them. For example, "we say of [an area] that it is red, or white, if it has the disposition to *reflect* red, or white, light, and consequently the disposition to *look* in daylight red, or white" (LSD, 424f., i.a.). Now the former, physical disposition is as theoretical as the disposition of being liquid. But what about the latter, phenomenal disposition?

When we call an area "red" in the phenomenal sense, we attribute to it the disposition to arouse certain sense impressions – namely, the disposition always to look red in daylight. Hence we mean "This area *always* looks red [in daylight for people with normal colour vision]." This disposition continues to exist when the light changes and even when no light is thrown on the area. Even if we call the area red only after having seen it *often* in daylight, we assert more than we have perceived – indeed, more than we could ever perceive. Hence colour predicates, even when they are taken in the phenomenal sense, differ only in degree from the most abstract predicates.

(3) But if we insert a *reference to an individual space-time region* into a strictly universal statement that is only falsifiable, we turn it into a numerically universal statement that is also verifiable. In the same way, we may reduce the content of an observation statement. And isn't the transcendence of our description eliminated if instead of saying "This area *always* looks red," we only assert what we are presently perceiving, say, "This area *now* looks red"?

(4) At any rate, such transcendence is not completely eliminated if by "this area" we mean a part of the surface of a certain physical *body*, for the assumption that bodies exist is highly theoretical. However, as far as this kind of transcendence is concerned, it no longer inheres in our description if we identify the area by referring not to a body but to a *coordinate system*. But have we thus eliminated any remaining transcendence inherent in our description?

(5) Let us now assume that when I say "This area *now* looks red," I mean not only that it seems red *to me* here and now but also that it would seem red *to any other person* having normal colour vision who now stood here. Then I assert more than I could ever sense, for the simple reason that not all persons having normal colour vision could here and now have the same sensation.

(6) And how can I find out whether *an individual* person having normal colour vision who sees the same area under the same conditions has the *same colour impression* that I have? As I cannot sense his sensations, I have to rely on his statements. But how do I know that we have the same colour impression when both of us say here and now "This area now looks red"? For the sake of simplicity, we disregard the difficulties that may arise from lies, errors, and idiosyncratic usage of words.

Instead, we make the idealizing assumption that two observers A and B use the word "red" – without exception – under the same conditions. Does this imply that they have the *same colour impression* whenever they use the *same colour predicate* "red"? It is still conceivable that stimuli of type S – and only stimuli of this type – always cause colour impressions of type I in A, whereas they cause impressions of type J in B, and that A reacts to impressions of type I, while B reacts to impressions of type J – and that both react only to these impressions – always by uttering the word "red." Then we cannot in principle find out that they have different colour impressions when they are confronted with the same stimulus S. Hence their *indiscernible use of the word "red"* does not imply an equality, but only a *one-to-one correspondence of their colour impressions* (cf. Keuth 1993, 2.212.).

Accordingly, insofar as I imply by my statement "This area now looks red" that *all* persons having normal colour vision would have *the same colour impression* if they now stood here, I assert more than could ever be tested. But I also may easily avoid this transcendence inherent in my description if by the same statement I imply only that all persons having normal colour vision, if they now stood here, would have *colour impressions that can be mapped in a one-to-one manner.*

(7) Let us now assume that when I say "This area now looks red," I mean only that it appears red *to me* here and now. Have I thus finally eliminated *any* transcendence inherent in my description? By using the *predicate* "red," I presuppose that my present colour impression equals the impressions that I have had on other occasions when I have used the same word. Hence I try to use it *according to a rule.* However, I do not now have the other impressions; rather, I only remember them. Accordingly, I still assert more than I sense here and now. *As long as we are using predicates at all, we cannot avoid this kind of transcendence inherent in our descriptions.* But subject-predicate statements are the simplest kind of statements in our language. *For that reason alone, no perception can secure the truth of any statement.*

4.6. RESOLUTION OF THE TRILEMMA

Observations cannot prove basic statements. But are observations never rational reasons to take basic statements to be true? Popper writes: "Every test of a theory, whether resulting in its corroboration or falsification, must stop at some basic statement or other which we *decide to accept.* If we do not come to any decision, and do not accept some basic statement or other, then the test will have led nowhere" (LSD, 104). Does this mean that the theory is falsified if a (falsifying) basic statement is *accepted as true* on account of observations, and that the theory is corroborated if the basic statement is *rejected as false?*

Rather, Popper's argument takes a *conventionalist* turn. To begin with, he demands a *consensus* of the scientists. He expects us to arrive "at a procedure according to which we stop only at a kind of statement that is especially easy to test. For it means that we are stopping at statements about whose acceptance or rejection the various investigators are likely to reach *agreement*" (LSD, 104, i.a.). If they do not immediately agree, they will go on testing or will repeat previous tests. "If this too leads to no result, then we might say that the statements in question were not inter-subjectively testable, or that we were *not*, after all, dealing with *observable events*" (104, i.a.).

But why should events be nonobservable if their observation does not lead to a unanimous judgment; why should a statement not be intersubjectively testable if there is no agreement on the result of its test? After all, the history of science shows how often there is disagreement on theories and even on observation statements. So how long are we permitted to test and discuss? When, at the latest, do we have to come to an agreement? Obviously, Popper's new rule for the use of the word "observable" is most inappropriate.

But does his proposal dissolve Fries's trilemma, "dogmatism – infinite regress – psychologism"? As an infinite regress is out of the question and as Popper rejects psychologism, it seems that he has to accept dogmatism. At any rate, he writes: "The basic statements at which we stop, which we decide to accept as satisfactory, and as sufficiently tested, have admittedly the character of *dogmas*, but only in so far as we may desist from justifying them by further arguments (or by further tests)" (LSD, 105).

However, strictly universal statements and probability statements cannot be justified either. Does this mean that any statement that is accepted without being justified, any mere hypothesis, is a dogma? Popper would strictly reject this opinion. But why then should basic statements – which are, just on account of their universals, hypotheses as well – "have the character of dogmas" (cf. Andersson 1998, 160f.)?

Popper does not tell us why, but he reassures us by asserting that "this kind of dogmatism is innocuous since, should the need arise, [the basic statements] can easily be tested further" (LSD, 105). It is true that we may rely on sense experience for these further tests, whereas there is no such external corrective in the case of religious or philosophical dogmas. Still, he asserts: "*Basic statements* are accepted as the result of a decision or agreement; and to that extent they *are conventions*" (LSD, 106, i.a.).

If, however, basic statements "are accepted as the result of a decision," then decisions settle the fate of theories. What then is the difference between fallibilism and *conventionalism*? Both make their judgments contingent on considerations of expediency. But the conventionalist decides immediately on acceptance or rejection of *universal* statements, and his principle is *simplicity*. In contrast to this, Popper's fallibilist immediately decides on acceptance or rejection of *singular* statements, and his decision is motivated by *observations*. Only subsequently does he decide – indirectly – on universal statements (LSD, 109).

Obviously, the difference between fallibilism and conventionalism seems less important to Popper than the difference between fallibilism and *positivism*, for he repeatedly expresses himself approximately as follows: "I differ from the positivist in holding that basic statements are not justifiable by our immediate experiences, but are, from the logical point of view, accepted by an act, by a *free decision*. (From the psychological point of view this may perhaps be a purposeful and well-adapted reaction)" (LSD, 109, i.a.). Though experiences "can *motivate a decision*, and hence an acceptance or a rejection of a statement, . . . a basic statement cannot be *justified* by them – no more than by thumping the table" (105).

The positivists of the Vienna Circle knew very well that statements cannot, from the logical point of view, be *justified* by states of affairs or by sense perceptions. But for some time a number of them believed that immediate experiences may permit *infallible* judgments about observation statements of the simplest kind. On the other hand, judgments about observation statements are *free decisions* only insofar as they cannot, from the logical point of view, be justified.

But what does "From the psychological point of view the acceptance of a basic statement is *a purposeful and well-adapted reaction*" mean? Does the acceptance of a basic statement only further our chances for survival? In this sense, the reaction of an amoeba may be well adapted. (According to an addition to the tenth edition of the *Logik*, the reaction serves the search for truth [74].) Or does it result from a *rational decision* that we take, motivated by sense experiences, after having carefully considered all relevant elements of knowledge (e.g., memories, hypotheses, methodological rules)? This would presuppose a decision that is free in the stronger sense of being an act of *free will*. However, the assumption that there is a free will is certainly metaphysical (if it is not contradictory), because it implies unsolvable conceptual problems (cf. section 14.7).

We do not here intend to doubt the rationality of scientific decisions; rather, the essential thing is to bear in mind that the statement "We *rationally decide* on the acceptance of a basic statement" is as *theoretical* and *metaphysical* as the statement "The acceptance of a basic statement is *caused* by sense impressions." What then is the advantage of Popper's idea that "a decision [on basic statements is] reached in accordance with a procedure governed by rules" (LSD, 109)?

Obviously, a *decision* may be wrong. Hence Popper's idea takes the *fallibility* of our judgments into account. If, on the other hand, the acceptance of a basic statement should be *caused* by sense impressions, would it then not be *inevitable*, and would this fact not exclude the possibility of an *error*? Sometimes we cannot help having an impression even though we know *that* it is deceptive. This applies, for example, to the autokinetic effect. And sometimes we even cannot help having such a sense impression when we know how it arises, that is, *why* it is deceptive. This applies to contrast enhancement at edges, which is due to "lateral inhibition" among neurons with adjacent receptive fields.

On the other hand, it is conceivable that in a person unaware of the autokinetic effect the false *impression* of a moving light *causes* the *judgment* "There is a moving light," whereas in another person the same impression and the *knowledge* (the hypothesis) of the autokinetic effect together cause the judgment "There is a light which seems to move but is stationary." As taking the impression of a moving light to be false presupposes the (fallible) *hypothesis* of the autokinetic effect (or some other hypothesis), the *fallibility* of our judgments is taken into account just as well by the *thesis that judgments are caused* as it is by the *thesis that they result from free decisions*. We do not propose psychological or physiological hypotheses on the origin of statements of fact, nor do we defend determinism. We only want to explain why *the thesis that judgments are caused does not contradict the thesis that judgments are fallible*. Had Popper been more familiar with the physiology and psychology of perception, he might easily have avoided conventionalism insofar as the problem of the empirical basis is concerned.

4.7. WHY JUDGMENTS ON BASIC STATEMENTS DEPEND ON THEORIES

If it appears to be necessary, the basic statements at which we stop may be tested further. For this purpose, we derive (from those basic statements and other premises) new test statements, which we then test in their turn and then either accept or reject. But we needn't stop there either, for there is no proof of the truth or falsity of *any* basic statement. Doesn't this lead to an infinite regress as well? Popper admits "that this too makes the chain of deduction in principle infinite," but then he asserts that "this kind of '*infinite regress*' is also innocuous since in our theory there is no question of trying to prove any statements by means of it" (LSD, 105).

Still, continued testing involves *methodological problems*, for we cannot derive new test statements from the original basic statements without "the help of some theory, either *the one under test*, or another" (LSD, 104, i.a.). But when the *same* theory is taken as an additional premise, the judgment of its truth already relies on the assumption of its truth. Thus if the theory is actually *judged to be true*, then the underlying reasoning is *circular*.

Actually, Popper fears that we "*argue in circles*" (i.a.) when trying to *confirm* theories, and therefore he demands that we "adopt a highly critical attitude towards our theories . . . : the attitude of trying to *falsify* them" (LSD, 107 n*2). However, the risk of arguing in circles does not depend on our intention of confirming or falsifying theories; rather, it depends, as we shall see, on our coming across confirming or refuting instances. On the other hand, *not every* theory can serve as an additional premise for the derivation of new test statements from its basic statements. Rather, this holds primarily of theories referring to perception or to instruments that are used in observations or experiments (cf. Keuth 1989, 3.222.).

If we analyze test procedures with a little care, we can discover the conditions under which we really do argue in circles. This will keep us from generally prohibiting test procedures in which the theory being tested is repeatedly applied. When judging hypotheses, we may commit errors of two types: We may *reject a true hypothesis* – in statistics this is called a *Type I error* – or we may *accept a false hypothesis* – this is called a *Type II error*. We adopt this usage and propose a thought experiment to discover under which conditions one or the other of these errors occurs.

* Let *geometrical optics (G)* be our theory. This theory deals with all aspects of light except its wave and quantum nature. Let it imply that object lenses with certain properties produce undistorted real images. We take the statement

(1) If the object lens *O* having the properties *P* produces a real image *R* of the square *S*, then *R* is undistorted

to be one of its *instantial statements*. We shall now examine step by step what problems arise when we first test the instantial statement (1) – or, what amounts to the same thing, its negation, the basic statement (2) – on the basis of observations, then evaluate theory *G* according to the result obtained, and finally, in order to reexamine this evaluation, derive new test statements from the old ones – using the *same* theory *G* as an additional premise – and test the new ones. To begin with, we assume (i) that our first observation contradicts theory *G*; then we assume (ii) that it is compatible with *G*.

(i) Let a *real image R* of the square *S*, produced by the object lens *O*, appear to the *naked eye* to be slightly *barrel-shaped* (i.e., distorted). And let, consequently, the negation

(2) The object lens *O* having the properties *P* produces a *distorted* real image *R* of the square *S*

of the instantial statement (1) – that is, *an original basic statement falsifying theory G* – be accepted as true for the present. This, however, is no sufficient reason to immediately reject theory *G*, for *G* is very well corroborated. Rather, the question will be examined beforehand whether, contrary to all appearances, the object lens *O* lacks the properties *P*, or whether *S* is not really a square, or whether *R* actually is undistorted; that is, the basic statement (2) will be reexamined.

We assume, however, that *O* has the properties *P* and that *S* is square, and we only test again whether or not the real image appears distorted. In order to improve our assessment of *R*, we now look at *R* through a *magnifying glass*, and in order to keep our example simple, we assume that the magnifying glass produces undistorted images – more precisely, that it has those properties *P* that are prerequisites for producing undistorted images. Together with this assumption, theory *G* implies the statement

(3) The real image *R* appears distorted in the virtual image *V* of the magnifying glass if, and only if, *R* is distorted.

For the sake of brevity, we call (3) a *theorem* of *G*. Theorem (3) and the original basic statement (2), which asserts that the real image *R* is distorted, together imply the *derived basic statement*

(4) The real image *R* appears distorted in the virtual image *V*

$[(2) \wedge (3) \Rightarrow (4)]$. Now the derived basic statement (4) must in its turn be tested on the basis of observations, and the test will have one of two possible results.

(i,i) Let us first assume that *the real image R* in fact *appears distorted in the virtual image V* of the magnifying glass and that the derived basic statement (4) is therefore accepted as true. Then, if theorem (3) is considered true (and, as presupposed, the object lens *O* has the properties *P* and *S* is square [(PS)]), the original basic statement (2) will still be accepted as true [for $(4) \wedge (3) \wedge (PS) \Rightarrow (2)$]. Thus *theory G is also indirectly refuted* [as $(2) \Rightarrow \neg(G)$].

This argument is conclusive, but is it unproblematic to assume that theorem (3) is true? Obviously, this is the case if (3) has been tested independently of theory *G* and has been corroborated. Then the *problem of circular reasoning*, which we are analyzing, does not arise. If, however, *(3) has not been independently tested but is only inferred from G*, then the renewed judgment that *G is false* presupposes along with the assumption that (3) is true the additional assumption that *G is true*. But in spite of this presupposition, the argument in this case is *not circular*.

Nevertheless, let us examine under which circumstances *the assumption that* (3) *is true because G is true* results in a *misjudgment* about theory *G*:

(a) If *theorem* (3) is *false*, then the assumption that the derived basic statement (4) supports the original basic statement (2) is erroneous. Should we, because of this erroneous assumption, stick to the original basic statement (2) and therefore reject theory *G*, we would still not make a mistake, as *theory G* must be *false* if theorem (3) is false. [For we assume that the magnifying glass has the properties *P*, and together with this assumption, theory *G* implies theorem (3).]

(b) If, however, *theorem* (3) is *true*, then, as the derived basic statement (4) is accepted, the original basic statement (2) must be accepted as well. If theory *G* is therefore rejected,

(ba) no error has been committed if *G* is *false*.

(bb) If, on the other hand, *G* is *true*, a *Type I error* has been committed, that is, a true theory has been rejected. But this error *cannot result from – for the very reason that theory G is taken to be true – erroneously taking theorem* (3) *to be true*. On the contrary, as both theorem (3) and theory *G* are true, the acceptance of the original basic statement (2) as well as the acceptance of the derived basic statement (4) must be mistaken.

(i,ii) Let us now assume that *the real image R* instead *appears undistorted in the virtual image V* of the magnifying glass and that the derived basic statement (4) is therefore rejected. Then if theorem (3) is considered true, the original basic statement (2) must be rejected as well [for $\neg(4) \land (3) \Rightarrow \neg(2)$]. Thus *theory G is still unrefuted*; it even has *once more been corroborated*.

But in this case, the judgment that theory *G* is still *unrefuted* presupposes – along with the assumption that theorem (3) is true – the assumption that *G* itself is *true*. Hence the argument resulting in this judgment is *circular*. Let us now examine under what conditions this circumstance will lead to a misjudgment about *G*:

(a) If *theorem* (3) is *true*, then an argument rejecting the original basic statement (2) along with the derived basic statement (4) is valid. If theory *G* therefore remains accepted,

(aa) no error has been committed if *G* is *true*.

(ab) Though theorem (3) is true, *theory G* may be *false*. If *G* still continues to be accepted, a *Type II error* has been committed. But this error *does not result from the circular argument*, for we assume that (3) is in fact true. [Thus independent tests of (3) would show that (3) is true, and therefore we would not have to base our assumption that (3) is true on the derivation of (3) from *G*, which, as we now assume, is false. However, the rejection of the derived basic statement (4) may be mistaken, or *G* may give rise to false predictions in other cases.]

(b) If, however, *theorem (3) is false*, then, on the one hand, *theory G* must also be *false* [as (3) follows from *G* and the – by supposition true – assumption that the magnifying glass has the properties *P* that are prerequisites for producing undistorted images], and, on the other hand, *the argument* rejecting the original (falsifying) basic statement (2) along with the derived basic statement (4) must be invalid. But it *is erroneously considered valid, because the false assumption that (3) is true is based on the false assumption that G is true.* As we, based on this argument, erroneously consider theory *G* to be unrefuted, *the circular argument here results in a Type II error.*

(ii) Our argument runs analogously if the *real image R* appears to the *naked eye* [not, as in (i), barrel-shaped but] *undistorted*, theory *G* therefore continues to be accepted, and new observations with a magnifying glass are later made in order to review this judgment.

(ii,i) If the real image *R* appears *undistorted in the virtual image V of the magnifying glass* as well, the argument is analogous to (i,ii).

(ii,ii) If, on the other hand, the real image *R* appears *distorted in the virtual image V of the magnifying glass*, the argument is analogous to (i,i).

For we always evaluate the theory according to the later, more precise observation. **

Let us now sum up the results of our thought experiment. There are theories that permit the derivation of additional test statements from their original basic statements. Our model of such a theory is geometrical optics (*G*), and "theorem" (3) is the weakest consequence of *G* (and the assumption that the magnifying glass has the properties *P* that are prerequisites for producing undistorted images) permitting the derivation of such additional test statements. On their basis, we may reevaluate *G*. In order not to exclude circular arguments from the outset, we assume that *G* is considered true on account of its corroboration so far, and that (3) has not been independently tested but is taken to be true because (3) follows from *G*.

If the new observations are incompatible with *G* and the *derived basic statements* are therefore *accepted*, then *theory G* is *refuted* by means of theorem (3), that is, indirectly on the basis of the assumption that *G* is true. But *the argument leading to this refutation of G is not circular, nor does the assumption that G is true diminish the refutability of G.* Any Type I error (a true theory is rejected) that may occur must result from erroneously accepting basic statements.

If, on the other hand, the new observations are compatible with theory *G* and if the *derived basic statements* are therefore *rejected*, then the judgment that *theory G* remains *unrefuted* presupposes along with theorem (3) the assumption that *G* is true. Therefore, *the argument leading to this judgment is circular*. This does not entail a misjudgment if theory *G* is true. If *G* is false, a Type II error has been committed. But *only if both theory G and theorem (3) are false does the error result from the circularity of the argument.*

Popper "summarizes" his exposition on the problem of the empirical basis as follows:

The empirical basis of objective science has thus nothing "absolute" about it. Science does not rest upon rock-bottom. The bold structure of its theories rises, as it were, above a swamp. It is like a building erected on piles. The piles are driven down from above into the swamp, but not down to any natural or "given" base; and when we cease our attempts to drive our piles into a deeper layer, it is not because we have reached firm ground. We simply stop when we are satisfied that they are firm enough to carry the structure, at least for the time being. (LSD, 111)

5

Corroboration

Popper's "negative methodology" (cf. section 3.5) is complemented by his "*positive theory of corroboration*" (LSD, 265ff.), whose *fundamental idea* is simple: *A hypothesis that withstands serious attempts to refute it is corroborated*; the more often it is tested, and the severer the tests are, the better it is corroborated. It is, however, not at all simple to determine under what conditions a test is severe or to what degree a hypothesis is corroborated. Therefore, we cannot expect a methodological rule that will be useful as a concrete directive either.

Still, Popper gives a definition of *degree of corroboration*. This, however, is not his real problem. Rather, "the task of finding an adequate definition of [degree of corroboration] (and of degree of acceptability) arose . . . [in] the last analysis . . . from the problems of *induction* and *demarcation*" (RAS, 233, i.a.). He believed he had found the solution to the problem of induction around 1927 (OK, 1 n1): An essential part of the solution is to realize that all of our "knowledge" is hypothetical. Thus the question "How do you know that the laws of nature will continue to hold tomorrow?" is replaced by the question "How can we distinguish between good and bad theories?"; and the latter question is answered by Popper's "positive theory of corroboration" (cf. section 5.5).

His "positive theory" is intended to show that a degree of corroboration is *not a probability* but is "incompatible with the rules of the probability calculus" (RAS, 232). (This is a criticism directed, above all, against Carnap and Reichenbach [1891–1953].) Popper instead defines the degree of corroboration "*in terms of content* – the content of the theory and that of the test statements" (232) – and he regards the degree of corroboration "merely as a *critical report* on the quality of past performance" of a theory

(PKP, 82, i.a.). Though a theory can help to "predict *future events*," he believes that a report on its past performance "*could not be used to predict* [*its*] *future performance*" (82). Still, he considers it *rational* "to act on that theory – if there was one – which *so far* had stood up to criticism better than its competitors" (82, i.a.).

Popper later attaches great significance to these considerations, asserting that the concepts "of *content* and of *degree of corroboration* are the most important logical tools developed in" his *Logic* (LSD, Appendix *IX, 395). As "corroboration" is a very complex topic, we first give an outline of the basic concept.

5.1. QUASI-INDUCTION BY TESTING HYPOTHESES

"Theories are not verifiable, but they can be 'corroborated'" (LSD, 251). In order to test a theory, we derive a prediction (from the theory in question, initial or boundary conditions, and perhaps other theories) and check whether the prediction is realized (cf. Chapter 2; section 4.7). If it is not realized, the system of its premises is *refuted* (cf. section 3.6); if it is realized, the system is *supported* – and so is the theory. It is true that judgments such as these can, in view of new observations, be reversed. But as long "as a theory withstands detailed and severe tests and is not superseded by another theory in the course of scientific progress, we may say that it has 'proved its mettle' or that it is '*corroborated*'" (LSD, 33).

Unlike the truth of a statement, its *corroboration* is *not timeless*. Hence "'[t]he corroboration which a theory has received up to yesterday' is *logically not identical* with 'the corroboration which a theory has received up to today'" (LSD, 275). Also, a theory is corroborated only "*with respect to some system of basic statements*" that are "accepted up to a particular point in time" (275). In addition, the corroboration of a theory depends not only on its own success but also on the success of its potential *rivals* (276ff.).

In spite of these qualifications, its corroboration is a "good reason" to retain a theory. Therefore, Popper gives the methodological *rule* (which we already know; cf. section 3.3):

(R_2) Once a hypothesis has been proposed and tested, and has proved its mettle, it may not be allowed to drop out without "good reason." A "good reason" may be, for instance: replacement of the hypothesis by another which is better testable; or the falsification of one of the consequences of the hypothesis. (LSD, 53f.)

But under what conditions does such a "good reason" suffice to abandon a hypothesis that has up until now been well corroborated? Even in the event of its refutation, the answer is not as simple as it may seem.

(a) If a hypothesis that was first corroborated is *refuted* later on, this may be a "good reason" to *abandon* it immediately, even if there is no other hypothesis to replace it. But even in this case, Popper hopes, we shall not have to get along indefinitely without any replacement. For what "compels the theorist to search for a better theory . . . is almost always the experimental *falsification* of a theory, so far accepted and corroborated" (LSD, 108). But until a better one is found, we often *continue to apply* the falsified theory. If it fails only in a certain field, it may in another field still be used to derive *predictions* or still be *technologically* applied. This holds, accordingly, if it permits quantitative predictions that deviate only slightly from the observed values. But because it has been falsified, it is no longer an adequate premise for an *explanation*.

(b) What then are the requirements that a theory must meet if it is to *replace* a *refuted* theory? Popper gives a dramatic example. He supposes "that the sun will not rise tomorrow (and that we shall nevertheless continue to live, and also to pursue our scientific interests)" (LSD, 253). In a case like this, science would try to explain the novel event, "*i.e.*, to derive it from laws." This would presuppose a revision of the existing theories, but "the revised theories would not merely have to account for the new state of affairs: *our older experiences would also have to be derivable from them*" (253). However, a new theory could not explain the old experiences if the fundamental laws of nature have changed. Does he therefore tacitly assume that the old laws continue to hold and that only some boundary conditions have changed? Instead of making such an *ontological assumption*, he formulates a *methodological demand*: He replaces "the principle of the uniformity of nature" with "the postulate of the *invariance of natural laws*, with respect to both space and time" (253).

Popper here alludes to the Humean thesis that from a present impression we infer the idea of an object that is its cause. If this inference is to be an achievement not of experience but of reason, then it would be possible only according to the principle that "*the course of nature continues always uniformly the same*" (Hume, 1739–40/1978, 89).

Hence the new theory is to comply with the methodological postulate that its domain of application should not be spatiotemporally restricted. Accordingly, it must also explain the former state of affairs (the sun regularly rises and sets) that used to be explained by the henceforth refuted theory. But the new theory would as well be false if it explained the former state in the same way that the old theory did. If we assume that the laws of nature continue to hold while the boundary conditions change, then the new theory may imply that the former state of affairs depended on conditions that no longer prevail or that the new state of affairs (the sun no longer rises) depends on conditions that formerly did not prevail.

A new theory explaining both the old and the new states of affairs has – in a sense to be specified – *greater content* than the old theory. Therefore, it is *better testable* and, if it passes additional tests in the new situation, also *better corroborated.* This holds even if the old theory does not, as in Popper's example, fail in the new situation, but does not refer to it at all.

(c) But when will an *unrefuted* hypothesis be *replaced?* If "a well-corroborated theory, and one which continues to be further corroborated, has been deductively explained by a new hypothesis of a *higher level* [, the] attempt will have to be made to test this new hypothesis by means of some of its consequences *which have not yet been tested*" – since they do not follow from the old theory (LSD, 77). Thus the new theory's risk of being refuted will increase. If it is refuted, the old theory remains intact and is therefore retained. If, on the other hand, the new theory is corroborated by the new tests, it is given preference, for

(R_{10}) We choose the theory which best holds its own in competition with other theories; the one which, by natural selection, proves itself the fittest to survive. This will be the one which not only *has hitherto stood up to the severest tests,* but the one which *is also testable in the most rigorous way.* (LSD, 108, i.a.)

Now the old theory can be dropped for the present, as the new one accomplishes more. It may, however, be necessary to reactivate the (still unrefuted) old theory if the new one should later fail where it seemed to surpass the old one. If, on the other hand, the new theory fails because of implications that it shares with the old one, then both are refuted.

But even if the new theory should *not* be *refuted*, it will one day be *superseded,* for science evolves in a "direction from theories of a lower level of universality to theories of a higher level" (LSD, 276). Though this may be called the "'*inductive*' *direction*," an advance in this direction does *not* "consist of a sequence of *inductive inferences*" (276, i.a.). On the contrary, Popper gives a noninductive explanation:

(R_{11}) A theory which has been well corroborated can only be superseded by one of a higher level of universality; that is, by a theory which is better testable and which, in addition, *contains* the old, well corroborated theory – or at least a good approximation to it. (276)

Therefore, Popper proposes "to describe that trend – the advance towards theories of an ever higher level of universality – as '*quasi-inductive*'" (276, i.a.).

5.2. NUMBER AND SEVERITY OF TESTS

When we try "to appraise the *degree of corroboration of a theory* we may reason somewhat as follows. Its degree of corroboration will increase with the *number* of its corroborating instances" (LSD, 269, i.a.). But it will not increase proportionally, for

we usually accord to the *first* corroborating instances far greater importance than to later ones: once a theory is well corroborated, *further* instances raise its degree of corroboration only very little [i.a.]. This rule however does not hold good if these new instances are very different from the earlier ones, that is if they corroborate the theory in a *new field of application*. In this case, they may increase the degree of corroboration very considerably. (269)

Hence "it is not so much the number of corroborating instances which determines the degree of corroboration as *the severity of the various tests* to which the hypothesis in question can be, and has been, subjected" (LSD, 267). Now, a *novel* test is riskier, hence it is more severe. This holds all the more if consequences (of the hypothesis in question) are tested that *contradict other theories*. In this case, the test is a *crucial experiment* (cf. section 3.61). It permits us to choose among the theories, for, whatever the result of the test, (at least) one of them will be refuted.

Also, in any other case a "*serious* empirical test always consists in the attempt to find a refutation, a counterexample" (CR, 240, i.a.). But how can a counterexample be found? When searching for it,

we have to use our background knowledge; for we always try to refute first the *most risky* predictions, the "*most unlikely* . . . consequences" (as Peirce already saw); which means that we always look in the *most probable kinds* of places for the *most probable* kinds of counterexamples – most probable in the sense that we should expect to find them in the light of our background knowledge. (240)

The unequal weight of earlier and later tests, of well-known and novel tests, seems to be plausible. But it makes sense only if we assume that the fundamental laws of nature do not change. For only then can we expect *like* tests to produce like results, whose marginal utility therefore decreases; and only then is it only *novel* tests that entail a new and therefore *greater risk* for the theory.

Popper wants to avoid the suspicion that he is arguing *inductively*. Thus he means by

the degree of corroboration of a theory . . . a concise report evaluating the state (at a certain time *t*) of the critical discussion of a theory, with respect to the way it solves its problems; its degree of testability; the severity of tests it has undergone; and the way it has stood up to these tests. Corroboration (or degree of corroboration) is thus an evaluating *report of past performance*. (OK, 18)

Accordingly, the report contains no (explicit) assumption about the future success of the theory. But can he thus completely avoid the assumption of a "uniformity of nature"?

Let us begin with a *methodological* consideration. If Popper assumed that *nature* is *constantly but randomly changing*, then he would have to consider any developing and testing of theories senseless, because statements could be true only for the moment. (There would not even be human beings to develop and test theories, as life is possible only where there are regularities.) If, on the other hand, he considered it just as *possible* that during a certain period of time nature *changes randomly* as that it is *uniform*, then it would make sense – expecting that nature is uniform – to develop and test hypotheses. If, finally, he assumed that nature *changes regularly*, he would postulate constancy at a higher level. However, it is not just the methodology of testing hypotheses that requires some uniformity of nature.

This is true as well of the use of *language*. As all predicates are *disposition predicates*, they imply universal hypotheses. Hence, anyone who utters a statement cannot avoid the assumption that there is some uniformity in nature. This holds as well of any report on the past performance of a theory. Whoever considers the *transcendence inherent in any description* inductive cannot, in this respect, avoid induction. On the other hand, Popper's tacit assumption of the uniformity of nature does not imply that his theory of corroboration involves a principle of induction, for this assumption is not suited to be such a principle.

But the severity of a test depends also on the *degree of testability* of the statement to be tested. Thus a statement that is "falsifiable in a higher degree" is also "corroborable in a higher degree" (LSD, 267). We shall deal with the "degrees" of falsifiability and of corroborability in sections 5.3 and 5.4.

5.3. DEGREES OF TESTABILITY

In Chapter 6 of his *Logic*, Popper inquires into *the comparison of* "*the various degrees of testability or falsifiability of theories*" (LSD, 112, i.a.). For this, he defines "the *empirical content* of a statement p as the class of its potential falsifiers" and its "*logical content* . . . as the class of all non-tautological statements which are derivable" from p (120). The potential falsifiers of p are those statements that contradict p and are empirically testable – that is, the falsifying basic statements of *p*, if *p* is a theory (90). (Quine considers it misleading to speak of the empirical content of a single statement; cf. section 3.62.)

The first of these definitions permits us to "regard the *comparison of the empirical content* of two statements as equivalent to the *comparison of their degrees of falsifiability*" (LSD, 121, i.a.). Thus the statement that has greater empirical content is better testable. But how can we compare empirical contents? As the class of the potential falsifiers of any theory is infinite, theories *cannot* be compared by the *number* of their potential falsifiers. Therefore, Popper considers comparing theories by their "*degree of composition*" (115 n*1) or by *subclass relations* between their contents (115ff.).

In order to compare the falsifiability of theories by their *degree of composition*, Popper needs a standard. He proposes (a) to "compare *theories* as to their degree of testability by ascertaining the minimum degree of composition which a basic statement must have if it is to be able to contradict the theory" (LSD, 127, i.a.), and (b) to "compare the degrees of composition of *basic statements* [i.a.] ... by selecting arbitrarily a class of *relatively* atomic statements, which we take as a basis for comparison" (128). But if the basis of the comparison is chosen *arbitrarily*, its result will also be more or less arbitrary. Hence this proposal is not promising either.

If, on the other hand, one statement logically follows from another, then their *empirical* contents can be indirectly compared by this relation of *entailment* or by the corresponding *subclass* relation between their *logical* contents (LSD, 119ff.). In order to make this more plausible, we first examine *how the logical and the empirical content of a statement* p *can be compared.*

If we negate a statement following from *p*, we get a statement contradicting *p*, and if we negate a statement contradicting *p*, we get a statement following from *p*. However, if the set of consequences of *p* is *finite*, this does *not* imply that the logical and the empirical content of *p* always are *equipollent* (as there exists a *one-to-one correspondence* between them). For the *logical* content of *p* can, as opposed to its empirical content, include *metaphysical* statements, whose negations need not be empirical. (Both the statement "The absolute is sleepy" and its negation "The absolute is not sleepy" are metaphysical.) Thus the empirical content of *p* cannot be mapped onto but only *into* the logical content of *p*, though this mapping is an injection. The same holds if the set of consequences of *p* is *infinite*, even though the logical and the empirical content of *p* are now *equipollent*. For in this case, not every *negation* of an *empirical* statement belonging to the logical content of p belongs to the empirical content of p. For if p implies strictly universal statements, their negations are strictly existential statements that, however, are not falsifiable and therefore cannot belong to the empirical content of p.

What does this imply with respect to *the comparison of the empirical contents of two statements* p *and* q? If q follows from p, but not conversely, then the logical content of q is a *proper* subset of the logical content of p (LSD, 120). Also, the empirical content of q is a subset of the empirical content of p, for any statement refuting q must refute p as well. But possibly the empirical content of q is only an *improper* subset of the empirical content of p – that is, is identical to the empirical content of p. This is easily seen, if we assume that p is equivalent to the conjunction of q and m, where m is a *metaphysical* statement. Hence, if q has less logical content than p, then q will never have greater empirical content than p. At best, both may have the same empirical content. If, on the other hand, the empirical contents of a number of statements are equal, then even a *simple ordering of their logical contents* implies only a *quasi-ordering of their empirical contents.*

In order to illustrate comparisons of testability, Popper formulates "conceivable natural laws" (LSD, 122). The deducibility relations among them depend on their *universality* and on their *precision*:

p: All *orbits of heavenly bodies* are *circles*.
q: All *orbits of planets* are *circles*.
r: All *orbits of heavenly bodies* are *ellipses*.
s: All *orbits of planets* are *ellipses*.

The arrows in his diagram show the deducibility relations: "From p all the others follow; from q follows s, which also follows from r; so that s follows from all the others" (122). And moving

from p to q the *degree of universality* decreases . . . because the orbits of the planets form a proper subclass of the orbits of heavenly bodies. . . . Moving from p to r the *degree of precision* (of the predicate) decreases: circles are a proper subclass of ellipses; . . . moving from p to s the degree of both universality and precision decreases; from q to s precision decreases; and from r to s, universality. To a higher degree of universality *or* precision corresponds a greater (logical or) empirical content, and thus a higher degree of testability. (122)

The *orderings of theories according to their empirical contents*, and hence according to their *testability*, are indirect consequences of their orderings according to their *logical contents* or according to the *deducibility relations* among them. However, we can seldom compare the testability of theories in this way, because deducibility relations are rare even among theories having the same subject matter.

In order to "*arrange the degrees of falsifiability* of various statements *on a scale*," Popper falls back on the idea of probability (LSD, 118, i.a.). For "[w]henever we can compare the degrees of falsifiability of two statements, we can say that the one which is the less falsifiable is also the more probable, by virtue of its logical form" (118f.). This

logical probability of a statement is complementary to its degree of falsifiability: it increases with decreasing degree of falsifiability. The logical probability 1 corresponds to the degree 0 of falsifiability, and *vice versa*. The better testable statement, *i.e.* the one with the higher degree of falsifiability, is the one which is logically less probable; and the statement which is less well testable is the one which is logically more probable. (119)

As science aims at better testability, it cannot prefer those hypotheses that are logically more probable.

However, only the tautology and the contradiction have definite numerical values, 1 and 0 respectively. Later, in Appendix *VII (1959), Popper tries to prove "that *in an infinite universe... the probability of any (non-tautological) universal law will be zero*" (LSD, 363). Accordingly, at best *probabilistic* hypotheses can be compared by their logical probabilities, whereas "the difference between a self-contradictory statement $a \wedge \neg a$ and a *universal* theory a remains unexpressed since $p(a \wedge \neg a) = p(a) = 0$" (374f., i.a.). On the other hand, only *some* subsets of the set of all synthetic statements can be *ordered* according to derivability, and usually the ordering is, as Popper's diagram shows, not even strongly connected. Here q and r are not comparable, as neither is derivable from the other. The diagram also illustrates how the derivability relations between the statements of a language form *lattices*. (A complete diagram [LSD, 117] would show how these lattices "are totally connected in the self-contradiction and in the tautology," as "a self-contradiction entails every statement and... a tautology is entailed by every statement" [121].) Hence the "*proper fractions*" (118) that Popper assigns to the empirical statements forming a sequence ordered according to derivability can only be considered *ordinals*, and they permit *comparisons only between statements belonging to a single sequence of one of those lattices*. On the other hand, the elements of different sequences are incommensurable, even if they have been assigned the same fraction. Hence real "*degrees of testability*" *are out of the question.*

5.4. THE DEGREE OF CORROBORATION

While the "*degree*" *of testability* of a theory is only one of its *logical properties*, its "*degree*" *of corroboration* mirrors (also) its *empirical success*. Popper gives his first *formal definition* in "A Second Note on Degree of Confirmation," which appeared in 1957 in *The British Journal for the Philosophy of Science* and which is now contained in Appendix *IX of his *Logic*. After 1958, he prefers the term "corroboration" to "confirmation." It would not make sense to report on every step that the development of his definition has taken since. Therefore, we rely primarily on its latest version in Chapter 4, "Corroboration," of his book *Realism and the Aim of Science*, which appeared in 1983 as the first volume of his *Postscript to the Logic of Scientific Discovery*. Popper here defines "degree of corroboration, *in terms of content* – the content of the theory and that of the test statements" (RAS, 232).

But this definition is primarily meant to be a criticism of the thesis that "*inductive logic is nothing but probability logic*" (RAS, 218). And he even doubts "whether a numerical evaluation of [the degree of corroboration] will ever be of practical significance" (221). Therefore, we take interest in only two aspects of his exposition: (a) his attempt at "clearing up the great muddle created by mistaken views on inductive probabilities" (221) and (b) the *conditions of adequacy* that he wants his definition to meet.

How then does he present the arguments of a *probability logic?* Suppose that *h* is a *h*ypothesis, or an "inductive conclusion," and that *e* is the "inductive *e*vidence" (the observations or the observation statements on which the induction is based). Then the problem of induction apparently is to determine the value of *r* in the equation

$$p(h, e) = r,$$

that is, the probability of the 'induced' hypothesis *h* relative to the evidence *e*. Here *r* is a real number in the closed interval from 0 to 1. Inductivists hope to solve the problem of induction by means of a logic of probability (RAS, 218). Of course, we cannot construct the 'induced' hypothesis *h* by means of an equation in which *h* occurs. At best, we can *assess* how well it matches the evidence *e*.

But what kind of judgments on *h* can we expect? According to Carnap's *theory of confirmation* (cf. Carnap 1950), *r* is greater the more *h* is supported by *e*; in other words, the greater relative probability $p(h_i, e)$ is assigned to that hypothesis h_i that is better confirmed by the available evidence *e*; and the – in this sense – (*relatively*) *more probable hypothesis is preferred*. Popper strictly opposes this view, because of two hypotheses, one of which entails the other, the latter has *less content* and thus is *more probable*, but science looks for hypotheses having the greatest possible content.

In order to show that probabilistic theories of preference (or of induction) are absurd, Popper introduces "the idea of *corroboration*, or '*degree of corroboration*'", and tries to prove that *a degree of corroboration cannot be a probability* (OK, 18). For example – in the material mode of speech – "the probability of a complex event consisting of the occurrence of several single events will in general be less than, and at most equal to, the probability of any of the component events" (RAS, 224, italics omitted); or – more generally, and in the formal mode of speech – the "probability of a statement describing an event *decreases with increasing logical content of the statement*" (224). He calls this the "'*rule of content*'" and points out that there is no corresponding rule for the "*degree of corroboration*" (224, i.a.; cf. section 5.4). Thus, unlike a probability, *the degree of corroboration may increase with increasing logical content.*

Originally, Popper assumed that "we cannot define a numerically calculable degree of corroboration, but can speak only roughly in terms of *positive* [or *negative*] degrees of corroboration" (LSD, 268, i.a.). But in a footnote added later, he declares "that it is possible to define 'degree of corroboration' in such a way that we can *compare* degrees of corroboration (for example, those of Newton's [1642–1727] and of Einstein's [1879–1955] theory of gravity)." He even considers it possible "to attribute *numerical* [i.a.] degrees of corroboration to statistical hypotheses, and perhaps even to other statements *provided* we can attribute degrees of (absolute or relative) logical probability to them" (268 n*2). But this condition is never met, for we lack both a suitable calculus of probability and convincing standards for assigning the required (absolute) "prior" probabilities to observation statements and theories. (Some authors say "*a priori* probabilities" instead of "absolute probabilities"; cf. Fisz 1973, 576.) Quite independently, Popper doubts whether a numerical evaluation of the degree of corroboration would ever be of practical significance (RAS, 221). Rather, he thinks that *corroboration* is, like *preference*, "essentially *comparative*" (OK, 18, i.a.). This holds as well for his definition of "degree" of corroboration (RAS, 220, 223ff.).

5.41. The Formal Definition

The probability logicians, whom Popper attacks, also contend with the problem that we lack both a suitable calculus of probability and convincing standards for assigning "prior" probabilities. But Popper wants to show that their situation is, quite independent of this, hopeless. To begin with, he formulates conditions that an adequate definition of the degree of corroboration has to meet. Then he expresses by means of relative probabilities the fact that the conditions are met. Thus he arrives at a definition according to which the numerical value of the degree of corroboration is derived from probabilities, but in such a way that *the degree of corroboration cannot itself be a probability*. Let us now look more closely at his argument.

We turn first to the *conditions of adequacy*. It would be *uncritical* to consider an observation (or an observation statement) *e* as supporting or confirming a hypothesis *h* "whenever *e* 'agrees' with *h*, or is an instance of *h*" (RAS, 233). For one who looks for *confirmation* eventually considers everything a confirmative instance, except the counterinstances. This leads to the paradox of confirmation (234; cf. section 3.5). On the other hand, one who is *critical* looks for counterinstances, for refutations (234), because only the results of *severe tests* can support *h* (235). But as the *sincerity* of a test cannot be logically analyzed, Popper believes that the *support* of *h* by *e* is not capable of complete logical analysis either (236).

By also including the *background knowledge*, Popper extends the question: When can we say that the observation statement *e* supports hypothesis *h* in the light of the background knowledge *b*? The background knowledge *b* contains all assumptions relevant to the test that we – perhaps only tentatively – accept when testing *h*. Thus *b* includes the initial conditions and possibly further hypotheses that are needed to derive *e* from *h*. Of course, *b* must be consistent with *h* (RAS, 236).

Considerations that we cannot describe here in detail suggest to Popper that "the following *definition of 'e supports h'* would be reasonably *adequate*:

> *e* supports *h* in the presence of the background knowledge *b* if, and only if,
>
> (a) *e* follows from *hb* [i.e., *h* and *b*]"
> (b) *e* is improbable on the background knowledge *b* alone

(RAS, 238f., i.a.). For only an experience *e* that has been predicted with the help of hypothesis *h* but is absolutely unexpected in view of the background knowledge *b* supports *h*. Hence the smaller $p(e, b)$ is, the more *h* is supported by *e* (238). But conditions (a) and (b) alone cannot secure the *severity* of the tests. Rather, *e* must also result from *genuine* attempts to refute *h* (252f.). The less *e* is to be expected, however, the riskier is the test of *h* by *e*. Therefore, we can, according to Popper, measure the *severity* of the test by the "(absolute) *improbability*" of *e* (247, i.a.). But we can never know the absolute improbability of a statement; at best, we can know its probability relative to our background knowledge.

Expressed in terms of probability theory, the first condition of adequacy reads:

$$\text{(a)} \; p(e, hb) = 1,$$

for if *e* follows from *h* and *b*, then the logical probability of *e*, relative to *h* and *b*, must equal one (RAS, 239). And the second condition of adequacy reads:

$$\text{(b)} \; p(e, b) \ll 1/2$$

where "$x \ll y$" means "*x* is considerably smaller than *y*" (238). Hence *h* is *significantly* supported by *e* only when

$$\text{(e)} \; p(e, hb) - (p(e, b) \gg 1/2.$$

Popper takes the difference $p(e, hb) - p(e, b)$ as "a measure of the *degree of support* given by *e* to *h*, in the presence of *b*, or of the *degree of corroboration* [*C(h,e,b)*] *of h by e in the presence of b*" (240, i.a.). By dividing the difference by a "normalizing factor," Popper arrives at the *definition of the degree of corroboration*:

$$\text{(D)} \; C(h, e, b) = p(e, hb) - p(e, b)/p(e, hb) - p(eh, b) + p(e, b).$$

While the numerator of the fraction has an intuitive significance, its denominator lacks such significance (240). Rather, the denominator is chosen because it entails certain desired properties of the degree of corroboration: $C(h,e,b)$ is *positive* when *e* supports *h*, *negative* when *e* undermines *h*, and equals *zero* when *e* is independent of *h* in the presence of *b* (241). In addition, one is the *maximum* value that $C(h,e,b)$ reaches if, and only if,

$$\text{(aa)} \; p(e, hb) = 1$$
$$\text{(bb)} \; p(e, b) = 0,$$

that is, when *e* follows from *h* and *b* but the evidence *e* is extremely improbable relative to the background knowledge *b*; and −1 is the *minimum* value that $C(h,e,b)$ takes on when e falsifies *h* in the presence of *b* (241f.).

5.42. Purpose and Appropriateness of the Definition

We need not deal with Popper's "further comments on the definition of degree of corroboration" (RAS, 244–255), as definition (D) has a decisive defect. It is *not applicable*, for the simple reason that we lack convincing standards for establishing the required "prior" probabilities. Hence the intended *quantitative* account of corroboration is *impossible*. Also, *comparative* accounts of corroboration that do not conform to the formal definition (D) but approximately satisfy Popper's conditions of adequacy are *seldom possible*. Only occasionally can we "say of two competing theories, *A* and *B*, that in the light of the state of the critical discussion at the time *t*, and the empirical evidence (test statements) available at the discussion, the theory *A* is preferable to, or better corroborated than, the theory *B*" (OK, 18f.).

Definition (D) also *does not meet all of the requirements* that Popper has considered essential. Already in his *Logic*, he makes *the degree of corroboration of a theory A also contingent on the success of a rival theory B*: The degree of corroboration of A is lowered not only when A is *undermined*, but also when A is "*superseded* by a better testable theory [B] from which it – or a sufficiently close approximation to it – can be deduced" (LSD, 268, i.a.). – At least more theories will be comparable as to their corroboration where instead of derivability only "sufficiently close approximation to it" is required.

But Popper thinks that he has achieved the main purpose of his formal definition of the degree of corroboration, which was "to show that, in many cases, the more *improbable* (improbable in the sense of the calculus of probability) hypothesis is preferable, and to show clearly in which cases this holds and in which it does not hold. In this way, [he believes he has shown] that *preferability cannot be a probability in the sense of the calculus of probability*" (OK, 18).

It is, however, doubtful that he did achieve this purpose. It is true that a degree of corroboration that meets Popper's conditions of adequacy is not itself a probability, though it is derived from probabilities. But in view of Popper's own restrictions, his choice of these conditions does not appear to be cogent. On the other hand, any new attempt at defining confirmation or corroboration as a probability would encounter the same difficulties.

As for the rest, Popper does not believe that his "definition of degree of corroboration is a contribution to *science* except, perhaps, that it may be useful as an appraisal of statistical tests" (RAS, 254, i.a.). He does not believe either that "it makes a positive contribution to *methodology* or to *philosophy* – except in the sense that it may help . . . to clear up the great confusions which have sprung from the *prejudice of induction*, and from the prejudice that we aim in science at *high probabilities* – in the sense of the probability calculus – rather than at *high content*, and at *severe tests*" (255, i.a.).

5.43. On the Revisability of Corroborative Appraisals

Already in his *Logic* – that is, long before he proposed the formal definition – Popper drew a surprising conclusion from his "positive theory of corroboration": "Yet we can lay down various *rules*; for instance the rule

[R$_{12}$] that we shall not continue to accord a positive degree of corroboration to a theory which has been falsified by an inter-subjectively testable experiment. . . . (We may, however, under certain circumstances accord a positive degree of corroboration to *another* theory, even though it follows a *kindred* line of thought. . . .) In general we regard an inter-subjectively testable *falsification* as *final* (provided it is well tested)." (LSD, 268, i.a.)

The first sentence (that . . . experiment) says something obvious; the sentence in parentheses suggests the ideas of "theory dynamics" and "problem shift" that Imre Lakatos (1922–1974) later elaborated. But the last sentence (In . . . final) seems to violate a central postulate of the *Logic*, for, as falsifying basic statements cannot be strictly verified, refutations must never be considered final.

Popper here refers to the replacement of Newton's corpuscular theory of light by Einstein's photon theory (LSD, 268). Does he want to say only that at present we do not have any reason to rehabilitate Newton's theory? We admonish the reader to consider the changeable fate of the heliocentric conception of the world and therefore not to take Popper's "last sentence" at face value. But he adds by way of explanation: This

is the way in which the *asymmetry between verification and falsification* of theories makes itself felt. Each of these methodological points contributes in its own peculiar way to *the historical development of science as a process of step by step approximations*. A corroborative appraisal made at a later date – that is, an appraisal made after new basic statements have been added to those already accepted – can replace a positive degree of corroboration by a negative one, but not *vice versa*. (268, i.a.)

This contradicts the fundamental idea of fallibilism, according to which every appraisal, including a negative one, is fallible.

But the passage quoted also contradicts his previous descriptions of the asymmetry between verification and falsification, for originally he had asserted that this asymmetry "results from the logical form of universal statements" (LSD, 41) and from the decision to take the falsifiability of a system as a criterion of demarcation (40). He had also considered it "*impossible*, for various reasons, that any theoretical system should ever be *conclusively* falsified" (42, i.a.). Both strictly universal statements and strictly existential statements are unilaterally decidable. They are "constructed *symmetrically*. It is only the line drawn by our criterion of demarcation which produces the *asymmetry*" (70, i.a.). In a footnote added later, he explains: "If it is the characteristic of empirical science to look upon *singular* statements as test-statements, then the asymmetry arises from the fact that, *with respect to singular statements*, universal statements are falsifiable only and existential statements verifiable only" (70 n*2; i.e., with respect to singular statements strictly universal statements are falsifiable, but not verifiable, and strictly existential statements are verifiable but not falsifiable). In section 81, he still asserts that "*the asymmetry between verification and falsification . . .* results from the logical relation between theories and basic statements" (265). But this asymmetry implies nothing as to the definiteness of falsifications. Only a rule demanding that we consider falsifications definite (possibly because an accepted basic statement contradicts the theory) but corroborations revisable (as no accepted basic statement can imply the theory) creates the *asymmetry between positive and negative corroborative appraisals.*

5.5. FOUR PROBLEMS OF INDUCTION

In the first chapter, "*Induction*," of his book *Realism and the Aim of Science*, Popper establishes a close connection between the problems of *induction* and *corroboration*. In doing so, he formulates "*A Family of Four Problems of Induction*" (RAS, 52ff.). He also speaks of *four* "*phases of the discussion of Hume's problem of induction*" or simply four "*phases of the problem of induction*." The first is an urgent *practical problem of method* (62):

(1) How can we distinguish between good and bad theories?

This problem is closely related to the *problem of demarcation*, that is, to the question "How can we distinguish between empirical and other theories?" The second is the "*'problem of rational belief'*" (53, 56ff.):

(2) Is it rational to believe in the truth of any particular theory?

The third is "'*Hume's problem of tomorrow*'" (53, 62ff.):

(3) How do you know that the future will be like the past?

or "'How do you know that the laws of nature will continue to hold tomorrow?'" (63). The fourth is the *problem of natural laws*:

(4) Do there exist regularities in nature?

This may be called the "*metaphysical phase of the problem of induction*" (53) and is at the same time an aspect of the realism-idealism controversy. Perhaps the reader will not subsume the first two problems under the heading "induction" but will recognize the classical problem of induction only in the third question.

5.51. On the Distinction Between Good and Bad Theories

Popper seems to side with Russell's thesis that our belief in science is *no longer reasonable*, if "Hume is right that *we cannot draw any valid inference from observation to theory*" (RAS, 54). In any case, Popper believes that he has solved Hume's *logical* problem of induction by pointing out that theories are *hypotheses* that cannot be verified but can be falsified and that, on the basis of the results of their tests, one hypothesis may be *preferred* to another (54f.). Basically, the whole chapter "Induction" is intended to convince the reader that Popper has in this way successfully solved the problem of induction.

According to Popper, an essential part of his solution "lies precisely in recognizing the *fundamental character of the first phase of the problem* [the distinction between good and bad theories, i.e., their *corroboration* or *refutation*] and the inferior character of its third phase [the "problem of tomorrow"]" (RAS, 63). When severe empirical tests decide against one of two competing theories, they show "that the other is '*better*'" (56, i.a.). And after many trials and errors, we may perhaps be able to say that "according to the present state of our critical discussion, including observational tests" *one* of the theories "appears to come *nearer to the truth than all the others* considered" (56, i.a.).

The real solution of the logical problem of induction consists, according to Popper, in replacing the question "How do you know that your hypothesis is true?" with the question "Why do you prefer this hypothesis to all others?" (RAS, 71). Hence *the problem of induction is replaced by the problem of comparing hypotheses with respect to their corroboration*. But this means that Popper did not *solve* the problem; rather, he *shifted* it.

On the other hand, Popper rightly indicates that "our belief in science" may be *reasonable* even if we cannot "draw *verifying* inferences" but only "*falsifying* inferences" from "observations [rather: observation statements] to theories" (RAS, 54). Of course, *Probability hypotheses* are not logically but only "practically" falsifiable (cf. section 8.3), and above all there are no valid inferences from observations to the truth or falsity of *observation statements* (cf. Chapter 4). Therefore, we cannot make the rationality of our attitude toward science contingent – only or even primarily – on the deductive-logical relation between basic statements and strictly universal hypotheses. Rather, the *merits* of rival hypotheses must be critically discussed (55f.; cf. Chapter 7).

5.52. On the Problem of Rational Belief

Popper considers the "problem of rational belief" less fundamental than that of "how to distinguish between good and bad theories," although he sides with Russell's criticism of Hume's alleged irrationality (cf. section 1.122) and at times even seems to identify science with rationality (RAS, 57). When, however, he speaks of "'rational belief' . . . in scientific theory, [he does *not* mean to say] that it is *rational* to believe in the *truth* of any *particular* theory" (57, i.a.). As he considers this point of greatest importance, he comes back to it several times (cf. sections 5.53, 5.54). Does he thus criticize only the imperturbable belief in a particular theory? Rather, he wants to say that it is not rational to *take* any particular theory – for the present – *to be true*, even if it has been most severely tested. (As we shall see [section 5.62], this thesis is too strong to be tenable.) According to Popper, "the object of our 'rational belief'" is "not the truth, but . . . the *truthlikeness* (*or 'verisimilitude'*)" of a theory (57). However, Popper's concept of truthlikeness or verisimilitude is – as opposed to Tarski's concept of truth – at best problematic (cf. section 7.2).

　　Popper gives a first example of rational belief: "What we believe (rightly or wrongly) is not that Newton's theory or Einstein's theory is true, but that they are *good approximations* to the truth, though capable of being superseded by better ones" (RAS, 57). Anyone who considers *both theories refuted* – perhaps because both predict values for the precession of the planetary orbits that differ from the observed values – would agree with a statement like this. (According to the *Brockhaus Enzyklopädie* [19th ed., vol. 16, 1991, 672), Einstein's general theory of relativity predicts that the orbit of the earth precedes by 3.8 arc seconds in 100 years, while a precession of 5.0 arc seconds is observed.) Still, he will consider Einstein's theory the *better approximation* to the truth, as the values that it predicts differ far less from the observed ones than those predicted by Newton's theory. But according to most sources, the values predicted by Einstein's theory have until now – within the inevitable variances of measurements – always equalled the observed values. Let us therefore consider *Einstein's theory still unrefuted.* We may then ask why we should not consider this theory *true until it is rejected* instead of considering it *from the outset only the better approximation to truth.*

Another example may give us a hint, though not an exhaustive answer. Because the Copernican model of the solar system is only a model "and therefore bound to be an *over-simplification and approximation,*" we "do not believe in its *complete truth*" but only in its *truthlikeness* (RAS, 59, i.a.). But is it a model that is too simple, or is the model qua model an oversimplification?

In a certain sense, *this model* is both too simple and too complex: too simple, because it still constructs the orbits of the planets on the basis of the simplest closed form, the circle; too complex, because it needs several epicycles (for most planets, two; for Mercury, four) to obtain good approximations to the observed values (cf. Teichmann 1983, 63). As it is *too simple*, it *cannot be true.* Hence it would be *irrational* to take it to be true.

But is *every model* qua model, as Popper seems to assume, too simple to be true? This is trivially the case if the concept "model" is defined in such a way that every model contains idealizing assumptions and hence *is a hypothesis deliberately made too simple.* Then Popper's example does in fact show that models must never be called "true," but it does not show that *hypotheses that are intended to describe reality exactly,* and hence are not models in this sense, cannot be called "true" either.

It is true that *every theory* – even if it is not a model in the sense indicated – simplifies, insofar as it does not describe reality completely. But is it also true that every theory is necessarily too simple to make a true assertion about that aspect of reality that it is intended to describe? This assumption would be contradictory, for anyone who makes a *statement* asserts a state of affairs. In the case of universal or probabilistic hypotheses, the state of affairs is a regularity. The statement, or an equivalent statement, *defines* this *state of affairs.* Hence it cannot be false for the reason that it somehow *deviates* from this state of affairs – for instance, because the statement is *too simple* to describe the state of affairs exactly. Rather, if the state of affairs exists – if it is a fact, if that part of the world to which the statement refers is as the statement says it is – then the statement is true.

If, on the other hand, the world is not as the statement says it is, this does not necessarily result from the statement's being too simple; the world may just as well be simpler than the statement says it is. For example, the adherents of various religions and philosophies "knew" (and "know") that the world is inhabited by a multitude of spirits. To other people, the world appears in this respect much simpler. (We shall return to Popper's ontological preferences; cf. Chapter 15.)

Popper also does not assert that every theory of physics is false. *Cautioned by the historical experience that until now all important theories have failed sooner or later, he only considers it irrational to take any particular theory to be true.* (This does not hold to the same degree of daily generalizations, such as "All men need air to breathe.") But it cannot be irrational to consider a particular theory true just because every theory is too simple to be true.

On the other hand, our "real *reasons for believing in the truthlikeness* [i.a.] of the Copernican model" consist, according to Popper, "in *the story of the critical discussion,* including the critical evaluation of observations, of all the theories of the solar system since Anaximander" (ca. 611–545) (RAS, 59). Popper lists the theories of Heraclitus (ca. 544–483), Democritus (460–371), Plato (427–347), Aristotle (384/3–322/1), Aristarchus (ca. 310–230), and Ptolemy (ca. 100–160). We prefer the model of Copernicus (1473–1543) to all of them. This preference "is *reasonable* because it is based upon the result of the present state of the critical discussion" (59, i.a.). Generally speaking, "a *preference* for a theory may be called '*reasonable*' if it is arguable [i.a.], and if it withstands *searching critical argument*" (59). An argument is "critical" when it ingeniously tries to show that a theory "is not true, or not nearer to the truth than its competitors," and Popper adds: "[*T*]*his is the best sense of 'reasonable' known to me*" (59).

Not only is our belief in the *truthlikeness* of well-corroborated theories rational, it also *remains* rational after they have been superseded. It is, however, no longer rational when they have been refuted. This belief is also "capable of *degrees*" (RAS, 58), and the same also holds of its rationality. Popper here calls the "degree of the *rationality* of our belief that a certain theory has achieved (a certain degree of) truthlikeness" the "'degree of *corroboration*'" (58, i.a.). Like the "degree of *truthlikeness,*" the "degree of *corroboration*" is not quantitative but only *comparative.* If the "degree of *corroboration*" of theory t_1 is greater than that of t_2, then we generally "have *reason to believe* that [t_1] is a better *approximation to the truth* [i.a.] than" t_2 (58).

This "positive" contribution to the "problem of rational belief" also has a "negative" side: "Though we may reasonably believe that the Copernican model as revised by Newton is nearer to the truth than Ptolemy's, there is no means of saying *how* near it is" (RAS, 61). Even if a metric for verisimilitude could be *defined*, which seems to be possible only for cases of little interest, we could not *apply* it, because we do not know the truth (61). We can *justify* neither our theories, nor our belief that they are true, nor even the belief that they are nearer to the truth than their rivals. But we can "*rationally defend a preference*...for a certain theory" (61, i.a.).

Popper gives a simple explanation for this: "*The method of science is rational: it is the best we have*" (RAS, 61, i.a.). And as the theoretician, as such, need not act, he need not believe in a theory either. For him, the theory that appears to come closest to the truth "is not one to believe in, but one which is important for *further progress*," and it is also the one that is most worthy of further criticism (62, i.a.). But not even the fact that the *critical method* has been very successful in the past permits us to conclude that it will continue to be so *in future* (60).

5.53. On Hume's Problem of Tomorrow

Popper considers the problem "of tomorrow" (the third phase of the problem of induction) even less fundamental than that of "rational belief" (the second phase). Once we have understood the first (the distinction between good and bad theories) and second phases, the problem "of tomorrow" seems to be "no more than a typical philosophical muddle" (RAS, 62). For if we ask "'How do you know that the future will be like the past?'" or: "'How do you know that the laws of nature will continue to hold tomorrow?,'" the answer can only be "'I do *not* know,'" as we know only the past and the present (63).

If, however, the *degree of corroboration* is "*nothing but*" a summarized report on the past performance of a theory, then the *problem of induction* seems to arise again (RAS, 64). For "does not the degree of corroboration of a theory...determine our expectation concerning its future performances?" (64) In fact, if Popper, because of the *past* success of a theory, immediately attributed to it the "disposition to survive *future* tests," this would be an *inductive inference* and would thus "amount to a *breakdown*" of his theory (methodology) (64, i.a.). But he does not even believe that the better-corroborated theory is more likely to survive future tests than the less-corroborated one, and therefore he does "*not* expect that a more highly corroborated theory will as a rule outlive a less well corroborated theory" (or at least that's what he says; 65).

But his attempt to dispense with all assumptions about the *future*, so as not to arouse the suspicion of arguing *inductively*, entails logical problems. Many authors object that he cannot avoid inductive elements in his reasoning and therefore has to admit them. We will have to examine whether this is true (cf. section 5.6.). But first we will examine some further examples.

Popper is willing to bet "on *the sun's rising tomorrow* (betting is a practical action), but not on the laws of Newtonian (or Einsteinian) mechanics to survive further criticism, or to survive it longer than, say, the best available theory of synaptic transmission, even though the latter has . . . a lesser degree of corroboration" (RAS, 65, i.a.). His refusal to make the latter bet is meant to show that he does *not draw inductive conclusions from the survival of a theory in the past to its survival in the future.*

But can his bet "on the sun's rising tomorrow" be *rational* if he does not assume that the (apparent) movement of the sun is *regular*? Doesn't he have to base his "practical action" of betting on the best theory available? This he admits. Even when he has "theoretical doubts," he bases his actions on the best-corroborated theory (RAS, 65). Doesn't this involve, at least *implicitly*, an *inductive* inference from that theory's past corroboration to its future reliability? In order to counter this objection, he first distinguishes between the "historical" question of the *survival* of a theory and its *use* for making predictions, and he then assesses, not the chances of a theory's surviving future tests, but only its usefulness for present application. He does not even consider these two questions to be intimately related, because we often apply *falsified* theories if they are "sufficiently good approximations for the purpose in hand" (65). But how does he know that a theory that in *past applications* was a sufficiently good approximation will be so in its *next application* as well? After all, this time it could be more radically refuted than it has been in the past.

Popper now examines Russell's inductivism and completes his deliberation with a thesis that is as momentous as it is problematic: "There simply is *no* reason to believe in the *truth* (or the probability) of any particular set of conjectures which we call a physical theory; though there may be reasons for preferring one theory to others as a better *approximation to the truth* (which is not a probability)" (RAS, 67). We will now examine this thesis more closely.

5.54. On the Problem of Regularities

Are there any *regularities in nature*? Popper is not prepared to say of any *particular* law of physics (expressing a regularity) "'*This law is true*, in its present formulation and interpretation:'". We already expect this assertion, but he continues: "'*I feel certain* that it will never be falsified, or modified, or recognized as merely conditionally valid, or as valid merely within certain limits'" (RAS, 72, i.a.). In view of the colon, we may consider the latter statement an interpretation of the former, and this interpretation appears to be the clue to his unfortunate refusal to take any particular universal hypothesis to be true.

In his favour, we assume that he does not confuse *truth* and *subjective certainty*, that is, that he does not interpret what at first seems to be a statement about the world ("This law is true" or "This regularity obtains") as a statement about his estimation ("I feel certain that this law is true"). But how much can our assumption strengthen his position? He would obviously be right if from the *assumption* that a law is true he inferred that it will not in the future be refuted or be considered valid merely within certain limits. But why does he have to *feel certain* that the law is true? Why shouldn't it be sufficient merely to *assume* its truth *with all due caution*? This would protect him against the reproach of a hidden inductivism.

On the other hand, he believes "that at least *some* of the laws of our present system of physics are true[;] ... [he] should even say many of them are, if we include those on lower levels of universality" (RAS, 72). This is a statement about the world. It implies the existence of at least *some regularities*. In order to refute this statement, it would be necessary to refute *all* of the laws of *present* physics. But how could we refute the old laws without having *new* laws? After all, in order to test physical theories we need measuring devices. They cannot be relied on, however, if the theories according to which they are made are all false. Thus we can at *no* time strictly refute the thesis that *some* of the theories accepted at *that* time are true. Hence this thesis is at least *quasi-metaphysical*. On the other hand, it is not verifiable either, because none of the theories are verifiable.

Popper rightly criticizes "many philosophers" who believe that the *law of "universal causation"* or of the *"uniformity of nature"* "may be used as a *principle of induction* whose validity would make inductive inferences valid" (RAS, 75, i.a.). According to most authors, this law says: "Every event has a cause." Popper's formulation is: "'For every event in this world, there exist true universal laws and true initial conditions from which a statement describing the event in question can be deduced'" (74). But if this were a principle of induction, it would long since have been refuted; to be more precise, it would have been "refuted by the first refutation of a theory which was induced with the inductive principle in question" (75).

But "even if we knew that there were *no* invariable regularities – even if there were counterexamples to *all* apparent laws – there would still be much sense in *trying* to rationalize such an ultimately irrational world as far as possible by the critical method of trial and error" (RAS, 76). However, if this attempt is to make sense, Popper must assume that there are enough regularities holding for a certain time and that they do not change to such a degree that we could not survive the change.

Hence the metaphysical *problem of the existence of natural laws* – according to Popper, the metaphysical phase of the problem of induction – "is largely academic" (RAS, 76). In order to solve it, Popper reformulates it. It thereby becomes apparent that "it is an aspect of the *problem of tomorrow*" (76). Thus if there are natural laws, he can argue: "[I]f *a* is such a law, *a* will continue to apply, or operate, in the future – say *tomorrow*" (77). On the other hand we may ask: "Why should not science and its method fail tomorrow completely because *all* regularities, whether previously thought of or not, fail? And why should it be reasonable to believe that this will not happen?" (77; cf. section 5.53).

However, speaking of "tomorrow" or "the future" takes "one regularity naively for granted: *the order of time*" (RAS, 77). Isaac Newton distinguished "absolute time" from "relative, apparent, and common time" as measured by clocks with all their irregularities. According to him, "'Absolute, true, and mathematical time flows equally of itself, and from its own nature, without relation to anything external'" (77). Metaphysically stated: "There is time (and presumably space), and everything in nature happens *in* time"; "*the future, or tomorrow, will come, independently of a change in the laws of nature*" (78).

Leibniz (1646–1716) criticized this concept of absolute time because it is compatible neither with the "principle of sufficient reason" nor with the "principle of the identity of indiscernibles." Instead, he proposed a *relational theory of space and time*. According to this theory, events are not *in* a time but exist *together with* their temporal relations, and "*time*" is only the "name for the abstract system of these temporal relations" (78). The difference between the absolute and relational theories of time has been expressed as follows: "According to Newton the universe *has* a clock, according to Leibniz it *is* a clock." The relational theory of time was widely accepted in science even before Einstein.

5.6. PRAGMATIC INDUCTION OR REALIST TAKING TO BE TRUE

Obviously Popper's exposition – in particular, "on Hume's problem of tomorrow" (section 5.53) and "on the problem of regularities" (section 5.54) – is incongruous. On the one hand, he has no doubt that meta-physical positions such as *realism* (RAS, 83) and *indeterminism* (OU, 41) may be considered *true*. He also believes that at least *some* of the *laws* of contemporary physics are true (RAS, 72). This assumption too is at least quasi-metaphysical. On the other hand, he thinks there is no reason to believe in the truth of any *particular* physical theory (67). But the assumption that a particular theory is true would be empirical, because it would fail if the theory should fail. Does he think that we may consider certain (quasi-)*metaphysical* assumptions true, because they cannot be refuted, whereas we must not consider certain *empirical* hypotheses true, because they can be refuted? This would be a sin against the spirit of fallibilism.

On the other hand, considering a physical theory T_1 a *better approximation to the truth* than another theory T_2 does not give him any difficulty (RAS, 67). An assumption of this kind is also *empirical*, at least if both theories are still unrefuted, T_1 has the greater logical content, and the tests that T_2 has passed form a proper subset of the tests that T_1 has passed. His reason for believing in the greater truthlikeness of T_1 is the *history of the critical discussion* of T_1 and T_2, including the critical evaluation of the relevant observations (59). He thinks that he can therefore *rationally defend his preference for* T_1 (61) but that he must not, on account of the past success of T_1, expect that T_1 will also be corroborated in the *future*, because this would be an *inductive* inference (64). Still, he believes that T_1 can be used for prediction and can be applied technologically, because for those purposes T_1 need not be true (65).

5.61. On the Requirement of a Pragmatic Principle of Induction

We have already indicated that such arguments are not convincing. Their defects have occasioned several authors to reproach Popper for a *hidden inductivism*. Gerhard Schurz argues: Whoever selects from the theories available (for explanation, prediction, or technological application) that theory which has up to now been most successful, obviously assumes the following *pragmatic principle of induction*:

If a theory T_1 has *up to now* been more successful than T_2, then it is – though not logically cogent – probable that T_1 will also *in future* be more successful than T_2. (Schurz 1998, 37, m.t.)

Hence he infers the theory's better corroboration in the future from its better corroboration in the past. This pragmatic principle of induction resembles Russell's *logical principle of induction*:

[I]f *A* has been found very often accompanied or followed by *B*, and no instance is known of *A* not being accompanied or followed by *B*, then it is probable that on the next occasion on which *A* is observed it will be accompanied or followed by *B*. (Russell 1945, 673)

Accordingly, we make inferences from the past association of *A* and *B* to their future association. It is true that we will – for the reasons given in section 1.111. – dispense with a logical principle of induction, but *without the pragmatic principle of induction, the past success of a theory would –* according to Schurz – *be irrelevant to our future actions* (1998, 37).

Though, according to Schurz, it is evident that the pragmatic principle of induction is contained in Popper's idea of corroboration (or learning from trial and error), he refuses to acknowledge it. Rather, his *Logic* contains the thesis:

The procedure of comparatively assessing theories on the basis of their past success involves *no principle of induction at all*. . . . Nevertheless this procedure is the *best* we have. (Schurz 1998, 37, m.t.; cf. RAS, 61)

According to Schurz, "the reason for which this procedure is the best" must "of course be the assumption of the pragmatic principle of induction," because without this assumption there would not be the slightest reason to prefer this procedure to forming a random judgment (37, m.t.).

Do we therefore really need a *pragmatic* principle of induction in order to make "inferences" from the (greater) past success of theories to their future success? Is it only such "inferences" that make the past success of theories pertinent to our actions? An analogy will take us further. Do we need a (logical or) pragmatic principle of induction in order to "infer" that *A* will in the future be followed by *B* from the fact that *A* has in the past been followed by *B*? Instead of this direct "inference," Aristotle chooses a two-part argument (cf. section 1.1). First, the *previous* association of *A* and *B* permits or causes him to "conclude" (*epagoge*, induction) that *A* and *B* are *always* associated. From this, he then deductively infers that *A* and *B* will be associated *in the future*.

Suppose that we *consider* the universal hypothesis *H*, "If *A*, then always *B*," to be *true* – not because of an induction but because of its corroboration up to now. Then our assumption that *H* is true logically implies the further assumption that *A* and *B* will be *associated in the future*. Do we nevertheless need a *pragmatic* principle of induction to support the assumption that *H* will be *corroborated in the future*? This is not the case if we thereby mean only that *H will not be refuted*. For if *H* should be refuted, then *H* is not true; we only took *H* to be true by mistake. In this respect, *the assumption that H will be corroborated in the future does not add anything to the assumption that H is true*. But if we thereby mean also that *H will not be surpassed by a better hypothesis*, then we would also be asserting the absence of any theoretical progress. But no principle of induction – not even a pragmatic one – would support an assertion like this.

Have we really shown that we do not need a pragmatic principle of induction in order to make "inferences" from the (greater) past success of theories to their future success? This would presuppose, on the one hand, that we may consider hypotheses true at all, if only tentatively, and on the other hand, that we may do so merely on the basis of their past success without having to apply a pragmatic principle of induction.

5.62. Truth and Realist Interpretation of Statements

But may we consider universal hypotheses true at all? As already mentioned, Popper will, because of the hypothetical character of all laws, take no *particular* law to be true. On the other hand, he asserts: "[I]f *a* is a *law of nature*, then '*a* is true' follows from *a*" (RAS, 73, i.a.). Conversely, *a* follows from "*a* is true." Both implications hold correspondingly of all other statements, for they follow from Tarski's (1901–1983) definition of truth, which in turn is based on the customary use of the word "true" (cf. section 6.2). As *a* and "*a* is true" are logically equivalent, it is logically impossible for Popper to *assume that what a asserts is the case while avoiding the assumption that a is true*.

But why should he assume that a natural law *a* asserts something and that what it asserts is the case? Instead, he could interpret *a* "as an instrument, *and nothing but an instrument*, for the deduction of predictions of future events (especially measurements) and for other practical applications" (RAS, 111). In this case, *a* would be *useful or useless* but *neither true nor false* (112). If he were an instrumentalist, therefore, he certainly would not have to consider any particular law to be true.

Already in his *Logic*, however, he criticizes instrumentalism, and in *Realism and the Aim of Science* he continues to put forward arguments that, in his opinion, "amply justify the rejection of instrumentalism" (RAS, 117). Therefore, he is consistent in considering even "higher-level theor[ies] such as Newton's... *genuine conjectures about the structure of the world* that can be tested" (118, i.a.). But Newton's theory has already been falsified. Thus he may consider it *false*. Nevertheless, he can continue applying it as an instrument, even without interpreting it instrumentalistically. For in order to be a useful instrument, it must only come close to the truth.

But this way out isn't always available. For *he can never assert the existence of a particular regularity if he is not prepared to consider the corresponding theory true, at least at the time when he asserts it.* Are there still other reasons in favour of the realist interpretation of theories? If interpreted in the instrumentalist way, theories are useless as premises of deductive nomological explanations (cf. section 2.2). Besides, Popper expects that, at least "in a time of crisis," the realist will more easily abandon a theory that collides with experience than the instrumentalist or conventionalist, because the realist considers it refuted, while the instrumentalist only takes it to be no longer suited to particular applications (LSD, 80). Hence *Popper unnecessarily weakens realism, which is so important to him, when he refuses to consider any particular theory to be true.*

What about statements below the level of natural laws? Obviously, "to believe in a *statement* and to believe in the *truth* of [this] statement is the same" holds universally (RAS, 79, i.a.). Now, a fallibilist may consider it careless to *believe* in a particular statement. But can he always avoid *taking* at least *some particular singular statements to be true*? This would be possible only if he made no more statements, for *if he* – without any mental reservation – *states "It is so and so,"* then he cannot – without contradicting himself logically – *assume at the same time that this statement is not true.* He is just as unable to *leave it undecided whether it is true,* as the statements "It is so and so" and "'It is so and so' is true" are logically equivalent, and hence the statements "It remains undecided whether ›'it is so and so' is true‹" and "It remains undecided whether ›it is so and so‹" are also equivalent.

Of course, we may want to assert "It remains undecided whether it is so and so," but then we do not assert "It is so and so." On the other hand, someone who asserts "It is so and so" does not claim to know *for certain* that it is so and so, or that the statement "It is so and so" is true. In other words: Someone who says "It is so and so" does not say "*It is certain* that it is so and so" or "It is certain that (the statement) 'it is so and so' is true." He does not even say "*I feel certain* that it is so and so," for the epistemic terms "it is certain that" and "I feel certain that" are, as opposed to the semantic term "is true," genuine predicates. Hence "It is so and so" and "It is certain (or I feel certain) that it is so and so" are not equivalent.

If Popper intends to make any statements about the world at all, he must *take at least some particular singular statements to be true*, and obviously he is prepared to do so. But what reasons *not to consider any particular universal statement true* then remain? Suppose an impression that we just had motivates us to state "This sheet of paper is white." By so stating, we do not simply render the impression that we just had (say: "a moment ago, here, white"). Rather, our statement *transcends* what we experienced, as it postulates the existence of a physical *body* (this sheet of paper) and assigns to it a *property* (of being white, even if nobody is looking and even if there is no light falling on it so that nobody can see it) that remains well beyond the moment of perceiving and the moment of stating.

Accordingly, even the simplest subject-predicate statement implies universal hypotheses because of its *predicate* and its *subject*. Popper's analysis of *disposition predicates* in his *Logic* shows the former; the latter is indicated in his *Postscript*: "[T]he existence of physical *bodies*... entails that of objective physical *regularities*" (RAS, 80, i.a.). Hence even the simplest observation statements are theoretical, and their theoreticity differs only *in degree* from that of the most abstract physical theories.

Whoever makes an assertion by uttering our *observation statement* cannot at the same time doubt the *universal hypotheses* contained in its predicate ("is white") or in the description of its subject ("this sheet of paper") without *depriving the statement of its linguistic meaning*. Now, there is no fundamental difference between these implicit hypotheses and explicitly formulated universal hypotheses. Hence *if we are entitled to consider our singular observation statement "This sheet of paper is white" — on the basis of careful observations and for the present — to be true, then there is no reason not to take a well-corroborated universal or probabilistic hypothesis — for the present — to be true*, while at the same time acknowledging that we may be wrong.

Suppose that, motivated by careful observations, we take our (thus corroborated) observation statement to be true. Does this imply that we have *inductively* "inferred" it or its truth from our observations? The question of how this statement was *factually* developed can be answered only empirically, and there can be no "inductive inference" *justifying* the judgment that it is true. Rather, this judgment is – like the statement itself, for the two are equivalent – a fallible hypothesis. But does it not contain an *inductive element*, insofar as the description given by the statement – and hence also by the judgment that the statement is true – *transcends what has been observed*?

This would be the case if the concept "*inductive*" were extended so that it included *any transcendence inherent in a description*, for there would then be *no statement without an inductive element.* We may, however, doubt the practicality of this definition. And how should we imagine a corresponding *principle* of induction? After all, the transcendence inherent in all descriptions excludes any justifying induction. Would, therefore, a schema of the factual development (or of the acceptance) of observation statements on the basis of observations be sufficient? *If,* on the other hand, *we believe* – in the absence of adequate proposals – *that considering observation statements to be true does not presuppose a principle of induction, then there also is no reason to assume that considering universal statements to be true does presuppose such a principle.* Rather, they may be tentatively judged to be true merely on the basis of their corroboration (or reports on their past success).

Hence *the suspicion of a hidden inductivism in Popper's methodology is unfounded.* But he unnecessarily gave rise to it by refusing without good reason to provisionally call any particular theory true. *Neither did Popper solve the problem of induction,* as he claims, *nor need he implicitly use a principle of induction,* as some of his critics claim.

6

Realism and the Concept of Truth

Obviously, there is a close connection between the concepts "truth" and "reality," but views on its nature differ vastly. Realists such as Popper take truth to be a correspondence between our statements and a reality existing independently of our opinions. The pragmatist Peirce means by the truth "the opinion which is fated to be ultimately agreed to by all who investigate" and explains reality as "the object represented in this opinion." And according to the idealist Berkeley, all reality is mental. On the other hand, the relation between truth and reality is always discussed in a language whose sentences are interpreted in a realist way, unless the speaker is acting as an idealist. All philosophical theories of truth fail because of the peculiarities of our language. Though Popper is aware of this danger, his arguments do not take it into account.

6.1. CAN WE DO WITHOUT THE WORD "TRUE"?

In no other respect did Popper change his mind so fundamentally as with regard to the problem of truth. In his *Logic*, he writes: "*In the logic of science here outlined it is possible to avoid using the concepts 'true' and 'false'*" (LSD, 273f., i.a.). He begins his argument: "Their place may be taken by logical considerations about *derivability relations*. Thus we need not say: 'The prediction *p* is true *provided* the theory *t* and the basic statement *b* are true'. We may say, instead, that the statement *p* follows from the (non-contradictory) conjunction of *t* and *b*." (274, i.a.). This is certainly true, but how can we avoid the statement *that* the prediction *p*, the theory *t*, or the basic statement *b* is true?

According to Popper, we need not say of *singular observation state-ments* such as *b* and *p* "that they are '*true*' or '*false*', for we may interpret their acceptance as the result of a conventional decision, and the ac-cepted statements as *results of this decision*" (LSD, 274, i.a.; cf. section 4.6). (Accordingly, we say "*b* is accepted" instead of "*b* is true," and we say "¬*p* is accepted" or "*p* is rejected" instead of "*p* is false.") But what about the *theory t*? Instead of saying "*t* is *false*," we may say "[*t*] is contradicted by a certain set of accepted basic statements" (274). (Hence, if *b* ∧ ¬*p* is accepted, then *t* must be rejected.) But Popper does not indicate how to avoid saying "*t* is *true*." At any rate, he does not take theories to be conventions (72ff.). In his *Postscript to the Logic of Scientific Discovery*, he definitely rejects calling theories true (cf. sections 5.54, 5.62). Maybe he already had this idea when he was writing *Logik der Forschung*.

But even when we say that a theory *contradicts accepted basic statements*, this is not the same thing as saying that it is *false*, for we accept or reject falsifying basic statements only *temporarily*, whereas we use the words "true" and "false" *timelessly*. While the truth value of a statement cannot change, our opinion as to its truth value can (LSD, 275). So the conventional decision to accept a new basic statement changes our opinion about the theory that it contradicts, and the revision of our opinion about a basic statement may entail a revision of our opinion about a theory.

Hence Popper's reasons for doing without the words "true" and "false" are not sound. Frege, however, has a more convincing reason. He writes, "One can, indeed, say: 'The thought, that 5 is a prime number, is true.' But closer examination shows that nothing more has been said than in the simple sentence '5 is a prime number'" (Frege 1892/1966, 64). Com-parable theses can be found in Thomas Aquinas and Leibniz (cf. Keuth 1978a, 34). They are subsumed under the heading "*redundancy thesis*" or "*redundancy theory*." Frege's example illustrates why we can do without the word "true." But if we can do without it, then we need no *theory of truth* to define its meaning. And the discussion of the redundancy thesis shows that we can *always* do without it when we talk about single statements or about a finite number of statements. For this purpose we need none of the substitutes that Popper proposes ("conventional decision," "contra-dicted by") nor any other – as, for example, the words "confirmed" or "corroborated," which are not timeless. But the discussion shows as well that it may be very economical to use the word "true," even if we could in principle do without it (cf. Keuth 1993, section 3.12).

Why did Popper consider the words "true" and "false" dispensable, even though he continued to use them? He gives several reasons. The *correspondence theory* was contested, and according to Popper's view at that time, rightly so. According to the correspondence theory, a statement is true if, and only if, it corresponds to reality (or to the facts). But Popper was not so much impressed by the fact that the correspondence theory implies the *antinomy* of the liar and hence is inconsistent (OK, 320). Rather, it seemed impossible to explain what we could possibly *mean* "if we say of a *statement* that it corresponds with the *facts* (or with reality)" (LSD, 274 n*1). Furthermore, he felt unable to combat the view that "if we wish to speak about truth, we should be able to give a *criterion of truth*" (OK, 320, i.a.).

Popper changes his view fundamentally when, in 1935, he learns about Tarski's "concept of truth in formalized languages" (OK, 319; cf. Tarski 1936/1956). Since that time, he has no longer been afraid to say that he sees "*science as the search for truth*" (CR, 229, i.a.). Rather, he takes *objective truth* to be an unrenouncable *regulative idea* (234), "which makes rational discussion possible – that is to say, critical discussion in search of mistakes with the serious purpose of eliminating as many of these mistakes as we can, in order to get nearer to the truth" (229).

Undoubtedly, Tarski's definition of truth permits this new assessment, if we disregard the fact that Popper's idea of *approximation to truth* is problematic (cf. Chapter 7). Popper even maintains that Tarski's semantic definition of truth has rehabilitated a theory defining truth as *adaequatio rei et intellectus* (correspondence of world and intellect). Nevertheless, he still avoids *considering a theory "true" for the present*, even if it has been carefully tested (cf. sections 5.54, 5.62).

6.2. TARSKI'S SEMANTIC DEFINITION OF TRUTH

Tarski tries to give a *satisfactory definition* of the word "true," a definition that is *materially adequate* and *formally correct*. He means "to do justice to the intuitions which adhere to the *classical Aristotelian conception of truth*" (Tarski 1944, 342), which Aristotle put in these words:

(1) "To say that what is is not, or that what is not is, is false; but to say that what is is, and what is not is not, is true." (*Metaphysics* 1011 b 26ff.)

Tarski also considers the idea that "we could *perhaps* [i.a.] express this conception by means of the familiar formula: '*The truth of a sentence consists in its agreement with (or correspondence to) reality*'" (343). But he rejects the argument "that – due to the fact that a sentence like 'snow is white' is taken to be semantically true if snow is *in fact* white . . . – logic finds itself involved in a most uncritical realism" (361). Rather, "we may accept the semantic conception of truth without giving up any epistemological attitude we may have had; we may remain naive realists, critical realists or idealists, empiricists or metaphysicians – whatever we were before. The semantic conception is *completely neutral* toward all these issues" (362, i.a.). So Popper's assumption that Tarski intended to defend and refine the commonsense theory that truth is "the peculiar relation of *correspondence to a fact*" is mistaken (OK, 44, 46).

In order to find an aspect from which to judge the *material adequacy* of any definition of truth, Tarski asks on what condition the sentence

(2) Snow is white

is true. If we follow the classical conception of truth, we shall say that

(3) The sentence "snow is white" is true if, and only if, snow is white.
    (1944, 343)

(By placing our linguistic objects – names, predicates, statements – in quotation marks, we get their names.) This formulation resumes the Aristotelian idea (1). It may seem trivial, but, as we shall see, it implies that *any theory of truth is bound to fail if it assigns the word "true" a stronger meaning* (cf. sections 6.3, 6.4).

Now Tarski generalizes the procedure applied to (2) "Snow is white" and obtains the schema:

(T) X is true $\leftrightarrow p$

("$\leftrightarrow$" means "if, and only if"). If in (T) we replace the variable "p" with the sentence (2) "Snow is white," and the variable "X" with its name " 'Snow is white,' " we get the equivalence

(4) "Snow is white" is true $\leftrightarrow$ snow is white

(i.e., "The sentence 'Snow is white' is true if, and only if, snow is white"). Tarski wishes "to use the term 'true' in such a way that all equivalences of the form (T) can be asserted, and [he] *shall call a definition of truth 'adequate' if all these equivalences follow from it*" (1944, 344). But the schema (T) is not itself a definition of truth. Rather, every equivalence of the form (T) may [like (4)] "be considered a *partial* definition of truth, which explains wherein the truth of this one individual sentence [here (2)] consists. The *general* definition has to be, in a certain sense, a logical conjunction of all these partial definitions" (344, i.a.). This is sufficient to sketch the core of "*'the semantic conception of truth'*" (345).

In order to avoid *semantic antinomies* (like that of the liar), Tarski adopts the fundamental idea of Russell's theory of types. So he distinguishes an *object* language *about* whose sentences we say that they are true or false from a *meta*language *in* which we say so. Only in the metalanguage can we express the idea that a sentence of the object language is true. Thus *no sentence may purport to be true itself,* and hence the antinomy of the liar can no longer be formulated. (Strictly speaking, in natural languages only statements may be said to be true, but in Tarski, and in the discussion of the semantic conception of truth, "*statement*" and "*sentence*" are often used indiscriminately. We use them interchangeably here as well, mostly for stylistic reasons.)

If we adapt Tarski's example to the new situation what will be the result? Let English be our metalanguage and German the object language. Then

(5) Schnee ist weiß

is our statement of the object language. In order to speak about it, we form its name (by placing the statement itself in quotation marks)

(6) "Schnee ist weiß"

in the metalanguage. The *condition on which we call* (5) "*true*" is – as in the case of (3) or (4) – that snow is white. And this is what is stated by sentence (2) "Snow is white," which now belongs to the metalanguage. Thus we may again replace the variable "p" in schema (T) with (2). We may also say that (2) is the correct *translation* into the metalanguage of (5). If in addition we replace the variable "X" with the quotation name (6), we get the equivalence

(7) "Schnee ist weiß" is true $\leftrightarrow$ snow is white.

For the statement

(8) Der Mond ist rund

of the object language, we correspondingly get the equivalence

(9) "Der Mond ist rund" is true $\leftrightarrow$ the moon is round.

And the *general* definition of truth for the German language is equivalent to the conjunction of all the *partial* definitions that we get when we formulate "equivalences of the form (T)" for every sentence of this language.

However, we do not need the general definition, as compatibility with philosophical theories of truth is a problem for any partial definition. So in our first partial definition (7) "'Schnee ist weiß' is true ↔ snow is white," the phrase

(10) "Schnee ist weiß" is true

is the *definiendum* and correspondingly the phrase (2) "Snow is white" is the *definiens*. As definition (7) confers the meaning of its definiens (2) on its definiendum (10), (*10*) "'*Schnee ist weiß' is true*" and (2) "*Snow is white*" have by definition the same meaning. Hence they are logically equivalent.

On the other hand, we presuppose with Tarski that (2) "Snow is white" is the *correct translation* into the metalanguage of (5) "Schnee ist weiß," and hence that these two statements have the *same meaning* as well. If now, as is common usage, (5) "Schnee ist weiß" is a statement *about snow* but is *not* a statement *about any statement*, then (*10*) "'*Schnee ist weiß' is true*" is also a statement *about snow* but *not* a statement *about any statement*, and above all, (10) *does not assert that* (5) "*Schnee ist weiß" is true.*

Hence, when we use the expression "*X* is true," we say nothing about the objects whose names we substitute for its variable "*X*." Consequently, "*X is true*" *is not a genuine predicate*, though it has the form of a predicate. Rather, "the utility of the truth predicate is precisely the *cancellation of linguistic reference*" to the statements whose names are substituted for "*X*" (Quine 1970, 12). Thus Tarski's *semantic definition of truth* is an elaborate form of the *redundancy theory* (cf. Keuth 1993, section 3.12). For it "implies nothing regarding the conditions on which a sentence like [2] 'snow is white' can be asserted. It implies only that, whenever we assert or reject this sentence, we must be ready to assert or reject the correlated sentence [.]: 'the sentence "snow is white" is true'" (Tarski 1944, 361).

This seems to be the *price* we have to pay *for the extrication of the conception of truth from semantic antinomies.* Though other solutions to the problem of semantic antinomies have been proposed – for example, by Kripke (born 1940; 1975), none of them has been elaborated in detail. So we do not know whether any of them could really solve the problem. But what – according to the quotation in the last paragraph – is implied by the semantic definition of truth follows as well from the standard use of the word "true," which is exemplified by the Aristotelian phrase (1). So even if one of those proposals should work, *only the redundancy theory would be compatible with the standard use of the word "true."* We shall return to this question later (section 6.4).

6.3. POPPER'S VERSION OF THE CORRESPONDENCE THEORY

As Tarski writes "The word 'true'... expresses a *property*... of certain expressions, viz., of sentences" (1944, 345, i.a.), it is not surprising that many authors still take "*X* is true" to be a genuine predicate. Some of them think, moreover, that its meaning is defined by their respective *theories of truth*. So Popper now accepts "the commonsense theory (defended and refined by Alfred Tarski) that truth is correspondence with the facts (or with reality)" (OK, 44). This statement seems *acceptable* if we do *not* take the word 'correspondence' *in a literal sense*, especially since Tarski had considered whether the *Aristotelian* conception of truth, to which his definition was to do justice, could "*perhaps*" be thus paraphrased (cf. section 6.2).

But when Popper now specifies that "Tarski's theory more particularly makes clear *just what fact* a statement *P* will correspond to if it corresponds to *any* fact: namely the fact that *p*" (OK, 45f.), this is *hardly acceptable even as a metaphor*. Though (7) "'Schnee ist weiß' is true ↔ snow is white" states the necessary and sufficient *condition* on which (5) "Schnee ist weiß" is true, and (2) "Snow is white" asserts that the condition is satisfied, neither the word "*correspondence*" nor a substitute for it occurs in any of these statements. Contrary to appearances, (7) cannot assert the correspondence of a statement with a fact but only the equivalence of two statements – or the identity of two facts, if you like.

Not at all compatible with Tarski's definition, however, is Popper's proposal to "*define* [i.a.], purely verbally, yet in keeping with common sense: '*A statement is true if and only if it corresponds to the facts.*'" And his statement "This, as Tarski points out, is an objectivist or absolutist notion of truth" is false (OK, 46; see below). Probably this misunderstanding is the result of his high regard for the correspondence theory, for in his opinion "*it is not his successful description of a method for defining 'true'* which makes Tarski's work philosophically so important, but his *rehabilitation of the correspondence theory of truth*" (OK, 328; cf. CR, 223).

On the other hand, Popper's thesis that Tarski rehabilitated the correspondence theory could be interpreted in a less problematic way. He gives an example himself. Because "as Tarski's theory suggests, truth is correspondence to the facts," Popper proposes that we "for a moment abandon the word '*truth*' altogether and instead only talk of 'the *correspondence* of statements to the facts they describe'" (OK, 324, i.a.). Then he argues that it should be possible to introduce "such predicates as '*X* corresponds to the facts'" on the same linguistic preconditions on which

Tarski had introduced "*X* is true" by means of his schema (T) (325). We give Popper's *definitional schema introducing the predicate* "*X corresponds to the facts*" (326) the form

(C) *X* corresponds to the facts ↔ *p*.

Even if we substitute a false statement for "*p*" and its name for "*X*," we get a "true semantical assertion:

[11] 'The German statement "Der Mond besteht aus grünem Käse" corresponds to the facts if and only if the moon consists of green cheese'" (326).

This is undoubtedly correct, but what is it to show? Popper thinks that by "speaking of correspondence to the facts (instead of truth)" (326), we more easily understand why the statement that we substitute [in (C) and finally in (T)] for "*p*" "*must* be[.] a metalinguistic statement of some *fact* (or some purported fact)" (327).

If, however, Popper's schema (C) is but a didactically better version of Tarski's schema (T), then (11) is a *partial definition of correspondence to the facts*, in which

(12) "Der Mond besteht aus grünem Käse" corresponds to the facts

is the *definiendum* and

(13) The moon consists of green cheese

is the *definiens*. Definition (11) confers the meaning of its definiens (13) on its definiendum (12). And if (13) is about the moon and not about the statement

(14) Der Mond besteht aus grünem Käse,

then (12) as well is about the moon and not about the statement (14). Hence (12) does *not* assert a *correspondence between a statement and a fact*. Let us call this use of "*X corresponds to the facts*" its *interpretation A*. It is unproblematic, but does it do justice to Popper's intentions?

When Popper calls (11) a "*true semantical assertion*" instead of a "partial definition" (OK, 326, i.a.), this does not contradict our account. For as (11) follows from the definitional schema (C), (11) is *true* and is also *semantic* insofar as (11) states a sameness in meaning. But when he writes, that "a false statement . . . does not stand in the peculiar relation of *correspondence to a fact* to anything real" (OK, 46), he obviously is *not speaking metaphorically of correspondence.* Therefore, our interpretation A, according to which (12) "'Der Mond besteht aus grünem Käse' corresponds to the facts" is actually a statement about the moon but not about the sentence (14) "Der Mond besteht aus grünem Käse," is not correct. Instead, we must assume that (12) is meant to assert *the relation of correspondence between the statement (14) and the facts* (or the fact that the moon consists of green cheese). Let us call this *interpretation B of "X corresponds to the facts."*

The consequences of *interpretation B* become evident, when we consider *Popper's* definition "*A statement is true if and only if it corresponds to the facts*" (OK, 46). This obviously is his *definitional schema of the correspondence theory.* We give it the form

(CT) *X* is true ↔ *X* corresponds to the facts.

Popper goes on, "This, as Tarski points out, is an objectivist or absolutist notion of truth." But there is no such schema in Tarski, and given interpretation B, (CT) directly *contradicts Tarski's definition of truth.*

In order to show this more easily, we return to Tarski's example. If in (CT) we substitute the quotation name (6) "'Schnee ist weiß'" for the variable "*X*," we get *Popper's partial definition of truth as correspondence*:

(15) "Schnee ist weiß" is true ↔ "Schnee ist weiß" corresponds to the facts.

In (15), the phrase (10) "'Schnee ist weiß' is true" is, as it is in (7), the *definiendum*, but here

(16) "Schnee ist weiß" corresponds to the facts

is the *definiens*. Given Popper's partial definition of truth as correspondence (15) and interpretation B (of "*X* corresponds to the facts"), statement (10) "'Schnee ist weiß' is true" really asserts (16) "'Schnee ist weiß' corresponds to the facts," and hence (10) is a genuine *assertion about statement (5) "Schnee ist weiß."* However, according to *Tarski's partial semantic definition of truth* (7) "'Schnee ist weiß' is true ↔ snow is white," (10) only asserts (2) "Snow is white," and hence (10) is an *assertion about the snow*. Obviously, *Popper's and Tarski's partial definitions of truth contradict each other*. Consequently, Tarski's definition of truth cannot rehabilitate the correspondence theory to which Popper refers.

Of course, this contradiction may easily be avoided if the expression "*X* corresponds to the facts" is given *interpretation A*. But then (16) "'Schnee ist weiß' corresponds to the facts" asserts nothing else but (2) "Snow is white," and hence (15) in the final analysis asserts nothing else but

(17) Schnee ist weiß ↔ Schnee ist weiß.

What was supposed to be a *partial definition of truth as correspondence* [(15)] turns out to be reducible to a *tautology*. In this way it is of course compatible with Tarski's definition of truth and hence does not imply antinomies, but in this way it can hardly render the correspondence theory. So we are left with the *semantic definition of truth*, which is an elaborate form of the *redundancy thesis*.

6.4. ON THE STANDARD USE OF THE WORD 'TRUE'

Anyone who is not content with this solution but who wants to keep to the correspondence theory (or to any other definitional theory of truth) may of course reject Tarski's semantic definition of truth, if he is not afraid of antinomies. But he still does not escape a peculiarity of the *expression* "*is true*." According to its *standard use*, which is mirrored in Aristotle's statement (1) and in Tarski's schema (T), it is *inconceivable* that (2) "Snow is white" should not be true when snow is white, or that (2) "Snow is white" should be true when snow is not white. Hence (2) "Snow is white" *and*

(18) "Snow is white" is true

necessarily have the same truth value. Thus – according to the semantic concept of logical consequence – they follow from each other; they are *logically equivalent.* (And so they also have the same meaning [cf. Keuth 1996, 96f.].) Consequently, (4) "'*Snow is white*' *is true* ↔ *snow is white*" not only follows from Tarski's schema (T) but also *is implied by the standard use of the word* "*true*." Therefore, (18) can be replaced by (2) quite independently of (T), as the *redundancy thesis* asserts.

Let us now add to the equivalence (4) "'Snow is white' is true ↔ snow is white" a theory of truth – say, (CT) "*X* is true ↔ *X* corresponds to the facts" – that defines in its way the meaning of the expression "*X* is true." In our example, the result of this move depends on the interpretation of "*X* corresponds to the facts." First, we choose *interpretation A* – that is, we give the statement

(19) "Snow is white" corresponds to the facts

the standard meaning of (2) "Snow is white." Then (2) and (19) are equivalent not only *to each other* but also *to* (*18*) "'Snow is white' is true" [because of (T) or (4) and, independently, because of (CT)]. Hence the "*correspondence theory*" (*CT*) is *compatible with the standard use of the word "true"* [which implies (4), i.e., the equivalence of (18) and (2)], but it is *empty*, as it may – like (15) – be reduced to a tautology.

Now we choose *interpretation B* – that is, we take (19) "'Snow is white' corresponds to the facts" to express the relation of correspondence between statement (2) "Snow is white" and the facts (or the fact that snow is white). But this entails a *logical contradiction*, as according to (4) statements (18) and (2) are equivalent, and according to (CT) statements (18) and (19) are equivalent, but (2) and (19) are *not* equivalent. Hence *the "correspondence theory" (CT) is not compatible with the standard use of the word "true."* This holds, accordingly, for any other definitional theory of truth (cf. Keuth 1993, section 3.6). Therefore, *any definitional theory of truth must either be empty or be incompatible with the standard use of the word "true."* So Popper's attempt had to fail.

6.5. ON THE REALIST INTERPRETATION OF STATEMENTS

Why does Popper defend the correspondence theory so passionately? For one thing, the *regulative idea of truth* matters to him, but in the final analysis it is the *realist interpretation of statements*, even of theories, that counts. This interpretation, however, does not presuppose a correspondence theory. This becomes evident if we examine Aristotle's proposition

> (20) "It is not because *we are right in thinking that you are white* that you are white; it is because you are white that *we are right in saying so.*" (Metaphysics 1051 b 6, i.a.)

Even if we give this the form

> (21) It is not because *the statement that you are white is true* that you are white; it is because you are white that *the statement that you are white is true,*

it seems acceptable, just because the words "right" and "true" need not be interpreted in the same way that "true" is interpreted in modern theories of truth. On the contrary, two assumptions as to the meaning of "true" suffice: (a) *it is inconceivable that you are white when the thought – or the statement – that you are white is not true, or that this thought is true when you are not white,* and (b) *we answer the question whether the thought that you are white is true according to whether you are white, but we do not answer the question whether you are white according to whether the thought that you are white is true.*

Clause (a) exemplifies the standard use of the word "true." Clause (b) is a useful paraphrase of the *realist interpretation of statements*, though it may be philosophically unsatisfactory. But whoever attempts to give it the form of a theory of truth or a theory of meaning must somehow refer to the relation between language and the world (or our experience of the world), and every explicit reference is bound to fail for the reasons already given (cf. Keuth 1993, section 3.133).

7

Verisimilitude

In the Preface to the English Edition of *The Logic of Scientific Discovery* (1959), Popper writes: "The central problem of epistemology has always been and still is the problem of the growth of knowledge. *And the growth of knowledge can be studied best by studying the growth of scientific knowledge*" (LSD, 15). Obviously, his point of view had changed in the quarter-century since the publication of *Logik der Forschung* (1935), for originally he had taken it to be "the first task of the logic of knowledge to put forward a *concept of empirical science*, in order to make linguistic usage, now somewhat uncertain, as definite as possible, and in order to draw a clear line of demarcation between science and *metaphysical ideas* [i.a.] – even though these ideas may have furthered the advance of science throughout its history" (38f.). This last clause is a concession quite unusual at the time in the antimetaphysical Vienna Circle.

Why does he now take the *growth of knowledge* to be the central problem of epistemology? Because up until now all scientific theories have failed sooner or later, we must expect that those theories that are at present best corroborated will one day be refuted as well. Thus the evolution of science appears to be a succession of false theories. How then can we find out whether there is *progress* in this succession? False theories do not correspond to reality, even though they are successfully applied. Does this mean we have to assume that theories aren't statements that can be true or false but rather instruments for prediction that are more or less useful, or is there another explanation of the *applicability of false theories?*

In order to solve both problems, Popper introduces the idea of "*verisimilitude*" (OK). He also speaks of "*similarity to the truth*" (CR), "*approach to the truth*" (CR), or "*truthlikeness*" (RAS). He *considers the growth of knowledge a result of our theories' gradual approach to the truth* and *explains the applicability of false theories by their truthlikeness.* Though, strictly speaking, they are false, they come sufficiently close to the truth to be applicable. This explanation spares him the instrumentalist interpretation of theories, which, he fears, would lead to a conservative practice: When predictions fail, the realist will reject the theories used because they are false, but the instrumentalist will keep to them as long as they successfully predict events of different kinds.

Popper believes that "the notions of *objective truth,* and of *getting nearer to the truth*" will be "of great help in analysing the *growth of knowledge*" (CR, 216, i.a.). He wants to be able to say "that *science aims at truth in the sense of correspondence to the facts or to reality*" and also "that *relativity theory is* – or so we conjecture – *a better approximation to truth than is Newton's theory,* just as the latter is a better approximation to truth than is Kepler's theory" (OK, 59, i.a.). He considers verisimilitude, like truth, to be a commonsense notion that is "much needed for any critical commonsense realism" but that has "become suspect" (59). And he wants to achieve "for *verisimilitude* something similar to what Tarski achieved for truth," that is, "the rehabilitation of a common-sense idea which [he needs] for describing the aims of science, and which, [he asserts,] underlies as a *regulative principle* (even if merely unconsciously and intuitively) the rationality of all critical scientific discussions" (59, i.a.). The "search for verisimilitude is [even] a clearer and a more realistic aim than the search for truth," and "the *aim of science* is *truth in the sense of better approximation to truth,* or greater verisimilitude" (57, i.a.).

7.1. THE CUSTOMARY IDEA OF APPROXIMATION TO TRUTH

The idea of approximation to truth seems to be very old. According to Popper, "it has repeatedly been confused, at least since the time of Plato, with probability" (1974b, 1100). In any case, the idea of the *approximation of a statement to the true description of a state of affairs* has been known to scientists and laymen for a long time.

Suppose we want to check the precision of a (weighing) scale by means of a test body (standard weight). Then the scale is exact if it indicates the weight of the test body; and a statement assigning the test body a weight on the basis of the reading of the scale is true if, and only if, the scale is exact. But the reading of the scale can differ more or less from the real weight, and accordingly, a statement describing the indicated weight can differ more or less from a statement describing the real weight. As the weight is measured on a ratio scale (i.e., its value is indicated in rational numbers), both the absolute and the relative difference between the indicated value and the real value can theoretically be calculated with any desired accuracy (cf. Keuth 1978a, 113ff.).

Suppose also that the test body weighs 1 kilogram, but the scale indicates 1.02 kilograms. From this, we first calculate the absolute *deviation* of the measured weight from the real *weight*. It is 20 grams. Accordingly, the relative deviation is 20g ÷ 1000g = 0.02 = 2%. Instead of referring (in the material mode of speech) to states of affairs, as we have up until now, we could refer (in the formal mode of speech) to statements and assert that (the indication of weight contained in) the false *statement* "The body weighs 1.02 kilograms" deviates from (that contained in) the true statement "The body weighs 1 kilogram" by 2%. In this particular case, *the approximation of a false statement to a true one*, or, if you like, to the state of affairs that the true one describes, can be *measured on a ratio scale.* In other cases that permit comparable measurements, the *approximation to a respective "truth"* may be measured correspondingly.

On the basis of the deviations of predicted values from measured values, we may also assess the *relative preferability of false theories.* For example, Einstein's general theory of relativity permits us to predict the positions of celestial bodies with greater precision than Newton's theory of gravitation does. Einsteinian predictions deviate far less from the true descriptions of observed positions. The extent of the deviations can, as in the earlier case of the weight, be measured. (Many authors deny that any Einsteinian predictions have so far been found to deviate from observations. If there are no such deviations, then we are not comparing two false theories but a false [Newton's] and a possibly true [Einstein's] theory. But this does not alter the numerical result of the comparison.)

This does not even presuppose that the theories are considered statements about reality that, though being false, come more or less close to the truth. Rather, they may be considered mere *instruments* for predictions, for even though we need them to derive the predictions, they do not play a part in calculating the deviation of the predicted values from the "true" (observed) values.

On the basis of the deviation of particular *predictions* from the measured values – that is, from the respective "truths" – we can calculate a numerical value that, in a certain sense, may be assigned to the *theory* applied in the prediction. After all, it is also possible to assign to a set the property of containing as elements people who on the average have a certain height, even though the set, being an abstract entity, cannot itself have a height. By analogy, we can assign to a theory – even if it is considered a mere instrument and hence is neither true nor false – the property of permitting predictions that to a certain degree deviate from the respective "true" values.

Of course, we may be misunderstood when we speak of the verisimilitude of a *theory* that is considered a mere *instrument.* But neither does the realist interpretation of theories identify a "truth" that a theory could approximate in the sense in which a prediction can approximate the description of the real position of a physical body. Rather, the derived measure (of the verisimilitude of theories) cannot be more informative than its premises (the measures of the closeness to truth of the predictions), which, however, inform us only about the deviation of particular predictions from the *respective* "true" values.

But can *every singular statement* approach a respective "true" value? The statement "This raven weighs a grams" gives a *quantitative* account. Its test requires a measurement on a *ratio scale.* Accordingly, its approximation to the true value b of the raven's weight can in principle also be measured on a ratio scale. As opposed to this, the statement "This raven is black" gives a *qualitative* account. This is also called a measurement on a *nominal scale.* As its result can be only "black" or "nonblack" (or at best "white," "red," etc.), the account of the corresponding statement can only be "true" or "false." Hence we cannot say that such a statement more or less approaches truth.

The idea of approximation to the truth sketched in this section is well known in the empirical sciences. It seems to equal the idea that, according to Popper, "has been used, *intuitively*, by many philosophers, including [him]self" but has also "been regarded as suspect" (OK, 47, i.a.). Popper wants to "allay these suspicions" (47), but for philosophical purposes the idea is *not sufficiently universal.* It is not applicable to qualitative statements and is only indirectly applicable to (quantitative) theories. Therefore, Popper proposes a new definition of verisimilitude that, if it were tenable, would be a remarkable *improvement.*

7.2. POPPER'S IDEA OF APPROXIMATION TO THE TRUTH

Chapter 10 of Popper's *Conjectures and Refutations* (1963) is entitled "Truth, Rationality, and the Growth of Knowledge." It is based on lectures he delivered in 1960 and 1961, and it contains "some essential further developments of the ideas of [his] *Logic of Scientific Discovery*" (CR, 215n).

Popper here asserts that "continued growth is essential to the rational and empirical character of scientific knowledge; that if science ceases to grow it must lose that character" (215). But why should science lose that character if it ceases to grow? "It is the *way* of its growth which makes science *rational* and *empirical*; the way, that is, in which scientists discriminate between available theories and *choose the better one* or (in the absence of a satisfactory theory) the way they give *reasons for rejecting* all the available theories, thereby suggesting some of the *conditions with which a satisfactory theory should comply*" (215, i.a.).

7.21. Comparisons of Contents

Our knowledge grows as we learn by trial and error (CR, 216). But how do we assess the growth achieved? "Within the field of science we have . . . a *criterion of progress*: even before a theory has ever undergone an empirical test we must be able to say whether, provided it passes certain specified tests, it would be an improvement on other theories with which we are acquainted" (217). Do we thus have reason to expect a criterion of progress that will be as successful as the criterion of demarcation has proved to be?

Popper first proposes a *criterion of potential progressiveness*: "It characterizes as preferable the theory which tells us more; that is to say, the theory which contains the greater amount of empirical information or *content*; which is logically stronger; which has the greater explanatory and predictive power; and which can therefore be *more severely tested* by comparing predicted facts with observations" (CR, 217). Hence the criterion says approximately:

(1) Theory *B* will *potentially* be an improvement as compared to *A* if the (empirical) *content* of *B* is greater than that of *A*.

All the other assets mentioned are consequences of this *greater empirical content*, for greater empirical content means not only greater explanatory and predictive power but also better testability, to which Popper refers "as the '*criterion of progress*'" (217 n2, i.a.).

He compares *empirical* contents on the basis of *logical* contents. In most cases this is unproblematic, when synthetic statements are compared that have no or only a small metaphysical content. For the statement with the greater logical content never has the smaller empirical content; and among purely empirical statements, that with the greater logical content also has the greater empirical content (LSD, 120f.). In this case, the ordering according to logical content mirrors the ordering according to empirical content (cf. section 5.3).

Hence when theory A is replaced by theory B, which has a more comprehensive content, this *possibly* represents scientific progress. But there is real progress only when the additional consequences of B also pass empirical tests. Therefore, Popper adds a *criterion of actual scientific progress* (CR, 219f.), which says approximately:

> (2) Theory B will *actually* be an improvement as compared to A if the excess content of B over A passes empirical tests.

However, both criteria are applicable only to pairs of theories whose *contents* are *comparable* (i.e., one of which implies the other). And even then, they are directly applicable only to *true* theories. For if the more comprehensive theory B is *false*, or if both A and B are false, then we must, *when comparing them, weigh their true consequences positively and their false consequences negatively*. For this purpose Popper proposes the concept of *verisimilitude*.

Already in his *Logic*, he considers comparing the *degrees of falsifiability* of statements by their *logical probabilities*. But he still confines himself to the thesis:

The logical probability of a statement is complementary to its degree of falsifiability: it increases with decreasing degree of falsifiability. The logical probability 1 corresponds to the degree 0 of falsifiability, and *vice versa*. The better testable statement, *i.e.* the one with the higher degree of falsifiability, is the one which is logically less probable; and the statement which is less well testable is the one which is logically more probable. (LSD, 119)

Later he specifies the connection between degree of falsifiability and logical probability. For this purpose he proposes a measure of the *logical content* – and thus indirectly of the empirical content. He derives $Ct(a)$, the *measure of the content of a*, by the equation

$$(3) \quad Ct(a) = 1 - p(a)$$

from $p(a)$, the logical probability of a (LSD, 374; CR, 390). In "Truth, Rationality, and the Growth of Knowledge," he formulates the inequality

$$(4) \quad Ct(a) \leq Ct(ab) \geq Ct(b),$$

which "contrasts with the corresponding law of the calculus of probability,

$$(5) \quad p(a) \geq p(ab) \leq p(b)$$

where the inequality signs of [4] are inverted" (CR, 218). Hence a high logical content corresponds to a low logical probability, and vice versa. [Unfortunately, he chooses to write "$Ct(a)$ for 'the content of the statement a,'" although $Ct(a)$ here obviously serves as a *measure* of the content of a; CR, 218.]

As we want our *knowledge* to *grow*, we look for theories of *increasing content*, and this means theories of *decreasing probability* [cf. (4) and (5); CR, 218]. But people generally are inclined "to assume uncritically that a high probability must be an aim of science," and they expect "the theory of induction [to explain] how we can attain a high degree of probability for our theories" (219). There can, however, be "no doubt that the absolute probability of a statement a is simply the *degree of its logical weakness, or lack of informative content*," for the calculus of probability "in its ('logical') application to propositions or statements, is nothing but a *calculus of the logical weakness or lack of content of these statements*" (219).

7.22. The Comparative Definition of Verisimilitude

Let us now return to the *comparison of false hypotheses*. If statement a is *true*, then the *logical content of a* – that is, the class of all logical consequences of a – contains only true statements, for truth is transferred from any premise to its logical consequences. If, however, a is *false*, then the logical content of a contains not only false statements but also true ones. Popper gives an example: "'It always rains on Sundays' is false, but its conclusion that it rained last Sunday happens to be true" (CR, 233). Correspondingly, Popper divides the set of all consequences of a into the subset of all true consequences and the subset of all false consequences. If a happens to be true, then the set of its false consequences is of course empty. Popper calls "the *class of the true logical consequences of a* the '*truth-content*' of a ... [and] ... the *class of the false consequences of a* – but only these – the '*falsity-content*' of a" (233, i.a.). The word "class" is used synonymously with "set."

Any pair of hypotheses, one of which implies the other, may be compared as to their logical contents. If b implies a but not vice versa, then the logical content of a is a proper subset of the logical content of b. As truth contents and falsity contents are by definition sets or classes, relations of inclusion may hold as well between truth contents and between falsity contents (whereas truth contents and falsity contents are mutually exclusive). Therefore, Popper proposes that we compare the *verisimilitude* of two hypotheses by their truth contents and falsity contents:

Assuming that the truth-content and the falsity-content of two theories t_1 and t_2 are comparable, we can say that t_2 is more closely similar to the truth, or corresponds better to the facts, than t_1, if and only if either
   (a) the truth-content but not the falsity-content of t_2 exceeds that of t_1,
   (b) the falsity-content of t_1, but not its truth-content, exceeds that of t_2. (CR, 233, his italics)

This basic idea is the model for all his further attempts at the "idea of approximation to truth, or of verisimilitude" (234). *According to this idea, any (additional) true consequence makes a theory more similar to the truth, and any (additional) false consequence makes it less similar to the truth.*

Two additional points are important to Popper. First, his idea of approximation to truth is, like the idea of objective or absolute truth, both an *objective* and a *regulative idea*. It is also not "*an epistemological or an epistemic idea*" but "a 'semantic' idea, like truth, or like logical consequence" (CR, 234). Though "corroboration" is an objective concept too, it is historic, whereas approximation to truth is *timeless* (CR, 5th ed., 402). And just as it is decisive "to distinguish sharply between objective truth and subjective belief," so is it decisive to distinguish sharply between "verisimilitude as an objective idea" and "all such subjective ideas as degrees of belief,...or of probability in any one of its subjective meanings" (402). Second, according to Popper's definition "maximum verisimilitude would be achieved only by a theory which is not only true, but completely comprehensively true: if it corresponds to *all* facts, as it were, and, of course, only to *real* facts" (234). Such a theory would state the *whole truth* that can be expressed in a given language.

So far, Popper has only answered the question "*What do you intend to say* if you say that the theory t_2 has a higher degree of verisimilitude than the theory t_1?" (i.a.). The question "*How do you know* that the theory t_2 has a higher degree of verisimilitude than the theory t_1?" (i.a.) has to be answered in the same way as the question "How do you know that the theory t_3 is true?" Popper admits: "I do *not* know – I only guess" (CR, 234).

In order to examine Popper's idea of comparing the verisimilitude of two theories more closely, let us first define a few symbols:

A is the logical content of statement *a*.
T is the set of all true statements,

that is, the "whole truth" of the language in question. For simplicity, we take T to be finitely axiomatizable. If t is the axiom of T, then T is the logical content of t, just as A is the logical content of a.

Now Popper defines the "*truth-content* [A_T] *of the statement a* as the class of statements which belong to both, the (logical) content [A] of a, and to T" (CR, 392; cf. CR, 233; OK, 330), that is:

$$A_T = A \cap T \text{ is the truth-content of } a.$$

If we form the set theoretical difference between the set S of all statements (or sentences) of a language and the set T of its true statements, we get

$$F, \text{ which is the set of all false statements}$$

of this language (393). As F is the complement of T in S, we may as well write:

$$\neg T \text{ is the set of all false statements.}$$

(As F contains only false statements and as any false statement has true consequences as well, F does not contain all of the consequences of its elements. Hence F is not a deductive system, and as F or $\neg T$ does not have an axiom, $\neg t$ could not possibly be the axiom of $\neg T$.) The corresponding definition of the falsity content says: "[T]he *falsity-content* [A_F] *of the statement a* is the set of all statements which belong as well to the (logical) content of a as to the set $\neg T$ of all false statements," that is,

$$A_F = A \cap \neg T \text{ is the falsity-content of } a. \text{ (CR, 233)}$$

(Of course, the falsity content of a is not a deductive system either. Therefore this definition "is not quite satisfactory" [OK, 331].)

By means of these definitions we may now symbolize Popper's *comparison of the verisimilitude* of two theories a and b (CR, 233):

$$vs(a) < vs(b) \leftrightarrow (A_T \subset B_T \wedge B_F \subseteq A_F) \vee (A_T \subseteq B_T \wedge B_F \subset A_F),$$

that is, b is more closely similar to the truth than a if, and only if, either

(1) the truth content but not the falsity content of b exceeds that of a, or

(2) the falsity content of a, but not its truth content, exceeds that of b.

This *comparative definition of verisimilitude* seems to be a decisive improvement on the customary idea of approximation to the truth.

It may indeed seem plausible to expect the verisimilitude of false sentences to increase if their truth content, but not their falsity content, increases, or if their falsity content, but not their truth content, decreases. However, *the truth content and the falsity content of every false sentence* a *are equipollent* – that is, they have the same cardinal number:

$$|A \cap T| = |A \cap \neg T|.$$

Hence *to each (additional) true consequence of* a *that makes* a *more closely similar to the truth (gets* a *nearer to the whole truth* T*), there is* a *(an additional) false consequence of* a *that makes* a *less similar to the truth (gets* a *farther from the whole truth* T*), and vice versa.* This refutes the seemingly plausible expectation and shows that Popper's *comparative definition of verisimilitude is inapplicable,* if not contradictory.

In order to prove the equipollence of $A \cap T$ and $A \cap \neg T$, we take t to be the axiom of T. By presupposition, a is false.

[1] First we show [1.1] that *we may assign a true consequence of* a *to any false consequence of* a. This is simple, for if f_i is an arbitrary false statement implied by a, then the true statement $f_i \vee t$ is also implied by a – that is, if $f_i \in A \cap \neg T$, then $f_i \vee t \in A \cap T$. We also must show [1.2] that *to any pair of nonequivalent false consequences of* a *we may assign a pair of nonequivalent true consequences of* a. In order to prove this, we again need only propositional logic, for if f_j too is a false consequence of a and if f_i and f_j are not equivalent, then $f_i \vee t$ and $f_j \vee t$ are not equivalent either, and vice versa, as the analysis of the biconditional

$$\neg(f_i \leftrightarrow f_j) \leftrightarrow \neg((f_i \vee t) \leftrightarrow (f_j \vee t))$$

shows. (We must bear in mind that to the statement t we can assign only the truth value "true," and to f_i and f_j we can assign only the truth value "false.") Hence there is *an injective mapping* (or function) *from* $A \cap \neg T$ *into* $A \cap T$:

$A \cap \neg T$		$A \cap T$
f_i	$\longleftrightarrow$	$f_i \vee t$
f_j	$\longleftrightarrow$	$f_j \vee t$
f_k	$\longleftrightarrow$	$f_k \vee t$
.		.
	.	.

[2] Then we show [2.1] that *we may assign a false consequence of* a *to any true consequence of* a. As a is false, t implies $\neg a$. Hence a implies $\neg t$.

Now, if w_i is an arbitrary *true* statement implied by a, then the false statement $w_i \wedge \neg t$ is also implied by a – that is, if $w_i \in A \cap T$, then $w_i \wedge \neg t \in A \cap \neg T$. We also must show [2.2] that *to any pair of nonequivalent true consequences of a we may assign a pair of nonequivalent false consequences of a*. If w_j is also a true consequence of a, and if w_i and w_j are not equivalent, then $w_i \wedge \neg t$ and $w_j \wedge \neg t$ are not equivalent either, and vice versa, as the analysis of the biconditional

$$\neg(w_i \leftrightarrow w_j) \leftrightarrow \neg((w_i \wedge \neg t) \leftrightarrow (w_j \wedge \neg t))$$

shows. (This time we must bear in mind that to the statements t, w_i, and w_j we can assign only the truth value "true.") Hence there is also *an injective mapping from $A \cap T$ into $A \cap \neg T$*:

$A \cap T$		$A \cap \neg T$
w_i	$\longleftrightarrow$	$w_i \wedge \neg t$
w_j	$\longleftrightarrow$	$w_j \wedge \neg t$
w_k	$\longleftrightarrow$	$w_k \wedge \neg t$
.		.
.		.

Consequently, there is *a bijective mapping from $A \cap T$ onto $A \cap \neg T$*. Hence both are equipollent.

It has been objected that this *equipollence* is *irrelevant*, as the conditions of Popper's comparative definition of verisimilitude may nevertheless be satisfied. After all, it is said, A_T, A_F, B_T, and B_F are all denumerably infinite, that is, they are equipollent; – on the other hand, the set of all even numbers is a *proper subset* of the set of all natural numbers, although both are equipollent. Hence there may nevertheless be orderings among truth contents, such as $A_T \subset B_T$, and orderings among falsity contents, such as $B_F \subseteq A_F$. But can both $A_T \subset B_T$ and $B_F \subseteq A_F$ hold at the same time? How can Popper assert that $A_T \subset B_T \wedge B_F \subseteq A_F$ or $A_T \subseteq B_T \wedge B_F \subset A_F$ holds, if to each element of A_T there is an element of A_F and to each element of B_T there is an element of B_F, and vice versa? As the truth content and the falsity content of a statement are *mutually exclusive*, A_T and A_F as well as B_T and B_F can be compared only by their cardinal numbers. And as they all have the same cardinal number, in the best case we cannot know whether $A_T \subset B_T \wedge B_F \subseteq A_F$ or $A_T \subseteq B_T \wedge B_F \subset A_F$ is *satisfiable*. Actually, neither can be satisfied – that is, both are *contradictory* – as the following argument shows: To any true consequence w_i of b ($w_i \in B_T$), by which b surpasses a ($w_i \notin A_T$) so that $A_T \subset B_T$, there is the false consequence $w_i \wedge \neg t$ of b ($w_i \wedge \neg t \in B_F$). On the other hand, $B_F \subseteq A_F$ cannot hold if $w_i \wedge \neg t \in A_F$ does not also hold. But $w_i \wedge \neg t \in A_F$ would imply $w_i \in A_T$, in contradiction to our presupposition. (The same holds, correspondingly, for $A_T \subseteq B_T \wedge B_F \subset A_F$.) A similar argument has been proposed by Pavel Tichý (1974, 156f.).

Undoubtedly, Popper's comparative definition of verisimilitude is applicable if we want to compare *only true statements that are in pairs derivable from each other.* But then we do not need this definition at all, as the falsity contents of true statements are empty and their truth contents are identical to their logical contents. Thus the comparison of the verisimilitude of statements is reduced to that of their logical contents. *If, however, at least one of the statements compared is false, then the comparative definition of verisimilitude could not possibly be applied.*

7.23. The Numerical Definition of Verisimilitude

In the "Addenda" to *Conjectures and Refutations,* Popper admits that "a definition of 'falsity-content' on lines analogous to 'truth-content' appears not to be workable" (CR, 393). Still, he wants "to define $Vs(a)$ [the *verisimilitude* of a] as *something like the difference of the truth-content and the falsity-content of a*" (393, i.a.). However, this time he attempts from the outset to define not contents but *measures* of contents, truth contents, falsity contents, and thereby of verisimilitude. The measures are based on the logical probability of a.

If it were possible to assign to every statement a logical probability, then *all statements would be comparable on the basis of the measures of their contents* derived from their logical probabilities, and hence *the verisimilitude of any statement could be compared to the verisimilitude of any other statement.* (As opposed to their measures, the contents themselves are, as we have seen, comparable only insofar as relations of inclusion hold between them. And, at best, those statements whose truth contents and falsity contents are comparable may be compared on the basis of the comparative definition of verisimilitude. Thus a numerical definition of verisimilitude would be a remarkable step forward as compared to the comparative definition.)

Popper first defines the *measure Ct(a) of the content of a* by the equation

$$Ct(a) = 1 - p(a)$$

(CR, 390, 392). Then he defines *"the truth-content of a as the content of a_T"* (393), where

$$a_T = a \lor t$$

(392), and he defines *the measure $Ct_T(a)$ of the truth-content of a* by the equation

$$Ct_T(a) = Ct(a_T) = 1 - p(a_T) \; [= 1 - p(a \lor t)]$$

(393). When Popper speaks of the *falsity content of a*, he obviously still has in mind the set of all false consequences of *a*, but in this new proposal there is no longer a symbol for the falsity content. Rather, he defines from the outset a *measure $Ct_F(a)$ of the falsity content of a*:

$$Ct_F(a) = 1 - p(a, a_T) \; [= 1 - p(a, a \lor t)] = Ct(a, a_T)$$

(394). Finally, he derives the *verisimilitude Vs(a)* of *a* from the difference

$$Ct_T(a) - Ct_F(a) = p(a, a_T) - p(a_T) \; [= p(a, a \lor t) - p(a \lor t)]$$

of the measures of the truth content and the falsity content of *a* (396). He declares this sufficient as "long as we are merely interested in comparative values." But if "we are interested in numerical values, then it becomes preferable to multiply this by a normalizing factor" (396). Therefore, he proposes to take

$$Vs(a) = (p(a, a_T) - p(a_T)) \; / \; (p(a, a_T) + p(a_T))$$

as the *numerical definition of verisimilitude* (397). We need not examine his reasons for choosing just this normalizing factor.

Two central problems of this definition are easily recognized. We have already encountered the first one (cf. sections 5.3, 5.4). Though there are definite numerical values for the logical probability of tautologies and contradictions, there are no such values for the logical probability of synthetic statements. Rather, there is but one objective basis for assigning logical probabilities to synthetic statements: To partial orderings (where they are possible) according to derivability there correspond inverse partial orderings according to logical probability. Therefore, we may, on idealizing assumptions, meaningfully assign logical probabilities to some statements of simple model languages, but not to empirical hypotheses. This holds, correspondingly, for all measures that are based on logical probability – hence for Carnap's "degree of confirmation" as well as for Popper's "degree of testability," "degree of corroboration," and "degree of verisimilitude." And Popper is well aware of this.

The second problem is specific to this new measure of verisimilitude. If it is not to fail for the same reason that the original comparative definition of verisimilitude failed, then it must not assign the same value to both the falsity content and the truth content of *a*, even though the two are equipollent. Therefore, Popper assigns to the *falsity content* of *a* a value that is derived from the values of the *content* of *a* and the *truth content* of *a*. This is easily recognized when looking at his definitions. As $Ct(a) = 1 - p(a)$ defines the content, $Ct_T(a) = 1 - p(a \vee t)$ defines the truth content, and $Ct_F(a) = 1 - p(a, a \vee t)$ defines the falsity content of *a*, and as

$$p(a, a \vee t) = p(a \wedge (a \vee t)) \, / \, p(a \vee t) = p(a) \, / \, p(a \vee t),$$

we get

$$Ct_F(a) = 1 - p(a) \, / \, p(a \vee t).$$

Thus the intended comparison of the truth content and the falsity content of a *actually has become a comparison of the content and the truth content of* a.

This also affects substitutes for Popper's definition that have been proposed by various authors. Popper himself considers several other definitions possible, and his next attempt introduces *relative contents* (OK, 332). This was already apparent in the (earlier) equation $Ct_F(a) = Ct(a, a_T)$, for $Ct(a, a_T)$ is a relative content. However, this new attempt is not very successful either. It would take too many symbolic expressions to describe and comment on it here (cf., e.g., Keuth 1976, 1978a).

Popper's proposals have often been criticized, and there are numerous attempts to improve on them. Kuiper's collection of papers *What Is Closer-to-the-Truth?* (1987) contains "A Parade of Approaches to Truthlikeness." More recently there have been other new proposals, among them an unobtrusive one by David Miller (1994, Chapter 10). But the most exacting one is by Gerhard Schurz and Paul Weingartner (1987). The authors propose to *take* (not all consequences but) *only the "relevant" consequences of the theories to be compared into account* and to disregard the "irrelevant" ones. Those consequences are *irrelevant* that would "neither in any empirical science nor in arguments used in everyday life" actually be drawn. Their "common characteristic . . . is that they contain *components which completely lack connection with the premises*" (1987, 52, i.a.). But how can a logical consequence completely lack connection with its premise? Isn't that a logical contradiction?

The authors consider "*disjunctive weakening*" – that is, the inference $p \Rightarrow p \vee q$, which is based on the "law of addition" $p \to p \vee q$ of propositional logic – to be *a paradigm case of irrelevant deductions,* "because [q] is replaceable in [$p \lor q$] by any arbitrary formula [r] *salva validitate* of [$p \Rightarrow p \lor q$], i.e. also [$p \Rightarrow p \lor r$] is valid" (1987, 52). In fact, if all "disjunctive weakenings" are eliminated as irrelevant, then the proof (given in section 7.22) of the equipollence of the truth content and the falsity content of any false statement is no longer possible. But they will be equipollent as long as neither is reduced to a *finite* set. Hence it will hardly be possible to rehabilitate in this way Popper's "simple and intuitively plausible" idea that "a theory is the nearer to the truth the more true and the less false (logical) consequences it has" (48).

8

Probability

Chapter 8, "Probability," is by far the most extensive chapter of Popper's *Logic*. In Chapter 9, "*Some Observations on Quantum Theory*," he applies the instruments just developed "to one of the topical problems of modern science" (LSD, 215). And if we consider the numerous appendices, most of which deal with probability theory or its application to quantum theory, then probability is the subject of more than half of the *Logic*. Why does he pay so much attention to probability?

Probability theory plays a decisive part in modern physics, but according to Popper, "we still lack a satisfactory, consistent *definition of probability*" or "a satisfactory *axiomatic system for the calculus of probability*" (LSD, 146, i.a.). When writing this, he still did not know Kolmogorov's (1903–1987) set theoretical axiomatization of probability theory, which had been published in 1933 as "Grundbegriffe der Wahrscheinlichkeitsrechnung" in the journal *Ergebnisse der Mathematik* (1933/1956). Moreover, probability statements "turn out to be in principle *impervious to strict falsification*," and this "becomes a touchstone upon which to test" his falsificationist methodology (LSD, 146). Thus he is confronted with two tasks: "*The first is to provide new foundations for the calculus of probability*," and "[*t*]*he second task is to elucidate the relations between probability and experience*," that is, to solve what he calls "*the problem of decidability of probability statements*" (146).

8.1. INTERPRETATIONS OF THE CALCULI OF PROBABILITY

Various interpretations of axiom systems of probability have been proposed. For one thing, the interpretations vary with the subjects to which the systems are applied; for another thing, philosophical aspects of the concept of probability play their part. Popper mentions *subjective, logical,* and *objective* interpretations (LSD, 148ff.). In his article "The Propensity Interpretation of Probability," he classes the first two under a common heading and ends up with two main classes, *subjective* and *objective* interpretations (1959, 25). This roughly corresponds to Laplace's distinction between *probabilité* and *possibilité* and also to Carnap's modern distinction between *epistemological* interpretations, which refer to our knowledge of the world, and *objective* interpretations, which refer to the world independently of our knowledge (cf. Howson 1995, 1f.).

According to the *subjective* interpretations, probability theory is "a means of dealing with the *incompleteness of our knowledge*" (Popper 1959, 25). They treat "the degree of probability as a measure of the feelings of certainty or uncertainty ... which may be aroused in us by certain assertions or conjectures" (LSD, 148). But in this case, how can statements expressing uncertainty or lack of knowledge be so well corroborated empirically? Does the hypothesis "The probability of obtaining a 3 when throwing this die is 1/6" really express the same lack of knowledge before the first throw as it does after 6,000 throws, 1,000 of which produced the 3? Have we thus learned nothing from experience? As there seems to be no satisfactory answer to this question, Popper believes that "[c]onsiderations of the 'weight of evidence' lead, within the subjective theory of probability, to paradoxes which, in [his] opinion, are insoluble within the framework of this theory" (406).

However, the proponents of subjective interpretations do not take probability to be primarily "a measure of our ignorance"; rather, they consider it a measure "*of the degree of the rationality of our beliefs*" (LSD, 406f., i.a.; cf. Eells 1991, 35f.). According to Bruno de Finetti, "all the basic results of probability theory can [even] be formulated using the concepts of *decision theory*" (de Finetti 1972, 3, i.a.). But does the degree of rationality of our taking a statement to be true not have to grow with growing experience corroborating the statement?

According to the *logical* interpretation, probability statements are "assertions about what may be called the '*logical proximity*' of statements" (LSD, 148, i.a.). If *a* follows from *b*, then $p(a, b)$ – that is, the probability of *a* relative to *b* – equals 1. If *a* and *b* contradict each other, then the probability of one of them relative to the other equals 0. In all other cases, $p(a, b)$ is the greater the less the content of *a* goes beyond that of *b* (149) – that is, the more, in Carnap's words, the *partial implication* of *a* by *b* approaches logical implication. As the formula "$p(a, b) = r$" expresses a *logical relation* between *a* and *b*, it is either logically true or logically false.

If *h* is a hypothesis and *e* is some empirical evidence, then "$p(h, e) = r$" expresses the support given by *e* to *h*, or the *corroboration* (not in Popper's sense) of *h* by *e* (cf. section 5.4).

Popper notes a *kinship between the logical and the subjective interpretation*, as John Maynard Keynes (1883–1946) defines the logical probability $p(a, b)$ "as the '*degree of rational belief*'" that we accord to *a* in the light of *b* (LSD, 149, i.a.). But the idea of such a kinship is rather surprising, as there is nothing less dependent on subjective estimation than a formal logical relation, – that is, there is nothing that could, in this sense, be more objective.

According to the *objective* interpretations, statements such as "$p(a, b) = r$" are *statistically testable* (1959, 25), and Popper believes "that *only* an objective theory can explain the *application* of the probability calculus *within empirical science*" (LSD, 150, i.a.). Therefore, he is interested primarily in objective interpretations. As in the early thirties he only knows these in the form of *frequency interpretations*, he writes: "[T]he *objective interpretation* treats every numerical probability statement as a statement about the *relative frequency* with which an event of a certain kind occurs within a *sequence of occurrences*" (149).

Later, in his article "The Propensity Interpretation of Probability," he takes the statistical or *frequency* interpretation to be only the *simplest* objective interpretation (1959, 26). And in the new Appendix *VI to the *Logic*, he prefers the "'*measure-theoretical approach*'" (LSD, 361, i.a.), according to which probability is a measure defined on an algebra. After Kolmogorov, this is usually an algebra of sets and the measure is normalized, that is, it assumes values from 0 to 1 (cf. section 8.4; cf. Halmos 1950, 171). The reason for this preference is his assumption that only the measure-theoretical approach (a) permits an objective interpretation that is suited to the interpretation of quantum mechanics, namely the *propensity*-interpretation of probability, and (b) adequately solves the problem of the probability of *single events* (cf. section 8.51).

8.2. POPPER'S MODIFIED FREQUENCY THEORY

In his *Logic*, Popper still advocated a frequency theory, according to which the "calculus of probability is a theory of certain chance-like or *random sequences* of events or occurrences" (LSD, 151, i.a.). According to Richard von Mises (1883–1953), in order to pass for a random sequence a series of events has to satisfy the *limit axiom* and the *axiom of randomness* – that is, it must be a "*collective*" (cf. Mises 1928/1981, 11f., 28f.). Earlier versions of the frequency theory – for example, that of John Venn (1834–1923) – had contained only a limit axiom. By adding the axiom of randomness, von Mises implicitly turned his system into a theory of random sampling (Howson 1995, 15). Therefore, it is better suited to serve as a basis for statistics than earlier frequency theories. Nevertheless, Popper has reasons for criticism, and he proposes his own frequency theory *without a "limit-axiom"* or "axiom of convergence" and "*with a somewhat weakened 'axiom of randomness'*" (LSD, 146, i.a.). Why does he consider these modifications necessary?

8.21. Chance and Convergence

According to Popper, "[t]he most important application of the theory of probability is to what we may call '*chance-like*' or 'random' events, or occurrences" (LSD, 150). From their incalculability, it is concluded that probability theory is applicable to them. To Popper, this appears to be the "*paradoxical* conclusion from incalculability to calculability (*i.e.* to the applicability of a certain calculus)" (150, i.a.). He even considers "the fact that from incalculability – that is, from ignorance – we may draw conclusions which we can interpret as statements about empirical frequencies, and which we then find brilliantly corroborated in practice" to be "the *fundamental problem of the theory of chance*," and he believes that frequency theory "in its present form" cannot, because of its "axiom of convergence," adequately solve this problem (151). For how could we expect incalculable events to approach a limit?

Therefore, we must first examine whether and to what extent *chance-like events* may *occur regularly*. Richard von Mises devotes a section of his book *Probability, Statistics and Truth* (1928/1981, 181–183) to the *kinetic theory of gases*, which is based on the concept of probability. He reports on ways to calculate the movements of particular molecules in a closed volume by means of the – universal or deterministic – *laws of elastic collision*, and he indicates that such computations presuppose idealizing assumptions, for example, "Boltzmann's original model of a gas consisting of absolutely elastic spherical molecules" (182). But even if the movement of a ball in the direction of another ball that is at rest deviates only very slightly from the line joining their centers, the first ball may rebound in a direction forming a considerable angle with the original direction of its motion. This means "that the result of a molecular collision is decisively affected by the slightest change in the original conditions of the system" (182). Obviously, this is a kind of *deterministic chaos* arising from the fact that the initial conditions cannot be ascertained with sufficient precision.

Thus the movements in volumes of gases cannot actually be explained by the laws of elastic collision. Rather, it is appropriate "to consider the molecules as elements of a collective, and to apply to this collective the rules of *probability calculus*" (Mises 1928/1981, 181, i.a.). Moreover, according to von Mises, "a statistical gas theory no more contradicts the *causality principle* than does any other statistical explanation of observed phenomena" (183, i.a.). And, according to Popper, the concept of *chance* "is not opposed to the concept of *law*" (LSD, 206, i.a.), and it is not "the case that whenever in a particular field frequency statements are well confirmed, we are entitled to conclude that in this field *no precision* [deterministic] *statements can be made*" (246). Thus the *frequency theory* may be applied to *causally determined* events, and it does not seem paradoxical that sequences of such events approach *limits*.

But are *all* applications of the frequency theory of this kind? Popper might object that – as opposed to the kinetic theory of gases – quantum theory is *fundamentally probabilistic*, as microphysical processes are not only *chancelike* but really *random*, and that it would therefore be paradoxical to expect limits. However, is there any reason to expect that probabilistic quantum theory will never be superseded by a universal or deterministic theory? Even if no such theory should ever be found, this would not prove that microphysical processes are in fact *random*. If, on the other hand, all known applications of probability theory should equal that of the kinetic theory of gases, then *the "paradox," the "fundamental problem of the theory of chance," would result from the false assumption that at least some processes are absolutely random*. Should this assumption not be false, it is in any case *metaphysical*. And in the *Logic*, Popper still rejects "the metaphysical idea that events are, or are not, determined in themselves" (LSD, 206). Therefore the *limit axiom* is not as problematic as he suggests. When he later becomes a metaphysical indeterminist (cf. Chapter 14), he has also given up frequency theory (cf. section 8.4), so the limit axiom is no longer a problem for him (cf. LSD, 361).

8.22. Irregularity and Freedom from Aftereffects

Series of tosses of a coin are particularly simple examples of chancelike sequences, as they have only two outcomes or "events" – say, "heads" and "tails." Mises calls a collective like this "a '*simple alternative*'" (1928/1981,

34); Popper calls it "an '*alternative*'" (LSD, 152). He gives the following example:

(A) 0 1 1 0 0 0 1 1 1 0 1 0 1 0 …

Correlated with the property "1" of the alternative (A) is the sequence of relative frequencies or "frequency sequence"

(A') 0 $\frac{1}{2}$ $\frac{2}{3}$ $\frac{2}{4}$ $\frac{2}{5}$ $\frac{2}{6}$ $\frac{3}{7}$ $\frac{4}{8}$ $\frac{5}{9}$ $\frac{5}{10}$ $\frac{6}{11}$ $\frac{6}{12}$ $\frac{7}{13}$ $\frac{7}{14}$ ….

(152). Now "the *axiom of convergence* (or "limit-axiom") postulates that, as the event-sequence [A] becomes longer and longer, the frequency-sequence [A'] shall tend towards a definite *limit*' [$^1/_2$], and "[t]he *axiom of randomness* or, as it is sometimes called, 'the principle of the excluded gambling system', is designed to give mathematical expression to the chance-like character of the sequence" (153). Accordingly, "[*p*]*robability*, for von Mises, is…another term for 'limit of relative frequency in a collective'" (153).

We would have an effective *gambling system* if, on the basis of the results of past tosses, we could predict future deviations from the ideal equidistribution. We could then improve our chances by betting accordingly. More generally, we would have a gambling system if we could purposefully select subsequences in which a certain event has a relative frequency that differs from its relative frequency in the (whole) collective.

It is, however, impossible to prove that a particular sequence of events excludes *every* gambling system and thus satisfies the demand of the axiom of randomness. So how do we determine whether the frequency theory is applicable to a given sequence? Mises compares the "*principle of the impossibility of a gambling system*" to the "*law of conservation of energy*." This law excludes the possibility of "perpetual motion" machines, but it cannot be proved. Rather, it is "a broad generalization…of fundamental empirical results. The failure of all the innumerable attempts to build such a machine plays a decisive role among these" (Mises 1928/1981, 26). In the same way, the failure of all gambling systems so far "entitles us to assume the existence of *mass phenomena* or *repetitive events* to which the principle of the impossibility of a gambling system actually applies" (26f., i.a.). Only such phenomena and events are subject to his further exposition on probability theory.

Both the limit axiom and the axiom of randomness have been criticized – and, in particular, their combination, as it implies the application

of the mathematical concept of a limit "to a sequence which by definition (that is, because of the axiom of randomness) must not be subject to
any mathematical rule or law" (LSD, 154). Therefore, Kamke proposed
abandoning the axiom of randomness, and Reichenbach proposed replacing it with a weaker postulate. This is also Popper's intention, but he
considers "the improvement of the *axiom of randomness*" to be "mainly a
mathematical problem," while "the complete elimination of the *axiom of
convergence* [is] a matter of particular concern for the *epistemologist*" (LSD,
154, i.a.). For he fears that the axiom of convergence prevents the solution of the "fundamental problem of the theory of chance" (151). But a
limit *axiom* becomes superfluous if a limit *theorem* can be proved, and the
axiom of randomness may be dispensed with if certain sequences can be
found "which would pass statistical *tests* of randomness" (LSD, 361, i.a.).
In 1959, he no longer believes "in the importance of the undoubted fact
that a frequency theory can be constructed which is free of all the old
difficulties" (362). At any rate, it is only on the basis of such tests that we
could form an opinion as to whether a particular sequence satisfies the
axiom of randomness.

In order to replace the axiom of (strict) *randomness* with a weaker
requirement of *irregularity*, Popper introduces the concept of *freedom from
aftereffects* (LSD, 159ff.). Let

(α)   1 1 0 0 1 1 0 0 1 1 0 0 1 1 0 0...

be an alternative consisting of a thousand ones and zeros arranged as
shown. If we now "select from α all terms with the neighbourhood-
property [β] of *immediately succeeding a one*" (160), then we obtain the
subsequence

($\alpha \cdot \beta$)   1 0 1 0 1 0 1 0 1 0 1 0...

In both sequences, the relative frequency of 'one' and 'zero' are equal –
that is, $1/2$. Therefore, the alternative α is "*insensitive* to selection according to the property β" (160). Except for a slight deviation, this holds as
well for the property $\neg\beta$ "of being the successor of a zero." Thus we may
say that "α is insensitive to *every* selection according to the property of
the *immediate predecessor*" (161). Instead, Popper also says "'α is free from
any aftereffect of *single* predecessors' or briefly, 'α is 1-free'" (162).

Now, a sequence γ (with equal distribution) can also be insensitive to
selection according to *pairs, triples, . . . , n-tuples* of predecessors. Popper
then says "γ is 2-free," "γ is 3-free," . . . , "γ is *n*-free" (LSD, 162). But
sequences with these properties may be *systematically constructed*. We may,

for example, construct the 1-free alternative α "by repeating the *generating period*

(A)   1 1 0 0 . . .

any number of times" (162); and by repeating the generating period

(D)   0 1 1 0 0 0 1 1 1 0 1 0 1 0 0 1 0 0 0 0 0 1 0 1 1 1 1 1 0 0 1 1 . . .

we obtain a 4-free alternative. Popper states "that the intuitive impression of being faced with an irregular sequence becomes stronger with the growth of the number n of its n-freedom" (163).

This suits Popper's purposes, for he tries "*to trace the highly irregular features of chance sequences by means of mathematical sequences which must conform to the strictest rules*" (LSD, 172, i.a.). A *collective*, as defined by von Mises, *cannot* have a *generating period*, as it excludes *every* gambling system. Popper considers this requirement too strong. Therefore, he proposes "to replace von Mises's principle of the excluded gambling system by the less exacting *requirement of 'absolute freedom'*, in the sense of n-freedom for every n, and accordingly to *define chance-like mathematical sequences* as those which fulfil this requirement" (171, i.a.). We might also say that (truly) *random* sequences are replaced by (merely) *chancelike* sequences – that is, sequences that, though they are regular, exclude *simple* gambling systems "which could be used without knowing the first element of the sequence" (172). And while, according to von Mises's theory, only *infinite* sequences may be *irregular*, *finite* sequences may be *absolutely free* in Popper's sense. (Unfortunately, Popper in some places equates "chancelike" or "randomlike" sequences to "random" sequences (e.g., 173, 174f., 187), although in another place he emphasizes that he "called probability sequences chance-*like*," because the concept of chance "is not opposed to the concept of law"; if "[w]e encounter 'chance'" means "our probability estimates are corroborated" [206].)

The requirement of "absolute freedom" is intended to eliminate the "apparent paradox of an argument from unpredictability to predictability," for the paradox simply "disappears when we realize that the assumption of irregularity can be put in the form of a *frequency hypothesis* (that of freedom from aftereffects)" (LSD, 188f.).

8.23. Objective Probability

Popper's definition of a "chancelike" sequence serves as the basis for his (preliminary) definition of probability: "A frequency-limit corresponding to a sequence which is random [actually: "chancelike or randomlike"] is called the *objective probability* of the property in question, within the sequence concerned" (LSD, 173). Popper wants to show that this definition "suffices for the derivation of the main theorems of the mathematical theory of probability, especially *Bernoulli's theorem*" (173, i.a.). Applied to our case, this "Law of Large Numbers" states: "The probability P that the relative frequency of 1's in a group of n experiments lies between $(p - \varepsilon)$ and $(p + \varepsilon)$, tends toward unity as n increases indefinitely, however small the value of ε" (cf. Mises 1928/1981, 114).

So far Popper has restricted his "inquiry to alternatives with *frequency limits*, thus tacitly introducing an *axiom of convergence*" (LSD, 185, i.a.). In order to free himself from the axiom, he now eliminates the restriction. In order to replace the concept of a frequency limit, he constructs the concept "of a *point of accumulation of the sequence of relative frequencies*[:] A value a is said to be a point of accumulation of a sequence if after any given element there are elements deviating from a by less than a given amount, however small" (185). For brevity, he calls "every point of accumulation of the sequence of relative frequencies corresponding to an alternative α ... 'a *middle frequency of* α'" (185). Now he can modify his "definition of chance-like sequences, and of objective probability[:] Let α be an alternative (with one or several middle frequencies). Let the ones of α have one and only one middle frequency p that is 'absolutely free'; then we say that α is *chance-like* or random, and that p is the *objective probability* of the ones, within α" (187, i.a.).

As even these two definitions permit the derivation of Bernoulli's *limit theorem* (187), the "*axiom of convergence* is not a necessary part of the foundations of the calculus of probability" (LSD, 189, i.a.). According to Howson, however, "long-run frequencies cannot be shown to approximate probabilities without explicitly building that condition into the meaning of the probability function, in which case the limiting relative frequency definition becomes virtually obligatory" (1995, 17).

In Appendix IV to the *Logic*, Popper supplements his proposal to substitute the less exacting *requirement of freedom from aftereffects* for the *axiom of randomness* by introducing "a method of constructing models for random sequences" (LSD, 292). This proposal is soon criticized, and Popper tries to take these criticisms into account by adding notes (cf. Miller 1994, 180; LSD, 165 n*1, 171 n*1). Copeland and Reichenbach offer similar proposals (cf. Ackermann 1976, 77; LSD, 162 n*2).

But as Popper later comes to prefer the "*measure-theoretical* approach" to probability, he no longer thinks "that the elimination of the limit axiom from the frequency theory is very important" (LSD, 361). After all, frequency theory itself has become dispensable. Consequently, we need not examine further details of his proposal here. More detailed discussions may be found in Ackermann (1976), Miller (1994), and Schroeder-Heister (1998). Still, Popper has made an important contribution to our understanding of the frequency theories (Schroeder-Heister 1998, 187).

Kolmogorov's axiomatic theory, on which most contemporary expositions of probability are based, also counts among the "measure-theoretical approaches" (cf. Gnedenko 1968; Rényi 1971). Much like Popper, Kolmogorov developed a theory of *finite* random sequences, and, as Fine proved, randomness (in Kolmogorov's sense) *by itself* implies that relative frequencies obviously converge (Howson 1995, 17).

8.3. THE PROBLEM OF DECIDABILITY

Like universal hypotheses, *probability hypotheses* are *not verifiable*. But unlike universal hypotheses, they are *not falsifiable* either (LSD, 191), for "[p]robability hypotheses *do not rule out anything observable*; [they] cannot contradict, or be contradicted by, a basic statement [or] by a conjunction of any finite number of basic statements" (190). Therefore, the "indubitable fact that we use them empirically must appear as a fatal blow to [Popper's] *basic ideas on method* which depend crucially upon [his] *criterion of demarcation*" (191, i.a.).

Consider a series of 1,000 tosses of a coin. Even if we obtain exactly 500 "heads" and 500 "tails," so that the *relative frequency* $rf(h)$ of heads (in this finite subsequence or sample of the sequence [according to von Mises: collective] of infinitely many tosses of this coin) is exactly $\frac{1}{2}$, this does not prove that (the coin is symmetrical and homogeneous and therefore) the probability $p(h)$ of heads (according to von Mises: the limit of the relative frequency of heads in this infinite collective) is $\frac{1}{2}$. This holds correspondingly of arbitrarily large samples with the same relative frequency. Hence the hypothesis $p(h) = \frac{1}{2}$ is *not verifiable*.

Rather, we can say only that, in view of the hypothesis $p(h) = \frac{1}{2}$, the relative frequency $rf(h) = \frac{1}{2}$ is more probable than any other sample distribution, even though it is only minimally more probable than, say, the relation of 499 heads to 501 tails. Conversely, the equidistribution in the sample [$rf(h) = \frac{1}{2}$] is more probable in view of hypothesis $p(h) = \frac{1}{2}$ than it is in view of any other hypothesis $p(h) = r$, where $r > \frac{1}{2}$ or $r < \frac{1}{2}$.

If, on the other hand, in the same experiment we obtain 1,000 heads and no tails – that is, if in our sample $rf(h) = 1$, then this result still does not logically contradict our hypothesis $p(h) = \frac{1}{2}$. (One might think that this result would be compensated for when we continue tossing the coin and obtain more tails than heads. But in an infinite sequence of throws, the ratio of heads and tails does not change when an arbitrarily long but finite sequence of heads is inserted.) Hence the hypothesis $p(h) = \frac{1}{2}$ is *not falsifiable* either. Rather, a sample like ours $[rf(h) = 1]$ is only extremely improbable, if the hypothesis $p(h) = \frac{1}{2}$ is true.

As probability hypotheses are not strictly falsifiable, Popper "should . . . really describe them . . . as void of empirical content" (LSD, 190). But this would clearly be "unacceptable in face of the *success* which physics has achieved with predictions obtained from hypothetical estimates of probabilities. . . . Many of these estimates are not inferior in scientific significance to any other physical hypothesis (for example, to one of a determinist character)" (190f.). But how can the predictive success of probability hypotheses be assessed, if they are neither verifiable nor falsifiable? A "physicist is usually quite well able to decide whether he may for the time being accept some particular probability hypothesis as 'empirically confirmed', or whether he ought to reject it as 'practically falsified, *i.e.*, as useless for purposes of prediction" (191). How then does he draw this distinction? This "*'practical falsification'* can be obtained only through a *methodological decision* to regard highly improbable events as ruled out – as prohibited" (191, i.a.).

As is common practice in statistics, a region of acceptance and a corresponding region of rejection is defined. Occurrences that are very unlikely in view of the hypothesis fall within the region of rejection. If a test results in such a sample, then the hypothesis is rejected for the present; otherwise, it is accepted for the present. The definition of a region of acceptance and a region of rejection functions as a "*methodological rule* . . . which makes probability hypotheses falsifiable" (LSD, 191 n*1, i.a.). We need not follow Popper's considerations any further, for they add nothing to what we know from statistics textbooks. In order to be in accord with empirical science, *Popper modifies his criterion of falsifiability to a criterion of testability*. Here it becomes apparent how philosophy hastens after science. On the other hand, this modification – the introduction of an additional methodological rule permitting "practical" falsifications – is in accord with his methodology.

8.4. FORMAL SYSTEMS OF ABSOLUTE AND OF
RELATIVE PROBABILITY

In 1938, Popper's article "A Set of Independent Axioms for Probability" appeared in *Mind*. Its introductory text has been added to *The Logic of Scientific Discovery* (1959) as Appendix *II, "A Note on Probability." Here he states "that the mathematical theory of probability should be constructed as a '*formal*' *system*; that is to say, a system which should be susceptible of many different interpretations, among them, for example, (1) the classical interpretation, (2) the frequency interpretation, and (3) the logical interpretation" (LSD, 318). We shall return to Laplace's classical definition of probability later (section 8.52).

Popper discusses two ways of designing axiom systems of probability. On the one hand, we may construct a *system of conditional or relative probability*, in which the two-termed functor

$$p(x_1, x_2),$$

which can be read as "'the probability of x_1 with regard to x_2,'" appears as an "(undefined) primitive variable" (LSD, 320). Then a second, one-termed functor "'$pa(x_1)$'" may be introduced by the equation

$$pa(x_1) = p(x_1 \neg (x_2 \wedge \neg x_2)),$$

which defines the "'*absolute* probability'" of x_1 as the relative probability of x_1 with regard to the tautology or the necessary event (321).

On the other hand, we may construct a *system of absolute probability* "in which '$pa(x_1)$' appears as (undefined) primitive variable." Using the equation

$$p(x_1, x_2) = pa(x_1 \wedge x_2)/pa(x_2),$$

we may then define the *conditional* probability of x_1 with regard to x_2 (LSD, 321). Popper still thinks that this *second method* is *superior* to the first one, and so he designs an axiom system of absolute probability (319).

But the idea that he has developed, as he "believe[s] for the first time," a calculus of probability that is "susceptible of many *different interpretations*" is erroneous. It is true that in 1938 he did not know Kolmogorov's *Foundations of Probability*, "although it had been first published in German in 1933" (LSD, 318), but this doesn't explain his error. Rather, in 1959 he still thinks that Kolmogorov's system is "less 'formal' than [his], and therefore susceptible to fewer interpretations," for Kolmogorov "interprets the arguments of the probability functor as *sets*; accordingly, he assumes that they have members (or 'elements')" (318f.).

This, however, in no way restricts the possibilities of interpreting the probability functor, as a brief look at Kolmogorov's axioms of the elementary theory of probability shows (1933/1956, 2). Let *E* be the set {α, β, ..., τ} of the *elementary events* α, β, ..., τ (say, of all possible results of throwing a die), and let the field *F* be the set of all subsets of *E*. Then the elements of *F* (not those of *E*) are called "*random events*," and every random event *A* in *F* is assigned a non-negative real number *P(A)*, where *P(E)* = 1. Suppose we set up an experiment and are interested in the probability of the result σ. It is represented as the probability $P(\{\sigma\})$ of the random event $\{\sigma\}$, that is, of the set that contains the elementary event σ as its sole element. This representation, however, implies nothing as to the possible interpretations of "σ" and hence of "$P(\{\sigma\})$" (cf. Gnedenko 1968, 42). Hence *Kolmogorov rightly claims that his axioms admit, like every axiomatic theory*, "*of an unlimited number of concrete interpretations*" (1933/1956, 1).

Popper later develops *systems of relative probability* (cf. BJPS 1955b; *Logic*, Appendix *IV, "The Formal Theory of Probability"). Now he considers the *first method superior*. He also reverts to the problem of the *interpretations* and tries to show that Kolmogorov's axioms exclude some of them. According to Popper, Kolmogorov assumes that "in '*p(a, b)*' – [he is] using [his] own symbols, not [Kolmogorov's] – *a* and *b* are *sets*; thereby excluding, among others, the logical interpretation according to which *a* and *b* are statements" (LSD, 327). Popper admits that it is of no importance *what* the members of the set *E* represent. Yet he objects that "in some interpretations, *a* and *b* have *no members*, nor anything that might correspond to members" (327). In 1983, he even speaks of a "*set-theoretic interpretation*" of probability (RAS, 283, i.a.).

But just as we may take the *results* α, β, ..., τ *of random experiments* to be elementary events and mean their probability when we assign probabilities formally to the sets {α}, {β}, ..., {τ}, we may also take the *statements* *a*, *b*, ..., *t* to be elementary "events" and mean their probability when we assign probabilities to the sets {*a*}, {*b*}, ..., {*t*}. We may even write *A*, *B*, ..., *T* instead of {*a*}, {*b*}, ..., {*t*}. The fact that *A* is then a set whose sole element is the statement *a*, and so on, does not in any way exclude the logical interpretation. Rather, it permits the application of the algebra of sets to *A*, *B*, ..., *T*, and as the algebra of sets and propositional logic are homeomorphous (Boolean algebra may be interpreted both as a calculus of classes and as a sentential calculus), it also permits the application of propositional logic to $a, b, \ldots, t$. Nevertheless, there is a difference. Statements that are arguments whose values are *logical* probabilities may refer to *events* (Ceasar's death, the throw of this die made yesterday at 10:00 A.M.), while *empirical* probabilities are assigned to *kinds of events* (death, throw of this die) (Carnap 1950, 35; Eells 1991, 38). But this is quite independent of our representing events as sets or mapping events onto sets.

Popper believes that his system of axioms has still another advantage. While *Kolmogorov's axioms* for absolute probability *presuppose the algebra of sets, Popper's axioms* "for relative probability . . . alone *guarantee that all the laws of Boolean algebra hold for the elements*" (LSD, 328). Among these, for example, are the associative laws, the commutative laws, and the laws of tautology. If we presuppose these laws, then "we prevent ourselves from finding out *what kind of relations are implied by our axioms or postulates*. But to find this out is one of the main points of the axiomatic method" (329). However, is it therefore advantageous to formulate axioms with greater logical content than would be necessary for the purposes of probability theory (331), just in order to be able to derive as many theorems as possible?

In Appendix *V, "Derivations in the Formal Theory of Probability," Popper gives the most important derivations from the system of postulates explained in Appendix *IV. For example, he shows how the laws mentioned in the previous paragraph can be proved. Thus his system of *probability theory* is a genuine *generalization* of *propositional logic* and not just its extension (Miller 1997, 385). To show that this is possible remains, of course, an honourable goal.

While Popper considers the possibility of this generalization to be an important *advantage of a system of conditional probabilities*, other authors have developed similar systems for different reasons. For example, Rényi points out that certain problems cannot be dealt with, or present great difficulties, in Kolmogorov's theory of probability. In physics, in the theory of Markov chains, and in the application of number theory and integral geometry we find non-normalizable distributions – that is, unbounded measures – that [because of the postulate $P(E) = 1$] have no meaning in Kolmogorov's system (Rényi 1971, 56). On the other hand, we may obtain meaningful values corresponding to experience if we choose non-normalizable distributions. Therefore, Rényi develops an axiomatic theory of probability whose basic concept is relative probability and which contains Kolmogorov's theory as a special case. Leblanc (1989) compares the systems of Kolmogorov, Rényi, and Popper and is rather sceptical about Popper's attempt to keep probability theory autonomous by not presupposing Boolean algebra.

There is another reason why Popper prefers systems of *conditional* probability. It is indicated in his "A Note on Probability" (Appendix *II). Popper wants "to show that what [he] had called in [*Logic*] '*degree of corroboration*' (or of 'confirmation' or of 'acceptability') was *not a 'probability*': that its properties were incompatible with the formal calculus of probability" (LSD, 318, i.a.; cf. section 5.4). It is perhaps doubtful that he succeeds, but his later approach presupposes that the probability $p(e, h)$ of a fact or an observation statement e relative to a hypothesis h can be known. On the other hand, he wants to express the idea that a universal hypothesis h is logically so strong that its absolute probability $p(h)$ must equal 0. Though most authors, among them Carnap, share this assumption, it is not uncontested either. But – in view of the definition $p(e, h) = p(e \wedge h) \,/\, p(h)$ of conditional probability – $p(e, h)$ would then have no definite value. This problem can be avoided by choosing an axiom system of conditional probability.

In his article "A World of Propensities: Two New Views of Causality," Popper mentions another reason, which seems to be really decisive (WP, 1–26). He asserts: When probabilities change in the course of an experiment, "*a calculus of relative or conditional probabilities*" is required to render a propensity interpretation possible (15f.). This, however, is not at all obvious either (as we shall see).

8.5. THE PROPENSITY THEORY

In his article "The Propensity Interpretation of the Calculus of Probability, and the Quantum Theory" (1957b), Popper outlines the propensity theory of probability. He begins his exposition with eight theses. They describe the problem that his theory is designed to solve and may be summarized as follows: (1) The interpretation of probability theory is fundamental to the interpretation of quantum theory. (2) The statistical interpretation is correct but unclear. (3) Therefore, the interpretation of probability in physics oscillates between an objective, purely statistical interpretation and a subjective interpretation expressing our incomplete knowledge. (4) This holds also of the Copenhagen interpretation of quantum theory. Thus the observer intrudes into physics. (5, 6) In order to solve these problems, Popper proposes the purely objective propensity interpretation of probability. (7) The idea of propensities is "metaphysical" in the same sense that the ideas of forces or fields of forces are metaphysical. (8) The idea is also "metaphysical" insofar as it provides a coherent programme for physical research (1957b, 65).

In further articles, and above all in the three volumes of his *Postscript to the Logic of Scientific Discovery*, Popper elaborates the propensity theory. In 1956, a considerable part of the work had been done and a copyright was conferred. While the first part of the first volume, *Realism and the Aim of Science* (1983), returns to the most important themes of the methodology of critical rationalism, its second part deals uniquely with the propensity interpretation of probability. In the second volume, *The Open Universe* (1982), Popper wants to show that metaphysical determinism has stood in the way of the propensity interpretation; and in the third volume, *Quantum Theory and the Schism in Physics* (1982), he intends to show that "with the help of the propensity interpretation, a new metaphysics of physics can be constructed" (RAS, 361).

In 1988, Popper gave a lecture before the World Congress of Philosophy at Brighton that he elaborated and published in 1990 as "A World of Propensities: Two New Views of Causality" (WP, 1–26). His central problem now is "*causality* and the change of our view of the world" (7, i.a.). Here he develops his final, and philosophically most demanding, theses on propensity theory: Objective probabilities are measures of physically real *propensities*; classical physics is only apparently deterministic – rather, its *forces* are special cases of propensities; hence we live in a world of propensities.

Thus Popper also hopes to save his ideas of creativity and freedom of will (cf. 14.). For if, like Descartes, we regard the world as "an *ideally precise* clockwork" (WP, 7), then there is "no room for human *decisions*" (7, i.a.). According to this determinist worldview, we only believe that we are planning and acting freely. But quantum theory, in particular Heisenberg's uncertainty principle, has revealed a certain imprecision in the clockwork.

The interpretation of quantum theory is still controversial. For example, it is debated whether the processes of microphysics are in the final analysis *random*, or whether, as Einstein assumed, they are basically *causal*. In the first case, quantum theory would be irreducibly probabilistic; in the second case, a – logically stronger – deterministic theory of quantum physics would in principle be possible. The fact that we make do with the *probabilistic* hypotheses of quantum theory until a deterministic theory can be found would then – as in the case of the kinetic theory of gases – be due to our *lack of knowledge*. This was also Einstein's view, which Popper criticizes, asserting that Einstein "adopted a *subjectivist* theory of probability" (WP, 8). Popper himself wishes "to adopt an *objectivist* theory" (8).

But Popper's criticism is unfortunate, to say the least, as von Mises's argument shows. The kinetic theory of gases is a part of statistical mechanics. It explains properties of gases such as pressure and temperature by referring to the movements of molecules. Hence it does not *refer* to our knowledge or lack of knowledge. In this sense it is not "subjective" but "objective." However, we use it *because of* our lack of knowledge, for we lack the perfect methods of measuring and computation that would be required for explaining the properties of gases by means of classical deterministic mechanics. Popper seems to approve this argument (WP, 25), but he does not apply it to quantum physics.

This would be easily possible, even though a deterministic theory of microphysics is (still) lacking, if quantum theory were interpreted "objectively" – as a system of statements *about elementary particles* – and not "subjectively" – as a system of statements *about our knowledge of elementary particles.* On the other hand, the Copenhagen interpretation of quantum theory is "subjective" insofar as it postulates that the concept "event" must be restricted to observation, because quantum theory does not permit a spatiotemporal description of what happens between two observations. But Einstein never sided with this interpretation. Hence there is no reason to suspect that he "adopted a subjectivist theory of probability."

8.51. The Probability of Single Events

According to the *frequency theory*, which Popper initially favoured, "only the notion of *probability in a given collective*...is unambiguous" (Mises 1928/1981, 20). Therefore, statements such as " 'the probability of throwing five with the *next* throw of this die is 1/6,' " which ascribe probabilities to *single occurrences*, are, strictly speaking, incorrect (LSD, 209f., i.a.). This restricts the applicability of the frequency theory.

It is true that the *subjective* interpretation of probability admits singular probabilities, for it takes probabilities to be "measures of the strength of belief," and "an individual might have a belief about a single coin toss that he is willing to translate into a bet" (Ackermann 1976, 79; in analogy to "singular statements," Popper speaks of "singular events" and "singular probabilities" – 1959, 27). However, Popper needs a theory of *objective* probability in order to fight the subjective interpretation of quantum theory (Popper 1957b, 66). In particular, his reinterpretation of the double-slit experiment presupposes *probabilities of singular events*. It also convinces him "that probabilities must be '*physically real*,'" "*physical propensities*" *to realize singular events* (Popper 1959, 28, i.a.).

Initially, Popper had hoped to solve the problem of singular probability statements within the *frequency theory* by means of an appropriate definition. In his *Logic*, he calls "a probability statement '*formally singular*' when it ascribes a probability to a single occurrence" (LSD, 209, i.a.) and proposes a definition: "*The formally singular probability* that the event *k* [e.g., the *k*-th toss of this coin] has the property *β* [say, "heads"] – given that *k* is an element of the sequence *α* [of all tosses of this coin] – *is, by definition, equal to the probability* of the property *β within the reference sequence α*" (210, i.a.).

This definition implies that the *value* of the formally singular probability *equals* that of the objective probability: $_\alpha p(\beta_k) = {_\alpha p(\beta)}$, if $k \, \varepsilon \, \alpha$. Later, he puts his idea in more concrete terms: "[T]he statement 'the probability that the next toss will be heads is one-half' *means* the same as the hypothesis 'the relative frequency of the heads in a sequence (whether finite or infinite) of tosses with this coin is one-half'" (RAS, 387). Now it is clear that he postulates the *synonymy* of singular probability *statements* with statements on [objective probabilities or] *relative frequencies*: $_\alpha p(\beta_k) = {^1/_2}$ def.$\equiv [_\alpha p(\beta) = {^1/_2}$ def.$\equiv] \, _\alpha rf(\beta) = {^1/_2}$.

But in his article "The Propensity Interpretation of the Calculus of Probability, and the Quantum Theory," Popper himself constructs an *objection* to this proposal (1957b, 65f.), which he later reformulates several times (1959, 31ff.; RAS, 352ff.). Consider a sequence *c* of throws with a symmetrical and homogeneous die and another sequence *a* of throws with a loaded die. The probability of a six in *c* equals 1/6, and we let the probability of a six in *a* equal 1/4. What does it then mean to say "The *probability* of throwing a six *with the next throw* is *r*"? According to the definition in the last paragraph, it means "The *relative frequency* of throwing a six *in a sequence of throws* (with this or that die) is *r*." Hence *r* depends on the sequence.

In order to show that this answer is unsatisfactory, we select two or three throws from *c* and insert them into *a*. Thus we obtain a new sequence *b*. Which is now the probability of a six with respect to the inserted sequence $b \wedge c$? As $b \wedge c$ has at most three elements, it cannot be a collective. Hence, according to the frequency theory, a six cannot have a probability with respect to $b \wedge c$. Moreover, the relative frequency of a six in $b \wedge c$ can neither be $1/4$ nor $1/6$. On the other hand, the fact that the elements of $b \wedge c$ were taken from c leads us to expect the probability $1/6$, whereas the fact that $b \wedge c$ is part of b leads us to expect the probability $1/4$. But, according to Popper, we do not doubt that the probability of a six in $b \wedge c$ is to be estimated on the basis of the relative frequency of a six in sequence c, because $b \wedge c$ results from throws with the fair die (1959, 33).

Adherents of the frequency theory will argue that b is, because of the inserted sequence $b \wedge c$, not a genuine collective either, for a collective must result from a series of *repeated* experiments – say, throws with the *same* die. But this means that they define a *collective* "by its set of *generating conditions*," and, as they assume "that a probability is *a property of some given sequence*," a probability may, according to Popper, "now be said to be *a property of the generating conditions*" (1959, 34). This, however, "amounts to a transition from the *frequency* interpretation to the *propensity* interpretation" (34, i.a.).

At first sight, this seems to be only a shift of accent. But Popper concludes from this, on the one hand, that "a singular event may have a probability even though it may occur only once; for its probability is a property of its generating conditions" (1959, 34). And he believes that the problem of the *probability of a singular event* has thus been solved in a way that is no longer subject to his self-constructed objection. Von Mises, however, states explicitly that "[t]he rational concept of *probability*, which is the only basis of probability calculus, *applies only to* problems in which either the same event repeats itself again and again [*repetitive events*], or a great number of uniform elements are involved at the same time [*mass phenomena*]" (1928/1981, 11, i.a.); and most authors follow him.

On the other hand, Popper concludes that we therefore "*have to* visualise the conditions as endowed with a *tendency*, or *disposition*, or *propensity*, to produce sequences whose frequencies are equal to the probabilities; which is precisely what the propensity interpretation asserts" (1959, 35, i.a.). Thus, however, Popper takes a position that Hume had criticized as metaphysical. For, according to Hume, anyone who uses the hypothesis $(x)(Fx \rightarrow Gx)$ to state the exceptionless association of events of kind F with events of kind G need by no means assume a *cause*, say in F, that brings forth this association. Why should we then, when we assert an association between an experimental setup (a situation in the broadest sense) and a sequence of events, have to assume that the experimental setup is endowed with the *propensity* to produce this sequence?

8.52. From Causality to Propensity

Popper does not, however, propose a propensity interpretation of the frequency theory of probability. Rather, in 1955 he publishes his *measure-theoretical* formalism of conditional probability (cf. section 8.4; LSD, Appendix *IV). Its main significance "lies in the fact that measure-theoretical probability statements are *singular* probability statements"; and "*from the point of view of physics, a singular probability . . . can best be interpreted as a physical propensity*" (RAS, 347).

Therefore, he proposes "*a new physical hypothesis*" (RAS, 360). Parenthetically, he admits that this hypothesis might instead be *metaphysical.* He claims that it is "analogous to the hypothesis of Newtonian forces" and asserts "that every experimental arrangement (and therefore *every state of a system*) generates *propensities* [i.a.] which can sometimes be tested by [relative] *frequencies* [i.a.]." His new hypothesis is to be testable in its turn and could even be "corroborated by certain quantum experiments" (360). Furthermore, the "main argument in favour of the propensity interpretation is to be found in its power to eliminate from quantum theory certain disturbing elements of an irrational and subjectivist character," and it is "by its success or failure in this field of application that the propensity interpretation will have to be judged" (351f.).

While quantum theory is empirically successful, its interpretation is controversial. Popper sides with Born's (1882–1970) statistical interpretation of the quantum mechanical wave functions. But he rejects the explanation (the Copenhagen interpretation) of their statistical character as due to the fundamental inexactitude of every measurement of complementary magnitudes (Heisenberg's [1901–1976] uncertainty principle; LSD, 217ff.). Rather, he thinks that the uncertainty relations must be interpreted as statistical scatter relations, because the fundamental equations of quantum theory themselves – for instance, Schrödinger's (1887–1961) wave equations – are interpreted statistically. And since the theory, if it is statistically interpreted, does not rule out exact single measurements, he considers "Heisenberg's limitation upon attainable precision" to be a "dogma" that can be refuted by a thought experiment (LSD, 231). When Einstein criticizes it – his letter is reproduced in the *Logic* – Popper bases his thesis that a particle "has" both a precise position and a precise momentum on the experiment of Einstein, Podolsky, and Rosen (457ff.). In 1983, he still declares the *double-slit experiment* to be "something like a *crucial experiment* between the purely statistical and the propensity interpretation of probability," and he believes that it decides "the issue against the purely statistical interpretation" (RAS, 360). We cannot here examine his interpretation of the experiment. Among physicists, it did not exactly meet with general consent. Düsberg (1998) gives a short description.

In his article "The Propensity Interpretation of Probability" (1959), Popper proposes "a propensity interpretation of the neo-classical (measure-theoretical) formalism" (LSD, 165f. n*1). Eventually, in 1987, he realizes "its *cosmological significance*" [i.a.] – namely, "the fact that we live in *a world of propensities*" (WP, 9). Forces that we took to be the *causes* of events in our world now appear to be only special cases of *propensities*.

But what are *propensities*? In order to give an explanation, Popper first refers to *possibilities*, which he in turn expounds in the light of the *classical* definition of probability. Why does he return to this oldest definition? According to Laplace's definition, in an experiment with finitely many equally possible results the probability of an event equals the ratio of the number of results *favourable* to this event to the number of all *possible* results. Thus when throwing a fair die we have six equally possible results, three of which are favourable to the event "even number." But Popper *reifies* the attribute "possible" when he writes: " 'The probability of an event is the number of the favourable *possibilities* divided by the number of all the equal *possibilities*' " (WP, 9). And this is not merely an unfortunate mode of expression, for he continues: "Thus the classical theory was about mere *possibilities*" (9), and "a tendency or propensity to realize an event is, in general, *inherent in every possibility*" (11).

Probabilities are *weights* of these *possibilities*. If a die is fair, the six possibilities have equal weight; if it is loaded, they have different weights. Equal possibilities are special cases of weighted possibilities. They can obviously "be regarded as weighted possibilities whose weights happen to be equal" (WP, 10). Thus the classical definition of probability is only a special case that is to be generalized.

The "actual *weight* of the weighted possibilities" (WP, 10, i.a.) can be statistically estimated if "the situation that produces the probabilistic events in question" repeats itself (11). In this connection, "the greater or smaller *frequency of occurrences* may be used as a test of whether a hypothetically attributed weight is, indeed, an adequate hypothesis" (11). Hence probability is no longer *defined* – as it is according to the classical definition – with respect to relative frequencies, but it is still *estimated* by means of relative frequencies (e.g., statistical averages). This is unproblematic, but stronger theses now follow.

If we "can measure the weight of the possibility of '*two turning up*' in throwing a certain loaded die, and find it to be only 0.15 instead of

0.1666 = 1/6 [,] then there must be inherent in the structure of throws with this die...a *tendency or propensity* to realize the event '*two turning up*' that is smaller than the tendency shown by a fair die" (WP, 11). Accordingly, Popper's first point is "that a tendency or propensity to realize an event is, in general, *inherent in every possibility* and in every single throw"; and the measure of this propensity is estimated "by appealing to the relative frequency of the actual realization in a large number of throws" (11).

If all relevant conditions remain stable, then statistical averages tend to remain stable as well. Thus we

explain the tendency or propensity of a sequence of throws with a die to produce (from any starting sequence) stable statistical frequencies by (a) the inner structure of the die, (b) the invisible field of forces carried with it by our planet, and (c) friction, etc. – in short, by the invariant aspects of the physical *situation*: the field of propensities that influences every single throw. (WP, 12)

Only the propensity theory explains that "*tendencies* or *propensities* to realize themselves...are inherent in all *possibilities* in various degrees and...are something like *forces* that keep the statistics stable" (WP, 12, i.a.). This is "an *objective interpretation of the theory of probability*" (12). According to this interpretation, *propensities*

are not mere possibilities but *are physical realities*. They are as real as forces, or fields of forces. And vice versa: *forces are propensities*. They are propensities for setting bodies in motion. Forces are propensities to accelerate, and fields of forces are propensities distributed over some region of space.... Fields of forces are *fields of propensities*. They *are real*, they exist. (12, i.a.)

But can a physically real propensity be inherent in a mere possibility, or should possibilities be physically real as well? In *The Open Universe*, Popper in fact postulates "*physical possibilities*" (OU, 105; cf. section 14.62).

The *physical* "*propensity 1* is the special case of a classical *force* in action: a *cause* when it produces an effect" (WP, 13, i.a.). And a *propensity < 1* "can be envisaged as the existence of *competing forces* pulling in various opposed directions" (13, i.a.). But if we envisage the competition according to the parallelogram of forces, then its result would be determined. Hence chancelike events could be explained only by assuming that now one force prevails, now the other, each with its own probability. Thus Popperian forces would fundamentally differ from the forces of classical physics. (This objection seems to have been raised for the first time by Mellor; cf. O'Hear 1992, 136.)

On the other hand, "*zero propensities* are, simply, *no* propensities at all" (WP, 13, i.a.). This is not plausible either, for if we assume, as Popper does, competing forces, then the idea of two equal forces pulling in opposite directions suggests itself. But he refers to a *logically impossible event* – like that "of getting the number 14 on the next throw with two ordinary dice" (13) – which, as such, has zero propensity. On the other hand, even if their *probability* equals *zero*, logically possible events may actually happen. Do we thus have to assume that a *propensity 1* prevailed in this rare case and caused this effect?

Popper's *introduction of propensities* is intended to *generalize the idea of Newtonian forces* (WP, 14). We have already indicated that *forces always* have certain effects, whereas *propensities* obviously have effects only *with a certain probability*. But there is also an important *methodological* difference. Newton's laws imply *testable statements about forces and about the movements of bodies*. For example, his *second law of mechanics*, $F = ma$, asserts that the force F acting on a body is equal to the product of its mass m and its acceleration a. In order to compute the force, we must know the mass and the acceleration. And if we want to apply Newton's *law of gravitation*, $F = G \cdot m_1 \cdot m_2 / r^2$, we must know, apart from the gravitational constant G, the masses of the bodies, m_1 and m_2, and the distance between them, r. As opposed to this, statements about propensities can only be tested in the form of those very probability statements whose interpretations they are. Therefore, it is *in principle not empirically testable* whether these *probabilities* are effects of propensities or even are *propensities* themselves (cf. O'Hear 1992, 133).

Popper emphasizes that propensities are not "properties *inherent in an object*" but are "*inherent in a situation*" of which an object may be a part (WP, 14). According to him, this is "decisively important for a realist interpretation of quantum theory" (14). A change in a situation changes the possibilities, and thus the propensities. In order to illustrate this, he gives a simple example: "[T]he propensity of a penny to fall on a flat table with heads up is obviously modified if the table top is appropriately slotted" (15).

Does he really want to say that because of some slots in the surface on which the penny falls, heads could occur more frequently than tails, or vice versa? This effect could hardly be physically explained. Or does he mean that the penny comes to a halt on its edge when it falls into a slot? This is O'Hear's interpretation (1992, 133). But then the example is not well chosen, for in his *Logic* Popper takes tossing a coin to be a process that produces an "alternative," although it is neither logically nor physically impossible that on a perfectly even surface a penny should come to a halt on its edge. Gamblers and statisticians ignore such throws. Otherwise, they would have to consider not two but three possible results of tossing a coin; the third one would be extremely improbable, and it could only be a residual category such as "neither heads nor tails." For it would not suffice to consider "comes to a halt on its edge" the third result. After all, the penny could also be attracted by a magnet, fall into a waste pipe, and so on.

Popper now draws an important conclusion from his assumption that a *changing* "*situation* changes the possibilities, and thereby the propensities" (WP, 15): When the situation and thereby the propensities change, "we need a *calculus of relative or conditional probabilities*"; only when a situation does not change can we "work with *absolute* [i.a.] probabilities or absolute propensities, having once and for all described the conditions" (16). This statement has occasioned several objections, and Miller expects here "the most interesting line of criticism that the propensity theory has yet attracted" (1994, 187).

If, for example, we draw from an urn containing red and white balls without returning the balls we have drawn to the urn, then the probabilities of obtaining a red ball or a white ball on the next draw change with each draw. It is true that we need *conditional probabilities* to describe this process, but we may introduce them *by definition* into a *calculus of absolute probabilities*. Did Popper merely express himself in a misleading fashion?

Let us consider the experimental setup "throwing a symmetrical and homogeneous die." We expect that each of the events $\{1\}, \{2\}, \{3\}, \{4\},$ $\{5\}, \{6\}$ has the same absolute probability $1/6$, so that $p(\{6\}) = 1/6$. If we now shift to the experimental setup "throwing a loaded die," the set $E = \{1, 2, 3, 4, 5, 6\}$ of the elementary events remains the same, but now the same events have different *absolute* probabilities. Suppose that $p(\{6\}) = 1/4$. Thus *we may take changes in the experimental setup into account without using conditional probabilities* – probabilities relative to the respective conditions. We may even compute the probability of throwing a six four times in four throws, two of which are made with the fair and two with the loaded die; it is $1/6 \times 1/6 \times 1/4 \times 1/4 = 1/576$. This is a simple example of the *linkage of events of different experimental setups*. In principle, the probability that a machine will fail is computed in the same way.

But can we, conversely, take changes in the experimental setup into account *by using conditional probabilities?* This appears to be impossible with conventional systems of relative probability such as those designed by Popper (LSD, Appendix *IV) and Rényi (1971, 56ff.). Suppose that the formula $p(\{6\},h) = 1/6$ is meant to express that the probability of throwing a six with a *ho*mogeneous die equals $1/6$, and correspondingly that $p(\{6\},l) = 1/4$ is meant to express that the probability of throwing a six with a particular *l*oaded die equals $1/4$. These two formulas would express standard conditional probabilities only if the experimental setups h (throwing a *ho*mogeneous die) and l (throwing a *l*oaded die) were, along with their possible results, elements of the *same algebra*. This means that $E = \{1, 2, 3, 4, 5, 6\}$ would have to be replaced by $E' = \{1, 2, 3, 4, 5, 6, h, l\}$. [In Appendix *IV, Popper constructs a system of probability that is (i) formal, (ii) autonomous, and (iii) "*symmetrical*; that is to say, it is so constructed that whenever there is a probability $p(b,a)$ – *i.e.* a probability of b given a – then there is *always* a probability $p(a,b)$ also – even when the absolute probability of b, $p(b)$, equals zero" (326f., i.a.). Accordingly, whenever there is a probability $p(\{6\},h)$, there would have to be a probability $p(h,\{6\})$ also.] But as *an experimental setup is not one of its own possible results* (events), this is no solution. Would we therefore need a probability function that is defined on a *pair of algebras*, an algebra of events and an algebra of experimental setups?

    In his defence of the propensity theory, Miller proposes a different solution (1994, 186ff.). His *events* are "*completely specified situations*" – that is, states of the world – and all "propensities, absolute or conditional, are simply propensities of the present unique situation to develop into another" (189). Accordingly, $p(\{6\})$ is the probability that the present state of the world will develop into another state with "six turned up." If this solution is feasible, then our formal objection in the last paragraph will have to be dropped, for every new state of the world is also a new experimental setup. A "calculus of relative or conditional probabilities" that takes account of changing experimental setups would then be *possible*, but it would *not* be *necessary*, as the required conditional probabilities can be defined in a calculus of absolute probabilities.

PART II

THE SOCIAL PHILOSOPHY

9

Knowledge, Decision, Responsibility

Popper's social philosophy is better understood if its connection to his philosophy of science is seen: All *empirical knowledge* is fallible, but *ethical knowledge*, even fallible ethical knowledge, is impossible. In any case, all models of ethical knowledge proposed so far have failed. Hence, *as we cannot know what we ought to do, we must content ourselves with deciding what we want to do.*

In *The Open Society and its Enemies* (OS), the distinction between statements of fact, on the one hand, and value judgments, demands, and norms, on the other hand, plays a central part. Popper dedicates Chapter 5, "Nature and Convention," to this distinction. In the state of "'*naïve monism*,'" the "distinction between natural and normative laws" has not yet been made; naïve monism is "characteristic of the '*closed society*'" (OS I, 59, i.a.). Only "*critical dualism*, or critical conventionalism" consciously differentiates "between the man-enforced normative laws, based on decisions or conventions, and the natural regularities" that are beyond human power (60); it is "characteristic of the '*open society*'" (59, i.a.). Protagoras (480–410) reached this position, which holds us responsible for the standards that we choose and the norms that we follow.

It is true that "the *dualism of facts and standards*" – accentuated by Hume – is "*one of the bases of the liberal tradition*" (OS II, 392, i.a.). However, the idea that our standards – provided that they are not innate – are neither given to us nor knowably right or reasonable but must be chosen – consciously or unconsciously, independently or under the influence of others – has so far not overcome the resistance of religions and philosophies. Though their objections cannot withstand any serious criticism, anyone who succeeds in *making others believe* that he knows what God has

193

commanded, or what is good, or which norms and value judgments are right, succeeds more easily in his intentions. On the other hand, anyone who *believes others* when they claim to have such moral knowledge may imagine himself free from any responsibility for the choice of his standards and for those of his actions that are orientated according to them. This is what William James considered the "cash value" of believing in the absolute.

In his late philosophy, Popper postulates a "third world ... of objective tentative knowledge which includes *objective* new tentative aims and *values*" (OK, 149, i.a.; cf. Chapter 15). This does not, however, mean that he has come closer to a "non-formal ethics of value." Rather, in his world 3, false hypotheses exist along with true ones and values that we reject exist along with values that we accept. But there is an important difference: When selecting hypotheses, we are guided by an external criterion, the empirical test against physical reality (i.e., world 1); as opposed to this, there is no comparable external criterion for the choice of aims or values.

In order that the inevitable *decision* may be *rational*, we proceed as follows: First, we try to form a clear idea of our *aims* (or of the aims of other people). Then we apply empirical hypotheses in order to find out by which *means* the ends can be reached and what are the unwanted *side effects* of their use. In view of the predicted consequences, a decision is taken. But it is always *provisional*, for the decision must be *revised* if the prediction is false or if the aims change. This already follows from *The Logic of Scientific Discovery*. Basically, this consideration can be found in Max Weber, and in outline it is sketched in Spinoza's *Tractatus theologico-politicus* (caput xx; Chapter 20).

In this outline, we take the *aims* to be given. They can, however, be *rationally chosen* in their turn, although only indirectly. For if several aims compete, an actor or an institution may, in view of the available means and the expected side effects, decide which aim is to be realized and to what degree. Whoever makes the decision is *responsible* for the choice not only of the means but also of the aims.

Mistakes are inevitable whenever human beings act. Therefore, Popper formulates a "principle of permanent correction of errors: *the method of looking permanently for mistakes and to correct in good time small or beginning mistakes*" (EH, IX, m.t.). And as this is very important to him, he now becomes inconsequent. He abandons the idea of rationally *weighing* and instead dogmatically postulates a *duty*: "To apply this method of correcting mistakes in good time is not merely a rule of wisdom but nothing short of a moral duty: . . . Here ability becomes an obligation: we *can* learn from our mistakes; therefore *it is our duty* to learn from our mistakes" (IX, m.t.).

But social changes must be introduced only *gradually*, so that they remain open to revision if unintended side effects become apparent. Only "open" societies, which function on the basis of abstract relations such as social exchange or division of labour and thus require personal decisions, ensure revisability.

For this reason Popper also examines *totalitarianism* critically, and he is one of the few philosophers who criticize both fascism and communism. To begin with, he traces the *Marxist* philosophy of history – history is a struggle of classes for economical predominance – and the racial doctrine or *fascism* – the biological superiority of a particular race explains the course of history – back to Hegel. But Hegel in the main follows Plato (OS I, 9f.). Marx, Hegel, and Plato share *historicism*, the doctrine that there are universal laws of history that make its course inevitable and predictable. Popper attempts to refute these doctrines, because "historicist metaphysics are apt to relieve men from the strain of their responsibilities" (4).

The Poverty of Historicism

Popper's title "*The Poverty of Historicism* alludes to Marx's (1818–1883) *The Poverty of Philosophy*, which in its turn is an answer to Proudhon's (1809–1865) *The Philosophy of Poverty* (EH, viii). Thus Popper wanted to indicate that he intended a philosophico-methodological criticism of the Marxist philosophy of history (viii). But what is *historicism?* Out of several found ideas – above all those of Plato, Aristotle, Hegel, and Marx – Popper *builds up* "a well-considered and close-knit philosophy... [,] a position really worth attacking" (PH, 3). This philosophy he calls "historicism." It is "*a doctrine of method*" (58, i.a.) or "*an approach to the social sciences* [i.a.] which assumes that *historical prediction* is their principal aim, and which assumes that this aim is attainable by discovering the 'rhythms' or the 'patterns', the 'laws' or the 'trends' that underlie the evolution of history" (3).

What objections can be raised against a research program like this one? The "historicist visualizes sociology as a theoretical and empirical discipline whose *empirical basis is formed by a chronicle of the facts of history alone,* and whose aim is to make forecasts, preferably *large scale forecasts*" (PH, 39, i.a.). Its limitation to particular data and the ambition to make large-scale forecasts is a mistake. Above all, Popper criticizes "the historicist contention . . . that in the social sciences the *validity of all generalizations,* or at least of the most important ones, is *confined to the concrete historical period* in which the relevant observations were made" (98, i.a.). According to this contention, the empirical hypotheses of the social sciences are valid only within certain spatiotemporal limitations.

On the other hand, historicists "believe in trends which are unconditional (and therefore general); or, as we may say, in '*absolute trends*'; for example, in a general historical tendency towards progress" that is not at all limited to particular historical periods (PH, 128). But they "*overlook the dependance of trends on initial conditions* ... [and] operate with trends as if they were unconditional, like laws" (128). This is "*the central mistake of historicism*" (128, i.a.). "*Its* [supposed] '*laws of development*' turn out to be [merely] *absolute trends*" (128). Put in another way, the *poverty of historicism* consists in the fact that the historicist blindly trusts in supposed laws, "for he cannot imagine a change in the conditions of change" (130).

10.1. ON THE METHODOLOGY OF THE SOCIAL SCIENCES

Popper divides *The Poverty of Historicism* into four chapters. He intends to describe the anti-naturalist and the pro-naturalist doctrines of historicism in the first two chapters, and to criticize them in the remaining two. The *pro-naturalist* doctrines "favour the application of the methods of physics to the social sciences"; the *anti-naturalist* doctrines "oppose the use of these methods" (PH, 2). But Popper does not really distinguish the description of these doctrines, their criticism, and the description of his own position.

10.11. The Unity of Method

According to Popper, the philosophy of science or methodology developed in *The Logic of Scientific Discovery* and illustrated by examples taken from physics is also applicable to the *social sciences*. In particular, he overrules as irrelevant the objection that *predictions of singular events* are impossible in the social sciences, as opposed to the natural sciences. After all, quantum theory does not permit such predictions either, as it is probabilistic. Popper entertains the suspicion that the demand for a *special methodology of the social sciences*, as it was raised in the *explanation-versus-understanding controversy*, results from a positivist conception of physics and that if this error is corrected, that disposes of the demand.

However, a special methodology of the social sciences is also posited for quite different reasons. Empirical theories are not suited to *legitimizing political goals*. As opposed to this, philosophical and humanistic speculation on society often serves this very purpose. This holds not only of Popper's "false prophets" – Plato, Hegel, and Marx – but also, say, of the members of the "Frankfort School" – for example, Horkheimer, Adorno, and Habermas (cf. Keuth 1993).

Popper also applies his philosophy of science and methodology to *political proposals* – in particular, to the defence of democracy. But he does not attempt to legitimize democracy as the morally right form of government. For according to him, it can only be shown to be, in view of our actual purposes, a (by far) more appropriate *means* than the other forms of government.

In science as in politics, all activity begins with a *problem*. Then *solutions* are proposed – here theories, there measures – which first have to be *tested* and then perhaps can be *applied*. But the results of their application present new problems. Often they necessitate *revisions* of the theories or measures. This takes us to the next cycle of the process of problem solving. In order to preserve the possibility of such concerted solutions, political measures must not be so far-reaching that their *effects* cannot be *undone*. The possibility of *revisions without bloodshed* is Popper's central argument in his defence of *democracy* as a form of government.

10.12. Peculiarities of the Social Sciences

At the same time, Popper also assumes certain peculiarities of the social sciences. It is true that he criticizes "*methodological collectivism*" and "*holism*," which postulates a "general will" or a "national spirit," as in the case of Rousseau's and Hegel's romanticism. Instead, he favours "*methodological individualism*," which "insists that the 'behaviour' and the 'actions' of collectives, such as states or social groups, must be reduced to the behaviour and to the actions of human individuals" (OS II, 91). But he rejects "*psychologism*" – "the doctrine that, society being the product of interacting minds, *social* laws must ultimately be reducible to *psychological* laws" (90, i.a.) or, in other words, "that sociology must in principle be reducible to social psychology" (88). Rather, he postulates the "*autonomy of sociology*," for human beings are formed by social rules and traditions (89, i.a.). He even states: "To have questioned psychologism is perhaps the greatest achievement of Marx as a sociologist" (88). Here he alludes to Marx's famous epigram: "'It is not the consciousness of man that determines his existence – rather, it is his social existence that determines his consciousness'" (89).

Popper argues that human actions cannot be explained by *motives* alone. Rather, motives must be supplemented by reference to the *situation* in which the action takes place, and to social *institutions*. This is correct, but from this he concludes that *every psychological analysis of human actions* "*presupposes sociology*" and that it is therefore impossible "to reduce sociology to a psychological or behaviouristic analysis of our actions" (OG II, 90). And if sociology is not reducible, then it will have to be autonomous, no doubt.

But he misses two points. On the one hand, *individual psychologists* are not engaged exclusively in motivational research. On the other hand, already in the 1930s there had been *social psychological* inquiries into the formation of social norms in groups, among them the instructive experiments on the "autokinetic effect" (cf. Sherif 1956). The reports on their results contain statements not only about individuals but also about aggregates – to be more precise, about *groups* and about the foundations (of a kind) for institutions, namely *norms*. Social norms result from individual judgments, and they influence further individual judgments. Hence there are interactions between the level of individuals and the level of aggregates. The development of social norms is here explained in terms of individuals and their actions, and the retroaction of the norms on the individuals is also explained without presupposing sociology.

Popper's dislike of "psychologism" corresponds to his preference for *rational constructions*. In most social situations, he expects "an element of *rationality*" that permits us "to construct comparatively simple models of . . . actions and inter-actions, and to use these models as approximations" (PH, 140f.). This seems to him "to indicate a considerable difference between the natural and the social sciences – perhaps *the most important difference in their methods*." As opposed to this, "specific difficulties in conducting experiments" and "in applying quantitative methods" are differences only of degree (141).

He considers actions to be primarily determined by what he calls "the *logic of the situation*" (OS II, 97). Behaviour is called "*rational*" if it is in accordance with this logic. Therefore, the logic of the situation plays an important part both in social life and in the social sciences. In particular, it is "*the* method of economic analysis" (97, i.a.). In his lecture "On the Logic of the Social Sciences," given at the Tübingen working session of the German Sociological Association in October 1961, he even calls it "the method of *objective* understanding" (Adorno et al. 1976, 102). He explains:

Objective understanding consists in realizing that the action was objectively *appropriate to the situation*. In other words, the situation is analysed far enough for the elements which initially appeared to be psychological (such as wishes, motives, memories, and associations) to be transformed into elements of the situation. The man with certain wishes therefore becomes a man whose situation may be characterized by the fact that he pursues objective *aims*; and a man with certain

memories or associations becomes a man whose situation can be characterized
by the fact that he is equipped objectively with certain theories or with certain
information.

This enables us then to understand actions in an objective sense so that we
can say: admittedly I have different aims and I hold different theories (from,
say, Charlemagne): but had I been placed in his situation thus analysed – where
the situation includes goals and knowledge – then I, and presumably you too,
would have acted in a similar way to him. The method of situational analysis is
certainly an individualistic method and yet it is certainly not a psychological one;
for it excludes, in principle, all psychological elements and replaces them with
objective situational elements. (102f.)

Another method of rational construction is the "'*zero method*' . . . , [i.e.,]
the method of constructing a model on the assumption of *complete rationality* (and perhaps also on the assumption of the possession of complete
information) on the part of all the individuals concerned, and of esti-
mating the deviation of the actual behaviour of people from the *model
behaviour*, using the latter as a kind of *zero co-ordinate*" (PH, 141, i.a.).
Presumably he considers this method to be a special case of situational
logic, but it might as well be a complement. An example of this method
"is the comparison between actual behaviour (under the influence of,
say, traditional prejudice, etc.) and model behaviour to be expected on
the basis of the 'pure logic of choice', as described by the equations of
economics" (141, i.a.). The possibility of constructing rational models is
a good reason to believe "that social science is less complicated than
physics" (140).

So we explain and predict human behaviour on the basis of our idea of
"the rational thing to do in any situation," and we are able to understand
why people act as they do, "except when they deviate from the rational"
(O'Hear 1992, 163). Only deviations from the rational require psychological explanations. But do people mainly act rationally, and do they
perceive the situations in which they act in like manner? Popper does not
test these assumptions.

10.2. ON THE REFUTATION OF HISTORICISM

Popper's basic thesis says "that the *doctrine of a historical necessity* is and
will remain sheer superstition, even though it pretends to be 'scientific',
and that the course of history cannot be rationally predicted" (EH, VII,
m.t.). Strictly speaking, he seems to advance two theses. According to the
first, weaker thesis, the – strong – statement that there are *historical laws*

that *inevitably* force a certain course of history is sheer superstition. Such a superstition may be found in *Marx's historical materialism*. According to the second, stronger thesis, *the course of history cannot be scientifically predicted at all*, not even by means of – weaker – probabilistic hypotheses. But he does not think that far-reaching historical predictions fail just because there are no well-corroborated historical hypotheses or because small causes have great effects but cannot be ascertained completely or precisely enough. Rather, he claims to have definitely refuted historicism: "*I have shown that, for strictly logical reasons, it is impossible for us to predict the future course of history*" (PH, v).

He summarizes his refutation in five sentences (PH, vf.). The first two contain his *premises*:

(1) "The course of human history is strongly influenced by the growth of human knowledge" (v).

This can hardly be doubted.

(2) "We cannot predict, by rational or scientific methods, the future growth of our scientific knowledge" (vf.).

For this, he intends to give a logical proof. The remaining three sentences contain his *conclusions*:

(3) "We cannot, therefore, predict the future course of human history" (vi).

(4) "This means that we must reject the possibility of a *theoretical history*; that is to say, of a historical social science that would correspond to *theoretical physics*. There can be no scientific theory of historical development serving as a basis for historical prediction" (vi).

(5) "The fundamental aim of historicist methods . . . is therefore misconceived; and *historicism collapses*" (vi, i.a.).

This refutation of historicism is, however, *not* intended to exclude *all* kinds of social predictions. Rather, he considers it possible to test theories of economics by predicting with their help certain developments – say, an economic upswing – and then testing whether they come true. His argument only "*refutes the possibility of predicting historical developments to the extent to which they may be influenced by the growth of our knowledge*" (vi, i.a.).

Popper himself considers statement (2) the decisive premise of his argument. How can he *prove* it? He has made various attempts (cf. section 14.53). They have a basic idea in common: "[*I*]*f there is such a thing as growing human knowledge, then we cannot anticipate today what we shall know only tomorrow*" (PH, vi). At first sight, this seems unobjectionable. But the question is, how exactly are we to predict what we don't know today but shall know tomorrow?

After all, we can often predict within certain limits *that* a particular problem will have been solved by a particular time in the future, even though we cannot predict exactly *how* it will be solved. For example, it is possible to develop different parts of an aircraft not successively but in a parallel manner, even developing different parts in different countries.

10.3. PIECEMEAL SOCIAL ENGINEERING

Popper's methodological ideas are mirrored in his *social philosophy*. When testing hypotheses, an *experimentalist* in an empirical science will always try to change only *one* parameter of the experimental setup and to keep all others constant, so as to be able to estimate which effects are due to which causal factors. A scientifically advised *social engineer* will proceed in a similar way.

It does not matter on *which hypothesis* he relies – whether it says, for example, "'You cannot have full employment without inflation,'" or "'You cannot have a centrally planned society with a price system that fulfils the main functions of competitive prices,'" or something quite different (PH, 62). It matters as little *which aims* he pursues, for his ends are beyond the province of his technology (64). "All that technology may say about ends is whether or not they are *compatible with each other* or *realizable*" and which *unwanted side effects* their realization may have (64, i.a.).

As opposed to this, *historicism* "regards the ends of human activities as dependent on historical forces and so within its province" (PH, 64). For *philosophies of history* connect the question of identifying the historical *facts* with the question of how these facts are to be *evaluated*. Thus the conservative *Platon*ist philosophy of history identifies *what was* with *what is good*; the modernist *Hegel*ian philosophy of history identifies *what is* with *what is reasonable, right*; and the futurist – or, as its adherents say, progressive – *Marx*ist philosophy of history identifies *what will be* with *what ought to be*.

It matters, however, *how* the piecemeal social engineer *proceeds*. "Even though he may perhaps cherish some ideals which concern society 'as a whole' – its general welfare, perhaps – he does not believe in the method of re-designing it *as a whole*. Whatever his ends, he tries to achieve them *by small adjustments and re-adjustments* which can be continually improved upon" (PH, 66, i.a.). For *the "piecemeal engineer knows, like Socrates, how little he knows.* He knows that we can learn only from our mistakes. Accordingly, he will make his way, step by step, carefully comparing the results expected with the results achieved, and always on the look-out for the unavoidable unwanted consequences of any reform" (67, i.a.). Not only because of the consequences but also for methodological reasons "he will avoid undertaking reforms of a *complexity* and scope which make it impossible for him to *disentangle causes and effects,* and to know what he is really doing" (67, i.a.).

Opposite this *piecemeal social engineering* stands the *holistic theory of social experiments:* "Utopianism and historicism agree in the view that *a social experiment (if there is such a thing) could be of value only if carried out on a holistic scale*" (PH, 84). But as "*'planned experiments'*" on such a scale are hardly possible, the historicist must learn from the "*'chance experiments'*" on which history reports (85, i.a.).

Historicists reject the method of piecemeal social engineering as being too cautious and too modest. Instead, they want to redesign "society 'as a whole'" (PH, 66). But this *holistic method* proves to be *impossible* in practice, for

the greater the holistic changes attempted, the greater are their unintended and largely unexpected repercussions, forcing upon the holistic engineer the expedient of piecemeal *improvization.* In fact, this expedient is more characteristic of centralized or collectivistic planning than of the more modest and careful piecemeal intervention; and it continually leads the Utopian engineer to do things which he did not intend to do; that is to say, it leads to the notorious phenomenon of *unplanned planning.* (68f.)

Thus utopian and piecemeal engineering differ in practice "not so much in scale and scope as in *caution* and in *preparedness* for unavoidable surprises" (69, i.a.).

The fixation on redesigning society "as a whole" also has a very unpleasant by-product. The utopian engineer rejects sociological hypotheses stating that *institutions are effective only in a limited manner* if they ignore what people want. But this spares him neither indifference nor disapproval nor even resistance. Therefore he also attempts to control this "human factor" by institutional means. He must then "extend his programme so as to embrace not only the transformation of society, according to plan, but also the *transformation of man*" (PH, 70, i.a.).

But this implies the admission that his original program has failed. "For it substitutes for his demand that we build a new society, fit for men and women to live in, *the demand that we 'mould' these men and women to fit into his new society*" (PH, 70, i.a.). This not only betrays his original program, which he had passed off as philanthropic, but also "removes any possibility of *testing* the success or failure of the new society. For those who do not like living in it only admit thereby that they are not yet fit to live in it; that their 'human impulses' need further 'organizing'. But without the possibility of tests, any claim that a 'scientific' method is being employed evaporates" (70, i.a.). Hence holistic social engineering is – as opposed to piecemeal social engineering – *unscientific.*

11

The Open Society

As already mentioned, Popper wrote *The Open Society and Its Enemies* as his "contribution to the war efforts" (OG I, ix, m.t.). Its tendency was "against nazism and communism; against Hitler and Stalin, the former allies of the Hitler-Stalin-Pakt of 1939." He goes on: "I detested the names of both so much that I did not want to mention them in my book. So I started searching for traces in history; from *Hitler* back to *Plato*: the first great political ideologist who thought in classes and races and proposed concentration camps" (ix, i.a., m.t.). He means the prison "in the middle of the country, in some spot that is deserted and as wild as possible, having for its name some term of retribution" (Plato, *The Laws*, 908a). And "from *Stalin* I went back to Karl *Marx*. My criticism of Marx was intended to criticize myself as well, for in my early youth I had been a Marxist myself and for a few weeks even a communist" (ix, i.a., m.t.).

In *The Open Society*, Popper again criticizes *historicism*, the doctrine of an inevitable historical development. He examines the three forms that, according to him, historicism was given by Plato, Hegel, and Marx. Agassi writes, that being "a political best-seller for over four decades," *The Open Society* "has achieved its chief end, ... the public discrediting of the theory of historical inevitability or destiny" (Agassi 1993, 178). (He reports that "it has won the award of the American Political Science Association for a book over two decades in print" [182]. By now it has been in print for more than five decades.) But were these three authors actually historicists? Only Marx's philosophy of history is undeniably historicist. Its promises had obvious political effects. So *Popper may have overestimated the consequences of historicism for totalitarianism*, which he wanted to fight against.

But *theological* legitimation of totalitarian rule seems to be much older than its *philosophical* counterpart, and secular totalitarian organizations easily find models among religious communities that claim to set absolute standards for every aspect of life. Even at the outset of modern times, Jean Cauvin (Johannes Calvin) tried with his *Ordonnances ecclésiastiques* of 1541 to completely Christianize the Geneva community by means of courts of morals, domestic controls, and so on (Lutz 1964, 99). And he didn't rest with this objective: "Conscious of his divine mission the Reformer controlled and formed [beginning in 1555] every aspect of the life of the municipal republic. The principle of the identity of civil duty and religious order was applied so forcefully that executions of political and theological opponents increased" (99, m.t.). Thus *the Reformer installed a paradigm of totalitarian rule*, but he is not mentioned at all in The *Open Society*.

11.1. PLATO

The most controversial part of *The Open Society* is Popper's attack on Plato (Boyle 1974, 852). It occupies almost all of the first volume. Popper criticizes both Plato's (427–347) *political philosophy* and his *theory of ideas*. He considers *historicism* to be the theoretical core of Plato's political philosophy and *methodological essentialism* to be the correlate of his theory of ideas. His diagnosis of historicism and essentialism in Plato caused comment. His attempt to analyse and to criticize "the *totalitarian tendency* of Plato's political philosophy" in order to show that the most important Western philosopher was an archenemy of the open society gave offence (OS I, 34, i.a.).

Popper calls the doctrine of ultimate explanation by essences "*essentialism.*" According to this doctrine, the *"best, the truly scientific theories, describe the 'essences' or the 'essential natures' of things – the realities which lie behind the appearances"* (CR, 104, i.a.). And he uses "the name *methodological essentialism* to characterize the view, held by Plato and many of his followers, that *it is the task of pure knowledge or 'science' to discover and to describe the true nature of things, i.e. their hidden reality or essence* [i.a.]" (OS I, 31).

According to Aristotle (384/3–322/1), Plato's "*theory of Forms or Ideas* was originally introduced in order to meet a methodological demand, the demand for pure or rational knowledge which is impossible in the case of sensible things in flux" (OS I, 38, i.a.). The theory of Ideas also provides a *theory of change*, for Plato believed "that the Ideas or essences exist *prior* to the things in flux, and that the trend of all developments can be explained as a movement away from the perfection of the Ideas, and therefore as a descent, as a movement towards decay" (OS II, 36). This movement is described by his *"law of historical development"* (i.a.), according to which *"all social change is corruption or decay or degeneration"* (OS I, 19).

Thus Plato's *political philosophy* depends in the final analysis on his theory of Ideas:

Plato's political ends, especially, depend to a considerable extent on his *historicist doctrines* [i.a.]. First, it is his aim to escape the Heraclitean flux, manifested in social revolution and historical decay. Secondly, he believes that this can be done by establishing a state which is so perfect that it does not participate in the general trend of historical development. Thirdly, he believes that the *model or original* of his perfect state can be found in the distant past, in a Golden Age which existed in the dawn of history. (OS I, 24)

11.11. Totalitarian Justice

In his chief work, the *Republic* (better: *The State*), Plato unfolds the *Idea of the Good*. He begins with the Socratic inquiry into the essence of *justice*. Like every idea, it is seized in an intellectual act. What is just can be cognized only from case to case with respect to the idea of justice, and only by him who is able to do so, the philosopher (Heuß 1962, 373). Plato represents the philosopher's reflections in the form of dialogues.

As Popper has repeatedly been charged with employing "unorthodox translations," I use quotations from the translations by Waterfield (*Republic*) and Pangle (*The Laws*) in order to make Popper's most important comments on Plato intelligible. Quotations from the *Republic* take the form "(380e)"; the less frequent quotations from *The Laws* take the form "(L 739c)."

Morality (better: *justice*) "can be a property of whole communities as well as of individuals" but as "a community is larger than a single person," morality may be "easier to discern ... in the larger entity" (368e). So a community is designed. It "has *everything it takes to be good*," that is, "it has *wisdom, courage, self-discipline*, and *morality* [justice]," the four cardinal virtues (427e, i.a.). It is a strict class society, and some of the virtues are specific to certain classes. But within the ruling classes of the guardians (philosophers) and their auxiliaries (civil servants and members of the militia) there are equal rights for men and women.

The community is *wise* if some of its inhabitants have knowledge, "which enables [them] to think resourcefully about the whole community, not just some element of it, and about enhancing the whole community's domestic and foreign policies"; and the rulers, the guardians, have this knowledge (428c,d). Hence *wisdom* is the virtue of the ruling philosophers.

The community is *courageous* only insofar as "its defensive and military arm" may be so called (429b). The members of the militia are indoctrinated "so thoroughly that the laws take in them like a dye, so that their notions about what is to be feared and about everything else hold fast" (430a), and "this ability to retain under all circumstances a true and lawful notion about what is and is not to be feared" is *courage*, the virtue of the members of the militia (430b).

On the other hand, *self-discipline* is a virtue both of the rulers and of their subjects (431e), but in very different ways. "To be self-disciplined . . . is somehow to order and control the pleasures and desires" (430e). But this means that "in a person's mind . . . the part which is naturally better is in control of the worse part" (431a), and that in the community "the desires of the common majority are controlled by the desires and the intelligence of the minority of better men" (431c,d). So we may claim "that self-discipline was this *unanimity*, a harmony between the naturally worse and naturally better elements of society as to which of them should rule both in a community and in every individual" (432a, i.a.).

So "it seems likely that this is in a sense what *morality* is – doing one's own job" (433b, i.a.). Its principle is "that every individual has to do just one of the jobs relevant to the community, the one for which his nature has best equipped him" (433a). But

when someone whom *nature* has equipped to be an artisan or to work for money in some capacity or other . . . tries to enter the military class, or when a member of the militia tries to enter the class of policy-makers and guardians when he's not qualified to do so, and they swap tools and status, or when a single person tries to do all these jobs simultaneously, then . . . these *interchanges and intrusions* are disastrous for the community. (434a,b, i.a.)

"There's nothing more disastrous for the community, then, than the intrusion of any of the three classes into either of the other two, and the interchange of roles among them, and there could be no more correct context for using the term '*criminal*'" (434b,c, i.a.).

Popper comments: "The principle that every class should attend to its own business means, briefly and bluntly, that *the state is just if the ruler rules, if the worker works, and if the slave slaves,*" and "[t]he state is just if it is healthy, strong, united – stable" (OS I, 90). A few years before Plato's birth, Pericles (about 500–429) had formulated the equalitarian principle "that the citizens of the state should be treated impartially" (95). But "Equalitarianism was [Plato's] arch-enemy, and he was out to destroy it; no doubt in the sincere belief that it was a great evil and a great danger" (93).

Almost a half-century before, Windelband had written:

The teleological world view [of Plato] results in the norm that everyone has his destination and is good and perfect in so far as he follows it. So in the state the *teaching profession* (of the philosophers) is to rule and to devote itself to science, the *military profession* is to enforce the laws conscientiously and to defend the country valiantly, the *agriculture* and the *trade* are to be unconditionally obedient, submissive to the will of the ruling and to produce the goods which are necessary for the common life. The coordination, the 'harmony' of the three parts is an order required by their essences and constitutes *the perfection of the state*, and this is what Plato calls *justice*. (Windelband 1900, 159f., last italics in the original, m.t.)

Today, more benign interpretations prevail. So Höffe speaks of the "'*Idiopragieformel*', according to which the different men are to attend to their own businesses, i.e. do what corresponds to their *abilities*" (Höffe 1997, 343, i.a., m.t.). But could there "be no more correct context for using the term '*criminal*'" than the case of someone doing something that does not correspond to his abilities?

Plato analogizes the community and the individual or the parts of the soul. To the teaching profession corresponds what is "reasonable," to the military profession what is "courageous," to agriculture and the trades what is "desirous" in the individual soul (Windelband 1900, 159, m.t.). Even "the norms and the values are politically and morally the same: in the former sense they refer to the 'man on a large scale' [the state], in the latter to the 'man on a small scale' [the human being]. The fundamental principle remains the same . . . : the right life in the state as in the individual consists in the fact that each of the three parts does 'its own'" (159, m.t.). Plato then derives "the unjust, *inappropriate constitutions* and the corresponding *types of character* of the individuals from the same premises . . . : of course they result from the fact that in addition to or instead of reason the two other parts or forces . . . rule. In order to show this, Plato chooses a development beginning with the ideal state of 'justice' and, by gradual deterioration, forming the 'false constitutions and characters'" (160f., m.t.).

11.12. The Constitutions

From the succession of the constitutions, Popper infers what he calls Plato's "*law of historical development.*" According to the *Republic*, aristocracy is followed by timocracy, oligarchy, democracy, and finally by tyranny. (For a description of the historical constitutions of Athens, see Heuß 1962, esp. 302–400.) Closest to the Idea of a state is *aristocracy*, "a kingship of the wisest and most godlike men" (OS I, 39). Plato explains the decline of this "best state" by means of a general *law of political revolutions*, stating "that all political change is due to the actual power-possessing members of society themselves, when conflict arises among them," whereas "[e]ven if there are very few of them, instability is out of the question as long as they're of one mind" (545d). While Popper rejects Plato's law of historical development, he considers his law of political revolutions "most interesting" (OS I, 38).

But how does conflict arise among the aristocrats? Plato begins a strange, seemingly Pythagorean story: There are "*times of fertility*," and "a divine creature's cycle is defined by a *perfect number.*" The rule for its computation is hardly understandable, but the "geometrical number [thus] produced is responsible . . . – for the quality of children born – and when your guardians are unaware of this, they pair men and women sexually on the wrong occasions, and the resulting children will not be naturally gifted or fortunate" (546a–d, i.a.). "As a result, the next generation of rulers to be appointed will not be particularly good at guarding, in the sense that they won't be so good at assessing . . . the castes of gold and silver, of copper and iron" (546e, 547a). According to Schleiermacher, Plato assumes *historical cycles* that might last 36,000 years (Plato 1990, vol. 4, 546b, n10). Thus, Popper is not the only one to assume a *law of historical development* in Plato.

Testing the minds for their metals is part of Plato's "*Myth of Blood and Soil*" (OS I, 141, i.a.), which introduces two ideas. The first (414e) is supposed to strengthen the defence of the country and is comparatively harmless: "[I]t is the idea that the warriors of his city are autochthonous, 'born of the earth of their country', and ready to defend their country which is their mother" (OS I, 140). The second idea (415a) is prima facie a *class myth*: "'God . . . has put gold into those who are capable of ruling, silver into the auxiliaries, and iron and copper into the peasants and the other producing classes'" (140). Obviously, these metals are hereditary. Therefore, Popper calls them "racial characteristics" and calls this myth the "*myth of racialism*" (140, i.a.).

Plato concludes the explanation of the conflict (547a) with his "*story of the Fall of Man*": When the guardians are no longer able to assess the castes of gold and silver, of copper and iron, "'[i]ron will mingle with silver and bronze with gold, and from this mixture variation will be born and absurd irregularity; and whenever these are born they will beget struggle and hostility. And this is how we must describe the ancestry and birth of Dissension, wherever she arises'" (OS I, 141, i.a.). When dissension arises, because the class barriers become blurred, the fate of aristocracy is sealed.

Violent conflicts will now result in the introduction of private ownership (547b) and the suppression of the working class (547c). A new constitution will evolve, *timocracy*, which falls "between aristocracy and oligarchy" (547c) and is "the rule of the noble who seek honour and fame" (OS I, 40), a rule of the military. But private ownership involves the noble "in *making money*; and the higher they rate money, the lower they rate goodness" (550e, i.a.).

Plato repeatedly emphasizes the *economic background of historical developments*, "a theory revived by Marx under the name 'historical materialism'" (OS I, 38). This theory too causes Popper to praise "Plato's greatness as a sociologist," even though it is an example of Plato's "sociological and economic historicism" (38).

Once wealth is admired and poverty despised, they "enact the legislation which is the distinctive feature of an oligarchic political system" (551a) by announcing "that only those whose property attains the ordained value shall play a part in government" (551b). The members of an *oligarchy* accept wealth as "the *raison d'être* of oligarchy" (562b). But their "insatiable greed for wealth – being too busy *making money* to pay attention to anything else – . . . causes its downfall" (562b, i.a.).

For the poor begin to doubt the superiority of the wealthy; finally, there is an open revolt, and "*democracy* starts . . . , when the poor members of the community are victorious. They kill some of the rich, they expel others, and they give everyone who's left equal social and political rights: in a democratic system governmental posts are usually decided by lot" (557a, i.a.). Initially "the members of the community are autonomous . . . , and everyone has the right to do as he chooses" (557b). But they do not have to fulfil any duties imposed by law or custom, and violation of norms is not punished (557e, 558a,b). Thus it is their "insatiable greed for *freedom* and neglect of everything else which causes this political system [democracy] to change and creates the need for dictatorship" (562c, i.a.).

Plato assumes "three distinct components to a democratically governed community" (564c,d). Democracy turns into *tyranny* when two of its components collaborate against the remaining one. The *third* component is "the general populace – the smallholders, who don't spend all their time on politics and don't have a great deal of property" (565a). Because of their great number, "they are the most authoritative group" when "they gather in one spot" (565a). But in order to gather them, their votes must be bought. The *second* is "the moneyed class," and, "[a]lthough everyone is trying to make money, it's invariably the most disciplined people who do best financially" (564e). The *first* is "the drone element," the sophistic professional politicians (564d,e). The people are "always given to setting up [one of them] as their special champion" (565c), and "he's the one who stirs up conflict against the propertied class" by "hinting at the cancellation of debts and the reassignment of land" (566a). Thus he will finally "become a *dictator*" (566a, i.a.). Then he will surround himself with Praetorian guards (567d,e) and will "eliminate" everyone who is "of any value" and therefore might become dangerous to him (567b). Thus "excessive freedom, at both the individual and the political level, [will] change into excessive slavery" (564a). This portrait of a dictator shows some traits of Lenin and Stalin.

Does Plato's description of the succession of constitutions justify the assumption that he postulates a *law of historical development*? While, according to Schleiermacher, Plato believes in a cyclical course of history (discussed earlier), the third part of the *Republic* contains, according to Russell and probably also to Windelband (1900, 160f.), only Plato's "discussion of various kinds of actual constitutions and of their merits and defects" (Russell 1945, 108). Still, Plato intended his description of the unjust constitutions to be "*paedagogical*," and "the history of their metamorphoses also has a *diagnostic value*, as far as *predictions* in historical situations are concerned. Therefore Plato can expect that from his model we can draw conclusions concerning the *actual course* of history, even if his thesis is not historicist in the strict sense of the word" (Frede 1997, 269f., i.a., m.t.).

11.13. Plato's Political Programme

Popper is numbered among the authors who assume that Plato intended a political reform. Windelband (1900, 160f., m.t.) also considers "the ideal state of the *Republic*" a "serious proposal for a political reform," and Russell (1945, 108) at least gives reasons to take this into account.

Popper portrays Plato as a *utopian social engineer* striving for a complete transformation of the social order – not as a radical historicist postulating "that we cannot alter the course of history," but rather as a moderate historicist considering "*human interference*" possible (OS I, 157, i.a.).

According to Popper, two demands underlie Plato's proposal for reform. The first corresponds to Plato's "*idealist theory of change and rest*" (i.a.), and it says: "*Arrest all political change!* Change is evil, rest divine" (OS I, 86). In order to achieve divine rest, the state must be made "an exact copy of its original" – that is, the *Idea* of the state. The second demand corresponds to Plato's *naturalism*, and it says: "*Back to nature!* Back to the original state of our forefathers" with its "natural class rule of the wise few over the ignorant many" (86).

From these two demands, Popper first derives *the principal elements of Plato's political programme* (OS I, 86f.):

(A) The *strict division of the classes*; i.e. the ruling class consisting of herdsmen and watch-dogs must be strictly separated from the human cattle. (i.a.)

(B) The *identification* of the fate of the *state* with that of the *ruling class*; the exclusive interest in this class, and in its unity; and subservient to this unity, the rigid rules for breeding and educating this class, and the strict supervision and collectivization of the interests of its members. (i.a.)

From these principal elements he then derives *further elements*, as for example:

(C) The ruling class has a *monopoly* of things like military virtues and training, and of the right to carry arms and to receive education of any kind; but it is excluded from any participation in economic activities, and especially from earning money. (i.a.)

(D) There must be a *censorship* of all intellectual activities of the ruling class, and a continual *propaganda* aiming at moulding and unifying their minds. All innovation in education, legislation, and religion must be prevented or suppressed. (i.a.)

(E) The state must be self-sufficient. It must aim at economic *autarchy*; for otherwise the rulers would either be dependent upon traders, or become traders themselves. The first of these alternatives would undermine their power, the second their unity and the stability of the state. (87, i.a.)

Popper calls this program "*totalitarian*" and explains it as resulting from Plato's "*historicist sociology*" (87, i.a.).

This explanation has been attacked. For example, it has been argued that a historical, eschatological way of thinking was only later taken over from Judaism and Christianity. If Plato did not postulate a "law of historical development," Popper's explanation fails; and if Plato did not devise a "political programme," his description of the unjust constitutions was at least intended to be "paedagogical." In any case, we have to judge whether the dialogues in the *Republic* and in *The Laws* favour an authoritarian, reactionary, or even totalitarian state.

11.14. Plato's Anti-individualism

In Plato's late work *The Laws*, the "*reactionary trait*" of his political philosophy becomes even more prominent (Windelband 1980, 109, i.a., m.t.). In Book IV, he begins his outline of model legislation for the founding of a state. First, we learn that the *best state* is most easily realized under the leadership of a *tyrant* having the traits of the *philosopher-king* depicted in the *Republic* (473b ff.). The tyrant, however, must be "young, moderate, a good learner, with an able memory, courageous, and magnificent" – and not least, "'with good luck'" (L 710c). Then the constitutions of *Lacedaimon* and *Knossos* are taken as examples, because they emulate the "very happy rule and arrangement under Kronos" (L 712c–714b).

Where the legal position concerning property is concerned, Plato first describes the ideal state of affairs, that of the best state – namely, the abolition of all private property (L 739c,d). He refers to the old proverb that "the things of friends really are common" (L 739c). Then comes one of the passages that Popper cites as proofs of Plato's "truly astonishing *hostility towards the individual*" (OS I, 102, i.a.). This judgment does not presuppose Popper's "unorthodox" translation; rather, Pangle's translation suffices:

> If this situation exists somewhere now, or if it should ever exist someday – [if women are common, and children are common, and every sort of property is common]; if every device has been employed *to exclude all of what is called the 'private' from all aspects of life*; if, insofar as possible, a way has been devised *to make common somehow the things that are by nature private*, such as the eyes and the ears and the hands, so that they seem to see and hear and act in common; if, again, everyone praises and blames in unison, as much as possible delighting in the same things and feeling pain at the same things, if with all their might they delight in laws that aim at making the city come as close as possible to unity – then no one will ever set down a more correct or better definition than this of what constitutes the extreme as regards virtue. (L 739c,d, i.a.)

The passage within brackets refers to the well-known demands in the *Republic* (416d ff., 457c ff., 460b ff.), which there concern only the guardians, whereas in *The Laws* they are to hold "as much as possible throughout the whole city" (L 739c). Though "[s]uch a city is inhabited, presumably, [only] by gods or children of gods," it is *"the model*, at any rate, *of a political regime"* (L 739d,e, i.a.).

The second passage in which Plato turns out to be a *"totalitarian militarist[.] and admirer[.] of Sparta"* (OS I, 103, i.a.) is part of a general foreword to the regulations concerning military offences:

[T]he most important thing is that no one, male or female, should ever be without a ruler, and that no one's soul should acquire the habit of doing something on its own and alone, either seriously or in play; at all times, *in war and peace*, it should live constantly looking to and following the ruler, governed by that man in even the briefest matters – such as standing when someone gives the order, and walking and exercising in the nude and washing and eating and getting up at night to guard and carry messages, and in dangers, not pursuing someone or retiring before another without an indication from the rulers. *In a word, one should teach one's soul by habits not to know, and not to know how to carry out, any action at all apart from the others*; as much as possible everyone should in every respect live always in a group, together, and in common – for there is not nor will there ever be anything stronger, better, and more artful than this for producing security and victory in war. This ought to be practiced *during peacetime, from earliest childhood*: ruling the rest and being ruled by others. And *anarchy ought to be removed from the entire life of all human beings* and of all beasts that are subject to human beings. (L 942a–d, i.a.)

Popper comments: "These are strong words. Never was a man more in earnest in his hostility towards the individual" (OS I, 103).

11.15. Rule and Lying Propaganda

As Plato's theory of justice shows, he thinks that the fundamental problem of politics is the question, *"Who shall rule the state?"* (OS I, 120). He answers: *"The wise shall lead and rule, and the ignorant shall follow"* (120, i.a.). Modern substitutes for the wise are "the master race," "the proletariat," and "the people." But such an aggregate never rules; persons always rule, and political leaders are not always "good" or "wise." Therefore, we should "prepare for the worst leaders, and hope for the best" (121). This "forces us to replace the question: *Who should rule?* by the new question: *How can we so organize political institutions that bad or incompetent rulers can be prevented from doing too much damage?"* (121)

Popper quotes extensively from the famous funeral oration of Pericles, emphasizing that *"although only a few may originate a policy, we are all able to judge it"* (OS I, 186). But this estimation is far too optimistic. For example, not every voter – not even every minister of finance – is able to judge measures in the field of monetary policy. After all, the minister has not been appointed because he has distinguished himself as an economist but because of his great influence as a politician – say, as the chairman of a party. Should the limits of his discernment become too obvious, it will be argued that he is a "generalist" and that his officials have the required knowledge and skills. In fact, democracy functions tolerably well, even though most citizens – so far as they (can) exert any influence at all – in most cases give their opinions on matters of which they know little or nothing. It is true that the social costs of this incompetence are enormous, but the costs of other forms of government are far higher. What is crucial – also for Popper – is not so much that we are all *able* to judge (even though this would be desirable) but that we all have the *right* to judge, for "of all human 'rights', the most essential is *the right to criticize one's rulers*" (Boyle 1974, 853).

Plato's position is quite different. We already mentioned two "*stories*" (415c) that he uses, the "class myth" and the "story of the Fall of Man." Not only does he consider "*noble . . . lies . . .* which crop up as the occasion demands" (414b, i.a.) permissible, he also recommends them emphatically. It is true that the philosophers who are to rule Plato's state search for truth (475e), but while "the gods really have no use for falsehood, . . . it can serve as a type of medicine for us humans" (389b). First, "'[i]t is the business of the rulers of the city, if it is anybody's, to tell lies, deceiving both its enemies and its own citizens for the benefit of the city; and no one else must touch this privilege'" (OS I, 138; cf. 389b). As opposed to this, the dominated are obliged to tell the truth: "'If the ruler catches *anyone else* in a lie . . . then he will punish him for introducing a practice which injures and endangers the city.'" (138; cf. 389d). Popper comments: "*Totalitarian* morality overrules everything, even the definition, the Idea, of the philosopher" (138; i.a.). According to a later passage (414b f., i.a.), it is not just the people who shall be deceived: "Now . . . can we devise one of those lies . . . so that *with a single noble* lie we can *indoctrinate* the rulers themselves, preferably, but at least the rest of the community?" Accordingly, the ruling philosopher acts nobly when he deceives his subjects, for they need not know the truth, as he guides them for their benefit.

11.16. Conventional Criticism of Popper's Criticism of Plato

Many objections have been raised against Popper's criticism of Plato's *lying propaganda*. We will mention only two of them. The first is: "To justify this reproach one would have to prove that the belief in the truth of the story is primarily to the *advantage* of those who tell the story" (Schubert 1995, 46, i.a., m.t.). This objection seems to indicate that (Plato thinks) the lie is primarily to the advantage of the deceived, not of the liar – say, because it is not a privilege but rather a burden to rule for the common good. The other objection is: "This story [the allegory of the metals] is not a *lie* at all. It is a *truth* [i.a.] conveyed in fictional or mythical form," for it says: "In spite of their different hereditary endowments and the different functions that they perform, they are racially the same and the earth (their land) is their common mother" (Wild 1974, 868). It is easily seen what interpretation can achieve.

There are also more fundamental objections to Popper's criticism of Plato. For example, his knowledge of the Greek language has been called into question. In particular, Levinson criticizes *translations* that are unfavourable to Plato (1953, 153, 168, 523, 542). Popper admits that his translations "are biased," but he replies that "there are no unbiased translations of Plato and, [he] suggest[s], there can be none"; he adds that most translations have a "liberal bias" (A, 94). On the other hand, Robinson, a classicist, has "admitted that the unorthodox translations of crucial passages of Plato in *The Open Society* are both correct and crucial to the case against Plato" (Agassi 1993, 186). No particular translations are needed, however, to consider Plato's political ideal in the *Republic* and *The Laws* totalitarian. The quoted translations by Waterfield and Pangle make this quite clear.

Also, the same translations permit different *interpretations* of Plato's political ideas. For example, Bertrand Russell writes: "'[Popper's] attack on Plato, while unorthodox, is in my opinion thoroughly justified'" (Magee 1973, 93). And Russell's description of "*Plato's Utopia*" to a large extent falls in line with Popper's description (Russell 1945, Book I, Chapter 14). And "Gilbert Ryle, himself a notable Plato scholar, writes in his review of Popper's book in *Mind*: 'His studies in Greek history and Greek thought have obviously been profound and original. Platonic exegesis will never be the same again'" (Magee 1973, 93).

On the other hand, according to Agassi, Levinson "attacked the integrity of anyone who dared doubt that Plato was a *liberal*" and asserted "that what is illiberal in Plato was standard in Athens at the time" (Agassi 1993, 184, 187, i.a.). But would Plato be a liberal if he were only as illiberal as his contemporaries? It is true that Levinson does not explicitly call him a liberal; he also admits that Plato's political ideal is a highly differentiated variant of *authoritarian* government, which may be called "*totalitarian*" insofar as it abolishes the distinction between the domains of private judgment and public control (Levinson 1953, 573). But faced with *The Laws* 739c,d and 942b–d (discussed earlier), we will have to say that Levinson's interpretation is euphemistic. Höffe, who raises a series of objections against Popper and considers Popper's portrayal of Plato "hardly tenable" (1997, 360), even discovers *"decisive elements of the open society already in Plato"* (357, i.a., m.t.).

Windelband's judgment is quite different:

[T]he fundamental idea of the thing as a whole is that the uniform way of life, which alone makes a state strong and efficient, can only be founded in the *unity of the way of thinking* of its citizens: but according to socratic-platonic conviction this unity is possible only through the *absolute rule of a doctrine*, i.e. science [Plato's philosophy]. All personal interests are nil as compared to this highest requirement, and it is this way of thinking which causes Plato to demand that *the individual freedom of the citizens be extremely restricted.* Thus *the ideal state of the Republic* becomes a *military state* devoted to the service of a scientific doctrine. (Windelband 1980, 108, i.a., m.t.)

In no customary sense of the word could this be called "liberal." Even Levinson agrees with Popper "that Plato was proposing, in Popper's terms, to '*close*' *his society*, in so far as this denotes *regimentation of the ordinary citizens*" (Levinson 1953, 571, i.a.).

Does Popper's criticism of Plato result from a personal *animosity?* Popper calls *Plato "the greatest philosopher of all time"* (OS I, 98, i.a.). He also "subscribe[s] to Whitehead's dictum that the whole of Western philosophy is footnotes to Plato" (Magee 1973, 92). And he says that "of all works on philosophy ever written [he] like[s Plato's *Apology*] best" (Popper 1984/1992, 174). He even writes: "There is no reason to doubt that one of [Plato's] most powerful motives was to win back *happiness* for the citizens" (OS I, 171, i.a.). He originally commented on Marx in a similar benevolent way. And Crossman, who remarked "that 'Plato's philosophy is the most savage and most profound attack upon liberal ideas which history can show', seems still to believe that Plato's plan is 'the building of a perfect state in which every citizen is really happy'" (OS I, 87). This appears strangely naïve when we consider what Plato prescribes for the citizens. For it is not only in politics that we rather expect that anyone who claims to be acting only for the benefit of others in most cases is acting primarily in his own interest. Gadamer, however, considers such judgments pointless: *"In* [*Plato's*] *ideal state there is no privacy for the individual at all, and hence there is no question of the happiness of the individual"* (1978, 165, i.a., m.t.). But then we cannot assume that Plato is well disposed toward the individual.

11.17. Hermeneutical Criticism of Popper's Criticism of Plato

Hans-Georg Gadamer (1900–2002) seems to be the one who most radically criticizes Popper for proceeding in the manner of "Aristotle who always takes Plato all too much at his word" (Gadamer 1978, 181, m.t.) and therefore reads "Plato's *utopian construction of a state*, in spite of Plato's assurance to the contrary, as a *reform-programme*" (Gadamer 1983, 276, i.a., m.t.). Popper's errors result from this false preconception. This holds correspondingly of "the modern . . . biographic-political interpretation of Plato" (1983, 275, m.t.). Gadamer is not alone in holding this opinion. Heuß writes – without any reference to Popper or to hermeneutics – that the *Republic* was no recipe for political practice and must in any case not be taken literally (Heuß 1962, 375).

Gadamer's study of Plato's dialogues inevitably involved the *hermeneutic turn* (Gadamer 1983, 273). His teacher "Friedländer interpreted the dialogues like *poetry* and taught to observe the literary form" (Pöggeler 1997, 250, i.a., m.t.). Thereby influenced, Gadamer began "to pay attention to the mimetic happenings in *Plato's dialogues*" (Gadamer 1983, 274, i.a., m.t.), that is, to read them "as the mimesis of real conversations, playing among the partners, involving them all and jeopardizing them all, and *not* as *theoretical treatises*" (Gadamer 1978, 182, i.a., m.t.).

We may be surprised when Gadamer explains "how, in the case of the *Republic*, I interpret Plato's thinking in utopias" (Gadamer 1983, 275, m.t.). For he believes "that we must take Plato's ideal state as being meant *ironically*" (Pöggeler 1997, 252, i.a., m.t.); he even speaks of the "*satiric-utopian construction* which Plato puts together in *Republic* and in *The Laws*" (Gadamer 1983, 276, i.a., m.t.). And he sees it "almost as a certain wastage [of the logical criticism of Plato] to miss conclusiveness and to newly introduce conclusiveness where quite different claims of being convincing are raised, like '*persuasive arguments*' arising from the immediacy of a conversation" (275, i.a., m.t.).

For example, the mistake in the calculation of the "*times of fertility*" seems to him to be "*a masterpiece of a literary sense of humour*. . . . This comical failure of a comical institution shows in a symbolic way . . . why no system of human social order, as carefully and wisely planned it may be, can be permanent" (Gadamer 1978, 168, i.a., m.t.). This sounds quite modern, but why does Plato fill books with "persuasive arguments" if he does not think anything he might achieve could last long? Does he only want to complement the Socratic "I know that I do not *know* anything" with a Platonic "I know that I cannot *bring about* anything"?

In other respects as well Gadamer interprets Plato as being close to the spirit of our time. According to him, not enough attention has been paid to the fact "that in his *Republic* Plato did something absolutely outrageous, turning these traditional *virtues* upside down and turning them all more or less explicitly into *forms of knowledge*. . . . The most prominent example is *courage*. . . . True courage turns out to be something we would call *determination to stand up for one's convictions* or *nonconformism*" (Gadamer 1983, 285, i.a., m.t.). This is at least surprising, as Plato, according to his own words, demands extreme conformity. To understand him as Gadamer does seems to require "that one appreciates Plato's sense of humour" (285, m.t.).

But Gadamer takes his interpretation of Plato to be quite obviously correct, for "you can see with half an eye that such a city is impossible, and this is even underscored by the complicated line of argumentation for its possibility" (Gadamer 1978, 166, m.t.). At any rate, Gadamer concludes: "*We will have to read the whole book as one single great dialectical myth*" (167, i.a., m.t.). What then does Plato really mean?

The institutions of this model-city are not themselves intended to incorporate reform-ideas. Rather they are to show *contrariwise* the real defects and dangers for the survival of a 'city', for example, to show by the total abolition of the family the pernicious role of family policy, of nepotism and dynastic accumulation of power in the so-called democracy of Athens at that time (and not only there). (167, m.t.)

The *epistemological* statements contained in the *Republic* must also be considered dialectical (Gadamer 1978, 169). For example, we must do without an exact "epistemological interpretation" of the *parable of the cave*. Rather, we must pay attention to its role in the course of the conversation: "But there it is quite clear: [the parable] is to dissipate the semblance, as if the devotion to 'philosophy' and 'theoretical' life were incompatible with the requirements of political practice in society and the state" (169).

If Gadamer's interpretation is correct, then Popper's criticism results from the misunderstanding that Plato must be taken at his word, and Plato is thereby relieved of any grave reproach. But this appears insignificant if we take into consideration that the *main work of the greatest Western philosopher* is now known for *a single myth*. For thereby the whole of *Western philosophy* is exposed as *a collection of footnotes to a myth that has erroneously been taken to be a theory*. Neither can *idealist epistemology* be taken seriously any longer. This holds as well of its close relative, the *philosophy of mind*; and anyone who asserts that virtue is knowledge – or that any other cognitive ethics is possible – actually argues only persuasively. Wittgenstein's *Tractatus* (1921/1922), Carnap's *The Elimination of Metaphysics through Logical Analysis of Language* (1932a/1959), and other philosophical contributions from the vicinity of the Vienna Circle regain topicality. Who would have thought that "philosophical hermeneutics" could become an ally of (analytic) philosophy of science?

But if we take into account the fact that Plato has erroneously been taken at his word for more than 2,000 years, then we obviously must assume that he expressed himself in a very misleading fashion. This too may have enhanced the reputation of the totalitarian state, either, because Plato could easily be taken to be its supporter or because his formulations invited interpretations that made him appear to be its supporter, even though his (different) real intention had been recognized. Plato would certainly as G. C. Field claims, "not have approved of Fascism or Nazism" (Boyle 1974, 852). But Popper doesn't suggest that he would. Marx probably would not have approved of Stalinism, even though there is a connection between Marx's doctrine and Stalin's rule. At least the doctrine of the former can be and has been used to support the rule of the latter. In the same way, Plato's philosophy can be and has been used to support totalitarian ideologies. In his *Der Mythus des Zwanzigsten Jahrhunderts* (The Myth of the Twentieth Century), Alfred Rosenberg could make honourable mention of Plato, and no attentive reader of the *Republic* and *The Laws* could easily give him proof of a misinterpretation; and the national socialist race theoretician Hans Friedrich Karl Günther wrote a book on Plato's ideas on breeding (Kaufmann 1956, 198, 219).

Plato has also been monopolized in school editions of the *Republic*. For example, concerning the fixing of the city's border (423b) we are taught: "Still today, Plato's point of view is of utmost importance: the homogeneity of the state must not be endangered by rivalries of the poor and the rich or of parties or by the fact that various hostile sections of the population are only nominally united in the state" (Maaß 1934, Kommentar, Teil 1, 76, set off in the original, m.t.). Maaß first gives the obligation to further the public interest (519e) an explicit time orientation (1934!): "We too learn from Plato again and again that happiness and well-being of the individual or of a single class do not count at all, but only the weal of the whole state counts." Then follows an implicit time orientation: "Plato first teaches, but he does not stop at compulsion"

(Maaß 1934, Kommentar, Teil 2, 74, set off in the original, m.t.). On the necessity of a standing army of professional soldiers (374) – still unknown during the Peloponnesian War – Maaß states: "The [guardians] are similar to the medieval armies of knights. Above all, they may in many ways be put on an equal level with the organizations of the SA and the SS, in which what is valuable in Plato's thoughts has been put into effect" (Maaß 1934, Kommentar, Teil 1, 51, m.t.). Obviously, classical education immunized neither Maaß nor a sufficient number of his contemporaries against national socialism; rather, it enabled them to take advantage of the opportunities that national socialism offered them. This holds as well of philosophers. Heidegger (1889–1976) provides a particularly unpleasant example.

Anyone who sides with Gadamer's interpretation may, even when reading *The Laws* (730d, 731b, 735d f., 736a), believe that Plato lacks only a double name – say, "Plato-Socrates" – to be a Constitutional Liberal. [Members of the left wing of the German Freie Demokratische Partei (Free Democratic Party) call themselves "*Rechtsstaatsliberale*" (Constitutional Liberals), and prominent members of this wing used to have double names indicating their social backgrounds.] He is also likely to side with Hölderlin, who wrote: "I believe, finally we all will say: holy Plato, forgive! grave sins have been committed against you" (Kobusch and Mojsisch 1997, 1, m.t.). We are all the more apt to apologize if we consider how enlightening, even liberating, the new understanding of philosophy – in particular, of Idealism – is, that we owe to Gadamer's interpretation of Plato.

11.2. ARISTOTLE

Popper also devotes a short chapter to Aristotle. He calls it "The Aristotelian Roots of Hegelianism." It is true that Aristotle "made no direct contribution to historicism" (OS II, 7), but "his version of Plato's *essentialism* has influenced the *historicism* of Hegel, and thereby that of Marx" (1, i.a.). While Plato considers "the Forms or essences or originals . . . as existing prior to, and therefore apart from, sensible things" and assumes that the things "move further and further away from" the Forms, Aristotle "makes sensible things move towards their final causes or ends" (6). For "one of [Aristotle's] four causes of anything – also of any movement or change – is the *final cause*, or the end towards which the movement aims" (5, i.a.), and he identifies the *ends* of the sensible things "with their Forms or *essences*" (6, i.a.).

But "[i]n so far as it is an aim or a desired end, the final cause is also *good*" (OS II, 5). Hence something good can be not only at the beginning but also at the end of a movement: "The Form or Idea, which is still, with Plato, considered to be good, stands at the end, instead of the beginning. This characterizes Aristotle's substitution of optimism for pessimism" (5).

Aristotle's theory of change "contains all the elements needed for elaborating a grandiose historicist philosophy" (OS II, 7). For example, "[t]hree *historicist doctrines* which directly follow from Aristotle's *essentialism* may be distinguished" (7, i.a.): (i) Only if persons or states develop and we know their history can we learn about their "'hidden, undeveloped essence.'" (ii) Only change reveals "what is hidden in the undeveloped essence." This assumption "leads to the historicist idea of an historical fate or an inescapable essential destiny" (7). (iii) "In order to become real or actual, the essence must unfold itself in change" (8). A slightly different form of this doctrine can later be found in Hegel. Popper's "irreverence towards Aristotle (not Plato)" was one of the reasons it proved so difficult to find a publisher for *The Open Society* (A, 95).

11.3. HEGEL

Popper judges Hegel almost as critically as he judges Plato. He writes: "The historical significance of Hegel may be seen in the fact that he represents the '*missing link*', as it were, between Plato and the modern form of totalitarianism" (OS II, 31, i.a.). But while he devotes ten chapters to Plato, there is only one on Hegel: Chapter 12, "Hegel and The New Tribalism." In the "Addendum" (1961), he asserts that he wrote his Hegel chapter in a "scherzo-style . . . , hoping to expose the ridiculous in this philosophy which [he] can only regard with a mixture of contempt and horror" (OS II, 394). Later, he confessed to Agassi that "he was sorry that the style of his attack on . . . Hegel . . . was so acrimonious" (Agassi 1993, 185).

11.31. Dialectics and Philosophy of Identity

According to Popper, Hegel's philosophy rests on two pillars. The first is *dialectic*. According to Hegel, dialectic represents the unity of the analytic and the synthetic methods and permits us to interpret a real antagonism as a logical contradiction and to dissolve it. With dialectic begins, according to Popper, what Schopenhauer called Hegel's charlatanism

(OS II, 38). Popper's description of a "dialectic triad" reminds us of the evolution of theories by conjectures and refutations:

This development [of reason] proceeds *dialectically*, that is to say, in a three-beat rhythm. First a *thesis* is proffered; but it will produce criticism, it will be contradicted by opponents who assert its opposite, an *antithesis*; and in the conflict of these views, a *synthesis* is attained, that is to say, a kind of unity of the opposites, a compromise or a reconciliation on a higher level. . . . And once the synthesis has been established, the whole process can repeat itself on the higher level that has now been reached. (39)

The other pillar is the *philosophy of identity*. Plato "had said that the Ideas alone are real, and that perishable things are unreal. Hegel adopts from this doctrine the equation *Ideal = Real*"; and from Kant's doctrine of the "'Ideas of pure Reason,'" he adopts the thesis "that the Ideas are something mental or spiritual or rational, which can be expressed in the equation *Idea = Reason*" (OS II, 41). But "[c]ombined, these two equations, or rather equivocations, yield *Real = Reason*; and this allows Hegel to maintain that everything that is reasonable must be real, and that the development of reality is the same as that of reason" (41). This result also has moral and political implications: As there is no higher standard than the latest development of reason, "everything that is now real or actual exists by necessity, and must be reasonable as well as good" – in particular, "the actually existing Prussian state" (41).

11.311. Popper had already dealt with *dialectic* – in particular, Hegelian dialectic – in a lecture he had given in 1937 in Christchurch, New Zealand. This lecture has been published in *Mind* under the title "What Is Dialectic?" (1940; CR, 312–335). Dialectic is supposed to solve a problem posed by *idealism*, which springs from *rationalism*. Descartes believes "that we can construct the explanatory theories of science without any reference to experience, just by making use of our reason" (324). Summed up in Hegelian terms, this kind of "rationalism" or "intellectualism" says: "'That which is reasonable must be real'" (324).

This has always been contested by *empiricism*, which "is the only interpretation of scientific method which can be taken seriously in our day" (CR, 324). Kant attempted a synthesis of rationalism and empiricism, but his *criticism* "was, more precisely, a modified form of empiricism" (324). Starting from the fact that there is science, Kant asked, "'How is science possible?'" or "'How can our minds grasp the world?'"; and he answered: "The mind can grasp the world, or rather the world as it appears to us, because this world . . . is mind-like" (325) – for the world, as it appears to us, results from the mind's processing of the material that the senses provide. This answer contains both a realistic and an idealistic element. The realist element is "the assertion that the world, as it appears to us, is some sort of *material* formed by our mind, whilst its idealist element is the assertion that it is some sort of material *formed by our mind*" (325).

The German Idealists after Kant also asked, "How can our minds grasp the world?," but they gave different answers. Fichte answered "'[b]ecause the mind *creates* the world,'" and Hegel answered "'[b]ecause the mind *is* the world'" or because "'[t]hat which is reasonable is real . . .'" (CR, 326, i.a.). Hegel's "'*philosophy of the identity of reason and reality*'" attempts to reconstruct rationalism on a new basis. But in order to be credible, Hegel had to refute Kant's refutation of rationalism. In the section on "Transcendental Dialectic" of his *Critique of Pure Reason*, Kant had argued:

> If we try to construct a theoretical system out of pure reason – for instance, if we try to argue that the world in which we live is infinite (an idea which obviously goes beyond possible experience) – then we can do so; but we shall find to our dismay that we can always argue, with the help of analogous arguments, to the opposite effect as well. (CR, 326)

Hence reason contradicts itself "if used to go beyond possible experience" (326).

In objecting to that, Hegel argues something like this:

> "Kant refuted rationalism by saying that it must lead to contradictions. But it is clear that this argument draws its force from the law of contradiction: it refutes only such systems as accept this law, i.e. such as try to be free from contradictions. It is not dangerous for a system like mine which is prepared to *put up with contradictions* – that is, for a *dialectical* system." (CR, 327, i.a.)

Thus Hegel protects his system against any conceivable criticism. As a result, Popper accuses him of "'reinforced dogmatism'" (327). After all, a logician must answer Hegel: "Anyone who accepts contradictions accepts everything, for a logically contradictory statement logically implies any statement, hence to every statement it implies its negation. Therefore he is no longer able to distinguish between a true and a false statement."

11.312. Popper later came to think that in Chapter 12 he "did not analyse the fundamental issue – the philosophy of identity of facts and standards – quite as clearly as [he] ought to have done" (OS II, 395). He makes up for that in section 17 of the "Addendum" (1961) (393ff). Kant had supported a "*dualistic view of facts and standards.*" Hegel's philosophy of identity tries to "'transcend'" this dualism (394f.). According to Hegel, standards too are historical facts; hence there are only facts. It is true that Hegel did not express this so clearly – rather, his formulation is "surpassingly vague" (395) – but he supports a *monism*, a *"philosophy of identity of facts and standards"* (some social or historical facts are at the same time standards; 395, i.a.). And this monism has evil consequences.

Popper brings three *charges* against the philosophy of identity: (1) "It played a major role in the downfall of the liberal movement in Germany" (OS II, 395). (2) By "contributing to *historicism* and to an *identification of might and right*, [it has] encouraged *totalitarian modes of thought*." (3) Because "Hegel's argument...was full of logical mistakes and of tricks,... [it] undermined and eventually lowered the *traditional standards of intellectual responsibility* and honesty" (395, i.a.).

Popper's criticism of Hegel has in turn been attacked. For example, Kaufmann objects that in Hegel's writings there is no evidence for Popper's derivation of the equation *Real = Reason* (Kaufmann 1951, 469). On the other hand, Kaufmann's quotation from Hegel "the rational (which is synonymous with the Idea)" (469) supports the second premise, *Idea = Reason*, of Popper's derivation. Also, according to Kaufmann, Hegel's expression *"wirklich"* must not be translated as "'real,'" as in Popper, but as "'actual'"; and Hegel's *"wirklich"* is the opposite of "'potential'" rather than of "'unreal'" (469).

However, anything real as well as anything actual must be possible. Moreover, anything real or actual must be possible not only logically, but also factually. Hence neither "real" nor "actual" can be the opposite of "possible" or "potential." Does this mean that Kaufmann misunderstood Hegel, or is this another contradiction in Hegel? Windelband seems not to side with Kaufmann's interpretation, for he writes: "According to [Hegelian] philosophical knowledge, what is reasonable, is real and, what is real, is reasonable. The system of reason is *the sole reality*" (Windelband 1980, 530, i.a., m.t.). Accordingly, there is evidence in Hegel's writings for Popper's conclusion *Real = Reason*.

11.32. Historicism

In his *Philosophy of History*, Hegel postulates a "'principle of *Development*'" (OG II, ch. 12, n26). But is he also a *historicist*, as Popper asserts when comparing Plato's and Hegel's philosophies of history? While Plato believes "that the Ideas or essences exist *prior* to the things in flux, and that the trend of all developments can be explained as a movement *away* from the perfection of the Ideas, and therefore as a descent, as a movement towards *decay*," Hegel believes, like Aristotle, "that the Ideas or essences are *in* the things in flux; or more precisely . . . that they are identical with the things in flux: 'Everything actual is an Idea'" (36, i.a.). This corresponds to Popper's first premise, "*Ideal = Real.*" Hegel also teaches "that the general trend is . . . *towards* the Idea; it is *progress*" (36, i.a.).

Hegel's historicism is optimistic. . . . We can say that Hegel's world of flux is in a state of "emergent" or "creative evolution"; each of its stages contains the preceding ones, from which it originates; and each stage supersedes all previous stages, approaching nearer and nearer to perfection. The *general law of development* is thus one *of progress*; but . . . not of a simple and straightforward, but of a "dialectic" progress (36f., i.a.).

Kaufmann admits that Hegel believed "in a *rational world order* and in his ability to understand it" (Kaufmann 1951, 470, i.a.); more precisely, Hegel "believed that history has a *pattern* and made bold to reveal it" (473, i.a.). But how did Hegel come to know this pattern? Had it first been revealed to him? Kaufmann concedes: "Hegel's conception is *dated today*: we know more than he did about the history of a great number of civilizations. We can no longer reduce world history to a straight line which leads from the Greeks, via the Romans, to ourselves" (467, i.a.). But why should we think that Hegel could do so? Was his idea of a pattern not already *false in his own day*? And could not its dissemination have done political harm, as Popper suspects? After all, the philosophy of history of the Hegelian-Marxist "Frankfort School" still profited from Hegel's influence on German intellectuals.

But, according to Kaufmann, Hegel "did not attempt to play the prophet and was content to *comprehend the past*" (Kaufmann 1951, 473, i.a.), and therefore, "in Popper's sense of the term, Hegel *was no historicist* at all: he was not one of those who 'believe that they have discovered laws of history which enable them to *prophesy* the course of historical events'" (473; quotation from: OS I, 3, i.a.). But even if Hegel only tried to comprehend the past and perhaps his time, he still shared, according to Popper, "the *fundamental position of historicist method,* that the way of obtaining knowledge of social institutions such as the state is to study its history, or the history of its 'Spirit'" (OS II, 37, i.a.).

11.33. State and Society

Popper states: "Plato's philosophy, which once had claimed mastership in the state, becomes with Hegel its most servile lackey" (OS II, 46). He looks for Hegel's motives and reaches the conclusion "that Hegel's philosophy was inspired by ulterior motives, namely, by his interest in the restoration of the Prussian government of Frederick William III, and that it cannot therefore be taken seriously" (32). In order to show that this assumption is not new, he quotes Hegel's disciple Schwegler, who in his *Geschichte der Philosophie im Umriß* (History of Philosophy in Outline) writes that Hegel in Berlin " 'acquired, from his connections with the Prussian bureaucracy, political influence for himself as well as the recognition of his system as the official philosophy; not always to the advantage of the inner freedom of his philosophy, or of its moral worth'" (33). It is true that a political interest on the part of an author may arouse distrust of his theses, but that doesn't give us sufficient reason not to take them seriously.

After all, Popper himself examines Hegel's theses (see above) and criticizes the means that Hegel uses to safeguard his political interests: Hegel starts "from *a point that appears to be progressive* and even revolutionary, and proceeding by [his] general *dialectical method* of twisting things . . . , [he] finally reaches a surprisingly *conservative result*" (OS II, 49, i.a.). Such results can be found in his *Philosophy of Law*, as for example: " '[T]he "sovereignty of the people" in opposition to the sovereignty of the monarch . . . turns out to be merely one of those confused notions which arise from the wild idea of the "people." Without its monarch . . . the people are just a formless multitude'" (56). And they can be found in his *Encyclopædia*, as for example: " 'The monarchical constitution is therefore the constitution of developed reason; and all other constitutions belong to lower grades of the development and the self-realization of reason'" (45f.). We need not add further examples here.

Kaufmann accuses Popper of misrepresenting Hegel's theses by piecing together quotations and by omitting parts of quotations. Taking Popper's exposition on "how Hegel twists equality into inequality" (OS II, 44) as an example, Kaufmann shows that Hegel *can* be understood differently if he is quoted in full and with his own accentuations (Kaufmann 1956, 221). We cannot now settle the question of how Hegel *must* be understood, particularly since Kaufmann himself admits the darkness of Hegel's language and thought (1956, 222). Instead, we will juxtapose Kaufmann's judgments on Hegel, which he added to the German version of his article (1956, 221ff.), and Popper's judgments quoted earlier. Astonishing parallels will become apparent.

11.34. Greatness and Dangers of Hegel's Way of Thinking

Kaufmann begins by indicating "*the real dangers of Hegel's way of thinking*" (1956, 221, i.a., m.t.; quotations are from section 12, which he added to the German version). First, there is "*the tremendous complicatedness of Hegel's style*" resulting from his "peculiar way of thinking" (221, i.a., m.t.). In this respect, Hegel's influence was disastrous (221), for his "*darkness*" (*Dunkelheit*) "shaped the lasting image of a German philosopher, and this necessity has gradually become a virtue – a virtue which should be done away with" (221f., i.a., m.t.). As opposed to this, it is "*Hegel's great merit*" that he "did not recoil from any difficulties and fearlessly attacked problems left in the dark by authors which are more easily readable" and that again and again he succeeded in saying "something interesting and important" about them (222, i.a., m.t.).

A second danger is the "*pseudo-precision of Hegel's dialectic*," particularly in his *Phenomenology of Mind* (Kaufmann 1956, 222, i.a., m.t.). Hegel secured for the "apparent discipline of Fichte's dialectic" an influence that it never would have won without him (223, m.t.).

This is an essential limit of his greatness, a defect of all his books and a singular danger of his way of thinking, even though he again and again formulated ideas of lasting value in his dialectic. Probably the gravest reproach we can rage at Hegel is this: not only Marx and Kierkegaard but also, though indirectly, their modern successors have learnt from Hegel the *art of apparent demonstration*. (223, i.a., m.t.)

A third danger "is *Hegel's traditionalism*, which teaches *understanding* to such a degree that criticism comes off badly" (Kaufmann 1956, 223, i.a., m.t.).

Under the sway of Hegel, *sympathetic understanding* became a real virtuosity, especially in Germany, whereas *critical thinking*, which in Lessing and Kant really had not been shallow, became atrophied, so that nowadays asking whether a great philosopher could not have drawn a false conclusion or whether some of his central ideas might be untenable, is almost considered naïve. *Also politically this lack of critical potential had disastrous consequences.* (223f., i.a., m.t.)

The "three dangers named are closely connected. The darkness . . . ; the pseudo-precision and apparent demonstration; and finally the demand of sympathetic understanding and of uncritical after-thinking: this is almost the formula of the *authoritarian obscurantism* which Kafka satirically-prophetically depicted in his *Das Schloß* [The Castle]" (Kaufmann 1956, 224, i.a., m.t.). We can, however, "admit the dangers of Hegel's thinking without denying Hegel's greatness: greatness in particular is connected with danger" (224, m.t.). On the other hand, the work of a philosopher "must also be considered quite independently of his influence" (224, m.t.). This, however, is difficult, because "*many people assume that philosophers discover truths*, just as, say, Columbus discovered America. *This misunderstanding is one of the main reasons why the influence of a philosopher, if it is great, is often so bad*" (224, i.a., m.t.).

But how did Hegel "make mankind richer" (Kaufmann 1956, 226, m.t.)? Above all, he took *belief in the spirit* over into a seemingly enlightened world. According to Hegel, the spirit is "'the absolute substance'" (HWP 3, 192, m.t.), "'the absolutely restless, the pure activity,'" and "'the absolute *self-determining*'" (191, m.t.). The word "spirit" (*Geist*) is combined with numerous adjectives – for example, "'subjective,' 'objective,' 'absolute,' 'theoretical,' 'practical,' 'finite,' 'infinite,' 'sleeping,' 'free,' 'true,' 'alienated from itself,' 'being sure of itself,' 'universal,' 'living,' 'self-conscious,' 'concrete,' 'abstract'" (192, m.t.). In Hegel's philosophy of history there appear also the "*world-spirit*" (*Weltgeist*), the "universal reason of the world" (*allgemeine Weltvernunft*) (EPW 4, 656), and the "*spirit of the time*" (*Zeitgeist*) (EPW 4, 834); in his early theological writings there appears as well the "*spirit of the people*" (*Volksgeist*) (Hoffmeister 1955, 652). As Hegel instead of "spirit" also uses "idea" or "God" (cf. Windelband 1980, 526ff.), we may assume that he made mankind richer insofar as he *disguised religious belief as a rational philosophy*. German Idealism is not without reason considered the continuation of Protestantism by other means.

11.4. MARX

Popper devotes chapters 13–22 – that is, most of the second volume of *The Open Society* – to Karl Marx. For a long time, Popper believed in "the humanitarian impulse of Marxism" (OS II, 81). He attributed to Marx "sincerity in his search for truth and . . . intellectual honesty" as well as "a burning desire to help the oppressed" (82). Only in 1965 does he admit "that Marx was by far less humane and freedom-loving than he appears to be in my book" (OG II, 494 [Addendum II, "A Remark on Schwarzschild's Book on Marx"], m.t.). But from the beginning he deplored the fact that "in spite of his merits, Marx was . . . a false prophet" (82). For, on the one hand, his *prophecies* on the course of history did not come true, and, on the other hand, he popularized the *historicist way of thinking* and "misled scores of intelligent people into believing that historical prophecy is the scientific way of approaching social problems" (82). Thus *Marxism* became "so far the purest, the most developed and *the most dangerous form of historicism*" (81, i.a.).

11.41. Sociological Determinism

Popper believes that "*Marxism* is, fundamentally, a *method*" (OS II, 84, i.a.). Being "purest historicism[,] ... the Marxist method" appears to Popper "to be very poor indeed" (84). Marx "says in the preface to *Capital*, 'It is the ultimate aim of this work to lay bare the ... *law of motion of modern society*'" (87, i.a.). But the plausible assumption that the future can be *predicted* only if it is *predetermined* misled him into believing "that a rigidly scientific method must be based on a *rigid determinism*" (84f., i.a.). Thus he postulated "'inexorable laws'" not only "of nature" but also "of historical development" (85).

It is true that "[t]he abstract idea of 'causes' which 'determine' social developments is ... harmless as long as it does not lead to historicism" (OS II, 85). For though it may be possible to *predict* singular future events *scientifically*, "*large-scale historical prophecy*" of "the main tendencies of the future development of society" will fail (86). But the historicist idea of a *natural law determining the movement of society* excludes *rational political intervention*. Thus Marx writes: "'When a society has discovered ... the natural law that determines its own movement, ... even then it can neither overleap the natural phases of its evolution, nor shuffle them out of the world by a stroke of the pen. But this much it can do; it can shorten and lessen its *birth-pangs*'" (86, i.a.).

11.42. The Autonomy of Sociology

As already mentioned (section 10.12), Popper praises Marx for criticizing psychologism and for defending the autonomy of sociology. It is true that psychologism rightly supports *methodological individualism* – that is, asserts "that the 'behaviour' and the 'actions' of collectives, such as states or social groups, must be reduced to the behaviour and to the actions of human individuals" (OS II, 91). However, according to Popper, there are two decisive arguments against psychologism.

On the one hand, "*psychologism is forced to adopt historicist methods*," for it must speculate about the origins and development of the human way of acting (OS II, 92). This forces upon psychologism "not only the idea of historico-causal development, but also the idea of the *first steps* of such a development" (92). Thus it ends up with the idea of a "*pre-social human nature* which explains the foundation of society" (93, i.a.). The latter idea, in particular, seems so entirely mistaken to Popper that he believes "it would ... be more hopeful to attempt a reduction or interpretation of psychology in terms of sociology than the other way round" (93). But why would sociology be autonomous if society and human nature have developed *together*? Or would Popper be prepared to postulate a *preindividual society* just in order to save the autonomy of sociology?

At the same time, and above all, psychologism misunderstands "*the main task of the explanatory social sciences*" (94, i.a.). Their task is not the prediction of the future course of history, as the (psychologist as a) historicist assumes, but rather "the discovery and explanation of the less obvious dependences within the social sphere" (94). But whoever tries to reduce sociological theories to theories of social psychology clearly need not accept the historicist assignment. Hence neither of Popper's two "decisive arguments" against "psychologism" and for the "autonomy of sociology" holds good.

11.43. Economic Historicism

Marx replaces Mill's psychologism, which corresponds to Hegel's idealism, with his "*materialism.*" He asserts "that 'in Hegel's writing, dialectics stands on its head; one must turn it the right way up again. . . .'" (OS II, 102). His philosophy of history is called the "'*materialistic interpretation of history*'" or "'*historical materialism*'" (100). He believes that phenomena such as war, depression, unemployment, and hunger are not consciously brought about by "'big business'" or "'imperialist war-mongers'" but are "the unwanted social consequences of actions, directed towards different results" (101). The actors on the stage of history are "mere puppets, irresistibly pulled by economic wires – by historical forces over which they have no control" (101). The stage of history "is set in a social system which binds us all; it is set in the '*kingdom of necessity*'. (But one day the puppets will destroy this system and attain the '*kingdom of freedom*.')" (101, i.a.)

Like Hegel, Marx takes *freedom* to be the aim of human development and takes the dialectic of history to be the way that is leading there. Marx "describes the material side of social life and especially its economic side, that of production and consumption, as an extension of human metabolism, i.e. of man's exchange of matter with nature" (OS II, 103). As we are not pure spiritual beings, we will never be able to "emancipate ourselves entirely from the necessities of our metabolism, and thus from productive toil," but we may succeed in reducing "drudgery to such an extent that *all of us can be free for some part of our lives*" (103f.). According to Popper, this is "*the central idea of Marx's 'view of life'*" (104, i.a.).

Marx's "view of life" must be combined with his *methodological determinism*, according to which scientific explanations and predictions of social occurrences are possible only insofar as society is determined by its past. Hence social science can deal only with the *"kingdom of necessity."* As opposed to this, the results of *free* spiritual activity cannot be predicted. As our *thoughts* are tied to the material "necessities," they must be considered *"'ideological superstructures* on the basis of economic conditions'"* (OS II, 104, i.a.). Therefore, Popper calls Marx's form of historicism *"economism"* (104). This is Popper's word for what Marx calls "materialism" (106).

According to Marx, it is the central task of social science to explain the development of the conditions of production. And his conception of *man's history* goes something like this:

"Just as the savage must wrestle with nature in order to satisfy his needs, to keep alive, and to reproduce, so must the civilized man; and he must continue to do so in all forms of society and under all possible forms of production. This kingdom of necessity expands with its development, and so does the range of human needs. Yet at the same time, there is an expansion of the productive forces which satisfy these needs." (OS II, 105)

But why then does Marx not recommend that we simply wait for circumstances to improve in this way?

While Popper rejects Marx's *historicism*, he considers Marx's *economism* "an extremely valuable advance in the *methods of social science*" (OS II, 107, i.a.). For Popper too believes that "the economic organization of society... is fundamental for all social institutions" and that therefore "practically all social studies... may profit if they are carried out with an eye to the 'economic conditions' of society" (106f.). But Marx pays attention *only* to the economic conditions, for he believes that all thoughts and ideas have to be explained "by reducing them to the underlying *essential* reality, i.e. to economic conditions" (107, i.a.). Popper comments critically: "This *philosophical* view is certainly not much better than any other form of *essentialism*" (107, i.a.). Now, is Marx's economism a *"method* of social science," or is it, because it considers economic conditions to be essential, a *philosophical view*, a kind of "essentialism"?

Marx asserts

that every social revolution develops in the following way. The material conditions of production grow and mature until they begin to conflict with the social and legal relations, outgrowing them like clothes, until they burst. "Then an epoch of social revolution opens," Marx writes. "With the change in the economic foundation, the whole vast superstructure is more or less rapidly transformed.... New, more highly *productive relationships*" (within the superstructure) *"never* come into being before the *material conditions for their existence* have been brought to maturity within the womb of the old society itself." (OS II, 109, i.a.)

In this case, however, Popper argues, the *Russian Revolution* has no similarity to the social revolution prophesied by Marx (OS II, 109). It is true that "Marx's *idea* 'Workers of all countries, unite!'" was very influential down to the beginning of the Russian Revolution (107). It also influenced economic conditions. With the revolution, however, the economic situation deteriorated, because "as Lenin himself admitted, there were no further constructive ideas." Lenin then advanced some *ideas* that may be "summarized in the slogan: '*Socialism* is the dictatorship of the proletariat, plus the widest introduction of the most modern electrical machinery'" (108, i.a.). These *ideas* – not the *material conditions*, as Marx had postulated – triggered a development that changed the material background of one-sixth of the world. Thus the Russian Revolution was not a *social* but a *political* revolution – that is, "a mere exchange of the persons who act as rulers" (109). Therefore, Marx's "materialistic interpretation of history" must not be taken too seriously.

11.44. Classes

An important formulation of Marx's "*historical materialism*" is the statement: "'*The history of all hitherto existing society is a history of class struggle*'" (OS II, 111, i.a.). Class struggle advances history. "The *interest of a class* is simply everything that furthers its power or its prosperity" (112, i.a.). It is not a subjective motive of the members of the class but rather the objective situation of the class that determines the consciousness of its members. This holds just as much of the rulers as of the ruled (113). Both are determined by the situation of their class, and because the system forces on both of them what they *believe* to be their interests, both act according to the "'*logic of a social situation*'" (114).

The "social systems or class systems change [always and only] with the conditions of production, since on these conditions depends the way in which the rulers can exploit and fight the ruled" (OS II, 113). Therefore, the circumstances cannot be improved by improving men; rather, men will improve only when the circumstances improve (114). As our actions depend on the social system, "social engineering, and consequently, a social technology, are impossible" (114f.). But, thanks to Marx's theory, the workers become aware of their class situation. Thus a revolutionary situation is prepared in which the conditions of production can change (115f.).

11.45. The Legal and Social Systems

According to the *Communist Manifesto*, "'Political power, properly so called, is merely the organized power of one class for oppressing the other'" (OS II, 118). Popper concludes that Marx and Engels ask *essentialist* questions such as "'*What* is the state?'" and give essentialist answers (119): Gradually reforming politics are impotent. Even democratic government is a form of class dictatorship. Under capitalism, the state is a dictatorship of the bourgeoisie; after the social revolution, it will at first be a dictatorship of the proletariat. But when the resistance of the bourgeoisie breaks down, only one class will be left; in other words, society will be classless and therefore there will no longer be a class dictatorship. According to Engels, the state "'*withers away*'" (120).

Marx's *historicism* leads him to misjudge the possibilities of *social engineering* (OS II, 125f.). After all, legislative steps or their prevention can also be a means of class struggle. For example, "it is only the active intervention of the state – the protection of property by laws backed by physical sanctions – which makes of wealth a potential source of power" (128). On the other hand, only until 1833 were capitalists able to prevent any labour legislation from being passed. Therefore, Popper assumes, unlike Marx, that political power can control economic power (126). But he also recognizes the dangers of political intervention. Such interventions extend the *power* of the state, and "state power must always remain a dangerous though necessary *evil*" (130, i.a.).

Faced with the unendurable working conditions of early capitalism, Popper underestimates another danger: Politically controlled prices lose their steering function. The socialist countries and the agricultural commodities market of the European Community show what results when state interventions impair free price formation. On the other hand, our concern for economic efficiency may pale into insignificance after globalization has affected the Western European labour market for another decade. By then, the number of unemployed will have increased further and the working conditions in quite a few trades will again have become – according to our present standards – unbearable. And if ordinary people will not be content with living conditions closer to those of early capitalism, then this will also have political consequences.

11.46. Marx's Prophecy

Popper calls Marx's *Capital* "the great work of his life" (OS II, 135). As already mentioned, it is intended "'*to lay bare the economic law of motion of modern society*', in order to prophesy its fate" (135f., i.a.). Popper portrays this prophecy "as a closely knit argument," even though only its first step is fully elaborated in *Capital*; the remaining two "are only sketched" (136).

In his "first step," Marx analyzes capitalist production. It tends "towards an *increase in the productivity of work*" and toward "the increasing *accumulation* of the means of production" (OS II, 136). From this, he infers tendencies toward an *increase* (a) of the *wealth in the bourgeoisie* and (b) of the *misery of the workers* (136f.). From these tendencies, he infers in his "second step," (c) that all classes except a small bourgeoisie and a large working class will disappear and (d) that growing tension between these two classes will inevitably lead to a *social revolution*. From this, finally, he infers in his "third step," (e) that after the victory of the working class society will consist of *one class* only and (f) that this society will hence be *classless*, without exploitation, "that is to say, *socialism*" (137).

Popper begins with a discussion of the "*third step*," that is, the *prophecy of socialism*. From its premises [the conclusions (c) and (d) of the "second step"], he admits, follows the first conclusion (e), insofar as it asserts the *disappearance of the bourgeoisie*; but it does not follow (f) that the *new society* will be *classless*. Rather, the leaders of the revolution will most likely "form a *New Class*: *the new ruling class of the new society*" (OS II, 138). And nobody could ignore that this was exactly what had happened in Russia after the October Revolution and had repeated itself in every other socialist country. In Korea, even the communist Kim dynasty emerged.

Then Popper discusses the "*second step*" leading to the prophecies of (c) the *development of the class structure* and (d) the *proletarian social revolution*. He finds that neither (c) nor (d) follows from premises (a) and (b). Even if premises (a) and (b) are true, quite different class structures might evolve instead of (c) (i.e. the confrontation of the bourgeoisie and the proletariat) (OS II, 148f.), and premises (a) and (b) would not cause us to expect (d) the social revolution either. If, on the other hand, we accept not only premises (a) and (b) but also the "consequence" (c), "then the prophecy of the social revolution would indeed follow" (154).

Popper considers the prophecy (d) "of a possibly *violent revolution* . . . by far the most harmful element in Marxism" (OS II, 151, i.a.). But Marxism cannot do without it, for "the sole basis of the prophetic argument is the assumption of an increasing class-antagonism"; an evolutionary interpretation of the "social revolution" would "destroy the whole prophetic argument" (155). Popper also criticizes "*the ambiguous attitude* [of Marxist parties] *towards the problem of violence*" (156f.). Here he inserts reflections on tyrannicide and parts of his theory of democracy, to which we shall return (in section 11.6.).

The "*first step*" in Marx's argument is "the *analysis of the fundamental economic forces of capitalism* and their influence upon the relations between the classes" (OS II, 136, i.a.). Competition, accumulation, and increasing productivity are the *fundamental tendencies* of capitalist production (167). These are the *premises* of the "first step." Competition forces accumulation of the means of production, of capital, which in turn increases productivity but also results in the concentration of capital in fewer and fewer hands.

So we have arrived at *conclusion (a)*, the increasing wealth of a small bourgeoisie. Thus far, Popper accepts "Marx's analysis as a *description* of an unrestrained capitalism," but not as a *prophecy* (OS II, 169, i.a.), for concentration can be limited by legal regulations, as has long been known. Hence conclusion (a) need not be true, and it does not follow from the premises either.

This holds all the more of *conclusion (b)*, "the *law* of increasing misery which Marx claimed to have discovered" (OS II, 169). It excludes the idea that capitalism could "afford to decrease the misery of the workers," and on this law "*the whole prophetic argument hinges*" (169, i.a.). When Marx began writing *Capital*, he already knew of political interventions by means of laws that were intended to lessen the misery of the workers. It is true that these regulations were still weak and that they were often violated, as the reports of the factory supervisors on which he based his theory showed. But from this he should not have inferred that in a capitalist society more effective laws cannot be passed and enforced. Marx himself lived to see this come to pass.

As Marx relied on an incomplete set of premises about the influence of politics on capitalism – some of which were even false – his "*derivation* of [(b)] the historical law of increasing misery is . . . *invalid*" (OS II, 179, i.a.). History has also *refuted* this *law*, for the "standard of living of employed workers has risen everywhere since Marx's day" (189). Thus "none of Marx's more ambitious historicist conclusions, none of his 'inexorable laws of development' and his 'stages of history which cannot be leaped over', has ever turned out to be a successful prediction" (197). Marx's *prophecies* fail because of the "poverty of historicism" – that is, because we do not know whether a trend observed today will continue tomorrow (193).

Only some of his less central prophecies were successful. Thus, "for the time being; the tendency towards an increase of productivity continues," and "the trade cycle also continues" (OS II, 196). But both developments had been predicted by other economists long before Marx. There is more reason to call Marx the author of the prophecy "that the association of the workers would be another important factor in this process [the downfall of the unrestrained system of capitalism]" (196). On the other hand, even though Marx's sociological and economical *analyses* of contemporary society were somewhat one-sided, they were nevertheless excellent insofar they were *descriptive*. However, "*it was nowhere his historicist method which led him to success, but always the methods of institutional analysis*" (197).

11.47. The Moral Theory of Historicism

According to (the early) Popper, Marx "took the ideals of 1789 seriously" and did not just preach freedom and equality (OS II, 207). Only "his hatred of hypocrisy . . . led him to veil his moral beliefs behind historicist formulations" (207). According to Popper's reconstruction, Marx's fundamental decision appears to have been not a "sentimental decision to help the oppressed, but *the scientific and rational decision not to offer vain resistance to the developmental laws of society*" (204, i.a.). Only after he had taken this decision did he accept his moral feelings and use them as a weapon in the class struggle (204).

But a *historicist moral theory* precludes any moral criticism of the past (Plato), present (Hegel), or future (Marx) *state of affairs* by which it orients itself, "since this state itself determines the moral *standard* of things" (OS II, 206, i.a.). Hence this theory is a form of "*moral positivism*" (206). Had Marx considered this consequence, he surely would have rejected historicist moral theory (207).

Popper's thesis that *Capital* is "largely a treatise on social ethics," even though "these ethical ideas are never represented as such" but "are expressed only by implication" (OS II, 199) – namely, as a historicist moral theory – and that Marx chooses this camouflage only in order to conceal his sincere moral feelings, which Popper shares, is a remarkable contribution to the veneration of Marx. And only those who do not know Marx's biography will share Popper's view: "It is certain that in the practical decisions of his life Marx followed a very rigorous moral code" (203).

11.5. THE AFTERMATH

Chapters 23 and 24 of *The Open Society* are devoted to the "aftermath" of Hegel's and Marx's philosophy. First, Popper deals with "the sociology of knowledge" (Chapter 23). Here he primarily concerns himself with the problem of *objectivity*. Then he turns to the "oracular philosophy and the revolt against reason" (Chapter 24), upon which he brings his *critical rationalism* to bear.

11.51. The Sociology of Knowledge

Popper considers Hegel's and Marx's historicist philosophies, to be "characteristic products of their time" (OS II, 212); Hegel even asserts "that *all* knowledge and all truth is 'relative' in the sense of being determined by history" (214, i.a.). This view is sometimes called "*historism.*" Obviously, it is not identical to what Popper calls "*historicism.*" Rather, it is "very closely related to or nearly identical with" the "*sociology of knowledge* or '*sociologism*'" (214, i.a.). It intends to make possible objective judgments in the social sciences, by enabling authors to see through their historical and social restraints. However, this kind of *sociotherapy* is obviously not very successful, for the sociologists of knowledge do not see through their own dependence on Hegel (216).

Hence there would be no objectivity in science if it depended on the impartiality of the scientists. Rather, "[s]cientific *objectivity* can be described as the *inter-subjectivity* of scientific method" (OS II, 217, i.a.). The attitudes of *persons* do not matter so much; rather, everything depends on "the working of the various *social institutions* which have been designed to further scientific objectivity and criticism; for instance the laboratories, the scientific periodicals, the congresses" (218).

11.52. A Plea for Critical Rationalism

Against oracular philosophy and the revolt against reason Popper sets his plea for critical rationalism. He uses the words "reason" and "rationalism" in a broad sense, comprehending not only purely intellectual activities but also observations and experiments. Accordingly, "*rationalism*" is the opposite of "*irrationalism,*" whereas in the common, narrower sense it is the opposite of "*empiricism.*" Thus rationalism comprehends empiricism and (classical) rationalism (such as, say, that of Descartes), which Popper calls "*intellectualism*" because it "extols intelligence above observation and experiment" (OS II, 224). As for the rest, Popper uses "rationalism" to denote "an attitude or readiness to listen to critical arguments and to learn from experience," "an attitude of admitting that '*I may be wrong and you may be right, and by an effort, we may get nearer to the truth*'" (225).

Popper subdivides rationalism in the broad sense into "'*critical ratio-nalism*' and '*uncritical rationalism*' or '*comprehensive rationalism*'" (OS II, 229, i.a.). Uncritical rationalism adopts the *principle* "that any assumption which cannot be supported either by argument or by experience is to be discarded" (230). This principle, however, is *inconsistent*, "for since it can-not, in its turn, be supported by argument or by experience, it implies that it should itself be discarded" (230). Hence "neither . . . argument nor experience can establish the *rationalist attitude*"; thus "comprehensive rationalism" is untenable (230, i.a.).

Popper therefore advocates "a modest and self-critical rationalism which recognizes certain limitations," and which he labels "'*critical ra-tionalism*'" (OS II, 229, i.a.). He shares the "*rationalist attitude*," which "*attaches [great importance] to argument and experience*" (230, i.a.), but he "recognizes the fact that the fundamental rationalist attitude *results from an (at least tentative) act of faith* – from faith in reason" (231, i.a.). His crit-ical rationalism "frankly admits its origin in an *irrational decision*" (231, i.a.). In a lecture given in 1960, he stresses that the rationalist demand to *justify* all assumptions is untenable. *Rational discussion* is now character-ized as a "*critical discussion* in search of mistakes with the serious purpose of eliminating as many of these mistakes as we can, in order to get nearer to the truth" (CR, 229, i.a.). And in his autobiography, he gives *criticism*, in retrospect, the greatest weight: In *The Open Society*, he reminds us, he had argued "that one of the best senses of 'reason' and 'reasonableness' was openness to criticism" and had suggested that the demand to "extend the critical attitude as far as possible might be called '*critical rationalism*'" (A, 92, i.a.).

The decision to adopt critical rationalism "is a *moral* decision" that "will deeply affect our whole attitude towards other men, and towards the problems of social life" (OS II, 232, i.a.). The analysis of the con-sequences of a moral decision (OG II, 273) such as this "has a certain analogy in scientific method" (OS II, 233). As "uncritical rationalism" is inconsistent, we are left with the choice between "irrationalism" and "critical rationalism." In order to rationally consider this choice, Popper examines the consequences of both positions. Then he makes his moral decision (OG II, 273); and each other person must make a moral deci-sion as well.

But isn't this choice more likely to be (means-end) *rational* than moral? After all, the methodology of critical rationalism is a modern form of empiricist epistemology. It shows what we can still do to avoid errors once we have given up the illusion of certain a priori or a posteriori knowledge.

Here we need only indicate Popper's description of the respective consequences: While the *critical rationalist* is "always ready to submit to facts" (OS II, 245), adopts the "humanitarian attitude of impartiality" (234) and consequently accepts the idea "of responsibility" (238), the *irrationalist* "can hardly avoid becoming entangled with the attitude that is opposed to equalitarianism" (235), for, being a mystic, he "escapes into dreams" (243) – as, for example Plato, who escapes into "the myth of the lost tribal paradise" (245) – or he joins the "oracular philosophy [e.g., of Hegel] which escapes into verbiage" (243). Popper also warns us about Marx, because "the attempt to make heaven on earth invariably produces hell" (237). And he criticizes Whitehead and Toynbee, "two of the most influential irrationalist authorities of our time" (247).

11.6. ON THE MEANING OF HISTORY

As *The Open Society* criticizes an influential political philosophy, historicism, it cannot avoid offering for its part "a kind of critical introduction to the philosophy of society and of politics" (OS II, 259). The title of its last chapter, "Has History Any Meaning?," is a surprise. In order to prepare the answer, Popper gives – in sections I–III – a short introduction to his methodology. Explanation, prediction, and the testing of hypotheses are briefly discussed. The discussion concentrates on the peculiarities of the *historical sciences*, which are interested "in specific events and in their explanation" (264), while the generalizing natural sciences are interested "in testing universal hypotheses, and in predicting specific events" (263).

His central thesis says: "[*T*]*here can be no history of 'the past as it actually did happen'*" (OS II, 268, i.a.). Though some matters of fact can be ascertained, *every description is necessarily selective* and in this sense contains an implicit *interpretation*. In addition, there are explicit interpretations in the form of attempts at explanation. By asking questions, we select some facts of history, and by giving explanations we order them (269). Therefore, a historical description can never be *objective* in the sense of being independent of any "*'point of view'*" (267, i.a.). Nevertheless, it can be *true* in the sense of corresponding to *reality*.

But historicist interpretations try to extract the unavoidable point of view from the tendencies of historical development. They are "out to discover... The Meaning of History" (OS II, 269). Popper comments: "*History has no meaning*" (269). *There is not even a concrete "history of mankind, there is only an indefinite number of histories of all kinds of aspects of human life*" (270, i.a.) – for every such aspect, we write a different history. And we compensate for the lack of a given meaning by choosing aims ourselves: "[*A*] *lthough history has no meaning, we can give it a meaning*" (278). Here we meet again "the problem of nature and convention," the "dualism of facts and decisions" (278), which historicism tries to get over because "it shrinks from realizing that we bear the ultimate responsibility even for the standards we choose" (279).

11.7. THE THEORY OF DEMOCRACY

Popper considers *The Open Society* "a theoretical defence of democracy against the old and new attacks of its enemies" (1999 [LP], 93; literally translated: "a *theory of democracy* and a defence of democracy" – 1994, 207, i.a., m.t.). There have been many editions of this book, but its *most important point* is seldom completely understood. Though "*democracy*" means in English "rule by the people," "the people do not rule anywhere; it is always governments that rule" (93). Does this mean that there are no democracies, or is the rule of the people not necessary for the existence of a democracy?

Popper states:

There are in fact only two forms of state: those in which it is possible to get rid of a government without bloodshed, and those in which this is not possible. This is what matters – not what the form of state is called. Usually the first form is called "democracy" and the second "dictatorship" or "tyranny." But it is not worth arguing over words (such as the German "Democratic" Republic [GDR]). *All that counts is whether the government can be removed without bloodshed.* (LP, 94, i.a.)

When he wrote this in 1987, Popper – like almost all politicians – probably considered it impossible to remove the government of the GDR without bloodshed. But in 1989, this is exactly what happened. This was possible, however, only in the presence of a particular historical event, the inner decay of the Soviet Union. Lest the GDR be considered a democracy just because of the way it ended, Popper's definition must be amended. It must stipulate that the possibility of removing a government without bloodshed recur at *regular intervals*. Of course, the intervals need not be as brief as they used to be in Italy.

Therefore, his answer to Plato's question "*Who should rule?*" is: "*[I]t does not matter who rules if it is possible to get rid of the government without bloodshed*" (LP, 94, i.a.). For he thinks: "Any government that can be thrown out has a strong incentive to act in a way that makes people content with it. And this incentive is lost if the government knows it cannot be so easily ousted" (94).

Though this is obviously correct, it does not save us further deliberation, for a steady succession of incapable or corrupt governments also endangers the citizens' security and welfare. And what's the use of voting when all eligible parties pursue an aim that the majority of the voters do not share, as was the case in Germany when the decision was made to introduce the Euro? We have to read Popper's answer as being the result of *balancing* one thing against another: If we can choose between, on the one hand, a government by the most capable people harbouring the best intentions, as sketched in Plato's utopia, which, however, cannot be replaced without bloodshed, and, on the other hand, a government by selfish people who are – except for their ability to influence others – only moderately gifted, as we know from our own experience, but which can be voted out, then the latter represents by far the lesser danger. For experience has shown that power corrupts; in fact, it corrupts the more the longer it lasts and the less it is open to attack. Even Kant writes – in Addendum II to his otherwise rather optimistic treatise on *Perpetual Peace*: "It is not to be expected or even desired that kings should philosophise, or that philosophers should become kings; for the possession of power inevitably destroys the free judgment of reason" (Kant 1927, 43).

But what shall we do when the existing circumstances seem unbearable? As we know, Popper answers: "Try piecemeal reforms!" But how – if the existing government prevents reforms and cannot be voted out? In extreme cases, his political program admits exceptions:

I am not in all cases and under all circumstances against a violent revolution. I believe with some medieval and Renaissance Christian thinkers who taught the admissibility of tyrannicide that there may indeed, under a tyranny, be no other possibility, and that a violent revolution may be justified. But I also believe that any such revolution should have as its *only* aim the establishment of a democracy. (OS II, 151)

The "use of violence is justified only under a tyranny which makes reforms without violence impossible, and it should have only one aim, that is, to bring about a state of affairs which makes reforms without violence possible" (151). And "[t]here is only one further use of violence in political quarrels which I should consider justified. I mean the resistance, once democracy has been attained, to any attack (whether from within or without the state) against the democratic constitution and the use of democratic methods" (151). By the attack from within, he obviously means above all Hitler's "seizure of power" of 1933.

12

The "Positivist Dispute"

During the 1960s, there was a revival of the classical "dispute on value judgments" in the form of the "positivist dispute in German sociology" (cf. Keuth 1989). At the Tübingen conference of the German Sociological Association in October 1961, Popper gave a lecture on "The Logic of the Social Sciences," and Adorno gave the supplementary lecture, "On the Logic of the Social Sciences" (Adorno et al. 1969/1976, 87ff., 105ff.). The discussion was friendly and resulted in a partial clarification of the respective points of view. A dispute arose only when Habermas, in his paper "The Analytic Theory of Science and Dialectics," criticized Popper and when Albert, in his "The Myth of Total Reason," made a counterplea (131ff., 163ff.). A second exchange followed in the form of Habermas's "A Positivistically Bisected Rationalism" and Albert's "Behind Positivism's Back?" (198ff., 226ff.). Then additional authors took part in the dispute.

Details on the case history of this conference may be found in Dahms's article "Der Positivismusstreit der 60er Jahre: eine merkwürdige Neuauflage" (The Positivist Dispute in the Sixties: A Curious Re-edition; 1991). Dahms does not, however, mean a re-edition of the "dispute on value judgments," which had raged since the 1870s and had reached its climax in the 1914 "discussion on value judgments" in the "Verein für Sozialpolitik" (Society for Social Politics; cf. Nau 1996b). Rather, he means a quite different controversy: In the thirties, the *Critical Theory of Society* had developed, for the most part already in exile but initiated by work at the Frankfort Institute for Social Research. After the return of its authors in the late forties, "critical theory" was ascribed to the *Frankfort School*. Its representatives severely, but not very knowledgeably, criticized the empirical sciences and "positivism" (see the following discussion). With political intentions, they also engaged in social research, and they imputed opposing political intentions to social scientists who criticized their methodical procedures. Obviously, Dahms means the re-edition of this controversy.

At the time of the "positivist dispute," Habermas adhered to this "critical theory of society." And Hans Albert became, as a consequence of his role in the "positivist dispute," the leading representative of critical rationalism in Germany. Critical theory attacks the empirical sciences and all realist versions of empiricism, which it indiscriminately labels "positivism." Above all, critical theory claims to provide not only factual but also ethical knowledge. But Horkheimer's and Adorno's contributions show their general ignorance of the neoempiricist positions they attack; Habermas at least knows a little about them. Their lack of competence, however, does not impair the political effectiveness of their criticism.

12.1. HORKHEIMER'S CRITICISM OF "POSITIVISM"

In his article "Materialismus und Metaphysik" (1933/1975), Horkheimer resumes Lenin's criticism of empiriocriticism (1909) and asserts that positivism may be characterized by "the belief that the world can be composed of elements, the ultimate of which are 'for the time being' our sensations" (1933, 86, m.t.). But, on the one hand, this statement is based only on *The Analysis of Sensations* (1886/1959) and *Erkenntnis und Irrtum* (Knowledge and Error; 1905) by Ernst Mach; on the other hand, it does not even give a correct account of Mach. For according to Mach, the *elements* (e.g., primary colours), as opposed to the sensations (e.g., colours), are already the *results* of an analysis – namely, "ultimate component parts, which *hitherto* we have been unable to subdivide any further" (1886/1959, 5f., i.a.). Horkheimer also refers to Wittgenstein's *Tractatus* (1921/1922), but he quotes only 6.52 and 6.522. Apparently, he doesn't know any other works from the vicinity of the Vienna Circle. At any rate, he mentions neither Schlick's *General Theory of Knowledge* (1918/1985) nor Carnap's *The Logical Structure of the World* (1928/1967).

Years before Horkheimer published his programmatic article "Traditionelle und kritische Theorie" (1937), Carnap had reacted to criticisms by Neurath and Popper. And as early as 1932 he had given up the phenomenalism of his *The Logical Structure of the World* (cf. section 4.1). Horkheimer calls the empirical sciences "*traditional theory*"; the "new dialectical philosophy," which "is based on Marx's criticism of political economics," he calls "*critical theory of society*" (1937, 57ff., m.t.). He considers "critical theory" to be "the most advanced way of thinking of the present time" (48, m.t.). In contrast to "traditional theory," "critical theory" produces not only statements but also value judgments and demands; and in contrast even to traditional philosophy, it includes political activities, even struggle (35). It is true that "critical theory" sides with Marx's philosophy; however, it does not see itself as an alternative to, but rather as the heir of, German Idealism (58). Thus Adorno also calls it "Hegelmarxismus."

While "traditional theory" may serve the reproduction of what exists as well as its alteration, the aim of "critical theory" is "the happiness of all individuals" (1937, 60, m.t.). However, it cannot achieve this goal by redressing some grievances – that is, by reforming society – but only by changing the whole construction of society (27). Hence "critical theory" too advocates utopian social engineering (cf. Chapter 10; for Horkheimer's description of "critical theory," see Keuth 1993, Chapter 1).

According to Horkheimer, the structure of "critical theory" results from its political task. From the "fundamental relation of exchange," it infers capitalist society (1937, 43), which at the present time (1937) leads to wars, revolutions, a new barbarism. However, "critical theory" also asserts that it is now (1937!) possible to change this development (44 n20). To the extent that statements of "critical theory" are derived from the concept of exchange, the states of affairs they express "appear necessary" (44, m.t.). With respect to this "necessity in the logical sense," the structures of "traditional theory" and of "critical theory" are similar (44f.). But they differ with respect to "factual necessity," because "traditional theory" does not take into account changes resulting from interventions (45, m.t.). For this, we need the critical concept of a "necessity . . . in the sense of events which we force ourselves" (47, m.t.). However, so long as society has not been changed according to "critical theory," this theory lacks "confirmation by victory" and even continues the "struggle for its correct wording and application" (55, m.t.).

But how does "critical theory" know what is morally right? It "devises" the aim of critical thinking (1937, 35, m.t.) that is, "the emancipation of man from enslaving circumstances" (58, m.t.). The word "devises" may sound decisionistic. However, "critical theory" recognizes a tendency in history that will lead to this state of affairs, and it proves that this state can now (1937) be realized (38). The devised aim is morally right, because it is "immanent to human labour" (38, m.t.), and what is more, "every man is really predisposed to it" (63, m.t.). Hence Horkheimer's "critical theory" too is historicist (cf. Chapter 10). But he is mentioned neither in *The Poverty of Historicism* nor in *The Open Society*. When Horkheimer's article appeared in 1937, Popper had already left Vienna, and in New Zealand it probably was inaccessible to him.

However, only a subject who is interested in this aim and in this tendency find them by historical analysis. Marx ascribes this interest to the proletariat (1937, 32); Horkheimer ascribes it to the spirit (40f.). By "spirit" he means society, whose activity appears as a transcendental power (24), for the idealist concept of reason has become the materialist concept "of a free self-determining society" (60).

12.2. HABERMAS'S CRITICISM OF CRITICAL RATIONALISM

At the time of the "positivist dispute," Habermas still claims that one can acquire practical, ethical knowledge by means of the neo-Marxist dialectic theory of society. He postulates "historical laws of movement" that, on the one hand, "signify developments which, mediated through the consciousness of the acting subjects, gradually prevail" and, on the other hand, "claim to articulate the objective meaning of a historical life-context" (1963/1976, 138f.; cf. Keuth 1989, Chapter 3).

Hence at this time (1963), Habermas too is a historicist. In 1980, he still strives "to carry on the Marxian tradition under greatly changed historical conditions" (1984, 477, m.t.). What already separates him from Marx "are historical evidences, e.g. the insight that in developed capitalist societies there is no identifiable class, no clearly defined social group, which could without further ado be considered the representative of a hurt common interest" (479, m.t.). These evidences have destroyed the "certainty of the philosophy of history" in which Marx's prophecies partake (479, m.t.). Only in 1981 does Habermas too admit that "*the way of thinking of philosophy of history*" results from "*confusions of fundamental concepts*" (1981, vol. 2, 562, i.a., m.t.). But even then he is not content with openly *deciding* for or against political aims. Rather, he still claims to *know* that his aims are morally right. Now he bases this claim on ideas belonging to the philosophies of language and of communication. But these ideas are no less confused than those of the philosophy of history (cf. Keuth 1993).

According to Habermas, the empirical and the dialectical social sciences disagree above all on "the problem of the so-called *value freedom* of historical and theoretical research" (1963/1976, 143ff., i.a.). But what does Habermas mean by "value freedom"? Undoubtedly, he pleads for *value judgments in academic teaching*, rejects Max Weber's (1864–1920) thesis that *scientific value judgments* are impossible, and considers Weber's demand for a *clear distinction between statements of facts and value judgments* unnecessary, if not unwelcome. Whether he also considers it unrealizable is left open.

At any rate, Habermas tries to take away the basis of the demand for value freedom by attacking the *"dualism of facts and decisions"* – that is, the "separation between science and ethics," the "dualism of descriptive and normative knowledge" (1964/1976, 215f., i.a.). In order to refute the assumption that the "bas[e]s" of natural laws and of social norms are "independent of one another" (1963/1976, 144), he interprets the empirical sciences pragmatically and emphasizes the idea that empirical science is not "released from every normative bond" (149). However, on the one hand, the dependence of science on choices and thus on evaluations had already been emphasized by Max Weber; and on the other hand, it is irrelevant to the problem of "normative knowledge."

Habermas examines the normative bond "in connection with Popper's suggestions for the solution of the so-called *basis-problem*" (1963/1976, 149, i.a.). According to Habermas, Popper's proposal does not take into account the *circle* that is unavoidable, when "law-like hypotheses" or "juridical legal norms" or simply "general rules" are applied (152). He owes this assumption to Gadamer. Habermas considers the circle inevitable because "[o]ne cannot apply general rules if a prior decision has not been taken concerning the facts which can be subsumed under the rules; on the other hand, these facts cannot be established as relevant cases prior to an application of those rules" (152; on the theory-dependence of judgments on basic statements, cf. section 4.7).

He takes the "inevitable circle in the application of rules [to be] evidence of the embedding of the research process in a context which itself can no longer be explicated in an analytical-empirical manner but only hermeneutically" (1963/1976, 152), and he believes, accordingly, that "the empirical validity of basic statements is measured against a behavioural expectation governed by social norms" (153). A pragmatist interpretation of the process of scientific discovery will show which are the expectations: "[T]he empirical validity of basic statements, . . . is related to the criteria for assessing the results of action," and "[t]he so-called basis-problem simply does not appear if we regard the research process as part of a comprehensive process of socially institutionalized actions" (154). Thus "*a connection* [is] demonstrated *with the social labour process,* a connection which penetrates the innermost structures of the theory itself and *determines what shall empirically possess validity*" (156, i.a.).

These theses have been criticized by Hans Albert (1964/1976). In his rejoinder, Habermas asserts that he does not attack empirical research but criticizes its "positivistic interpretation" in order to question the separation between science and ethics (1964/1976, 198). He admits that Popper has efficiently criticized neopositivism, but asserts that Popper "does not see through the objectivistic illusion which suggests that scientific theories represent facts" (199). According to Habermas, the thesis that "tests examine theories against 'independent' [of the theories tested] facts... is the pivot of the *residual positivistic problematic in Popper*" (203, i.a.). And he suspects that (in 1963/1976) he did not succeed "in even making [Hans Albert] aware of what is at issue here" (1964/1976, 203). Contrary to what Popper and Albert assume, "[t]he experiential basis of the exact sciences is not independent of the standards which these sciences themselves attribute to experience" (201). But in *The Logic of Scientific Discovery*, Popper discusses these standards. So, what does Habermas mean?

"Moral feelings, privations and frustrations, crises in the individual's life history, changes in attitude in the course of reflection – all these mediate different experiences. Through corresponding standards they can be raised to the level of a validating instance" (1964/1976, 201). In fact, the adherents of the moral sense school – in particular, Francis Hutcheson (1694–1746) and David Hume (1711–1776) – take moral judgments to be based on a feeling. But Habermas does not side with Hume. Rather, he claims that the "critique of an empirical-scientific hypothesis and the critical discussion of the choice of a standard... [have] the same... logical structure" (216). If the "logical structure" is that of a hypothetico-deductive argument, then Popper can accept this statement. Nevertheless, there remains a difference between (a) the "validation" of the statement "There is a feeling" by the feeling itself or by indicators of its existence and (b) the "validation" of a moral norm (say, "Act in such a way that your action gives to a spectator the pleasing sentiment of approbation") by a (the spectator's) feeling or by indicators of its existence. While validation (a) is based on the empiricist model of knowledge, there is no corresponding model of knowledge in case (b). Habermas ignores this difference and continues: "Popper terminates this reflection by reference to the correspondence theory of truth" (216). This criticism shows that Habermas also misunderstands the realist interpretation of statements (cf. section 6.5; Keuth 1989, sections 3.6, 3.7).

Hans Albert examined Habermas's arguments critically (1965/1976), without, however, producing any perceptible effect on Habermas, on other proponents of "critical theory," or even on its (at that time) numerous adherents. Other critics of "critical theory" had as little success. It did not matter that the criticism that "critical theory" directed against empirical science and against critical rationalism proved untenable and that its philosophy of history results from confusions of fundamental concepts. As long as its untenable criticism and its confused philosophy could be used to "legitimate" political demands and thus improve the chances of realizing political aims, the adherents of "critical theory" saw no reason to abandon their positions.

PART III

METAPHYSICS

13

Natural Necessity

According to David Hume, "a characterization of laws of nature as universal statements is *logically sufficient* and also *intuitively adequate*" (LSD, 427; cf. section 2.1). In his *Logic*, Popper had adopted this thesis, and William Kneale had criticized him for it (Kneale 1949). In the new Appendix *X, "Universals, Dispositions, and Natural or Physical Necessity" (first added to LSD in 1959), Popper (in part) accepts this criticism. He restates its fundamental idea as follows: "Although universal statements are *entailed* by statements of natural law, the latter are logically stronger than the former. They do not only assert 'All planets move in ellipses', but rather something like 'All planets move *necessarily* in ellipses'" (426).

But Kneale's "positive theory of natural laws" seems to him unacceptable (LSD, 427), because Kneale assumes "that laws of nature are necessary in the same sense in which logical tautologies are necessary" (430). Popper criticizes this view as "a particularly severe form of . . . 'essentialism,'" because "it entails the doctrine of the existence of *ultimate explanations*" (431). In its stead, he postulates that "[c]ompared with logical tautologies, laws of nature have a contingent, an accidental character" (429). Therefore, Popper develops his own version of "the idea that there are necessary laws of nature" (438). In section 12 of the *Logic*, he had still proposed excluding the "principle of causality," which asserts "that the world is governed by strict laws, . . . that *every* specific event is an instance of a universal regularity or law, . . . as 'metaphysical', from the sphere of science" (61, i.a.; cf. section 2.1). But now he emphasizes "that the *metaphysical* character . . . of the *assertion that* [*necessary*] *laws of nature exist* need not prevent us from discussing this assertion *rationally* – that is to say, *critically*"; he also considers this idea "metaphysically or *ontologically important,* and of great intuitive significance in connection with our attempts to understand the world"; he even believes "that it is *true*" (438, i.a.). It implies, however, that at least *some* events are *physically determined* – even if not all of them are, as the "principle of causality" asserts.

13.1. NATURAL LAWS AND STRICTLY UNIVERSAL STATEMENTS

In order to explain his change of mind, Popper constructs an example. It relates to the moa, an extinct bird. He uses the *word* "moa" "as a universal name . . . of a certain biological structure" – not as the proper name of the totality of those running birds that once lived in New Zealand (LSD, 427; he refers to section 14, "Universal Concepts and Individual Concepts"; cf. section 2.5). In addition, he makes the following *assumptions*: (1) "[T]he biological structure of the moa organism is of such a kind that under very favourable conditions, a moa might easily live sixty years or longer." (2) "[N]o moas have ever existed in the universe, or will ever exist, apart from those which once lived in New Zealand." (3) "[T]he conditions met by the moa . . . were far from ideal . . . [so that] no moa ever reached the age of fifty." Accordingly, "the strictly universal statement 'All moas die before reaching the age of fifty' will be true" (427). That no moa did live longer is, however, "only due to *accidental or contingent* conditions – such as the co-presence of a certain virus" (427f.).

The moa example is meant to show "that there may be *true, strictly universal statements* which have an *accidental character* [i.a.] rather than the *character of true universal laws of nature* [i.a.]" (LSD, 428). But by supposition, the statement "All moas die before reaching the age of fifty" is true only of the finite number of moas that once lived in a certain spatiotemporal region. Doesn't this mean that it is only *numerically universal* after all? In that case, however, even "statements of natural law" might be only numerically universal, for they would also be true only of a finite number of cases, should our world be finite. Actually, the statement "All moas die before reaching the age of fifty" is *strictly universal,* for the fact that it applies only to a finite number of birds is due not to its *meaning* but to the additional *factual* premise (2) that in the entire universe moas exist only for a certain time and in a certain place.

Popper considers "the characterization of laws of nature as strictly universal statements . . . logically insufficient and intuitively inadequate," because strictly universal statements may be true on some physically possible conditions – for example, the co-presence of the moas and the virus – while on other conditions they may be false (LSD, 428). Accordingly, it is important to distinguish "*the universality of laws* from '*accidental*' *universality* [i.a.]" (438). Therefore, he introduces his concept of *natural necessity*. Tarski's explanation of *logical necessity* (a statement is logically necessary if, and only if, it is deducible from a "*universally valid*" statement function, 432) serves as his model. By analogy, Popper proposes that:

(N°) *A statement may be said to be naturally or physically necessary if, and only if, it is deducible from a statement function which is satisfied in all worlds that differ from our world, if at all, only with respect to initial conditions.* (433)

In a world identical to ours but in which that virus did not occur, the strictly universal statement "All moas die before reaching the age of fifty" would be false. Hence it is not naturally necessary.

Along with the laws of nature, all their *logical consequences* are *naturally or physically necessary* (LSD; 433). Carnap calls them all "*causally true*" (1966, 214). If there are physically necessary natural laws, then there are also physically necessary *particular* statements. But their derivation must not depend on additional premises that are not themselves physically necessary. Trivially, the *instantial statements* of natural laws satisfy this condition.

As natural laws postulate necessities, they are *logically stronger* than the strictly universal but "accidental" statements that they imply (LSD, 426, 431). Now, Popper demands that we always choose the logically strongest hypothesis, because it is best testable. But is the excess content of natural laws empirical? How can we test their physical necessity? The three assumptions mentioned earlier, taken together, imply that the strictly universal statement "All moas die before reaching the age of fifty" is not "necessarily" but only "accidentally" universal. But the second assumption, "[N]o moas have ever existed in the universe, or will ever exist, apart from those which once lived in New Zealand," is *in principle not empirically testable*; hence it is metaphysical. Therefore, the distinction between "necessarily" universal and "accidentally" universal statements is *methodologically irrelevant*, as Popper admits (432). This will become clear in yet another way (see the following discussion).

13.2. DEGREES OF UNIVERSALITY AND STRUCTURAL PROPERTIES OF THE WORLD

According to Popper, the idea that there are physically necessary natural laws implies a change "on an ontological, a metaphysical level," which may be described by saying that a natural law "expresses a *structural property of our world*" (432). Thus he emphasizes "*the peculiar ontological status of universal laws*" (438, i.a.). On the other hand, he regards "'necessary' as a mere word – as a label useful for distinguishing *the universality of laws* from 'accidental' universality" (438).

However, *any* statement – when interpreted in the usual realist way – expresses a "property of our world," either a state of affairs or a regularity. Why should this property be called "*structural*" in the case of natural laws? The only reason seems to be that natural laws hold independently of any initial condition of still more universal laws (cf. LSD, 433, 438f.). Hence when he calls universal laws of nature "structural theories about the world" (434), this means only that laws of nature are the *most universal* laws.

In order to express a naturally necessary connection, Popper introduces a *modal operator*. Let *N* be the class of naturally necessary statements, that is, those statements that are "true whatever the initial conditions may be" (LSD, 433). Then, by definition,

(D) $a \rightarrow$N b is true if, and only if, $(a \rightarrow b) \in N$,

that is, "'If *a* then necessarily *b*' [$a \rightarrow$N b] is true if, and only if, 'If *a* then *b*' is necessarily true" [$(a \rightarrow b) \in N$] (433). Popper calls $a \rightarrow$N b "a '*necessary conditional*' or a '*nomic conditional*'" (434, i.a.). This formula expresses what other authors call a "subjunctive conditional" or a "counterfactual conditional" (434) – as, for example, "If *a* were the case, then *b* would be the case." (Carnap considers any genuine law a sufficient justification for a counterfactual conditional [1966, 210].)

On the other hand, Popper thinks he can say "that a law of nature is *necessary* in its turn because it is logically derivable from, or explicable by, a law of a still *higher* degree of universality, or of greater 'depth'" (LSD, 438f., i.a.). Obviously, the law "of a still higher degree of universality" must be necessary itself. If, however, it is necessary because it in turn follows from an even more universal law, then Popper's explication of the concept "law of nature" leads into an *infinite regress*.

As we never know that a particular strictly universal statement is true, and as at most some of the true strictly universal statements are necessary, we never know that a strictly universal statement is necessary. Hence there is no "*positive criterion* of natural necessity" but only a "*negative*" one: "[B]y finding initial conditions under which the supposed law turns out to be invalid, we can show that it was not necessary; that is to say, not a law of nature" (LSD, 433). Of course, no false lawlike hypothesis can be a law of nature. But this "negative criterion" does not permit us to refute the assumption that a lawlike hypothesis *is necessary* independently of the assumption that it *is true*. Accordingly, it is *methodologically irrelevant* to distinguish the universality of laws from "accidental" universality, and the assumption that a universal hypothesis is a law of nature is *metaphysical*.

Carnap shares this view. He constructs an example: If we add the phrase "and this holds with necessity" to a universal hypothesis (1966, 200), then the hypothesis says no more than it did before, for "no more can be predicted *in principle*." It has become stronger only in its "ability to arouse an emotional feeling of necessity" (201). Nevertheless, he also believes that it is possible to define causal modalities by way of analogy to logical necessity (215). But what are such definitions good for?

Like the "principle of causality," Popper's "idea of natural necessity" is metaphysical. And while the "principle of causality" may be regarded as the metaphysical version of the "methodological rule not to abandon the search for universal laws," the "*idea of natural necessity*" may be considered the metaphysical version of the "*methodological rule not to abandon the search for ever more universal laws*." But there are other reasons to adopt this rule: A more universal hypothesis has greater explanatory power and is better testable. Hence we need not assume natural necessity in order to justify the introduction of this rule. In Popper's methodology, the "*idea of natural necessity*" is *superfluous* (cf. LSD, 432), a metaphysical luxury. Moreover, it is incompatible with his indeterminism (cf. section 14). Nor has any other author succeeded in defining a methodologically relevant concept of natural necessity; and Hume showed, why this is impossible.

14

Determinism versus Indeterminism

Popper's book *The Open Universe: An Argument for Indeterminism* is the second part of his *Postscript to the Logic of Scientific Discovery*. Though written before 1956, it was not published until 1982. In his "Editor's Foreword," W. W. Bartley III writes that this second volume contains "the centerpiece" of Popper's argument in the *Postscript*, "the most sustained and important treatment of the problems of determinism and indeterminism" of which he knows (OU, xi). And Popper writes in his "Preface 1982" that when he wrote the book, he did not intend "to discuss human freedom and human free will, even though these were really the problems that stood behind it" (xix). For, on the one hand, the *Postscript* was intended "to discuss the physical sciences, their methods . . . , physical cosmology, and the role of the theory of knowledge in the physical sciences"; on the other hand, the complex of problems surrounding the idea of human freedom was "somewhat muddled by what philosophers ha[d] written" (xix). But already in *The Open Society* and *The Poverty of Historicism* it had become apparent how deeply interested Popper was in the defence of "*human freedom, creativity,* and *responsibility*" "and of what is traditionally called *free will*" (xx, xxi, i.a.). Thus *The Open Universe* finally became "a kind of prolegomenon to the question of human *freedom* and *creativity*" (xxi, i.a.).

The philosophical muddle that Popper complains about is connected to a commonsense muddle. On the one hand, common sense tends to assume that *every* event "is *caused* by some preceding events, so that every event can be explained or *predicted* if we know all the relevant preceding events in sufficient detail"; on the other hand, common sense "attributes to mature and sane human persons . . . the ability to *choose freely* between alternative possibilities of acting; and hence *responsibility* for such action" (OU, xix, i.a.). However, these two assumptions seem to contradict each other. In order to save the latter, the thesis of free will, Popper intends to undermine the former, determinism. In fact, he takes it as his task "to *make room* within physical theory, and within cosmology, *for indeterminism*" (xxi, i.a.).

This aim fundamentally changes his attitude toward the determinism–indeterminism problem. In the *Logic*, he still doesn't want to examine "the metaphysical idea that events are, or are not, *determined in themselves*" (LSD, 206, i.a.). In accordance with the Humean tradition, he instead emphasizes: "If we are successful with our prediction, we may speak of 'laws'; otherwise we can know nothing about the existence or non-existence of laws or of irregularities" (206). Rather than accepting a "principle of causality" that asserts "that any event whatsoever *can* be causally explained – that it *can* be deductively predicted," he instead proposes "a methodological rule which corresponds so closely to the 'principle of causality' that the latter might be regarded as its metaphysical version" – the rule "that we are not to abandon the search for universal laws" (61). Hence already in the *Logic* Popper rejects ontological determinism; instead, he proposes a *methodological determinism*.

This becomes evident in Chapter 9, "Some Observations on Quantum Theory," and above all in section 78, "Indeterminist Metaphysics." He regards the question "Is the world ruled by strict laws or not?" as being metaphysical (LSD, 247). Thus if we are to choose between determinist and indeterminist metaphysics, we must do so according to their expected fruitfulness. While, on the one hand, the belief in causality "is nothing but a typical metaphysical hypostatization of a well justified methodological rule," "denying causality would," on the other hand, "be the same as attempting to persuade the theorist to give up his search" for strict laws (247f.). Therefore, Popper proposes "to *dissent from the indeterminist metaphysic* so popular at present" (216, i.a.). Denying causality would probably not have quite as serious consequences, for the theorist could search for probabilistic hypotheses instead of universal laws. But as universal laws are logically stronger, it is appropriate to search for them first and to content oneself with probabilistic hypotheses only if need be.

In the new Appendix *X that he first added to the English edition of *The Logic of Scientific Discovery* (1959), Popper even returns to a position that Hume had overcome when he asserts that "*natural laws* may be described as '*principles of necessity*' or 'principles of impossibility'" (LSD, 428, i.a.). According to Popper, "laws of nature are ... *logically stronger* than the corresponding universal statements" (431), and they express "a *structural property of our world*," and this requires changes "on an ontological, a metaphysical level" (432; cf. section 13.2). This idea of "*natural necessity*" (432) implies that at least *some* physical events are *determined*.

All the more surprising, then, his change of mind. In the *Postscript* and in his article "Of Clouds and Clocks" (1966), Popper defends a *metaphysical indeterminism* "because it seems to [him] to open new vistas, to suggest the resolution of serious difficulties, and to be, perhaps, true," as he writes in a note that he also adds to *Logic* in 1959 (LSD, 206 n*2). Hence he is now an *ontological* or "*metaphysical*" *indeterminist*, and since he assumes that even classical physics is only prima facie deterministic (cf. section 14.4), the character of his methodological determinism also changes.

14.1. KINDS OF DETERMINISM

In seeking to characterize the *intuitive idea of determinism*, Popper makes use of an analogy: The world is like a motion picture film. The frame just being projected corresponds to *the present*; the frames that have already been shown correspond to *the past*; and the frames that have not yet been shown correspond to *the future*. In this film, the past and the future coexist, "and *the future is fixed*, in exactly the same sense as the past" (OU, 5, i.a.). In *The Open Universe*, Popper differentiates three kinds of determinism – *religious*, '*scientific*,' and *metaphysical* determinism; in his article "Of Clouds and Clocks," he differentiates *physical* and *philosophical* or psychological determinism. All of these forms either state or imply that every event of the (physical) world is *predetermined*.

The "idea of determinism is of religious origin," and *religious determinism* "is connected with the ideas of divine omnipotence . . . and of divine omniscience" (OU, 5). God *knows* the future now; hence it can be known in advance, and it is "*fixed* in advance" (5, i.a.). As Popper says little more about religious determinism in *The Open Universe*, and as he doesn't mention it at all anywhere else, we too shall discuss it no further.

14.11. 'Scientific' Determinism

'*Scientific*' *determinism* replaces God with nature and divine law with natural law (OU, 5). According to this doctrine, "the structure of the world is such that *any event can be rationally predicted, with any desired degree of precision, if we are given a sufficiently precise description of past events, together with all the laws of nature*" (1f.). But in this form it is not supported by scientists.

Rather, Popper extremely sharpens the idea of the predictive power of classical physics in order to show that even in this strong form it does not support (ontological) determinism. To mark his construct, he always puts the attribute 'scientific' in the name "'scientific' determinism" in single quotation marks.

A prediction is rational if it conforms to the deductive-nomological model (cf. 2.3.). Accordingly, 'scientific' determinism says: "To each event there are at least one law of nature and one initial condition which, if they are sufficiently precisely known, permit the derivation of an arbitrarily precise description of that event." How can 'scientific' determinism then be tested? The main clause of its characterization ("To each event there are...") is a mixed (universal and strictly existential) statement and is therefore *neither verifiable nor falsifiable*. In addition, 'scientific' determinism would not be refutable for the simple reason that we never have reason to believe we know "all the laws of nature." Hence it would be *metaphysical* according to the definition given in the *Logic* (cf. section 1.21). But Popper strengthens it by introducing additional assumptions so that it becomes *contradictory* (cf. section 14.53). For this reason alone 'scientific' determinism could not support ontological determinism. Thus Popper need not undermine it in order to weaken ontological determinism.

Its negation, *'scientific' indeterminism*, says that *at least one event cannot be rationally predicted with any desired degree of precision, even if we are given a sufficiently precise description of all past events and know all the laws of nature*. Being the negation of a mixed (universal and strictly existential) statement, it is itself a mixed (strictly existential and universal) statement. Therefore, it would also be *neither verifiable nor falsifiable*, hence *metaphysical*, if it were not *analytic* – being the negation of a contradictory statement.

But 'scientific' determinism *concerns* our *knowledge*. For this reason, it would have been more appropriate to call it "*epistemic* determinism." The same holds correspondingly of 'scientific' indeterminism.

14.12. Metaphysical Determinism

If all events are to be exactly predictable, they must be *predetermined*. As Popper wants to avoid the term "ontological" (OU, 7 n3), he calls this determinist doctrine "*metaphysical determinism*" (7). This weakest form of determinism says only "that *all events in this world are fixed, or unalterable, or predetermined*. It does not assert that they are known to anybody, or predictable by scientific means. But it asserts that the future is as little changeable as is the past. Everybody knows what we mean when we say that the past cannot be changed. It is in precisely the same sense that the future cannot be changed, according to metaphysical determinism" (7f., i.a.; later Popper expresses less doubt about the word "ontological").

Where the word 'metaphysical' is used as a substitute for "ontological," it is not used in the way in which it is defined in the *Logic*. Therefore, we put it in single quotation marks wherever it is part of the name "'metaphysical' determinism." As we cannot empirically show that all events are predetermined, 'metaphysical' determinism is *not verifiable*; and as we cannot show that a particular event is not predetermined, it is *not falsifiable* either; hence it is also *metaphysical* according to the definition in the *Logic* (OU, 8). This becomes even more evident if we give it the classical form of a mixed (universal and strictly existential) statement, "Every event has a cause" (cf. section 14.14).

Its negation, '*metaphysical' indeterminism*, says that *at least one event in this world is not fixed, or unalterable, or predetermined*. As we cannot empirically show that all events are predetermined, it is *not falsifiable*; hence it is also *metaphysical* in the sense of the *Logic* (OU, 8); and because we likewise cannot show that a particular event is not predetermined, it is *not verifiable* either. (It can be given the form of the mixed statement "There is at least one event that does not have a cause.")

'*Metaphysical' determinism follows logically from 'scientific' determinism*, but *not vice versa* (OU, 8). If everything can be exactly predicted, then everything must be predetermined; but from the fact that everything is predetermined alone it does not follow that anything could be predicted. Actually, '*metaphysical' determinism is compatible with 'scientific' indeterminism*.

14.13. Physical Determinism

In his article "Of Clouds and Clocks," Popper writes: "My *clouds* are intended to represent physical systems which, like gases, are highly irregular, disorderly, and more or less unpredictable" (OK, 207, i.a.). On the other hand, his *clocks* are intended to represent physical systems "which are regular, orderly, and highly predictable in their behaviour" (207). In this paper, he confronts physical determinism with philosophical or psychological determinism.

Physical determinism says that "'[*a*]*ll clouds are clocks*'" (OK, 210, i.a.) or that "*all* events *in the physical world* are predetermined *with absolute precision*, in all their infinitesimal details" (220, i.a.). Like 'metaphysical' determinism, it refers to the world, is ontological, whereas 'scientific' determinism refers to our knowledge, is epistemic. And as physical determinism differs from 'metaphysical' determinism only in its restriction to events "in the physical world" and in the qualification "with absolute precision," physical determinism is for the same reasons not verifiable and *not falsifiable*, hence *metaphysical*.

The success of Newton's theory made physical determinism "the ruling faith among enlightened men" (OK, 212). On the other hand, Popper writes: "*Physical* determinism, we might say in retrospect [i.e., after it has been superseded by physical indeterminism], was a daydream of *omni-science* which seemed to become more real with every advance in physics until it became an apparently inescapable nightmare" (222, i.a.). Here he obviously makes no clear distinction between *physical* determinism, which says something about the world, and '*scientific*' determinism, which says something about our knowledge of the world.

Physical determinism – unlike 'metaphysical' determinism – admits that *mental events may not be predetermined*. Hence there might be decisions of *free will*, but they could have no effect on our behaviour, because that is physically determined. Does, however, as Popper's formulation suggests, physical determinism also postulate a more complete or exact determination of physical events, while '*metaphysical*' determinism admits *small regions of random scattering*, because it considers all events predetermined but not predetermined with absolute precision?

14.131. Like the physicist Arthur Holly Compton (1892–1962), Popper believes that the *fundamental question of morality* goes: "Is man a *free* agent?" (OK, 217, i.a.) Compton asks rhetorically: "'If . . . the atoms of our bodies follow physical laws as immutable as the motions of the planets, why try? What difference can it make how great the effort if our actions are already predetermined by mechanical laws . . . ?'" (217)

What Compton describes here Popper calls

"*the nightmare of the physical determinist.*" A deterministic physical clockwork mechanism is, above all, completely self-contained: in the perfect deterministic physical world there is simply no room for any outside intervention. Everything that happens in such a world is physically predetermined, including all our movements and therefore all our actions. Thus all our thoughts, feelings, and efforts can have no practical influence upon what happens in the physical world: they are, if not mere illusions, at best superfluous by-products ("epiphenomena") of physical events. (OK, 217)

Does this mean that physical determinism implies *fatalism*? At any rate, it confronts us, Popper believes, with the alternative of either supposing "that the *feeling of freedom* is *illusory*" or assuming "that the statements of the *laws of physics* [are] . . . *unreliable*" (OK, 218, i.a.). What is even worse, physical determinism "destroys, in particular, the *idea of creativity*" (222, i.a.). For when Popper speaks of freedom, it is true that he also means *free will or moral freedom*, but above all he is interested in the *freedom to create works of art or scientific theories* and in the *freedom to evaluate reasons or arguments* (cf. 223 n35; OU, 41f.).

But Compton's deliberation is not conclusive. Even in a *completely determined* world, our thoughts, feelings, and efforts could have effects on what happens. They would, however, be predetermined in their turn. If they didn't occur, chains of determination, whose links they are, would break. Hence our effort would make a difference, but we would be determined to make the effort. And no doubt some of us would be determined erroneously to take our will to be free.

What, then, turns complete determination into a nightmare? What would change for us if we *were* determined without knowing it? Obviously, nothing would change in the world or in our condition, for it is conceivable that we (and the rest of the world) are determined. In this case, our actual condition is that of people who are determined without knowing it.

And what would change if we also *learned that* we are determined but *not how* we are determined? Possibly, some of us would then be determined to abandon the philosophical postulate of free will, and to some of us, especially to Kantians, man would therefore appear less dignified. Possibly, some would no longer consider themselves the authors of their works to begin with; but things would soon change, once they got accustomed to their knowledge about determination, for *they*, and not their colleagues, would then be determined to have new ideas and to write them down. On the other hand, while this idea of being determined would be *new for us*, it would *not appear emergently*. Rather, the idea of creating something not predetermined and insofar completely new would be as false as the idea of having a free will.

Only if I *knew how* I am determined might I, if my fate were such, have a nightmare. This would be the case, for example, if I knew that I will have a terrible accident tomorrow but could not avoid it. Then nothing would be left for me but fatalism. If, on the other hand, I knew, because God has treated me very well so far, that I am destined to attain eternal bliss, then it would hardly be a nightmare. But in any case, the scientific predictability of the details of my fate would be limited, for the reasons that Popper works out when he examines 'scientific' determinism (cf. section 14.5). And this would limit the danger of nightmares, should God not completely reveal my fate.

To Herbert Feigl and Paul E. Meehl, "Popper's 'nightmare of determinism'" seems "to rest on identifying determinism with strict predictability" (PKP, 520). According to them, only "the attainability of a World Formula . . . leads to absurdly paradoxical and abhorrently unpalatable consequences" (521). The idea of this World Formula is to be understood as the conjunction of three theses: "(1) The doctrine of the deterministic form of all basic natural laws. (2) The precise, complete (and simultaneous) ascertainability of all initial and boundary conditions. (3) The mathematical feasibility of the hopelessly complex computations necessary for precise and complete predictions (or retrodictions)" (521f.).

Like Popper, they assume that it will never be definitely decidable whether the basic laws of nature are deterministic or statistical (PKP, 522). But while Popper intends to refute the thesis of complete predictability ('scientific' determinism) in order to undermine thesis (1), the deterministic form of all basic natural laws ('metaphysical' determinism), Feigl and Meehl attack only thesis (2), the ascertainability of all initial conditions. If (2) is refuted, the nightmare is overcome. According to them, there is no need to examine whether the mathematical problems of (3) are soluble (525). Thus we don't have to assume, just in order to avoid nightmares, that our will is free.

14.132. Popper's "brief formulation of the view which [he calls] '*physical determinism*'" is: "'*All clouds are clocks*'" (OK, 210). Accordingly, its negation, *physical indeterminism* ("*Not all* events in the physical world are predetermined with absolute precision" [220]) would have the form: "*Not all clouds are clocks.*" But what does Popper mean when he writes that "to some degree *all clocks are clouds*" (213)? He shares Peirce's view that all physical bodies are "subject to molecular heat motion" and that hence there is "a certain *looseness or imperfection* in all clocks, and that this allow[s] an *element of chance* to enter" (213). Peirce's criticism was mostly ignored. It was only the rise of quantum theory that caused physicists to abandon determinism. But is their decision compelling?

The physical theory of molecular heat motion has been well corroborated. Has therefore Peirce's argument *empirically refuted physical determinism?* It is true that the thesis of *random* molecular heat motion would contradict physical determinism; but is heat motion actually random? After all, we can take it to be *determined* by the laws of classical mechanics, and we can explain our application of the probability calculus to the collective of molecules by our ignorance of the initial conditions (necessary for the application) of the classical laws (cf. section 8.21). Even if these laws were refuted and could not be replaced by other deterministic theories, this would not refute physical determinism. Nor is it refuted by the indispensable statistical element in quantum theory, for this theory is, like any other system of hypotheses, fallible, and it is conceivable that, as Einstein believed, the fundamental laws of microphysics are deterministic. As no observation could show that any particular event is not completely predetermined either (cf. Hume 1970), *physical determinism* not only has not been refuted but remains irrefutable, *metaphysical*. This holds correspondingly of its negation, *physical indeterminism*.

14.14. Philosophical Determinism

Philosophical or psychological *determinism* – which Popper ascribes to Hume – says: " '*Every event has a cause*' " or " 'Like effects have like causes' " (OK, 220, i.a.). These two formulations are not completely equivalent. If, for the sake of simplicity, we consider only the first, we immediately recognize that it is a mixed (universal and strictly existential) statement. Hence philosophical determinism is also *neither verifiable nor falsifiable*, that is, it is likewise metaphysical according to the definition given in the *Logic*. And this must hold correspondingly of its negation, *philosophical* or psychological *indeterminism* (cf. sections 14.11, 14.12).

In contrast with physical determinism, Popper considers philosophical determinism *harmless*, for it "is so vague that it is perfectly compatible with physical *in*determinism" ["Not all events in the physical world are predetermined with absolute precision"] (OK, 220). As "the terms 'event' and 'cause' are vague enough," physical indeterminism does not, after all, entail "that there are 'events without causes' " (i.e., philosophical indeterminism) (220). Obviously, he means that an event may have a cause without being completely predetermined by that cause.

Prima facie philosophical determinism (" 'Every event has a cause' ") seems not to differ from 'metaphysical' determinism ("All events are predetermined"). But we must assume that Popper differentiates between them, for he considers philosophical determinism harmless, whereas he intends to undermine 'metaphysical' determinism by refuting 'scientific' determinism and thus eliminating its only support. The difference could be that philosophical determinism is defined by means of the "vague" expression "cause."

But is philosophical determinism really compatible with physical indeterminism, as Popper claims? The wording of *physical indeterminism,* "Not all events in the physical world are predetermined with absolute precision," is equivalent to "There is at least one event in the physical world that is not predetermined with absolute precision." If this is not to entail *philosophical indeterminism* ("There is at least one event that does not have a cause") – philosophical determinism and physical indeterminism would then be *in*compatible – then there must be causes that do not predetermine an event with absolute precision.

Popper seems to explain how this is possible when he asserts that the terms "event" and "cause" are vague. But an event [*Fa*] that – in view of a deterministic regularity $[(x)(Fx \to Gx)]$ – sets off another event [*Ga*] is, according to common linguistic usage, its cause. Whether the effect *Ga* will occur when its cause *Fa* is present is not left unclear. The event *Ga* is also (thought to be) predetermined "with absolute precision" by its cause *Fa*. On the other hand, the event *Ga* ∧ *Ha* is – in view of the same regularity – predetermined by *Fa* only in its aspect *Ga*, but not in its aspect *Ha*, hence not "with absolute precision." Obviously, the terms "cause" and "event" are sufficiently clear. *Hence Popper fails to show that philosophical determinism and physical indeterminism are compatible.* (However, philosophical determinism and "*scientific*" indeterminism are compatible; cf. section 14.12.) Whether our theories determine particular causes and other events (their effects) sufficiently precisely to be successful is of course another question.

Popper even asserts: "[T]he formula 'every observable or measurable *physical* event has an observable or measurable *physical* cause' is still compatible with physical indeterminism, simply because no measurement can be infinitely precise" (OK, 220). But the inaccuracy of a *measurement* concerns only the *ascertainability* of a cause – our knowledge of it, not its existence or its effect.

14.2. POPPER'S CRITICISM OF METAPHYSICAL DETERMINISM

Having examined the criticism of physical determinism (in "Of Clouds and Clocks"), let us return to the criticism of 'metaphysical' determinism (in *The Open Universe*). Although 'metaphysical' determinism is irrefutable, we can *argue* for or against it. It is true that arguments never show *what is the case* – hence they cannot show whether everything is predetermined either – but they may show that an assumption cannot be true because it is self-contradictory, or, as in the present case, that we cannot hold to an assumption if we do not want to give up another one that it contradicts.

According to Popper, the strongest arguments *in favour of 'metaphysical'* determinism are those that *support 'scientific'* determinism. This is certainly correct, for 'scientific' determinism entails 'metaphysical' determinism. If everything can be exactly predicted, then everything must be determined. If, however, these arguments collapse, "little is left to support metaphysical determinism" (OU, 8).

This would have to be shown in detail, for 'metaphysical' determinism is logically far weaker than 'scientific' determinism. Hence from the fact that there is no tenable argument supporting 'scientific' determinism we cannot infer that there is none supporting 'metaphysical' determinism either. But why does Popper look for *supportive* arguments? After all, the methodology of his *Logic* demands that we try to discover what tells *against* our views. And in the present case, this would not by any means be hopeless, for the fact that 'metaphysical' determinism is irrefutable does not entail that there can be no arguments against it. Besides, the search for supportive arguments leads easily into the well-known paradoxes of confirmation (cf. section 3.5).

In fact, there are models for the discussion of metaphysical assumptions (cf. section 1.23). For example, Popper and other authors, such as Victor Kraft, succeed in showing that *metaphysical realism* is preferable to metaphysical idealism, because only realism permits the construction of a simple consistent conception of the world. Popper also tries to show that only *metaphysical indeterminism* permits us to adhere to the ideas of creativity and freedom of will. But we can more easily dispense with these ideas than with an appropriate conception of the world. On the one hand, such a conception can be important for survival, whereas only he who has survived up to now and does not consider his further survival immediately threatened may ask whether his will is free and his ideas are new. On the other hand, there are also ideas of freedom that are compatible with 'metaphysical' determinism (cf. section 14.7). They are classed under the term "compatibilism."

Let us now consider a first argument *against* 'metaphysical' determinism. "In a deterministic physical world there is . . . [no] indeterministic behaviour; for all behaviour consists of events within the physical world" (OU, 25). This does not exclude undetermined states of consciousness, but they cannot influence behaviour. Therefore, we also cannot talk about them, for "if we did, undetermined [mental] events would have some causal influence upon the physical world of sounds [speech]" (25f.).

According to Popper, this shows that the commonsense arguments from behaviour (behaviour can be predicted, hence it is determined [15]) and from psychology (our will is also caused [20]) used to support determinism are invalid (26). Actually, only two commonsense ideas clash in his argument, the idea of a determined physical world (which he rejects) and the idea of undetermined states of consciousness that influence physical events such as our speech (which he defends). Hence they cannot both be true. But this need not tell against 'metaphysical' determinism.

14.3. THE DETERMINIST'S BURDEN OF PROOF

In order to convince us that not all behaviour is determined, Popper chooses a strategy of reasoning that results in a *shift of the burden of proof*, an aid all too well known from moral philosophy. He writes: "An important reason for accepting indeterminism, at least tentatively, is that *the burden of proof rests upon the shoulders of the determinist*" (OU, 27, i.a.).

But all of the versions of determinism presented here are neither provable nor refutable, if we disregard the fact that 'scientific' determinism turns out to be contradictory (cf. section 14.53). What then is the burden of proof? Popper gives four reasons for the shift of the burden of proof:

(1) [*U*]*nsophisticated common sense* [i.a.] favours the view that there are clocks *and* clouds, that is to say, events which are more *predictable* [i.a.], and events which are less predictable; that predetermination and predictability are matters of degree. (OU, 27)

Instead of giving a reason for shifting the burden of proof, Popper seems here to introduce a standard for the assessment of ontological ('metaphysical') determinism: It is to be measured by unsophisticated common sense. But how can this be done? After all, it is compatible with *any* experience, as it is empirically neither verifiable nor falsifiable. If, however, we counterfactually assume that it is an empirical hypothesis, then daily experience obviously does not support it. Rather, experience makes us assume that there are random events, and this supports indeterminism. Is it therefore the burden of the determinist to prove the falsity of the assumption that there are random events by explaining the presumed random events causally?

(2) [*T*]here is a *prima facie* case for the view that organisms are less predetermined and predictable than at least some simpler systems, and that the higher organisms are less predetermined and predictable than the lower ones. (27)

But more complex systems would also be less predictable if they were predetermined; and independently of predictability we cannot find out anything about predetermination.

(3) If determinism is true, it should in principle be possible for a physicist or a physiologist who knows nothing of music to *predict*, by studying Mozart's brain, ... *Mozart's action* and write his symphony even before it is consciously conceived by Mozart. ... [This result *appears* to Popper] *intuitively as absurd.* Absurd or not, [it goes] *far beyond anything known to us*; thus, again, the burden of proof rests upon the determinist. (28, i.a.)

But why should a determinist assume that Mozart's composing at time t_1 is predetermined solely by the state of his brain at time t_0? If, on the other hand, he intended to take into account *everything* that could influence Mozart's brain between t_0 and t_1, then, according to Popper's own considerations, he would not be able to predict even a single note before Mozart actually wrote it down (cf. section 14.53). In this respect, at least, an ontological determinist can agree with Popper, for, unlike Popper, he does *not* assume that he must be able to predict Mozart's compositions just because they are predetermined.

(4) [I]ndeterminism, which asserts that there exists *at least one* event that is not predetermined, or predictable, is clearly a weaker assertion than 'scientific' determinism, which asserts that all events are in principle predictable. ... In any case, he who proposes the stronger theory accepts the burden of proof. (28)

What does Popper expect him to prove? That determinism has explanatory power (28). Couldn't determinism explain the apparent existence of deterministic regularities? Popper thinks it "has no explanatory power," as it "does not belong to science" (28). But then indeterminism has no explanatory power either. So why does Popper defend it so vigorously?

Moreover, the phrase "predetermined, *or* predictable" blurs his distinction between 'metaphysical' and 'scientific' determinism. Already in the *Logic* Popper had asserted that the "principle of causality" ("[A]ny event whatsoever *can* be causally explained" ['scientific' or epistemic determinism]) is synthetic if the word "'can' is meant to signify that the world is governed by strict laws" ('metaphysical' or ontological determinism). As in this case the statement is not falsifiable, he proposes "to exclude it, as '*metaphysical*' from the sphere of science" (LSD, 61, i.a.). Here he seems to share Hume's "regularity theory" of causality.

14.4. ARGUMENTS AGAINST 'SCIENTIFIC' DETERMINISM

While quantum theory "is a probability theory," classical physics is, according to Popper, "*'prima facie* deterministic'" (OU, 29). But this assertion about the statements of classical physics is not based simply on their *logical form* – say, the fact that they are universal statements or Hamiltonian functions. Rather, he claims that "the *'prima facie* deterministic character' of classical physics may best be described with the help of the so-called 'Laplacean demon'" – that is, the notion of an *idealized predictability* (29). Thus he makes great demands on scientific predictions that no empirical scientist considers satisfiable in his work.

14.41. Laplace's Demon and the Principle of Accountability

To begin with, Popper quotes Laplace (1749–1827):

"We ought ... to regard the present state of the universe as the effect of its anterior state and as the cause of the one which is to follow. Assume ... an intelligence which could know all the forces by which nature is animated, and the states at an instant of all the objects that compose it; ... for [this intelligence], nothing could be uncertain; and the future, as the past, would be present to its eyes." (OU, xx)

Laplace speaks about an *intelligence* that recognizably is not an object of physics or biology. Others speak of the Laplacean *spirit*; Du Bois-Reymond even speaks of the Laplacean *demon*. But Popper considers it crucial that Laplace's argument "*makes the doctrine of determinism a truth of science rather than of religion*. Laplace's demon is not an omniscient God, merely a super-scientist" (OU, 30).

Accordingly, the demon predicts future events by means of theories and initial conditions. Popper calls theories that answer this purpose "*'prima facie* deterministic,'" and he proposes the following definition:

A physical theory is *prima facie* deterministic if and only if it allows us to deduce, from a *mathematically exact* description of the initial state of a closed physical system which is described in terms of the theory, the description, *with any stipulated finite degree of precision*, of the state of the system at any given future instant of time. (OU, 31)

For the purpose of his argument, Popper assumes that Newton's and Maxwell's theories are prima facie deterministic in the sense of this definition. Then he asks: "Assuming that [such a] theory is *true*, are we entitled to infer from this assumption the truth of 'scientific' determinism?" (OU, 32) Of course we are not, for "'scientific' determinism could, if at all, follow only from a system of physics which was *complete, or comprehensive*, in the sense that it would allow the prediction of all kinds of physical events" (38).

The motion picture analogy is only a vague metaphor of certain foreknowledge. 'Scientific' determinism replaces it with "the more precise idea of *predictability in accordance with rational scientific procedures of prediction*" (OU, 33). Hence it asserts more than the mere "motion-picture character of the world," for it asserts "that the events shown in the film are never haphazard but always subject to rules, so that each picture or shot belonging to the film allows us to *calculate by rational methods* any of those which follow, with the help of the rules or laws connecting successive shots" (33).

Popper does not demand absolute precision of a prediction, but *every theory* "*will have to account* for the imprecision of the prediction" (OU, 11). Before testing the result of a prediction and possibly drawing conclusions from it, we must know "whether or not the initial conditions are sufficiently precise" (12). To this end, we must be able to "*calculate from our prediction task (in conjunction with our theories, of course) the requisite degree of precision of the initial conditions.*" To begin with, this "*principle of accountability*" seems to be the basis on which Popper's definition of "scientific determinism" rests (12). But if we actually want to test the determinist character of a theory, it will not suffice to know the requisite "*precision of the initial conditions*"; rather, we will have to know "*the precision of the results of possible measurements from which the initial conditions can be calculated*" (13). Thus "scientific" determinism requires accountability in the sense of this *stronger principle of accountability* (13).

According to Popper, Laplace assumed that the demon's powers "were to be unlimited only in fields where there were *no definite limits* to the human scientist's powers" (OU, 34). In order to put this idea more precisely, Popper formulates two conditions: (1) The demon must not "be able *to ascertain initial conditions with absolute mathematical precision*" – as empirical tests are the matter at issue, the word "mathematical" should be omitted – but he must be able to "make the range of imprecision of his measurements as small as he likes" (34). (2) The demon must "belong himself to the physical world," that is, he must "*predict the system from within*"; hence his prediction must be a physical process, for the demon's powers must not "*in principle* surpass all human powers" (35).

After these preparations, Popper can *define 'scientific' determinism* as

the doctrine that the state of any closed physical system at any given future instant of time can be predicted, even from within the system, with any specified degree of precision, by deducing the prediction from theories, in conjunction with initial conditions whose required degree of precision can always be calculated (in accordance with the principle of accountability) if the prediction task is given. (OU, 36)

This is the *weakest* definition that permits us to formulate the idea of a 'scientific' determinism. It incorporates the weaker principle of accountability and the two conditions indicated in the paragraph before last. Actually, "'scientific' determinism requires accountability in the stronger sense" (OU, 13). The definition just given also does not comprehend other desirable properties of a 'scientific' determinism. Therefore, Popper proposes a *stronger* definition that in addition demands "that it can be predicted, of any given state, *whether or not the system in question will ever be in this state*" (36f.). This definition comes very close to Laplace's idea.

14.42. Limits of Accountability

Popper now presents arguments that are intended to *refute* 'scientific' determinism. (They would have to fail if 'scientific' determinism were *metaphysical*, as its original formulation suggests [cf. section 14.11].) For example, he believes that the *stronger* version of 'scientific' determinism is refuted by the findings of the mathematician Hadamard (1865–1963), who anticipated as early as 1898 part of the theory of *deterministic chaos* (OU, 39f.). For where deterministic chaos prevails, it is impossible to predict of *every* given state whether the system will ever be in this state. But this refutes the *stronger* version of "scientific" determinism only *if* nature is such that the preconditions of Hadamard's results are satisfied, or *if* there is deterministic chaos – in other words, *if* physical theories are true whose deterministic equations entail chaotic results.

On the other hand, where such physical laws obtain, *both* versions of 'scientific' determinism fail because of *problems of computation*. For the inevitable rounding errors exclude – particularly in the case of recursive operations – both arbitrarily precise predictions and the sufficiently precise determination of the requisite initial conditions.

But refutations such as these would not serve Popper's purpose, for by supposition, those events that cannot be predicted are predetermined. Hence what refutes 'scientific' determinism at the same time *supports* physical and 'metaphysical' determinism. It could hardly be more clearly shown how problematic Popper's idea is – to undermine 'metaphysical' (ontological) determinism by refuting 'scientific' (epistemic) determinism.

14.5. ARGUMENTS FOR INDETERMINISM

Popper personally believes "that the doctrine of *indeterminism is true*, and that determinism is completely baseless" (OU, 41, i.a.). Having criticized determinism, he now formulates three "positive arguments in favour of indeterminism": the argument "from the approximate character of scientific knowledge" (section 14.51), the argument "from the asymmetry of the past and the future" (section 14.52), and the argument that "we cannot predict, scientifically, ... the growth of our own knowledge" (section 14.53; OU, 62). He considers these "positive" arguments supporting indeterminism more important than his "negative" arguments criticizing determinism. But the first of the arguments resumes his criticism of 'scientific' determinism, and the third carries it on.

14.51. The Approximate Character of Scientific Knowledge

The "approximate character of all scientific knowledge" seems to Popper to provide "*the philosophically most fundamental argument* against 'scientific' determinism, and in favour of indeterminism" (OU, 55, i.a.). Theories are human inventions, nets that we mesh to catch the world. We shouldn't mistake them for *complete* representations of the world in all its aspects, "not even if they are highly successful; not even if they appear to yield excellent approximations to reality"; for they are *fallible* (42f.). Therefore, we should take care not to assume that "their *prima facie deterministic character* [corresponds] to features of the real world" (43, i.a.). Rather, science is "the art of systematic over-simplification" (44).

How sound is this argument? After all, quantum theory is also fallible. Therefore, we should take care not to consider it a complete representation of microphysical processes and not to assume that its *prima facie indeterministic character* mirrors their randomness. Neither the incompleteness nor the fallibility of our assumptions about the world is a reason to believe that any events in the world are random (not predetermined). They are not even reasons to assume that there are events that we will never be able to predict with the help of deterministic hypotheses.

There is a connection between this inevitable *simplification* and the problem of *accountability* (OU, 44). As every prediction "operates with a simplifying *model*" (45), it provides only approximate values; and as there is "no absolute measure for the degree of approximation achieved," we must always take into account that the net of our theories "is too coarse for ['scientific'] determinism" (47). Actually, not even classical physics is accountable. This follows not only from Hadamard's results but also from the fact that Newton's theory does not provide a complete analytic solution of the three-body problem (Earth, moon, sun; 49ff.). In the light of this problem, Popper constructs for classical physics a counterpart of Heisenberg's principle of indeterminacy that is intended to show that classical physics is not accountable in the stronger sense (51ff.).

All this would speak against Popper's 'scientific' determinism, if it were not already a logically contradictory construct (cf. section 14.53), but how is it that it speaks in favour of Popper's ontological indeterminism? And as *'scientific' determinism* is contradictory, Popper cannot take it to be "*the view that* [physical or 'metaphysical'] *determinism is backed by human science, by human experience*" (49f., i.a.). On the other hand, he rightly suspects that this view is problematical.

This is easily seen, even if we consider only the range of application of a *single* hypothesis. As well corroborated as it may be, it is still *fallible*, and therefore we cannot be sure that it provides correct information about the real state of the world. If it is *deterministic*, then its success is compatible with the assumption that *fundamentally probabilistic* processes are the basis of the *prima facie deterministic* courses of events within the range of its application. For, because of contingent boundary conditions, probabilistic processes could result in events whose quantitative attributes deviate only within the range of errors of measurement from those values that the deterministic hypothesis predicts.

On the other hand, deterministic processes may be the basis of the distributions of events that a *probabilistic* hypothesis predicts. We may simply not know the laws describing the deterministic processes, or, if we know them, we may not be able to determine their initial conditions or to compute the predictions sufficiently precisely. As ontological determinism implies that all laws of nature are deterministic, it is, even if we consider it counterfactually empirical, not supported at the present level of research, and we cannot expect that it will be supported in the future.

14.52. The Asymmetry of the Past and the Future

Less fundamental than the argument "from the approximate character of scientific knowledge" but still important enough, as it seems to Popper, is the argument "from the asymmetry of the past and the future" (OU, 55ff.). According to this argument, "*the past*" cannot be changed but rather "*is completely determined by what has happened*" (55), whereas the *future* is *open* (48). Determinism, however, considers *the future* "also completely determined by what has happened"; it thereby "wantonly destroys a *fundamental asymmetry in the structure of our experience*" and thus comes into "striking *conflict with common sense*" (55, i.a.). We do believe "that what will happen in the future is *largely determined* by the past or the present"; after all, we try to influence the future by our present actions; but in doing so we also consider the future "*open to [our] influence*" (ontologically open), "*not yet* [in another way] *completely determined*" (56, i.a.).

Popper again judges the tenability of determinism by its compatibility with common sense. If our attempts to influence the future should be successful, then *the future* would be (ontologically) *open to our influence*. Nevertheless, *our attempts to influence it* could be *completely predetermined* in their turn. Popper's arguments, however, are intented to undermine precisely this assumption. Therefore, he would do better to speak of "*freedom of will*" instead of the "*openness of the future*."

Einstein's "*prima facie*" *deterministic special theory of relativity* implies an (epistemic) *asymmetry*, in the sense that *past events can in principle be completely retrodicted*, whereas *future events cannot be completely predicted*. (Here a "retrodiction" is the computation of an earlier event on the basis of a later event. The computation of a later event, which has already occurred, on the basis of an earlier event would be called a "postdiction," i.e., a belated prediction. However, these two expressions for the most part are used indiscriminately.) According to the special theory of relativity, for every (observer or) space-time point there is an "(absolute) past" consisting of all the space-time points from which it can be influenced (from which signals can reach it), and there is also an "(absolute) future" consisting of all the space-time points that it could, in principle, influence. All other space-time points form its "possible contemporaneity" (OU, 57). Popper illustrates this by means of world lines in Minkowski space-time. The (epistemic) asymmetry results from the (ontological) fact that a signal (or a causal chain) could from every point in the "past" (of the present observer or space-time point) reach every point in the "future," but could from no point in the "future" reach any point in the "past" (58).

From this, Popper infers that "the future becomes [epistemically] '*open*' to us in the sense that it cannot be fully predicted *by us*, while the past is 'closed'" (OU, 59; but he leaves it open whether he contrasts the epistemically open future with an epistemically closed past, which can be completely retrodicted, or with an ontologically closed past, which can no longer be influenced).

Now he wants to show that, on account of the (epistemic) asymmetry between the past and the future, Einstein's *special theory of relativity* "is no longer *prima facie* deterministic," because "there is no longer a Laplacean demon in special relativity" (OU, 60). The reason is that all signals emanating from past or present events that could possibly influence a future event take time to reach this event and also to reach the demon, and not all of them can reach the demon earlier than the event. The demon also needs time after all the necessary information has reached him to make his prediction. Therefore, his prediction will be ready only after the event has occurred. Hence it actually is only a postdiction (Popper writes "retrodiction"; 60f.). Thus "the demon of special relativity is no longer that of Laplace" (61). Therefore, special relativity, "in spite of its *prima facie* determinist character, cannot . . . be used to support 'scientific' determinism" (61).

But what does this argument contribute to the assessment of ontological determinism? According to its form, the special theory of relativity is deterministic. If it should be *true*, the events to which it refers would be *determined*. This would *support "metaphysical" determinism,* which Popper wants to undermine, and physical determinism, which he takes to be refuted. He does not, however, doubt the truth of special relativity, but he considers it "not *prima facie* deterministic," because, when we predict an event, we can never know all the other events that might possibly influence the event to be predicted. This, he thinks, *weakens "scientific" determinism* (the future is epistemically closed), and if it fails, *the most important argument supporting "metaphysical" determinism* (the future is ontologically closed) *is dropped.* Obviously, this strategy of reasoning is a failure.

14.53. On the Prediction of Future Knowledge

Popper considers a third argument even less fundamental. But it is still very important because it is meant to help us "construct *a formal refutation of 'scientific' determinism*" (OU, 62, i.a.). Basically, it says that "*we cannot predict, scientifically, results which we shall obtain in the course of the growth of our own knowledge,*" for the "idea of predicting today what we shall know only tomorrow" is *contradictory* (62). If, however, Popper succeeds in logically refuting 'scientific' determinism, then the criticisms that he has already presented are, at the least, superfluous.

But what ensues from the fact that *no scientist can "predict all the results of all his own predictions"* (OU, 63)? On the one hand, he cannot predict "some of his *own* future states"; on the other hand, he cannot predict "all the states of his own '*neighbourhood.*'" For "if he does not know what he will know tomorrow, he cannot know how he will act tomorrow upon his environment." Thus he cannot himself completely predict the state of his environment *from within,* while observers may be able to predict it *from without,* if they do not influence him or his environment noticeably. More generally stated: "[*N*]*o physical system can be completely predicted from within*" (63, i.a.). This argument is also intended to refute historicism (cf. section 10.2).

There are two aspects of predicting *the growth of our theoretical knowledge:* (1) the prediction of *the exact content of a still unknown theory,* and (2) the prediction of *the acceptance of a new theory that is incompatible with already accepted theories, on the basis of new tests* (OU, 64ff.). The idea of predicting the exact *content* involves the contradiction we have already mentioned: As the content to be predicted must be described at the time of the prediction, it can no longer be unknown, and hence it can no longer be predicted (65).

More important, therefore, is the prediction of the *acceptance* of a new theory that is incompatible with already accepted theories. This requires the prediction of the results of future tests. However, an event *predicted with the aid of already accepted theories* corroborates those theories but doesn't corroborate that part of the content of a new theory that is incompatible with them. For each theory implies its own truth and therefore does not predict events that will refute it (OU, 67). If, on the other hand, *the new, not-yet-accepted theory predicts* results that speak in its favour but against the accepted theories, we must, for this very reason, expect that the predictions will *not* come true. According to Popper, this argument "suffices for a *refutation of the influential doctrine of historicism;* for it shows that we cannot, by scientific procedures, predict the growth of our theoretical knowledge" (67, i.a.; cf. Chapter 10).

But what would happen if our knowledge ceased to grow, because our theories were true and completely described the regularities of the universe? Let us assume that we had complete knowledge of the laws of nature and of their past and present initial conditions. Could we then "predict, by *deductive methods,* our own future states for any given instant of time, and more especially, our own future predictions" (OU, 68)? Owing to our assumption, the prediction "becomes a problem of mere calculation" that could in principle be solved by a machine, "a 'calculator' or a 'predictor.'" Therefore, Popper can give the intended proof of the impossibility of self-prediction the form of the "proof that *no calcula-tor or predictor can deductively predict the results of its own calculations or pre-dictions*" (68).

As a way of offering this proof, Popper designs a *thought experiment.* The predictor knows all true universal (deterministic) laws of nature and all requisite calculation methods of logic and mathematics (OU, 70). Its task is to predict the state of a system at time t_1 on the basis of the description of its state at time t_0. It is given this task by means of a punched tape, and it gives its reply in the same way. This predictor "may be considered *as a . . . perfect physical embodiment* [] *of Laplace's demon*" (70), and its behaviour could be predicted *from without* (69).

The result of the thought experiment essentially depends on two assumptions: (A_1) If the task is sufficiently clear, the predictor will al-ways provide a correct result (OU, 70). (A_2) The predictor *takes time* for its prediction. Hence the predictor is "not disembodied, but a physical machine" (71). According to Popper, these two assumptions suffice to prove that the predictor's reply "can only be complete *after* the event pre-dicted, or at best at the same time," and hence that it "cannot predict the *future* growth of its own knowledge" (71).

In order to show this, Popper now considers two structurally iden-tical predictors. One of them, "Tell," is to predict the future states of the other, "Told." Let us assume that Told is to predict some event and that Tell is to predict what Told will predict, and let both of them have all the information necessary for their respective tasks. If both of them begin to calculate at the same time, Tell's prediction will at the earliest be completed simultaneously with Told's prediction, because Tell, in or-der to predict Told's result, has to go through the same operations as Told and needs as much time for them. This is the basic idea of a proof that is considerably more complex (OU, 74f.) and whose result Popper makes even more momentous by introducing two additional assumptions (71, 76f.).

Popper's 'scientific' determinism requires "that in principle we should be able to predict, from within, everything in our world with any de-gree of precision we choose" (OU, 78). But the proofs we have just sketched show why this is impossible. Hence '*scientific' determinism* is false. As the proofs were furnished by *logical* means alone, it is even *self-contradictory* (79). However, this holds only if the *synthetic* assump-tions (A_1) and (A_2) are part of the definiens of the concept "'scientific' determinism."

But the refutation of (epistemic) 'scientific' determinism by no means entails the refutation of ('metaphysical,' i.e., ontological) determinism – which Popper himself considers "irrefutable" (OU, 79). He even admits that this "*proof cannot... be used to refute determinism*," because, by supposition, the predictor knows all true universal (deterministic) laws of nature – that is, the world is determined (77f.). (As we have seen, this holds as well of the argument "from the asymmetry of the past and the future," which rests on the deterministic special theory of relativity; cf. section 14.52.) What benefit then does Popper derive from *this thought experiment*? He thinks that it *refutes* "*those who say that* [*ontological*] *determinism... is justified by scientific experience*" (79f., i.a.). But how could they be refuted by his construction of an admittedly *self-contradictory* model of science?

The refutation of "scientific" determinism is also intended to show that "the existence of rational knowledge itself" is "*the decisive argument for indeterminism*" (OU, 80f., i.a.). How is that? *We* "*are* '*free*' . . . , not because we are subject to chance rather than to strict natural laws" but *because our* "*foreknowledge...* [*is*] *so limited as to leave room for action – that is, for 'free' action*" (81, i.a.). Hence, even though we may be ontologically determined, we are free in the sense that we cannot exactly predict the results of our actions. The limitation of our foreknowledge gives us the *appearance* of acting according to our free will. That Popper is aware of this becomes immediately apparent.

14.6. METAPHYSICAL ISSUES

Some events depend on our knowledge, but it is impossible to predict our future knowledge exactly. Therefore the *exact prediction* of *arbitrary* future events *from within* the world is impossible. But this does not affect the possibility that the world "is completely determined if seen *from without*" – say, by a God (OU, 87). Hence Popper has not quite reached his aim. Therefore, he now examines '*metaphysical*' *determinism* (87ff.).

14.61. On the Motion Picture Analogy

To this end, he goes back to the motion picture analogy. In the eyes of God, who knows the whole film, the future is as present as the past. From this, Popper infers that "*nothing ever happened in this world*, and change was a human illusion, as was also the difference between the future and the past" (OU, 90, i.a.). However, his inference from "God's knowledge of the whole film" to the assertion that "nothing ever happens in this world" is already invalid. It is true that God knows all the frames, but this does not imply that they are equal to each other. Only if they were equal to each other would Popper be entitled to say that nothing happens in the world that the film depicts.

Now he raises two *objections to the determinism* of the motion picture analogy. The *first* says that "nothing in our experience" warrants a deterministic metaphysics of this kind (OU, 90). But what in our experience warrants Popper's indeterministic metaphysics? Obviously, he believes that *indeterminism* – as opposed to determinism – *needs no warrant* whatsoever, for he insists that his "argument that the determinist should carry the burden of proof... applies not only to 'scientific' determinism but also to its metaphysical version" (89).

The *second* objection points out three consequences of the motion picture analogy (OU, 91f.):

(1) As *the future* is "causally entailed by the past, [it] could be viewed as contained in the past" (91). Thus the future *becomes redundant,* for it makes no sense to watch a film whose later frames are entailed by its first frame and a universal theory.

But, on the one hand, we do not know any such theory, and on the other hand, it would not enable us to describe the future frames perfectly before they are shown, if Popper's argument of the impossibility of a perfect prediction is sound. Thus the film is full of surprises for us, and this makes it exciting.

(2) Our perception of change and of the flow of time must be an illusion, and the arrow of time is only *subjective.* This is an *idealist's* position (91).

But, if the content of the frames changes, then there is objective change, even if it should be predictable.

(3) Finally, Popper even believes that he notices a *contradiction:* If we see successive frames depicting an unchanging world, something changes *for us* and therefore also *in the world;* whereas, according to the motion picture analogy, nothing changes in the world (91f.).

However, the first clause, "If... in the world," contradicts the second, "according... world," only because the latter relies on consequences (1) and (2). In order to avoid these self-made problems, Popper proposes "to accept an indeterminist view of the world" (92).

14.62. The Physical Theory of Propensities

What could be said *in favour of 'metaphysical' indeterminism?* It could be useful, for example, to common sense, *ethics*, or philosophy of science. But if it should turn out to be "*a gain . . . to science itself*," this would perhaps be "the strongest positive argument in favour of indeterminism" (OU, 93, i.a.). Popper thinks that "a physical interpretation of probability theory in the form of a *physical theory of propensities*" would be such a gain (93, i.a.). For he fears that determinism could prevent us from seriously examining the idea of *physical propensities*. This idea may best be explained by analogy with the idea of *physical forces*. A force is an unobservable *hypothetical entity* even though it is *empirically accessible*, since we can test hypotheses involving the force. This holds correspondingly of propensities.

Being a convinced indeterminist, Popper even goes one step further and postulates that an "*objective situation*, all of whose conditions we have kept constant, determines *propensities rather than forces*" (OU, 94). He considers the idea of propensity "a kind of generalization of – or perhaps even an alternative to – the idea of force" (95). The hypothesis that somewhere there are propensities at work is to be tested statistically. It also sufficiently explains why the same test conditions "*may produce fluctuating results*," whereas a determinist, in order to explain the same effect, would have "to postulate *fluctuating initial conditions*" (94).

If, for example, the determinist wants to apply the prima facie deterministic laws of classical mechanics to tosses of a coin, he may assume that there are "*hidden fluctuations of the initial conditions*" – say, of the impulse that the coin is given when it is thrown (OU, 94). From this, Popper infers that the determinist needs "*a probabilistic assumption about 'hidden' initial conditions*" and that he thus only *shifts* the problem, because he must now deterministically explain the probabilistic character of the "hidden" initial conditions (97).

Popper here relies on an argument by Alfred Landé (1888–1975) that is designed to show that "we must accept *probabilities* of single events as *fundamental*" (i.a.), that probability statements can be replaced only by other probability statements, and that we get an *infinite regress* "if we combine a *prima facie* deterministic theory with statistical assumptions concerning initial conditions" (OU, 100).

The core of the argument may be summed up as follows: Balls are dropped through a tube on the centre of a blade and then fall either to the right or to the left. A naïve observer may take the actual path of a particular ball to be random, but a physicist may be able to predict that it will fall to the right, because he detects the fact that it collides with a group of molecules when leaving the tube and thus receives an impulse in this direction (OU, 100). But how does he explain the position and momentum of the molecules before the collision? And how can he causally – that is, deterministically – explain the statistical distribution of the balls after a series of experiments?

Suppose that after a series of 1,000 trials we observe that exactly 500 balls have fallen to the right and 500 to the left. When a determinist is asked to explain this distribution, he will assert that it "*was predetermined* long before the tube and the blade ever existed'" (OU, 100). But this is not sufficient. He must also postulate "'a corresponding random distribution of causes at an earlier time, and from there back to a still earlier time'" (101). This leads to an infinite regress. As he must again and again go back to an unexplained statistical distribution of initial conditions, "the strangely law-like behaviour of the statistical sequences remains, for the determinist, *ultimately irreducible and inexplicable*" (102). His explanation that "many small causes or 'errors' will (by partly cancelling each other, etc.) produce the random result" also proves to be empty (101).

This becomes even more obvious when we consider that the probabilities change if we readjust the blade. Instead of a 50:50 ratio, we could then obtain 40:60, or 52:48, and so on. In order to explain these ratios deterministically, they must be reduced to distributions of earlier events that cause, among other things, the respective positions of the blade. But the determinist can never have access to all those distributions. Therefore, his explanations, if not impossible, must seem "miraculous, since they would have to assume a 'pre-established harmony' in the initial conditions" (OU, 103).

However, Landé's and Popper's argument only varies an old objection to determinism. It says that the principle of causality, "*Every* event has a cause," leads into an infinite regress, which is traditionally broken off by referring to some *first* cause – an unmoved mover or the absolute spontaneity of a cause. Hence if the determinist tries to explain *any* event *completely*, he will *always* end up in an infinite regress – not only, as Landé and Popper suggest, when he tries to explain a random event.

In any case, in order to avoid the regress it is not sufficient to convert to 'metaphysical' indeterminism in the *weak* form, "*Not every* event has a cause." For in this form it does not preclude the possibility that in some – perhaps even in most – cases we may still end up in a regress. Would it make a difference if we instead adopted 'metaphysical' indeterminism in the *strong* form, "*No event has a cause*"? That would preclude any *causal explanation* and hence any infinite regress of causal explanations. But would it also preclude any, possibly infinite, *concatenation of events*? This would certainly be the case if in addition we assumed that each event is *random* in the sense of being *statistically independent* of *all* other events. But in circumstances like these, there would be no regularities and hence no life. Therefore, we may take this assumption to be refuted.

Where there are no causal connections there may still be probabilistic, or statistical, connections. Even the strong form of 'metaphysical' inde-terminism, "No event has a (deterministic) cause," is compatible with the assumption "Some events are subject to probabilistic influences" and, in-deed, with the assumption "*Each event is subject to probabilistic influences.*" Both of these assumptions allow infinite *concatenations of events*; and just as we can ask for the (deterministic) cause of the (deterministic) cause of an event, we can ask for the *probabilistic "causes"* of its probabilistic "causes" and thus begin an infinite *regress of explanations*.

Does this mean that the indeterminist Popper is in no better position than his determinist counterpart? Obviously, the determinist must stick to the thesis of an infinite chain of causes, whereas the indeterminist may assume not only that some events are completely accidental, but also that each probabilistic concatenation of events ends after a finite number of steps with one or more completely accidental events.

We need not examine here whether this assumption is compatible with well-corroborated physical hypotheses. For if we examine not only the *con-sistency* of the competing philosophical theories but also their *compatibility with widely accepted empirical theories*, then the astrophysical thesis that our universe has existed only for a finite time also saves the determinist from an infinite regress. It even suggests that at the time when laws of nature of the type on which the determinist relies began to hold, there existed that random distribution of initial conditions that he needs in order to explain random events causally.

Landé's argument is intended to refute determinism, but Popper thinks that it also shows the advantages of the *propensity interpretation* of probability. If we change the position of the blade, the relative fre-quencies of balls falling to the right and to the left change as well. The propensity interpretation provides a simple explanation of this effect: "Any change of the position of the blade changes the *possibilities* inherent in the experimental set-up. . . . More precisely, it changes the measure of these possibilities" (OU, 104, i.a.). Popper calls theses measures "objec-tive probabilities or *propensities*" (104) in order to point out "that these 'possibilities' are now considered as *physical magnitudes*" that interact like forces and can therefore be considered "as *physically real*: they are not merely logical possibilities, but *physical possibilities*" (105).

Propensities are *singular* probabilities "in so far as they are inherent in the experimental set-up which is assumed to be the same for each experiment" (OU, 105). As the test conditions "are objective physical conditions, the propensities or probabilities are also objective." They are objective probabilities not of the ball under investigation but "of the whole experimental set-up," including the ball. If the setup always produces the same result – say, all balls fall to the right – "then it may be ... *prima facie* deterministic"; if it always produces relative frequencies differing from both 1 and 0, then it is "probabilistic" (105). Hence *propensities are generalizations of forces* (WP, 13f.). Popper proposes that we admit their existence, just as we admit the existence of forces.

14.7. INDETERMINISM IS NOT ENOUGH

While the success of Newton's theory of gravitation made determinism for centuries the dominant position, indeterminism won favour when quantum theory became successful. Now, at last, the "nightmare of determinism," or rather of fatalism, seemed to dissolve. According to indeterminism, however, "sheer *chance* plays a major role in our physical world," and chance appears even less satisfactory than determination (OK, 226). For in order to be able to act *rationally* and *responsibly*, we must know the consequences of our behaviour, at least approximately. But this is impossible if everything is accidental. Popper quotes Schlick: "'[F]reedom of action, responsibility, and mental sanity, cannot reach beyond the realm of causality: they stop where chance begins. . . . a higher degree of randomness . . . [simply means] a higher degree of irresponsibility'" (226f.).

Actually, the matter is even more complicated. If I behave purely accidentally, I do not act. For *acting* presupposes an aim, and the choice of a means that is suited to this aim presupposes that the behaviour of my fellow beings and of my environment is not random. Where there are no regularities, nothing can serve as a means to an end. And only if we "know" and weigh the consequences of various possible ways of behaving can we ask whether we act *rationally* and *responsibly*.

But if responsibility presupposes regularity, how much regularity is then admissible without endangering freedom? David Hume gives a surprising answer. In section VIII of his *Enquiry Concerning Human*

Understanding, he examines "*the doctrine of necessity*," the thesis "that the conjunction between *motives and voluntary actions* is as regular and uniform as that between the *cause and effect* in any part of nature" (EHU, 81, 88, i.a.). Accordingly, our actions are caused by our motives. This does not, however, mean that they are determined, for Hume considers "the probability of causes" (57). He also supports "*the doctrine of liberty*" (94 n1, i.a.), and by "liberty" he means "*a power of acting or not acting, according to the determinations of the will*; that is, if we choose to remain at rest, we may; if we choose to move, we also may. Now this hypothetical liberty is universally allowed to belong to every one who is not a prisoner and in chains" (95).

Nowadays this "hypothetical liberty" is usually called "*freedom of action*." It is compatible with determination of will. *If nothing prevents me from acting in the way in which I am determined to want to act, then I am free in the sense of freedom of action*. But Hume knows that theologians and philosophers are not content with freedom of action and therefore postulate *freedom of will*. Theologians consider this important for theodicy, and philosophers above all for the justification of punishment. They believe that "I am responsible for my actions only if my will is not determined; and I deserve praise or punishment only insofar as I am responsible." Hume, however, regards the idea of freedom of will as erroneous, and he explains the error as follows: "We feel, that our actions are subject to our will, on most occasions; and imagine we feel, that the will itself is subject to nothing" (EHU, 94 n1).

On the other hand, even the most convinced adherents of freedom of will have noticed limitations. Some quote the Apostle Paul: "For the good that I will *to do*, I do not do; but the evil I will not *to do*, that I practice" (Epistle to the Romans 7:19). Obviously, something in Paul prevents him from executing his original laudable intention. In order to take this problem into account, Donald MacKay distinguishes between the *freedom to choose what we want* and the *freedom to want what we ought to do* (1967, 35). But thereby he seems only to double the problem of free will.

We cannot here examine the question of what it means to say that we *ought* to do something (God commands us to do so; everybody can see that it is right, etc.). Also, Paul's problem is not that he doesn't want what he ought to want, but that (in the end) he doesn't do what he (originally) wants to do. Obviously, the *choice* that we make before we act is subject to various *influences*. According to Hume, when we feel "the sentiment of approbation or blame," this results "from a reflection of . . . opposite interests" (those contributing to "the peace and security of human society" or to "public detriment and disturbance"; EHU, 102). But in the present context we are not so much interested in *what* influences the choice but in whether it is *completely determined* by these influences (which would exclude freedom of will) or, if that is not the case, whether it is *accidental* (which would exclude responsibility).

But why does Popper state: "Hume's and Schlick's ontological thesis that there cannot exist anything intermediate between chance and determinism seems to me . . . clearly absurd" (OK, 228)? After all, he himself describes *determinism* and *indeterminism* in such a way that one of them is the negation of the other. Hence there is no third possibility. Nevertheless, Popper believes that "we need for understanding rational human behaviour . . . something *intermediate* in character between perfect chance and perfect determinism" (228).

His problem cannot be to decide, whether all physical events are determined or all are accidental, or whether some of them are determined and others are accidental, but only whether *a particular event* can only be either completely determined or completely accidental. For in neither case could we "understand how such non-physical things as *purposes, deliberations, plans, decisions, theories, intentions,* and *values,* can play a part in bringing about physical changes in the physical world" (OK, 229). Rather, this requires something intermediate, which Popper calls "*plastic control*" (cf. section 15.53).

Plastic control in its turn contains a strong presupposition. Obviously, "a *physically closed* system containing chance elements . . . would not be deterministic"; yet "purposes, ideas, hopes, and wishes could not in such a world have any influence on physical events" (OK, 219 n29). Thus physical indeterminism does not suffice to save the idea of freedom of will. Rather, we must abandon the idea of the *seclusion* of the physical world. And with "this statement, *indeterminism is not enough,*" Popper has arrived "at the very heart of [his] problem" (226).

He even asserts "that the problem of determinism versus indeterminism enters into [his] argument . . . as a merely *subsidiary problem,* subsidiary to the problem of the closedness or openness of world 1" (PKP, 1075). But in what respect can the *physical world* be open? According to Popper, it *interacts with* other worlds, a second *world of mental entities* and a third *world of objective thought contents* (cf. sections 15.12, 15.52).

Already Popper's formulation of the problem tacitly presumes that purposes, theories, and so on do not belong to the physical world and hence are not states or occurrences in the central nervous system. But this has yet to be shown. If they should nevertheless be of a physiological nature, his *thesis of the openness* of the physical world would *not* be *appropriate* for saving the ideas of creativity and freedom of will.

There is also reason to suppose that Popper's *thesis of the openness of the physical world is untenable*, as it *contradicts the conservation laws of physics* – in particular, the conservation-of-energy principle (the first law of thermodynamics), which, after the discovery of relativity, has developed into the principle of the conservation of mass-energy (because according to Einstein's law $E = mc^2$, the mass m is equivalent to the energy E).

Obviously, Popper has recognized this problem, for he argues that

> if we bring in (at least) *two* particles, then the laws of conservation of momentum and of energy certainly do not fully determine their direction, although they do determine, after the direction of one of them has been chosen, the speed of both particles, and the direction of the second particle. Now...a moving animal...chooses its direction.... Its choice of speed, however, is...limited...by the available muscular energy...and thus, by the energy principle. (If we take the animal as one of these two particles, then the second particle whose presence makes it possible to satisfy the law of conservation of momentum is, as a rule, the earth.)

From this he concludes: "I do not think that any physical law is violated here" (QTSP, 192 n1).

If this argument is to be relevant to his theory of three worlds, then he must assume that an *animal's* choice of its direction also involves *mental* entities. But even then his argument is not sound. For what is decisive is after all an interference originating from the mental world that induces the change in direction. In order to have a physiological effect, the interference would have to change the position or the impulse of at least one particle of the animal's central nervous system. But – if we follow well-corroborated theories of physics – this is impossible without the transfer of an impulse that cannot come *from* the physical world and therefore must change the quantity of energy *in* the physical world.

Even if we assume that purposes are mental entities and that the physical world is open toward the mental world, that is *not sufficient* to make freedom of will possible. To begin with, the openness of the physical world implies only that it is not completely determined by *its own* laws or causes. For should certain occurrences in the mental world that influence our physical behaviour be determined in their turn, then our behaviour, though not physically determined, would be *mentally determined*. This too would *exclude freedom of will.* On the other hand, in order for acts of will to be free, it does not suffice that some mental occurrences are *not determined*. Rather, within the scope that their indeterminacy leaves, *a new first cause* must be created in a *nonaccidental* way. Popper thinks that "plastic control" will make this possible.

What is needed in the present case is a "*plastic control*" *of the occurrences in the second world*. According to Popper, this plastic control becomes possible owing to the *openness* of the second, mental world toward the third world of objective thought contents, for world 3 theories plastically control the mental self (KBMP, 115; cf. section 15.53). But these theories are not considered unmoved movers, nor are they taken to be plastically controlled in their turn by entities of a fourth world. Rather, all plastic controls are, according to Popper, "of the *give-and-take*, or *feedback*, type." Thus we – that is, our mental self – can "change the controlling world 3 theories" (115, i.a.).

We are well acquainted with interactions between physical entities. If they make plastic control possible, then the physical world need not be open toward the mental world. The same holds, correspondingly, of interactions within the mental world and its openness toward the world of objective thought contents. If, however, interactions between entities of the *same* world are not sufficient, then it is not understandable how the fact that interacting entities belong to *different* worlds could make plastic control possible. Hence the idea of "plastic control" does not solve the problem of creating an uncaused first cause either.

It is also hard to imagine how the problem could be solved, for, on the one hand, *the new first cause must not be merely accidental.* If *acts of free will* were *statistically independent of everything else*, then not only would they be completely unintelligible and therefore could not be called "rational" – which, on the contrary, presupposes that to a certain degree they correspond to our expectations, that is, show regularities – we would also have no reason to praise or blame them morally. Moreover, the *behaviour* resulting from them would then also have to be statistically independent of everything else, except for the acts of free will. Actually, our behaviour normally is not even statistically independent of everything observable. This too speaks against the thesis of first causes that are created by acts of free will.

If an *act of free will* is *not* to be *completely accidental*, it must *statistically depend on at least one state or occurrence in any of the worlds.* On the other hand, *a new first cause must by definition not depend on anything else.* It is true that not every statistical dependence expresses a "real" dependence; some of them are only "spurious correlations." However, not all correlations can be spurious. Rather, a correlation is spurious only if it can be explained by another, "genuine correlation."

If we do not, like Kant, use transcendental evasions, either we must abandon the concept of free will, or we must *limit the requirements of free will* so that an act of will that *statistically depends* on the needs of the acting subject and on the circumstances of the action may nevertheless be called "free." But how close then may the conditional probability of an act of will, given certain needs and outer circumstances, come to the value 1 that it would assume if it were completely determined? By the way, not even the Kantian can escape such dependences. If he wants to follow the categorical imperative, "Act only according to that maxim by which you can at the same time will that it should become a universal law" (*Groundwork of the Metaphysic of Morals*, B 52), then he must make his action dependent on what he wills (can will) and on his expectations concerning the effects of the law.

15

The Body-Mind Problem and the Third World

In his article "Language and the Body-Mind Problem" (1953; CR, 293–298), Popper supports a *body-mind dualism*. It is true that he does not, like Descartes, postulate two *substances*, a thinking substance and an extended substance, but only physical and mental *states* that *interact* (OK, 231 n43). However, he attributes these states to *bodies* or *minds* and constructs universes or *worlds* containing them. For example, physical entities "belong to the [first,] *physical world*" (CR, 298, i.a.); and soon he also speaks of a *second world of mental entities*. His *central thesis* says that "a physicalistic causal theory of the human *language*" is impossible (293, i.a.; cf. section 15.4), and it implies that we must therefore assume the existence of mental entities as well.

In a very short paragraph (6.2), he already indicates entities of another kind: "*Logical relationships*, such as consistency, do not belong to the physical world." Neither are they subjective thought contents; hence they do not belong to the world of mental entities either; rather, they "are abstractions (perhaps '*products of the mind*')" (CR, 298, i.a.). And he postulates that our minds may be influenced by logical relationships as well as by physical objects. If, for example, I recognize a contradiction, this may prompt me to act in the physical world (298).

In his Arthur Holly Compton Memorial Lecture "Of Clouds and Clocks" (1966; OK, 206–255), Popper explicitly postulates a "*universe of abstract meanings*," the third world (230). His *central problem* is "*whether the physical world is closed or not*" (PKP, 1073, i.a.). He searches for an answer to "Compton's problem" of the influence of the world of abstract meanings on human behaviour, and he wants to show "that the physical world is not *closed*, but that *reasons . . . can have physical effects . . .* , at any rate *after having been grasped by some mind"* (1073). Accordingly, his *central thesis* asserts *"the influence of reasoning (worlds 2 and 3) upon the physical world 1"* (1075, i.a.). He also touches upon the problems of determinism versus indeterminism, of *freedom,* and of *rationality.* However, "the *problem of determinism versus indeterminism"* (i.a.) is "a merely *subsidiary problem"* (1075; cf. section 14.7).

The main subject of his articles "Epistemology without a Knowing Subject" (1968a; OK, 106–152) and "On the Theory of the Objective Mind" (1968b; OK, 153–190) is "*'the third world,'*" or "world 3," of "'*objective contents of thought,'*" which, above all, contains theories (106). Here the matter at issue is not, as in Descartes, the knowledge of particular subjects but a knowledge that is independent of particular subjects, that is, intersubjective. World 3 has much in common with "Plato's theory of Forms or Ideas" and "Hegel's objective spirit"; it has more in common with "Bolzano's theory of a universe of propositions in themselves"; and it comes closest to "the universe of Frege's objective contents of thought" (106). But for Popper, contenting himself with only three worlds is a matter of convenience. He might easily "distinguish more than three worlds" (107).

Together with John Eccles he writes *The Self and Its Brain* (1977). As its subtitle, *An Argument for Interactionism,* indicates, the authors try to corroborate their common *main thesis* of *psychophysical interaction.* Eccles presents his thesis of a *liaison brain,* where the interaction takes place, and Popper develops – in the context of his criticism of materialism – his version of the thesis of "*downward causation"* (the mind [world 2] and theories [world 3] influence the body and its behaviour [world 1]). According to him, the neo-Darwinian *theory of evolution* "together with the fact that conscious processes exist, lead[s] beyond physicalism"; and together with the thesis of "the existence of an evolved consciousness," it leads to interactionism (1977, 99).

Popper's last contribution to the body-mind problem can be found in his book *Knowledge and the Body-Mind Problem* (1994b; KBMP). It is based on a series of lectures given in 1969 and on subsequent discussions with the public. The transcriptions of the tape recordings were revised first by Popper during the 1970s and later by the editor, M. A. Notturno; the subsequently published version has been approved by Popper. In a nutshell, the *main thesis* of his lectures is: "[I]n order to understand the relationship between the body and the mind, we must first recognize the existence of objective knowledge as an objective and autonomous product of the human mind, and, in particular, the ways in which we use such knowledge as a control system for critical problem-solving" (Author's Note, 1993). In the lectures he touches upon almost everything he had ever written on the subject. Therefore, we shall orient ourselves by the course of these lectures. But he also dispenses with some more sophisticated arguments that he had put forward earlier. Therefore, we shall from time to time go back to older texts.

15.1. OBJECTIVE AND SUBJECTIVE KNOWLEDGE

In *Knowledge and the Body-Mind Problem,* Popper discusses first and foremost two complexes of problems, the *problem of two kinds of knowledge* and the *body-mind problem* (KBMP, 3). His *main thesis* is: "We cannot understand world 2, that is, the world inhabited by our own mental states, without understanding that its main function is to *produce* world 3 objects, and to be *acted upon* by world 3 objects" (7).

15.11. The Problem of Two Kinds of Knowledge

To begin with, Popper gives an introduction to the problem of two kinds of knowledge. (He obviously relies on his article "Epistemology without a Knowing Subject.") He distinguishes between "*knowledge in the subjective sense*" and "*knowledge in the objective sense*" (KBMP, 3, i.a.). Subjective knowledge consists of dispositions – above all, expectations; objective knowledge "consists of problems, theories, and arguments" (24). Various examples illustrate this distinction: The statement "'*It is well known that* water consists of hydrogen and oxygen'" explains what he means by "knowledge in the objective sense," while the statements "'*He knew* he was exceeding the speed limit,'" "'*He thought* that elementary particles have an internal structure,'" and "'*He saw* a yellow flash'" refer to cases of subjective knowledge (3). "Knowledge in the objective sense is ... *knowledge without a knowing subject*" (OK, 109). But how can anything be known without being the knowledge of some knowing subject?

With the aid of the distinction between subjective and objective knowledge he formulates three *epistemological theses* (OK, 111f.):

(1) "[T]raditional epistemology, with its concentration on the second world, or on knowledge in the subjective sense, is irrelevant to the study of scientific knowledge."

(2) "[T]he study of a *largely autonomous* third world of objective knowledge is of decisive importance for epistemology."

(3) "An objectivist epistemology which studies the third world can help to throw an immense amount of light upon the second world of subjective consciousness, especially upon the subjective thought processes of scientists; but *the converse is not true.*"

They are complemented by three *supporting theses* (112):

(4) The third world is a natural product of the human animal.
(5) The third world is largely *autonomous*, even though we constantly act upon it and are acted upon by it.
(6) Objective knowledge grows through the interaction between our-selves and the third world.

There is also "a close analogy between the *growth of knowledge* and biolog-ical growth; that is, the *evolution of plants and animals*" (112, i.a.).

Popper calls "the approach from the side of the products – the the-ories and the arguments – the 'objective' approach or the 'third world' approach [and he calls] the behaviourist, the psychological, and the so-ciological approach to scientific knowledge the 'subjective' approach or the 'second world' approach" (OK, 114). While the subjective approach is causal – proceeds from the causes to the effects – the objective approach "starts from effects rather than causes," and this is in "all sciences, the ordinary approach" (114f.).

Even a book that is never read contains objective knowledge. But in order to belong to the third world of objective knowledge, it "should – in principle, or virtually – be capable of being grasped . . . by somebody" (OK, 116). From this, Popper concludes: "We can thus say that there is a kind of Platonic (or Bolzanoesque) third world of books in themselves, theories in themselves, problems in themselves, . . . arguments in them-selves, and so on." And now he adds a particularly strong thesis: "[E]ven though this third world is a human product, there are many theories in themselves and arguments in themselves and problem situations in them-selves which have never been produced or understood and may never be produced or understood by men." The sceptic will consider this thesis to be "extremely metaphysical and dubious." But Popper defends it "by pointing out its biological analogue" (116): "The question of the ade-quacy of [a nesting] box is clearly an objective one; and whether the box is ever used is partly accidental" (117).

However, a nesting box is made to serve a specific purpose, and the only question is, whether it is suited for this purpose. But what is a "theory in itself" that possibly will never be "produced or understood"? Does every (universal or probabilistic) statement that might *possibly* be formulated in *a given* language constitute a theory *in itself*? Is this true even of every statement that might possibly be formulated in *any possible* language? What does Popper gain by existential postulates such as these? Obviously, only the ability to say that theories are not invented but discovered.

The real problem of the two kinds of knowledge is that "of the relation between knowledge in the objective sense and knowledge in the subjective sense" (KBMP, 24). Popper contends that *we can understand subjective knowledge only if we study "the growth of objective knowledge and the give and take between the two kinds of knowledge"* (4, i.a.). The growth of objective knowledge is "part of the growth of world 3" (10). Here the explanation of world 2 is the end to which knowledge of world 3 is the means.

15.12. The Body-Mind Problem

The sceptic may ask *whether* anything speaks for the distinction between body and mind and *how* they can be distinguished. He will consider *these* questions to be the body-mind problem. Popper, on the other hand, takes the first question (*whether*) to be answered in the affirmative. He is so much a convinced dualist that he considers it "*silly* to deny the existence of mental experiences or mental states or states of consciousness" (A, 149, i.a.). Here the sceptic misses Popper's critical rationalist attitude. Popper is hardly interested in the second question (*how*) at all.

But what does he state as his reason for being a dualist? When he talks to me, he does not address my body but my mind (cf. section 15.51). Accordingly, "in addition to the *first world* ... of physical bodies and their physical and physiological states ... there seems to exist a *second world* ... of mental states" (KBMP, 4). Consequently, *the question* arises *what kind of relations hold between the two worlds*, and, according to Popper, this *is the body-mind problem* (5).

If we follow Descartes, Popper's mind acts upon his body, which then produces a physical sound. This sound affects my ears (i.e., my body), which in turn affects my mind and makes me think. Accordingly, there is an *interaction between physical and mental states* (KBMP, 5). And if what *interacts* may be called *real*, then we may accept the reality of both worlds. In this respect, Popper is a Cartesian *dualist*.

Early on, he contented himself with Cartesian *dualism*, although since 1934 he has supported an epistemology that emphasizes "the status of objective knowledge and the hopelessness of any attempt to reduce it to subjective knowledge" (KBMP, 52). But he considers the idea of a third world "hot air" until he thinks he can explain "the status of world 3 and its relation to world 2" (52).

He also calls world 3 "the world of the *products* of our human minds" (KBMP, 5). At the same time, he considers some of these products physical objects. *Paintings*, for example, belong to world 1 *and* to world 3. However, Shakespeare's *Hamlet* and Mozart's *Symphony in G Minor* belong *only* to world 3, whereas their *reproductions* belong *both* to world 1 and world 3 (6). But double memberships like these blur the boundary between world 1 and world 3.

World 2 interacts not only, as Descartes assumed, with world 1 but also with world 3; and world 3 objects can affect world 1 only through the intermediary of world 2 (KBMP, 7). On the other hand, it is only by our actions that world 1 can affect world 3. *We* are the mediators. Thus we cannot get closer to the solution of the body-mind problem if we ignore world 3. But if world 2 is the intermediary between world 1 and world 3, "then the body-mind problem must remain incomplete . . . until we extend it to cover the interrelationships between all three worlds" (8).

Nevertheless, Popper considers the term "world 3" to be a metaphor, for "we could, if we wish to, distinguish *more than three worlds*" (KBMP, 25, i.a.). We might, for example, distinguish between a world of "*objective knowledge*" and a world of "*the arts*." Hence he is not simply a triadist but a *pluralist*. But he recognizes "how very abstract and abstruse and, indeed, 'philosophical' . . . this idea of a world 3" is (10).

Popper formulates the classical body-mind problem – or "*Descartes's problem*" – as follows: "[*H*]*ow can it be that such things as states of mind – volitions, feelings, expectations – influence or control the physical movements of our limbs?*" (OK, 231, i.a.). The other side of the problem – "[H]ow can it be that the physical states of an organism may influence its mental states?" – seems to him less important (231), for he is interested in the influence of *world 2* on *world 1*.

But another problem – he calls it "*Compton's problem*" – seems to him more important: "*How can it be that the content of a communication* (a letter) *prompts me to act* (travel)?" This is "the problem of the influence of the *universe of abstract meanings* upon human behaviour," that is, of the influence of *world 3* on *world 1* (OK, 230).

Every acceptable solution of Descartes' or of Compton's problem has to comply with what Popper calls "*Compton's postulate of freedom*": It must explain freedom, and it must explain "how freedom is not just chance but, rather, the result of a subtle interplay between *something almost random or haphazard*, and *something like a restrictive or selective control* – such as an aim or a standard" (OK, 231f.). In other words, it must "conform to *the idea of combining freedom and control,* and also to *the idea of a 'plastic control,'*" as Popper calls it, "in contradistinction to a 'cast-iron [deterministic] control'" (232). In order to solve both problems, Popper designs "a new theory of evolution" and "a new model of the organism" (232).

15.2. THE AUTONOMY OF WORLD 3

The objective world 3 contains, roughly, "the products of the human mind" – for example, works of "architecture, art, literature, music, scholarship," and, above all, "the problems, theories and critical discussions of the sciences" (KBMP, 25). Theories and arguments are by-products of human language, which, in turn, is an unintended by-product of actions directed at other aims (OK, 117). Central to Popper's theory of world 3 is the idea of *autonomy*: "[A]lthough the third world is a human product . . . , it creates in its turn, as do other animal products, its own *domain of autonomy*" (118).

But what constitutes the autonomy of the third world? Once we have begun to produce something – for example, a house – we cannot proceed in any way we like. Rather, the unfinished product obeys structural laws, which we discover rather than invent, which we cannot change, and which in this sense are *autonomous* (KBMP, 47f.). Other "world 3 inmate[s]," such as "objective problems, arguments, and theories," can also be *discovered* and *understood* (29).

Understanding an objective problem, an argument, or a theory is not the same as understanding other persons and their intentions, for *thoughts* in the objective sense are not the same as thoughts in the subjective sense. Rather, a *thought in the subjective sense* is "a *thinking process*" (i.a.) that "happens *at a certain time*" and may differ "from occasion to occasion and from person to person" (KBMP, 29). On the other hand, "the *content* of some statement" (i.a.), or "the connectedness of an argument, or the difficulty which constitutes an unsolved problem" is a *thought in the objective sense.* It may at *some* time have been invented or discovered, but "it can be plugged into or subjectively understood at *any* time after." Though it has a temporal history, it may, as "a world 3 inmate, . . . be called 'timeless'" (29). Elsewhere he numbers not only the *actual* theories but also all merely *possible* theories among the inmates of world 3 (OK, 116).

Popper gives geometrical and arithmetical examples to explain in what respect the term "world 3" is "more than a metaphor" and how world 3 itself is "more than a world of products of the mind" (KBMP, 26). If, for example, we "*invent* a method of naming natural numbers . . . we can, in principle, always add one, and so go on to infinity" (29). But this invention has unintended and unavoidable consequences that we do not invent but *discover*, just as we discover "unknown mountains and rivers" (29ff.). Thus we may discover that there are odd and even numbers as well as prime numbers. Along with the prime numbers a lot of solved and unsolved problems arise, among them the problem of whether there is a greatest prime number. Euclid solved that problem by proving that the number of prime numbers is infinite. Both the problem and the proof have been *discovered* (30). On the other hand, the problem of whether there are infinitely many twin primes is still unsolved – that is, the problem has been discovered but so far the solution hasn't.

The problems that we *discover* are *unintended* by-products of our world 3 products. Thus they are only *indirectly* products of the human mind. That is why Popper asserts only that world 3 contains, *roughly*, the products of the human mind. As these products are no longer subject to our control, he calls them "'*autonomous*'" (KBMP, 30, i.a.). On the other hand, "every discovery is *like* an invention" insofar as "it contains an element of creative imagination" (48).

As some problems and theories already existed before they were discovered, they cannot belong to world 2 – that is, they cannot be mental states, subjective thoughts. "This establishes precisely . . . the 'autonomy' of world 3" (KBMP, 31). Anyone who follows Euclid's proof plugs into Euclid's world 3 product. The proof itself belongs to world 3, but Euclid's thoughts, which produced it, and the thoughts of a reader, which follow it, belong to world 2. Hence there is an *interaction between two minds, mediated by a world 3 product* (27).

Animals too have developed *languages*. The song by which a bird marks the limits of its district is "an exosomatic instrument" and has, "like all animal instruments, an inborn genetic basis" (KBMP, 34). However, "*animal knowledge* is essentially *endosomatic*." It comprises "inborn or acquired dispositions" and thus is "very much like human *subjective* knowledge." As opposed to this, human language also permits "*exosomatic* knowledge" (34, i.a.). We can externalize our knowledge, and thus it becomes *criticizable*. This is the main difference between animal language and human language.

But how sound is Popper's argument? Does it really show why we must postulate the existence of world 3 entities? When he assumes that *natural numbers were invented* but *primes were discovered*, he doesn't mean that the primes 2, 3, 5, 7, 11, 13, . . . were at first omitted and have only later been discovered as additional natural numbers. Rather, he assumes that they have existed in world 3 since their *invention as natural numbers* so that mathematicians could *discover their being prime*. But what then existed in world 3 without having been discovered? Was it the *property* of these natural numbers *of being prime?*

Suppose that the natural numbers are constructed by means of the operation "plus 1" (i.e., they are invented). The (general) operation of addition "+" is introduced (on the set of natural numbers) as well as its inverse operation, subtraction; in order to avoid any limitations of subtraction, the negative numbers are invented; multiplication is defined as a repeated addition, and division is defined as its inverse operation; in order to avoid any limitations of division, rationals that are not integers are invented. Somebody *discovers*, when dividing, that the following divisions result in integers: $2 \div 1$, $2 \div 2$; $3 \div 1$, $3 \div 3$; $5 \div 1$, $5 \div 5$; . . . but that no division of 2, 3, 5, . . . by any other divisor results in an integer. Therefore, he *defines* the *predicate* "is a prime number" as "is greater than 1 and has only itself and 1 as positive divisors."

Does this imply that the results – that is, the *values of these quotients*, as such – already existed in world 3 before even the first division was carried out? Or did the *property* of being prime exist in world 3 before the predicate "is a prime number" was defined (i.e., invented)? And if this is the case, has this property existed not only since the invention of division but even since the invention of the natural numbers?

Any one who likes profuse ontologies will answer these questions with a hearty "yes." But one who follows Ockham's razor, "*Entities are not to be multiplied beyond necessity*," will ask whether anything can be explained *with* such postulates that can *not* be explained *without* them. Only on this condition will he accept them.

Popper's theory of world 3 appears to be even more problematic, when we leave the field of the formal sciences. Then we must ask not only in what the *content of a synthetic statement* consists but – in the context of the theory of world 3 – also in what the content of a *completely unknown* synthetic statement consists. Now, Popper defines the *logical content* of a statement p "as the class of all non-tautological statements which are derivable from the statement $[p]$" (LSD, 120). As this definition refers only to logical relations, it is insufficient once we leave the field of the formal sciences. For outside this field, it also matters what the premise of such a class of consequences *says* about the world.

The concept of the *content* even of daily statements is a problem for interpreters and linguists. Does a statement say what its *author* wants to express? Even then, Popper need not content himself with this "subjective sense" of the statement. Rather, he could assume that along with the expression of a "thought in the subjective sense" a "thought in the objective sense" having the same content originates, or that the latter arises from the former. But what would then be the content of a still-undiscovered theory? After all, it must exist independently of any author.

Or does a statement say what its *interpreter* associates with it? In this case, Popper could assume that its content – the "thought in the objective sense" – equals the "thought in the subjective sense" that the interpreter associates with it. And then could not the content of a still-unknown theory equal the "thought in the subjective sense" that an interpreter would associate with it if he came to know it? However, the same interpreter could at different times associate different "thoughts in the subjective sense" with the same statement. Moreover, different interpreters could at the same time associate different "thoughts in the subjective sense" with the same statement. Hence the "thought in the objective sense" would be neither timeless nor independent of the interpreter, as Popper assumes.

Hence if a statement is to have *but one single, timeless content,* then this "thought in the objective sense" must be conceived in a different way. On the one hand, Popper could try to identify a particular interpretation of the statement – that is, *a particular* "thought in the subjective sense" – as the one that equals the "thought in the objective sense." But it will prove difficult to find a definition that harmonizes with his world 3 theory. On the other hand, he could (therefore) try to construct on the basis of all possible interpretations of the statement – that is, of *all possible* "thoughts in the subjective sense" – a single "thought in the objective sense," its content.

Let us begin with simple logical connectives. The *conjunction* of all possible interpretations could not be the content, because it will be, for the most part, contradictory, even if all particular interpretations are consistent. On the other hand, their *disjunction* can be, at worst, analytic. But if the interpretations differ, the "thought in the objective sense" would, in consequence of the disjunction, also normally have far less content than the individual "thoughts in the subjective sense." Therefore, the construction of the "thought in the objective sense" must be more radical. It could identify the content of the statement with that fictitious interpretation that *an average interpreter, who is sufficiently versed in the language,* would give it, if he followed the "principle of charity."

But even this fiction would not suffice, for linguistic rules change. Hence the content would change as well. And a still-undiscovered theory has not yet been formulated in any language. According to the rules of which language should it be interpreted? A simple answer can be given only in the case of still-undiscovered consequences of theories that are already known. So what does Popper gain by postulating the existence of possible theories and their contents in world 3? Obviously, only the possibility of speaking of their discovery.

15.3. WORLD 3 AND EMERGENT EVOLUTION

Two "insights" encourage Popper to speak of world 3:

> First, the realization that world 3, though *autonomous*, was *man-made*, and that it was also fully *real*, since we could act upon it and could be acted upon by it: that there was a give and take, and a kind of feedback effect. And second, the insight that something closely analogous to world 3 existed already in the animal kingdom, and that the whole problem could therefore be surveyed in the light of evolutionary theory. (KBMP, 52)

15.31. On the Prehistory of the Theory of World 3

To begin with, Popper draws an outline of the prehistory of his theory of world 3 (KBMP, 49ff.). He cites many names but only briefly examines three authors – namely, Plato, whom he again calls "the greatest of philosophers" (50), Bolzano, and Frege. *Plato's* first world of Forms or Ideas "consists of deified concepts," whereas Popper's third world, in its "region of objective knowledge," contains not only concepts but also theories, open problems, and arguments (49). Moreover, Plato's theory is one of "descent or degeneration," while Popper's "is a theory of evolutionary ascent towards world 3" (49). *Bolzano* postulated a world of "'statements in themselves'" that are only represented in language. Popper considers this "a tremendous progress." Though Bolzano took this world to be real, he could not explain its relation to the physical world. Thus the impression was created that his world of "statements in themselves" is merely a philosophical fiction (50). *Frege* made the important distinction between subjective thought processes and objective thought contents. His "'third realm'" of objective thought contents comprises concepts as well as true and false propositions, but neither problems nor arguments. And he cannot substantiate the idea that his "third realm" is real (51).

However, Popper fails to notice *Carnap*, who, although he too calls himself a pluralist, does not distinguish between ontologically different *worlds* but only between *spheres* of objects that are all constituted on the same basis (Carnap 1928/1967).

15.32. Evolutionary Theory in General

Popper now adds some remarks about "evolutionary theory in general" (KBMP, 52). Though Darwin's theory of evolution by natural selection is most important, it is in many respects unsatisfactory. On the one hand, it is vague. For example, it relies on assumptions about the heritability of properties and about their mutability by the recombination of genes. The assumptions are correct, but they explain too much, as they permit him to explain any stability of properties from generation to generation by heritability, and any instability by mutability (53). On the other hand, Darwin explains the emergence of higher forms of organisms by "'the survival of the fittest.'" According to Popper, however, this explanation works only "if we add a proposition like this: by and large, a higher form tends to be more fit than a lower form" (53). But this proposition is untenable, because some lower forms have survived much longer than all higher forms. Above all, their fitness can hardly be ascertained independently of their survival and their proliferation. Thus Darwin's theory is almost a tautology. At most, it explains "an overall increase of *different* forms" (54). Later Popper weakens his objections.

But he hopes to improve Darwin's theory of evolution slightly by means of his old tetradic schema

$$P_1 \rightarrow TT \rightarrow EE \rightarrow P_2$$

(KBMP, 55). Here P_1 is a *p*roblem as we find it at the beginning of a development. *TT* is a *t*heory that is *t*entatively proposed or, more generally, an attempt to solve the problem (e.g., a mutation). *EE* is the *e*limination of *e*rrors that the attempt may have. It may result from critical discussion (in the case of theories) or from natural selection (in the case of biological species). In any case, it is a reaction to the failure of the attempt to solve P_1 by means of *TT*. P_2 is a new problem that results from either *TT* or *EE*.

Originally, Popper designed this schema in order to explain the development of theories, or the progress of knowledge. Now he tries to generalize it, to apply it to other problems. His aim is "*a theory of emergent evolution through problem-solving*" (KBMP, 63, i.a.). This may be considered a slight revision of Darwinism; it explains new forms "as tentative solutions to the emerging new problems" (63). His theory of evolution has six *main theses*:

(1) "*All organisms* are constantly engaged in problem-solving" (79).

Many of these problems are only remotely related to survival. The ability of organisms to solve problems can perhaps be explained as a result of evolution: Those that failed to solve problems were eliminated; those that did solve problems survived (55).

Insofar as thesis (1) refers to arbitrary problems, it is already *more general* than Darwin's idea that organisms constantly solve survival problems (KBMP, 57; actually it is *less special*). But Popper wants to make even stronger statements, as, for example:

(2) "*Individual organisms* solve their problems by tentative trials which consist of *behaviour* patterns" (79).

An amoeba, for example, may have a feeding problem. In order to solve it, the amoeba may tentatively extend its pseudopodium and thus increase the possibility of ingesting something. This behaviour is subject to error elimination and eventually results in new problems (55f.). The "*various behavioural patterns*" that an *individual* tries out are "*the 'spearheads' in [its] adaptation*" (56).

But in what sense does the amoeba have problems, try solutions, or commit errors? Sometime after its last ingestion, a physiological state of deprivation will return. It still makes sense to call this state the amoeba's individual (world 1) *problem* (P_1) and to call its extending the pseudopodium an *attempt to solve this problem* (*TT*). If the amoeba doesn't manage to ingest something, we may also say that its attempt failed. But the amoeba could commit a *subjective* (physiological world 1 or even mental world 2) *error* only insofar as it is perceptive and receptive. When hunting for something ingestible, it may also approach a natural enemy; but this becomes its new *subjective* (world 1 or world 2) *problem* only if it becomes aware of the enemy. On the other hand, we colloquially say that it runs into *danger* of being eaten, and thereby, according to Popper's world 3 theory, when it approaches its enemy an *objective problem* arises, just as the problem of the greatest prime number arises when the natural numbers are invented. When the amoeba accidentally moves toward its enemy, this may still be called an *objective error*, but could an accidental movement also be called an *objective attempt to solve a problem*?

It becomes evident how far Popper deviates from common usage when he speaks of problem solving in species:

(3) "*Species* solve their problems by tentatively composing genetic patterns, including new mutations. These are tried out in the *breeding of individuals*, and this is where natural selection comes in" (KBMP, 79).

Accordingly, the *individuals* are the *spearheads of the problem solving*, or the tentative trials, *of the species* (56). It is true that new genetic patterns arise with any sexual reproduction, but this happens, as far as we know, by *accidental* recombination of the genes. All the more, a physically or chemically induced mutation results only in accidental changes. Hence "by tentatively composing new genetic patterns" a species can *not* in the usual sense *solve* a problem.

Popper, however, considers "the *production* of the individual by the species . . . *not random*, because some genetic types are *eliminated* by natural *selection*" (KBMP, 56, i.a.). Accordingly, "the production of the individual" must be an episode of evolution that comprises both the individual's coming into being and its struggle with its environment. However, as the species does not take part in this struggle, it does not *solve* any problem of survival faced by a particular individual. But does the species *solve* the problem of its own continuation? As it is an abstract entity, it can only in a figurative sense *have* this problem. And if it composes *new*, fitter genetic patterns, this may mean *its* near end. Does this mean that the species *solves* the problem of the progress of evolution? At any rate, it is hard to see what problem Popper solves by asserting that species solve problems.

If an organism has a problem, P_1 (e.g., how to get food in a pool slowly drying up) and invents a new *aim* (getting from this pool to another over dry land), then it also invents a new problem, P_2 (*how* to get from one pool to another). Popper concludes: "Thus emergent evolution, the evolution of *novelty*, is explained by the possible novelty of P_2 as compared with P_1" (KBMP, 80).

(4) "The tetradic schema explains *emergent evolution*, that is, the emergence of something *entirely novel*. Since P_1 and P_2 are only loosely connected, P_2 will often be totally different – even qualitatively different – from P_1" (79, i.a.).

In order to solve new problems, *individuals* invent "*new behavioural patterns* by the method of trial and error elimination"; and *species* invent "*new individuals* by inventing new genetic patterns" (63, i.a.). According to Popper, this "*theory of emergent evolution through problem-solving*" turns (63), by means of the tetradic schema, the "hot-air term" "'emergent evolution'" into a "perfectly cool and solid" concept (62, i.a.).

Actually, the tetradic schema *permits* P_2 to be entirely novel relative to P_1, but Popper does not say when a problem may *be called* "entirely novel," nor does his schema tell us on which conditions P_2 *is* entirely novel. Popper himself admits: "New forms do emerge, but we don't know when and how" (KBMP, 64). For that reason alone, the schema could not *explain* the *rise* of an entirely new problem; all the less could it explain the development of a completely new *solution* to an old or a new problem.

At any rate, being the *schema* of a theory, it does not explain anything, for it is at best a sentential function and hence cannot even have a truth value. Only theories – that is, statements – constructed according to this schema could explain something. And what if the schema were read as a very general theory that says that all developments are of the form indicated? Then the theory would, because of the great scope of its concepts, probably be empty. After all, even a *random* recombination of genes is considered an *attempt* at solving a problem, and *any* change occurring after the confrontation with reality of such an attempt is considered an error *elimination*.

And if Popper says that a *species* – that is, an abstract entity – has a *problem*, this can only mean that its present situation may have consequences for its proliferation or its continuation. But he tries to put his schema into more concrete terms:

> (5) "According to our schema, new behavioural *aims* [i.a.], such as getting over land into another pool, will be followed by new *skills* – and these may become *traditional* in a population.... If they do, then those anatomic mutations which make it even slightly easier to practise the new skills will be of immediate advantage. They will be favoured by natural selection" (KBMP, 80).

Actually, this is a complementary thesis on evolution. Another one says: "[*A*] *behavioural tradition may also become the spearhead of a genetic entrenchment*" (61). This one need not be considered a concession to Lamarck, but, because of the word "may," it has little content. A further thesis appears more interesting: "[*E*]*very genetic entrenchment of a specialization is bound to be lethal in time, even though it may be extremely successful for the time being, and perhaps for a long time to come*" (61).

But as this one doesn't contain a time limit, it is still metaphysical. From thesis (5), Popper concludes:

(6) "[B]ehavioural changes are more important than anatomic changes [which] cannot succeed unless they favour existing behavioural patterns.... New behaviour is the ultimate spearhead of evolution" (KBMP, 80).

From these theses, he concludes that a typical evolutionary sequence goes like this:

"[F]irst the aim structure changes, then the skill structure changes. And only then does the anatomic structure change" (81).

But he expressly does not "assert that nothing else *can* happen." This is sensible, for how could we rule out the possibility that an accidental change in the anatomic structure bestows capabilities upon its bearer that he discovers by accidentally applying them, and that he only then develops new aims?

15.4. DESCRIPTION, ARGUMENTATION, AND IMAGINATION

Popper now applies his evolutionary theory to man (KBMP, 81ff.). His argument is based on the philosophy of language of his teacher Karl Bühler. In his *Sprachtheorie* (Theory of Language, 1934), Bühler distinguishes three functions of language: two lower functions – the *expressive function* and the *communicative function*, which can also be found in animal languages – and a higher function, the *descriptive or informative function* (84). Popper adds the *argumentative or critical function*, because giving reasons for an opinion distinguishes rational from irrational judgment (84; CR, 134f.).

In his article "Language and the Body-Mind Problem" (1953), he tries "a restatement of interactionism" (CR, 293ff.). To this end, he develops further language philosophical theses. The most important one says that "*a physicalistic causal theory of the human language*" – that is, of the descriptive and argumentative functions – *is impossible* (293, i.a.), in other words, that "[a] *ny causal physicalistic theory of linguistic behaviour can only be a theory of the two lower functions of language*" – that is, of the expressive and the communicative functions (295).

How could he show that a physicalistic (i.e., a world 1) theory of the two higher functions of language is impossible? Popper believes that "doubts about the existence of other minds become *self-contradictory* if formulated in a language" (297, i.a.). For whoever *argues* with other people "cannot but attribute to them *intentions*, and this *means, mental states*" (297, i.a.).

Because of the word "means," the statement "Whoever has intentions has mental states" is analytic. Possibly the same holds of the statement "Whoever argues with other people attributes to them intentions." Both of these statements together imply "Whoever argues with other people attributes to them mental states." Thus anyone who formulates a theory stating something about arguing but denying the existence of mental states becomes entangled in a contradiction. What is the consequence of that? The result depends on a *linguistic prescription* according to which intentions are mental states. But why should a linguist accept this prescription? Should he do it because he otherwise misses a traditional subject? After all, a language philosophical theory on "mental arguing" remains metaphysical, whereas an empirical theory on "nonmental arguing" might be corroborated. But Popper does not stop at the theses quoted.

15.41. The Machine Argument

In order support his central thesis of the impossibility of a physicalistic causal theory of the human language, Popper develops "the machine argument." It says that *a machine* may express an internal state and may signal but cannot describe (and even less argue), even if it writes something down. As "we do not attribute the responsibility for the description to it [but] attribute it to its maker ... , we see that it *does not describe*" (CR, 296, i.a.).

What does this argument show? Isn't the maker of the machine also responsible for its expressing and signalling? Accordingly, machines do not even express or signal. And isn't the almighty and omniscient God who made us also responsible for our describing and arguing? Accordingly, we too do not describe or argue.

Popper asserts that his result – a machine cannot describe – remains the same even when the machine becomes arbitrarily complex. In order to show this, he conceives *a machine* "*whose behaviour is very human*" (CR, 296, i.a.). We may then ask "whether it does not, perhaps, act *intentionally*, rather than mechanically (causally, or probabilistically), *i.e.* whether it does not have a *mind* after all" (296, i.a.).

Here Popper seems to identify "*mechanically*" with "*causally, or probabilistically*." But what does "causally, or probabilistically" mean? Does he want to say "*predetermined or accidental*," or "*universal or probabilistic*"? In

the first case, he confronts us with the problem of whether there is a
third possibility (cf. section 14.7); in the second case, with the question of what form statements about intentional acts can have if they are
neither universal (causal, deterministic) nor probabilistic. Then, obviously, they can only be *singular* subject-predicate statements or *existential*
statements. (Of course, the predicate can be polyadic – as, for example "*x* is the father of *y*" – and the subject term can be formed with a
functor – as, for example, "the product of 2 and 18 is a square number.") Accordingly, they cannot express any regular association, and this
means that they can neither explain something nor make it intelligible.
Rather, they merely describe singular events. The assumption that statements about intentional acts are neither universal nor probabilistic would
make the humanities purely idiographic disciplines. They could only state
events.

Another consequence is even more serious. If the assumption that
someone in some situation had an intention (of kind) *I* is to explain
(or make intelligible) the fact that in this situation his behaviour was
(of kind) *B*, then the following condition must be satisfied: In view of
intention *I*, we would rather expect behaviour *B*; or more precisely, the
conditional probability of *B*, given *I*, is greater than the absolute probability of *B*. Accordingly, whoever asserts both that some intention *I leads
to*, or at least *favours*, behaviour *B* and that *I* and *B* are nevertheless *statistically independent* of each other *contradicts* himself. If, on the other hand,
intention *I* and behaviour *B* are not statistically independent of each
other, then there is at least a *probabilistic*, possibly even a *deterministic,
dependence*. Therefore the reference to probabilistic or deterministic associations is not able to distinguish between *mechanical behaviour* (probabilistic or deterministic) and *intentional action* (neither probabilistic nor
deterministic). (For the problem of free will – or free intention – see
section 14.7.)

If Popper's attempt at distinguishing between mechanical behaviour
and intentional action fails, what still speaks in favour of his assumption of
mental entities? He could argue that there actually *is* a mentalistic theory
that explains the descriptive function of language using the hypothesis
of mental entities, whereas there is *no* physicalistic theory explaining the
same without any reference to intentions. But the latter claim (there is no
such physicalistic theory) would be trivial, as Popper defines "describing"
and "arguing" by reference to "intention" and "intention" by reference
to "mind"; and the former (there actually is such a mentalistic theory)
would be false, for there is still no explicitly formulated mentalistic theory,

much less a well-corroborated one, but only problems and terminological proposals, at best fragmentary sketches of theories.

We may have overlooked something important, for Popper writes: "Whether a person does in fact describe or argue,..., depends on whether he speaks intentionally *about* something" (CR, 295). Does his result depend on the emphasized word "about"? Does he share Brentano's view that *directedness to a content* is common to all acts of consciousness, and that this distinguishes them from physical processes? If Popper wants to say that only someone who directs an act of consciousness at something can describe it, then this *intentionality* entails the same problems as do our intentions. Is it *inconceivable* that someone can describe something without directing an act of consciousness at it, or is it *inconceivable* that this act of consciousness is a particular, very complex physical process? Then the machine would not describe for reasons of *linguistic usage* alone, and Popper would have to explain what speaks in favour of this usage. But he does not attempt to do this. If, on the other hand, either is *conceivable*, then the hypothesis that one or the other is *factually impossible* would have to be *empirically* corroborated before he could turn it against his opponent. But Popper does not remark on this point either.

There is still another problem. Anyone who, like Popper, postulates that intentions can *only* be *mentalistically* grasped will have to assume that someone may have an intention while in his brain there is no corresponding physiological state or process. What is intended here is not a process interacting with the intention. Rather, what is meant is that the intention neither *is* itself a brain process nor is *correlated* with a brain process in such a way that it could be identified by means of this process. But in order to defend his postulate, he would first have to show that there are in fact mental intentions without corresponding physiological processes. The same holds as well of intentionality. Hence the core of the machine argument is a *petitio principii*.

15.42. The Evolution of Human Language

On the basis of this philosophy of language and his theory of evolution, Popper later formulates the following main theses:

(1) "Man is distinguished from animals through ... the higher functions of his language, the '*descriptive*' or 'informative' function, and the '*argumentative*' or 'critical' function."

As opposed to this, animal languages contain only the "*expressive*" and the "*communicative*" functions (KBMP, 81; OK, 235f.). While these (latter) lower functions are merely *dispositional* in both man and animal, the (former) higher functions "*transcend* the region of dispositions, and so become basic for the third world" (KBMP, 81, i.a.). This results in the following layers:

3 – products (such as books, stories, myths: language)
2 – dispositions of the organism
1 – physical states

Popper's second main thesis draws conclusions from the existence of the higher functions of language:

(2) As the higher functions transcend the region of dispositions, the "imaginative power of man can . . . evolve in entirely new ways."

For, having invented descriptive language, man can make true and false statements, *invent* stories, "develop an entirely new kind of imaginative world," and give *explanations* (KBMP, 81). "Stories, myths, and explanatory theories are the first characteristic inhabitants of world 3" (82). Then Popper seems to take a step back: "They are followed by picture stories, such as reports of a hunt, as found in caves."

But could not *all* functions of language be dispositional? Then at least world 3 would be dispensable. And could not dispositions be physical states or processes in the organism? Then world 1 alone would be sufficient.

Popper now turns to "*the evolution of the specific human functions of language*": "Animal languages, including [the lower functions of] human languages, may be regarded as kinds of *subjective knowledge* – that is, as *dispositions to behave* in a certain way. They may also be regarded as something *physical* and *objective* – as *exosomatic tools*, tools developed outside the body, comparable to nests" (KBMP, 82, i.a.). Products of animal behaviour like these all have a genetic base, and some of them also have a traditional component (82). They may be considered "*animal third worlds*"; they are predecessors of the human world 3, and are equally *autonomous* (83, i.a.). This exposition is followed by two more main theses:

(3) "All animal knowledge is dispositional. And though some of these dispositions develop by *imitation* – that is by *tradition*, which admittedly comes near to objective knowledge – there is a gulf between this and human objective knowledge" (83, i.a.).

Thus objective knowledge is one of the few biological facts that sharply distinguish between animal and man:

(4) Among the exosomatic tools that man has developed, only the "specifically human functions of language which make *objective* [i.a.] knowledge possible *do* have a highly specific and... hereditary basis." (83)

From these four theses, Popper concludes that evolution has given us something specifically human – "a genetically based instinct to acquire, by imitation, a specifically human language which is fit to be the carrier of objective knowledge" (84).

Obviously, human language is far more efficient than any animal language. However, what empirical evidence shows that no animal produces something like *intersubjective* knowledge? After all, Popper admits that even bees can *describe* directions and distances (KBMP, 87). And what well-corroborated empirical theory supports the assumption of a world 3 – in particular, a specifically human world 3? Popper's strict distinction between man and animal seems only to disguise an old prejudice in terms of language philosophy. On the other hand, it is easy to see the *biological importance of the evolution of a descriptive language* (89). For example, bees can, using information obtained by their scouts – their *intersubjective* and in this sense *objective* knowledge – gather food much more efficiently, for the descriptions are sufficiently precise – and hence also *objective* insofar as they *correspond to reality*. Specifically human, no doubt, is the claim to differ not just incrementally but fundamentally from (other) animals.

15.43. The Ideas of Truth and Validity

Popper finally turns to "the development of the *regulative ideas* of objective *truth* and *validity*" (KBMP, 90, i.a.). He now resumes his earlier epistemological considerations. The idea of objective truth is already contained, even if in a confused way, in the idea of *subjective truthfulness* (90f.). Though the *idea of truth* pertains to stories and theories, descriptions and informations, it emerges only where there are arguments and criticism. For to say that a theory is true or false means to evaluate it critically. Just as the idea of truth relates to the descriptive or informative function of language, the *idea of validity* relates to the argumentative or critical function. For to call an argument or a criticism valid or invalid means to evaluate it critically (92).

According to Popper, "the descriptive function cannot *fully* develop without the critical function," for "only with the . . . critical function can *negation* [i.a.] . . . develop" (KBMP, 90). But what can it mean to say that an object has a particular property, if it is not yet possible to say that the object does *not* have this property? From a biological point of view, the argumentative function is still developing "and not so well entrenched in our heredity as the others." However, the critical and argumentative use of language has an obvious biological advantage: It "allows us to *let theories die in our stead*" (90, i.a.).

Also, "[t]he *objectivity* of the third [descriptive] level [of language] is only achieved when the fourth [argumentative] level comes into action" (KBMP, 99, i.a.). Therefore, Popper considers splitting the third level into two levels, "namely the '*not yet objectivized descriptive*' and the '*objectivized descriptive*'" (99, i.a.). Bees attain only the former, human beings the latter as well. Accordingly, subjects of statements are objectivized only if we do not simply state them but also *argue* about them. Obviously, this is a stronger version of "objectivity" in the sense of "intersubjectivity."

Popper uses the word "*emerge*" to express the notion that the ideas of truth and validity appear or develop on the argumentative level and that the argumentative function evolves from the descriptive function (KBMP, 91). Obviously, he wants to say that in both cases the appearance of the new cannot be explained by our knowledge of the old. This is obviously correct if he means only the knowledge that is *actually* available at the time of the appearance of the new. But he seems to mean as well that the new cannot *in principle* be explained. Possibly he even means that the new is completely *independent* of the old. But these are metaphysical hypotheses.

In the context of the idea of truth, Popper returns to *Tarski's definition of truth* (KBMP, 96ff.; cf. section 6.2). Tarski has designed a method of defining suitable concepts of truth in formalized languages, and he has shown how we can, with all due caution, apply the concept of truth even to natural languages (96; cf. Keuth 1978a,b). His proposal has an important consequence: "Although there is truth, there is no *criterion* of truth." But Popper adds: "If it did exist, we would all be omniscient"; and conversely: "Since we are not omniscient, there cannot be a criterion of truth" (96). But we would not be omniscient even if we had a criterion of truth applicable to all statements of all languages, because our limited life span would prevent us from applying it to all statements.

Popper also repeats his thesis that Tarski rehabilitated the correspondence theory of truth: "Tarski says very simply: the statement . . . 'Snow is white' ... *corresponds to the facts* if, and only if, snow is white" – and so on for all other statements (KBMP, 103, i.a.). According to Popper, "[t]his *explains corresponding to the facts quite generally*"; thus Tarski has shown "that we can give a definition of 'correspondence to the facts' for any given artificial language," and this "establishes very fully" both what "correspondence to the facts" means and what "truth" means (104, i.a.). We can only repeat that Tarski nowhere explains what "correspondence to the facts" means (cf. section 6.3).

15.5. INTERACTION AND CONSCIOUSNESS

Popper is primarily interested in the *body-mind problem*. The ideas of a *world 3* and of an *emergent evolution* as well as his theory of the *evolution of language* are the principal means by which he attempts to solve this problem. In Chapter 5 of *Knowledge and the Body-Mind Problem*, he outlines his solution. Though it cannot be compared to a physical theory, it is "a *testable* theory, and it has *passed some tests* in a way which has exceeded all [his] expectations" (KBMP, 105, i.a.). However, he admits that he is offering something "only in comparison with certain earlier [philosophical theories]" (105), which he considers "*false*, even though they are *irrefutable*" (106).

15.51. Monistic Theories

First Popper criticizes monistic theories, and he starts with *mentalistic monism*. One of its variants is *solipsism*, which says: "*Only I exist*, everything else is my dream." Though this theory is irrefutable, it is false and even silly. Nevertheless, there are no conclusive arguments against it, only ad hominem arguments (KBMP, 106f.). One of them says: "When I hear the music of a great composer, *I am conscious* of the fact that I would not be capable of composing it. But if only I exist, then, in dreaming it, I am its composer." Therefore, Popper thinks that "in order to believe seriously in solipsism, one would have to be a megalomaniac" (107). But what is megalomeniacal about the solipsist's dreaming that he hears music *he doesn't think he is capable* of composing?

Another variant, Berkeley's *idealism*, says: "[O]nly *minds* exist, and ... the existence of bodies and of a material world is a kind of dream which is, due to God's intervention, dreamt by all minds in unison" (KBMP, 107). Popper hopes to shake the bishop "by another *ad hominem* argument: his theory is incompatible with Christianity ... [which] teaches the reality of bodily suffering" (108). But owing to God's intervention, the minds only *dream* of bodies and their sufferings.

Both solipsism and idealism solve the body-mind problem by asserting that there are no bodies. But *materialism, physicalism,* and *radical behaviourism* solve it by the opposite stratagem. (Popper does not always strictly distinguish among these variants of materialistic monism.) They assert: "*Only bodies* (or physical states, or events) *exist,*" and they deny the existence of minds and of mental states. *Materialistic monism* is, like mentalistic monism, irrefutable. Therefore, Popper also addresses an ad hominem argument to the physicalist. He asks him: "'To whom do you address your theory? To my body? Or to my... behaviour?...It cannot possibly be your purpose to convince *me...*'" (KBMP, 108, i.a.). And he asserts that physicalism "denies *the obvious* – that is, the existence of mental states, or consciousness" (109, i.a.). But what makes their existence obvious? In order to counter Popper's argument, the physicalist need only answer: "I address my statement to your brain" or perhaps "to certain processes in your brain."

15.52. Dualistic Theories

Not only the monistic but also the well-known dualistic theories are problematic. *Descartes'* theory, for example, asserts that mental and physical states interact. Therefore, it is called "*interactionism.*" But as physical states are located in space and time, we may ask *where* the interaction takes place. According to Descartes, it takes place in the pineal gland. This thesis "has been much ridiculed," but Popper is going to "propose a very similar answer" (KBMP, 109). According to him, the interaction takes place in the speech centre of the brain (cf. sections 15.53, 15.61).

Spinoza proposes an alternative to interactionism. He takes the universe to be a single infinite substance with the dual attributes (or aspects) of thought (mind) and extension (matter). This is the simplest and best-known form of "'body-mind *parallelism.*'" In Popper's words, it says: "[I]f we look at reality from inside, it is mind, and if we look at reality from outside, it is matter" (KBMP, 109). According to Popper, this theory is ingenious and may be true, but it implies "that an electron is invested with consciousness" (109). Spinoza would probably reject this interpretation, but Popper now objects that electrons "can have no *memory* whatever," because "according to quantum physics all electrons are exactly alike" and must therefore be "unaffected by their history" (109f.). As a "consciousness without any memory... would be totally different from what we call 'consciousness,'" Popper cannot take parallelism seriously (110).

More serious is *epiphenomenalism*, which could be considered a variant of parallelism. It says "that minds do exist, but as epiphenomena" – that is, as irrelevant by-products of physical states or processes (KBMP, 110). Like Spinoza's parallelism, it takes the *physical world* to be "*closed* or complete" (i.a.) so "that in principle *everything* that can be explained at all can be explained in purely physical terms" (110).

But by his theory of world 3, Popper combats the idea that the physical world 1 is closed (KBMP, 110; cf. section 14.7). He believes:

The fact that there are objective problems, such as the problems of prime number theory, existing in world 3, together with the fact that the discovery of such a problem may lead to great and obvious changes in world 1, show…that world 1 is not closed or complete, but open towards world 3, with world 2 acting as intermediary. (110)

How does Popper know that these are *facts*? For the reasons given, epiphenomenalism must be false. Mind or consciousness cannot be an irrelevant by-product of physical states or processes (KBMP, 110f.). The *evolutionary approach* also speaks against it. Why should mind have evolved if it has no function (111)? There is a simple answer to this question: "Something enabling us to solve certain problems has evolved. There is, however, no reason to assume that it is not a physiological but a mental entity, a mind."

15.53. Popper's New Theory of the Mind and the Ego

Popper begins his new theory of the mind and the ego with the remark that the world 2 of consciousness is as inhomogeneous as world 1 or world 3. He then formulates more concrete conjectures, the first of which is basic (KBMP, 111):

(1) "To speak of body and mind is somewhat misleading, for there are many different *kinds and levels of consciousness* in the animal kingdom.

(2) We can distinguish between *full consciousness* – that is, the highest form of human consciousness – and lower forms, which may be vastly different" (111, i.a.).

But what is the biological significance of these various levels of consciousness? To this question Popper can only give a speculative answer, but he believes that some of his theses "have *testable consequences*" (111, i.a.)!

In order to explain the biological significance of consciousness, Popper introduces "the idea of a *hierarchy of controls*, and the idea of *plastic control*" (KBMP, 112; cf. section 14.7). In all higher organisms, there is a variety of controls regulating, for example, the heartbeat or the breathing; and there is a hierarchy among the controls. The highest position is held by the central control of the movements of an animal, and:

> (3) "[*M*]*ental states* are connected with this central and highest control system, and they help to make this system more *plastic*" (112, i.a.).

But what is plastic? A knee jerk is a case of "'non-plastic control'"; but where the reactions to a stimulus may differ considerably, Popper speaks of a "'plastic control'" (112). However, if we content ourselves with this sketchy explanation, and if we take into account the fact that this "plastic control" by no means must be deterministic, then it proves difficult to find any difference between "*plastic control*" and "*probabilistic causation*" (for the latter, cf. Eells 1991).

Now follow conjectures on the *emergent evolution of consciousness*: In animals, "first vague feelings emerge that reflect the expectation . . . of negative or positive events" (KBMP, 112). They "become feelings of pain and of pleasure." As they are mostly anticipatory, they in their turn "become the basis of a . . . system of interpretation or decoding of signals" that goes beyond the decoding by sense organs (112):

> (4) Thus world 2 may emerge from world 1,

and Popper claims he has already shown how world 3 ermerges from world 2. Misinterpretations, which often occur in unusual situations, lead to a wavering between different possible reactions, and from this "may evolve *anticipatory and tentative interpretations of a situation*" (113).

They are connected to "*the incipient innervation of movements*" and permit trying out possible reactions without actually carrying them out (KBMP, 113, i.a.). This is a decisive step, for the biological advantage of this process is that various possible modes of behaviour and their appropriateness to the given situation may be tried out without taking the risk of actual movements. But the process requires "a kind of *imagination*: the imagined anticipation of the expected result of the movements . . . and a consequent action. *This, then, is the way in which consciousness interacts with the body*" (113, i.a.). But nowhere does he show why this kind of imagination in particular, or this kind of consciousness in general, should be mental. Is this simply a matter of definition?

We now have a sketch of the *"general evolutionary background for [Popper's] new conjectural theory of the human mind and of the human ego"* (KBMP, 114, i.a.). According to this theory, the relation between *mental* and *physical* states is fundamentally the same as the relation between *controlling* and *controlled* systems. It is an interaction (114). But would any interaction do, or is this a special kind of interaction?

Human consciousness contains many relicts of lower forms of consciousness (KBMP, 114). It is also highly complex. Therefore, the well-known idea of a "stream of consciousness" is too simple. Undoubtedly, "we achieve full consciousness – or the highest state of consciousness – when we are *thinking* [i.a.], especially when we try to formulate our thoughts in the form of statements and arguments," and in "thinking articulately, we really *know* that we are conscious" (114).

Has Descartes' "I think, therefore I am" evolved into Popper's "I think articulately, therefore I know that I'm conscious"? But what does he mean? Can we unconsciously think articulately, or can we consciously think articulately without knowing that we are conscious? If neither is conceivable, then Popper, like Descartes, has made only an analytic statement.

Popper now formulates the five main theses of his *"theory of full consciousness and of the ego or the self"* (KBMP, 114f., i.a.):

(1) *Full consciousness* is *anchored in* world 3, the world of human language and of theories. It consists mainly of *thought processes*. The corresponding *thought contents belong to* world 3.

(2) The self, or the ego, is impossible without the intuitive understanding of certain world 3 theories and without taking them for granted. These theories are about space and time, about physical bodies in general, about people and their bodies, and about certain regularities of being awake or asleep. In other words, a self results from achieving a view of ourselves from outside, and thus from placing ourselves into an objective structure. This view presupposes a descriptive language.

(3) The *interaction* of the *self* with the *brain* takes place in the *speech centre*. This thesis is experimentally testable (115; cf. section 15.61).

(4) The self *plastically controls* some of our movements, which are therefore called *actions*. Some movements have been so well learned as to have sunk to the level of *unconscious control.*

(5) The *self* is not the highest control centre, since it is, in its turn, *plastically controlled by world 3 theories*. But this control is mutual, as we can change the controlling world 3 theories (115).

According to Popper, the emergent evolution has answered the question "whether there is an *interaction* between body and mind or a *parallelism.*" The new structures always interact with the physical structures from which they emerge; that is, the "controlling system interacts with the controlled system . . . , world 3 interacts with world 2 and through it with world 1" (115; on "plastic control," cf. section 14.7).

Although he presents these theses decisively, Popper sometimes fails to make a proper distinction between world 1 and world 2. When we acquire a capability – for example, riding a bicycle or playing the violin – there is a "process of becoming unconscious" (KBMP, 116). He comments: "[W]hen . . . everything connected with the technique of playing has sunk into the unconscious – or into the *physiology*, as I usually say – then you can concentrate on the presentation of the whole piece" (116). This may still be taken to mean that the conscious, world 2, has stored something like its records in physiology, world 1. But, to say the least, this interpretation is not supported by his apparently inconsistent statement "that skills which have been mastered, in so far as they are incorporated in our *physiology* [world 1], belong to this *second level*," world 2 (118, i.a.). Is this merely a lapse? After all, he admits, if only in the context of animal experiments, "*somehow something must be the carrier of these learned patterns*" (124, i.a.). If, however, human capabilities are not freely floating mental dispositions but have a physiological carrier, why does Popper not assume that they are physiological dispositions of this carrier? Obviously, it is more difficult to defend dualism than Popper thinks.

15.6. THE SELF, RATIONALITY, AND FREEDOM

In addressing a topic so vast, there is a danger of "degenerating into all kinds of vague generalizations" (KBMP, 129). Popper tries to avoid this by strictly organizing his argument.

15.61. The Self

Popper's central thesis on the ego or the self says that the self is anchored in world 3 and cannot exist without world 3 (KBMP, 129; cf. section 15.53). Before expounding the thesis more fully, he wants to clear away a problem that it seems to entail: How can world 3 be, roughly, the universe of the products of our mind, if our mind cannot exist without world 3? Popper believes that he has found a simple answer: "Our selves, the higher functions of language, and world 3 have all evolved and emerged together, in constant interaction. Thus there is no special difficulty here" (129).

But no matter how small he makes the steps of the evolution, he cannot solve the problem of why something could not possibly exist without *its own* product. Would it help if he contented himself with the thesis that nowadays an ego cannot exist without a product of a *predecessor*? This would presuppose either that at some time there was an ego that produced the first world 3 entity – that is, that could exist *without* such an entity – or that the first human ego depended on world 3 entities that were produced by Fichte's Ego (God) or by the non-Ego (nature).

As the self develops only with the higher – descriptive and argumentative – functions of language, Popper denies "that *animals* have . . . a conscious self" (KBMP, 129, i.a.). Their highly developed *spatial sense* is merely "the unconscious result of instinct combined with the results of spatial exploration." Animals and plants also have a *sense of time*. "They are . . . [even] conscious"! But they lack "the ability to see themselves as extending in time and space and as acting in time and space" (129f.). Popper provides no empirical basis, however, for these conjectures.

Instead, he develops a "*theory of animal anticipation*": Animals "anticipate movements of an enemy or prey . . . by a template effect, by a partial innervation of responding movements," which, according to Gomperz, is "represented in feelings" (KBMP, 130, i.a.). But partial innervations also occur in human beings. Their deliberate preparation plays an important part in competitive sports. What, then, is the decisive difference? A full (human) consciousness contains "a *knowledge* of ourselves stretching back in time," and our sense of location contains a "history of how we came to the place in which we are located" (130, i.a.).

But how does Popper know that even animals, which are nearly as complex as we are, completely lack this knowledge? After all, the relative stability of hierarchies of animal groups speaks against the assumption that animals have no knowledge of their stretching back in time. And a rat that has mastered a labyrinth knows the way leading to the food; it has a "cognitive map."

The knowledge of ourselves stretching back in time has the form of "dispositions to recall the past to our consciousness" (KBMP, 130). They are linked with other dispositions directed toward theories of space, of time, and of physical bodies. We see ourselves located in their frame. This gives our orientation "a *theoretical* character: *it depends upon descriptive language, and even on argumentative language*" (130). Thus the controlled recall of earlier experience "is made possible only through our links with

world 3 objects" (131). The role of memory in our conscious self is anchored in the world 3 of *criticizable knowledge in the objective sense*. Again,
Popper concludes that our ego is closely linked with the higher functions
of language: "And this suggests that *full consciousness interacts with the speech
centre of our brain*" (131, i.a.).

He adds three further theses. The first one summarizes what has already been said on the linguistic evolution of the species:

> (1) "In the evolution of the *species*, the ego or the self or self-
> consciousness emerges together with the higher functions of
> language – that is, the descriptive and the argumentative func-
> tions – and it interacts with these functions" (KBMP, 131).

To this thesis he adds nothing new.

> (2) "In the development of the *child*, the ego...develops with the
> higher functions of language, and therefore after the child has
> learned to express himself, and to communicate with other per-
> sons, and to understand his relations to other persons, and to
> adjust himself to his physical environment" (131).

On the second thesis he makes a few short remarks: The "common-sense
theory of knowledge is subjectivist and sensualist" (132). It is a "bucket
theory of the mind," which says that throughout our lifetime we "acquire
knowledge through our senses." Subjective idealists such as Berkeley believe that all knowledge consists of experiences, or of memories, is subjective. When speaking of experiences, they presuppose a self; and on
the basis of this self or of its thought contents, they "try to construct the
external world," including "other minds," but "they fail" (132).

As opposed to this, Popper considers it "a matter of psychological fact"
that in the development of a child the dispositional knowledge of the self
comes later than that of the external world and of "other persons and
other minds" (KBMP, 132). For the knowledge of the self is acquired together with descriptive and argumentative language. Therefore, animals
have knowledge only of the external world and of other persons, while
"the self emerges only on the human level" (132). But this "psychological
fact" is obviously merely a postulate of his language philosophy.

The third thesis is an alternative to Descartes' hypothesis of the pineal
gland (KBMP, 131f.):

> (3) "The self or the ego [world 2] is linked with the central control
> function of the brain [world 1] on the one hand, and it interacts

with world 3 objects on the other. In so far as it interacts with the brain, the *location of interaction* may be anatomically localizable. I suggest that the interaction is centred in the *speech centre* of the brain" (i.a.).

The main function of the self, or of consciousness [world 2], "is to establish a kind of remote and very plastic control of our speech centre [world 1] through world 3" (134, i.a.).

Popper takes his anatomical hypothesis of a mind-brain interaction in the speech centre to be empirically *testable* (KBMP, 132f.). He refers to observations of certain epilepsy patients whose "great cerebral commissure" – that is, the connection between the two hemispheres of the cerebrum – has been severed. Their speech centre is (mostly) in the left hemisphere, but what their left hand feels and what happens in the left half of their field of vision is represented in the right hemisphere. Thus their speech centre does not "learn" about it, as the commissure is severed. Consequently, these patients are unable to impart information about it. From this, Popper concludes that such tactile or optical sensations remain *unconscious* (133).

This does not, however, follow from Popper's assumptions alone, for it is conceivable that a split-brain patient is conscious in his right hemisphere of the movements of his left hand but cannot talk about it, because his speech centre does not "learn" about it. But let us assume, with Popper, that the speech centre is central for consciousness and that therefore we are conscious only of what is accessible to the left hemisphere. Nevertheless, an empirical examination of a split-brain patient relates only to his physiology or his behaviour. Hence reports of such an examination inform us only about world 1 events. Accordingly, they offer no clue whatsoever about the existence of a world 2 consciousness or even about an interaction between physiological processes in (or around) the speech centre and a mental consciousness. Hence Popper's thesis that the main function of consciousness is to establish a plastic control of our speech centre through world 3 remains entirely *metaphysical.*

15.62. Rationality

Popper cannot be numbered among those philosophers who define man as the rational animal. He considers rationality "not a property of men" but "a *task for men to achieve*" (KBMP, 134). For by "*rationality*" he means a critical attitude, "the readiness to learn from our mistakes" and to look consciously for mistakes and prejudices. In other words, rationality is "the attitude of conscious, critical, error elimination" (134).

However, "[a]ll *criticism* must be *piecemeal*," even revolutionary criticism in science (KBMP, 134, i.a.). Although our knowledge consists of numerous dispositions, expectations, and theories, we can at any given time consciously criticize only a few of them. In actual fact, we always *examine* only *one* theory *using part of the rest*, mostly unconsciously, as background knowledge. Insofar as we are conscious of the background knowledge used, we temporarily accept it uncritically for the purpose of the examination. For it is impossible to criticize all of our knowledge at once. As our subjective knowledge is mostly innate or handed down – that is, dispositional – it is not even explicitly formulated (135). For all these reasons, our criticism can be only piecemeal (136).

Hence the scope of our rationality is limited. But although we can deal only with one or two problems or theories at a time, there is no problem, no theory, no prejudice, and no element of our background knowledge that cannot be the object of our critical examination. Therefore, rationality is limited only insofar as we cannot criticize everything at the same time. On the other hand, we are far from being rational, and we are *fallible* not just with respect to everything we believe we know "but *even in our critical approach*" (KBMP, 136, i.a.). For we must *choose* the problems or theories that we want to criticize rationally, and the choice itself is a tentative conjecture. Hence we may waste a great deal of time on the wrong problem. But if we tried to do without all our fallible "knowledge," because it may contain prejudices, and to start again where Adam started, we probably would get no further than he did (136).

Popper now turns against "'*the myth of the framework*,'" according to which "all rational *argument* must always proceed within a *framework of assumptions* – so that the framework itself is always *beyond rational argument*" (KBMP, 137, i.a.). He takes this myth to be a variety of "'*relativism*'" – because it implies that every statement must be considered relative to a framework of assumptions – and he takes it to be "one of the great intellectual evils of our time," for "the alternative to critical discussion [including discussion of the framework] is violence and war," and vice versa (137, i.a.). Above all, the myth of the framework is false. It is an elaborate form of the doctrine that *rationality* consists in the *justification* of our assumptions. But this doctrine is untenable, for we cannot justify any theory – that is, show that it is true; we always justify only our "tentative *preference*" for one of the competing theories (138; cf. Chapter 5).

Some authors claim that individual frameworks are as different as individual languages. Therefore, those who have grown up in different frameworks cannot understand each other. Hence rational criticism is impossible (KBMP, 138). Kuhn (1962) is one of these authors. Wittgenstein also considers thought to be bound by language. He writes: "A *picture* held us captive. And we could not get outside it, for it lay in our language and language seemed to repeat it to us inexorably" (PI, 115). But he had proposed that we explore language in order to identify the problem and to dissolve it. Popper too proposes that we choose languages that are richer and less burdened with prejudices, and he demands that we criticize frameworks, for there is no basic difference between a framework and a theory. Though we cannot be sure that our attempts will succeed, they are always possible.

15.63. On Freedom and Responsibility

It is true that we are "the prisoners of our prejudices, or of our framework of assumptions" (KBMP, 139). But by using the world 3 method of formulating theories and other assumptions explicitly, so that they become criticizable, and by then criticizing them, we can "break out of this prison.... There is no question that we possess this *freedom*" (139, i.a.). Without it, our relation to world 3 could not be understood. If we hit on a world 3 object, we must first understand it. And in order to be able to prefer one theory to another, we must have understood *all* competing theories. There are also *degrees of understanding*. The lowest degree is the linguistic understanding of a theory (139). Then follows the understanding of the problem P_1 that it is to solve. Then we have to understand the various attempts at a solution – that is, the competing theories. Otherwise, we would not understand any of them, "since understanding, in this fuller sense, means appreciation, or appraisal" (140). Discovering the difficulties of the various theories – that is, the problems P_2 that they entail – is a still higher degree of understanding. This series may be continued indefinitely, for no theory offers an ultimate explanation. "All this means that there is a tremendous *range of freedom* in our relationship with world 3," and it becomes even greater "if we consider human *creativity*" (140, i.a.).

Popper's main thesis was "that all selves are anchored in world 3" (KBMP, 140). But this may be the case in many different ways. In almost everything we do, we explore world 3 and add to it. "And this means not only freedom but a great *responsibility*" (140, i.a.).

15.64. On Self-transcendence

Popper concludes his book "by discussing the relationship between a man and his work" (KBMP, 140). According to "the theory of self-expression," the quality of our work "depends only on our talents, on our psychological, and, perhaps, on our physiological states." Popper considers this theory "false, vicious, and depressing." According to his theory of world 3, there is no such unilateral relation but "a give-and-take interaction between a person and his work." The worker can grow with his work, do better work, and so on. In this process, the most active part of world 3 is "our own work, the product which we contribute to world 3" (140). Self-criticism may considerably increase this feedback. This interaction between our actions and their results, by which we transcend ourselves and our talents, is an astonishing characteristic of life, evolution, and mental growth: "This *self-transcendence* is the most striking and important fact of all life and all evolution. . . . It is contained in the move from P_1 to P_2" (141, i.a.).

Like children, theories become independent of their parents, and we may gain more knowledge from them than we put into them (KBMP, 141). We learn – our subjective knowledge grows – by *imaginative criticism*. We transcend "our local and temporal environment" by devising new test conditions, "*critical* situations," in order to detect and test our habitual assumptions and prejudices. Thus "we lift ourselves by our bootstraps out of the morass of our ignorance" (141). We test our possibilities almost entirely in world 3. To this end, we represent world 1 and world 2 in world 3 theories and thereby try to get nearer to the truth.

World 2 becomes "more and more the link between world 1 and world 3. All of our actions in world 1 are influenced by our world 2 grasp of world 3" (KBMP, 142). Therefore, it is impossible to understand the mind and the self without understanding world 3, or "to interpret either world 3 as a mere expression of world 2, or world 2 as a mere reflection of world 3." *Self-transcendence* is possible in all situations. We may fail, but we must never "give way to a feeling that we did not receive what was our due," for the world owes us nothing: "We all can participate in the heritage of man. We all can help to preserve it. And we all can make our own modest contribution to it. We must not ask for more" (142).

Résumé

It is impossible to pay tribute to Popper's extensive work in a few pages. But I will try to summarize what I think are its most important aspects. According to Popper, we advance knowledge by proposing bold hypotheses and testing them severely. My exposition of his philosophy adopts this idea and criticizes many of his theses. Thus the reader may ask: Is there anything that will last? However, becoming obsolete seems to be the fate of all theses. Hence any answer to this question will be only temporary. So what has lasted up to now?

ON METAPHYSICS

Let us begin with Popper's theory of three worlds (Chapter 15). He is not the first to postulate – in addition to the physical world – a second world of mental entities and a third world of objective thought contents, but he develops the idea of their evolutionary emergence. The idea of evolving capabilities is undoubtedly promising. But why should we assume that in the course of this evolution entities of a second and a third world emerge? Popper cannot show that this assumption explains anything that could not be explained without it. He primarily defends a traditional idea – body-mind dualism.

The same holds correspondingly of his argument for indeterminism (Chapter 14). He develops it with great intellectual effort, for he wants to save the ideas of free will, responsibility, and creativity. Nevertheless, he admits that it is only an ad hominem argument. As indeterminism is not enough for his purposes, he postulates that the physical world is open to influences from both the mental world and the world of objective

327

thought contents. But not only is the idea of "openness" problematic – because of the conservation principles – it also cannot solve the problem of the creation of new causes. Therefore, the problem of free will, which Hume discussed more sensibly, cannot be solved either.

Like other philosophers, Popper does not succeed in defining the concept of natural necessity (Chapter 13). But in the methodology of his *Logic*, this idea is dispensable, anyhow. Obviously, he only reifies the concept of a most general theory.

ON SOCIAL PHILOSOPHY

Popper's *Open Society* is intended to be both a theory and a defence of democracy (Chapter 11). According to him, democracy is a procedure that permits us to replace governments without bloodshed. Where this is not possible by means of recurrent elections, there is no democracy. While other authors charge the concept of democracy with ideas of "social democracy" and "political participation," Popper singles out this unrenouncable core (section 11.7).

His political philosophy has been severely criticized. He may not always correctly interpret the texts of his false prophets Plato (11.1), Hegel (11.3), and Marx (11.4). But which interpretation is correct? At any rate, the interpretation of Plato proposed by Popper's most severe critic does not seem preferable. For, according to Gadamer, Popper's critique of Plato stems from the misconception that Plato has to be taken at his word. But if, as Gadamer writes, Plato's chief work is one single myth, then Western philosophy is but a collection of footnotes (Whitehead) to a myth that has been mistaken for a theory. Popper may well overestimate the importance of "essentialism" and "historicism," especially since both concepts are his own constructs. Only Marx's philosophy of history is undoubtedly historicist in Popper's sense.

We do not need *The Open Society* to recognize how the works of Plato and Marx are well suited to support fascist and communist totalitarianism, respectively. It is more difficult to judge to what extent these authors intended to further totalitarian rule. But we must give Popper credit for reminding us of the suitability of their works to this purpose. For even nowadays we cannot be sure that among philosophers it is disreputable to have justified Stalin's terror and never to have withdrawn that judgement.

Because of the devastating consequences of "utopian social engineering," which – with reference to Marx – was to change society as a whole, Popper – in *The Poverty of Historicism* (Chapter 10) – proposes "piecemeal social engineering" (section 10.3). This reduces the risk of irreversible false decisions resulting from our lack of knowledge. But his logical refutation of the assumption that the course of history can be rationally predicted depends on his unrealistic demand for perfectly accurate predictions (10.2).

Popper defends the "unity of method," the thesis that research in both the sciences and the humanities is empirical (10.1). Scientific problem solving is to him the paradigm of decision making in everyday life and in politics. In this respect, he follows Max Weber. But his theses on some peculiarities of the humanities – for example, on the "autonomy of sociology," "situational logic," and the "zero method" – are less fortunate.

ON THE PHILOSOPHY OF SCIENCE

Popper's most important achievements are his contributions to the philosophy of science. He develops the Vienna Circle's neoempiricism further into critical rationalism. Here we can comment only very briefly on his philosophy of science, for the exposition of its problems cannot be shortened at will.

Popper's proposals to improve the frequency theory of probability appeared only shortly after Kolmogorov had published his set theoretical axiomatization of probability theory. Due to Kolmogorov's success, there was not much interest in Popper's proposals, only some of which were actual improvements. Popper's propensity interpretation of probability, and above all his idea that physical forces are special propensities, are purely metaphysical (Chapter 8).

He makes it clear that truth (Chapter 6) and approximation to truth (verisimilitude) (Chapter 7) are regulative ideas. On the other hand, his theses on the correspondence theory of truth and his definition of verisimilitude are not tenable. He examines the problem of the corroboration of theories and shows its difficulties (Chapter 5). But as he refuses to call well-corroborated hypotheses "true," at least temporarily, he arouses suspicion of being a covert inductivist. Neither does he succeed in proving that the degree of corroboration cannot be a probability.

His solution to the problem of the empirical basis ends the debate on protocol sentences (Chapter 4). But the conventionalism of this solution is unnecessary and unfortunate. His thesis of the "transcendence inherent in any description" gives a sufficient reason for the fallibility of all statements. Thus he repeats by means of linguistic analysis a result that Helmholtz had reached by physiological investigation (sections 4.2, 4.5).

Methodology (Chapter 3) is a necessary complement to the criterion of demarcation. Hempel and Oppenheim developed Popper's exposition of scientific explanation and prediction into the deductive nomological model (Chapter 2).

Popper separates the criterion of the scientific character of a statement from the criterion of its meaning, and he replaces the verifiability criterion of the scientific character with his falsifiability criterion (section 1.2). As to the logical and methodological aspects of the problem of induction (1.1), he adopts Hume's position and works it out in detail. But he fails in his attempt to prove that Hume's idea of empirical induction is untenable for logical reasons. And his claim to have solved the problem of induction by pointing out that we invent new hypotheses and afterward test them is not justified.

In particular, his contributions to the problems of demarcation and of the empirical basis were milestones in the development of neoempiricism. His replacement of the idea of refutation with the idea of criticism may be even more important, for criticism can be directed not only against assumptions but also against claims, dispositions, and activities.

Undoubtedly, there are not only achievements but also failures, especially in Popper's late work, which is predominantly metaphysical. But what does this prove, after all? Popper (and the author of these lines) considers Immanuel Kant to be the greatest German philosopher. Kant claims that his "transcendental philosophy" provides certain knowledge not only about the conditions of the possibility of any empirical knowledge but also about some objects of science. But it had been known long before Kant that such claims are untenable. So Kant's criticism is not at all a synthesis of empiricism and rationalism but a relapse into rationalistic metaphysics. This is not to detract from Kant's merits but to relativize our criticism of Popper.

Certainly, Kant's work is the zenith of German enlightenment. This speaks both in favour of Kant and against the culture of Germany, which did not permit of more enlightenment. The restrictedness of German enlightenment cannot be attributed to the political situation at Kant's time alone, for even after two world wars the culture in Germany is still impregnated with the German Idealists' belief in spirits. This is one of the reasons why in the Federal Republic the philosophy of the neo-Marxist "Frankfort School" gained great influence, while the empiricist philosophy of the "Vienna Circle" did not.

Bibliography

Ackermann, Robert John (1976). *The Philosophy of Karl Popper.* Amherst, MA.

Adorno, T. W., Albert, H., Dahrendorf, R., Habermas, J., Pilot, H., and Popper, K. R. (1969/1976). *Der Positivismusstreit in der deutschen Soziologie.* Neuwied / Berlin, 1969. / *The Positivist Dispute in German Sociology.* Translated by G. Adey and D. Frisby. London, 1976.

Agassi, Joseph (1963). *Towards a Historiography of Science.* The Hague.

Agassi, Joseph (1991). "Popper's Demarcation of Science Refuted." *Methodology and Science,* 24, 1–7.

Agassi, Joseph (1993). *A Philosopher's Apprentice: In Karl Popper's Workshop.* Amsterdam / Atlanta, GA.

Agassi, Joseph, and Jarvie, Ian C., eds. (1987). *Rationality: The Critical View.* Dordrecht.

Agassi, J., Ravets, J., Burgoyne, B., and Blackburn, R. (1995). "Karl Popper, 1902–1994." *Radical Philosophy,* 70, 2–8.

Albert, Hans (1964/1976). "Der Mythos der totalen Vernunft. Dialektische Ansprüche im Lichte undialektischer Kritik." *Kölner Zeitschrift für Soziologie und Sozialpsychologie,* 16, 225–236. Reprinted in Adorno et al. 1969, 193–234. / "The Myth of Total Reason: Dialectical Claims in the Light of Undialectical Criticism." In Adorno et al. 1976, 163–197.

Albert, Hans (1965/1976). "Im Rücken des Positivismus. Dialektische Umwege in kritischer Beleuchtung." *Kölner Zeitschrift für Soziologie und Sozialpsychologie,* 17, 879–908. Reprinted in Adorno et al. 1969, 267–305. / "Behind Positivism's Back: A Critical Illumination of Dialectical Digressions." In Adorno et al. 1976, 226–257.

Albert, Hans (1968/1985). *Traktat über kritische Vernunft.* Tübingen, 1968. *Treatise on Critical Reason.* Princeton, NJ, 1985.

Albert, Hans (1971). *Plädoyer für kritischen Rationalismus.* München.

Albert, Hans (1972). *Konstruktion und Kritik. Aufsätze zur Philosophie des kritischen Rationalismus.* Hamburg.

Albert, Hans (1978). *Traktat über rationale Praxis.* Tübingen.

Albert, Hans (1982). *Die Wissenschaft und die Fehlbarkeit der Vernunft.* Tübingen.

Albert, Hans (1986). *Freiheit und Ordnung. Zwei Abhandlungen zum Problem einer offenen Gesellschaft.* Tübingen.

Albert, Hans (1987). *Kritik der reinen Erkenntnislehre. Das Erkenntnisproblem in realistischer Perspektive.* Tübingen.

Albert, Hans (1990). "Der Mythos des Rahmens am Pranger: Anderssons Antwort auf die wissenschaftsgeschichtliche Herausforderung." *Zeitschrift für Philosophische Forschung,* 44, 85–97.

Albert, Hans (2000). *Kritischer Rationalismus. Vier Kapitel zur Kritik illusionären Denkens.* Tübingen.

Albert, Hans, ed. (1964). *Theorie und Realität. Ausgewählte Aufsätze zur Wissenschaftslehre der Sozialwissenschaften.* Tübingen.

Albert, Hans, and Salamun, Kurt, eds. (1993). *Mensch und Gesellschaft aus der Sicht des Kritischen Rationalismus.* Amsterdam / Atlanta, GA.

Alt, Jürgen August (1982). *Die Frühschriften Poppers.* Frankfurt am Main.

Alt, Jürgen August (1992). *Karl R. Popper.* Frankfurt / New York.

Andersson, Gunnar (1988). *Kritik und Wissenschaftsgeschichte. Kuhns, Lakatos' und Feyerabends Kritik des Kritischen Rationalismus.* Tübingen.

Andersson, Gunnar (1998). "Basisprobleme." In Keuth 1998, 145–164.

Aristotle (1966a). *Topica.* With an English translation by E. S. Forster. London / Cambridge, MA.

Aristotle (1966b). *Posterior Analytics.* With an English translation by Hugh Tredennick. London / Cambridge, MA.

Aristotle (1968). *The Metaphysics,* 6th ed. With an English translation by Hugh Tredennick. London / Cambridge, MA.

Ayer, Alfred Jules (1954). "The Terminology of Sense Data." In his *Philosophical Essays,* London, 66–104.

Ayer, Alfred Jules, ed. (1959). *Logical Positivism.* Toronto. Paperback edition: New York, 1966.

Barbosa de Oliveira, Marcos (1988). "Against Demarcation." *The Journal of Non-Classic Logic,* 5, 21–48.

Bartley, William W., III (1962). *The Retreat to Commitment.* New York.

Bartley, William W., III, and Radnitzky, Gerard, eds. (1987). *Evolutionary Epistemology, Theory of Rationality, and the Sociology of Knowledge.* La Salle, IL.

Bernard, Claude (1865). *Introduction à la Médecine expérimentale.* Paris. Translated into English by H. C. Greene as *An Introduction to Experimental Medicine,* New York, 1949.

Black, Joseph (1803). *Lectures on the Elements of Chemistry.* Edinburgh.

Bohnen, Alfred, and Musgrave, Alan, eds. (1991). *Wege der Vernunft, Festschrift zum siebzigsten Geburtstag von Hans Albert.* Tübingen.

Boyle, Edward (1974). "Karl Popper's *Open Society:* A Personal Appreciation." In Schilpp 1974, II, 843–858.

Brockhaus Enzyklopädie, 19th ed. Mannheim, 1986–1994.

Bunge, Mario, ed. (1964). *The Critical Approach to Science and Philosophy: Essays in Honor of Karl Popper.* Glencoe, IL.

Burke, T. E. (1983). *The Philosophy of Karl Popper.* Manchester.

Bühler, Karl (1934). *Sprachtheorie. Die Darstellungsfunktion der Sprache.* Jena.

Carnap, Rudolf (1928/1967). *Der logische Aufbau der Welt.* Berlin, 1928. Third ed. Hamburg, 1966. / *The Logical Structure of the World and Pseudoproblems in Philosophy.* Berkeley, 1967.

Carnap, Rudolf (1932a/1959). "Überwindung der Metaphysik durch logische Analyse der Sprache." *Erkenntnis,* 2, 1932, 219–241. / "The Elimination of Metaphysics through Logical Analysis of Language." Translated by Arthur Pap. In Ayer 1959, 60–81.

Carnap, Rudolf (1932b/1995). "Die physikalische Sprache als Universalsprache der Wissenschaft." *Erkenntnis,* 2 (1932), 432–465. / *The Unity of Science.* Translated and with an introduction by Max Black. London, 1934; reprinted: Bristol, 1995.

Carnap, Rudolf (1932c/1987). "Über Protokollsätze." *Erkenntnis,* 3 (1932/33), 215–228. "On Protocol Sentences." *Noûs,* 21, (1987), 457–470.

Carnap, Rudolf (1934/1937). *Logische Syntax der Sprache.* Wien, 1934. Second edition 1968. / *The Logical Syntax of Language.* Translated by Amethe Smeaton. London, 1937.

Carnap, Rudolf (1935). "Popper, Karl: Logik der Forschung. Zur Erkenntnistheorie der modernen Naturwissenschaft" (review). *Erkenntnis,* 5, 290–294.

Carnap, Rudolf (1950). *Logical Foundations of Probability.* Chicago.

Carnap, Rudolf (1961). *Introduction to Semantics* and *Formalization of Logic,* 2nd printing. Cambridge, MA.

Carnap, Rudolf (1966). *Philosophical Foundations of Physics.* Edited by Martin Gardner. New York / London. Republished as *An Introduction to the Philosophy of Science,* New York, 1995.

Cicero (1968). *Topics.* Translated by H. M. Hubbell. London / Cambridge, MA.

Chalmers, A. F. (1976). *What Is This Thing Called Science?* St. Lucia, Queensland.

Clark, Peter (1995). "Popper on Determinism." In O'Hear 1995, 149–162.

Colodny, Robert G., ed. (1965). *Beyond the Edge of Certainty: Essays in Contemporary Science and Philosophy.* Englewood Cliffs, NJ.

Colodny, Robert G., ed. (1970). *The Nature and Function of Scientific Theories: Essays in Contemporary Science and Philosophy.* Pittsburgh.

Cornforth, Maurice (1968). *The Open Philosophy and the Open Society: A Reply to Dr. Karl Popper's Refutations of Marxism.* London.

Currie, Gregory, and Musgrave, Alan, eds. (1985). *Popper and the Human Sciences.* Dordrecht.

Dahms, Hans-Joachim (1991). "Der Positivismusstreit der 6oer Jahre: eine merkwürdige Neuauflage." *Jahrbuch für Soziologie-Geschichte,* 119–182.

Dahms, Hans-Joachim (1994). *Positivismusstreit: Die Auseinandersetzungen der Frankfurter Schule mit dem logischen Positivismus, dem Pragmatismus und dem kritischen Rationalismus.* Frankfurt am Main.

Descartes, René (1983). *Principles of Philosophy.* Translated by Valentine Rodger Miller and Reese P. Miller. Dordrecht / Boston / London. Original edition: *Principia Philosophiae,* 1644.

Dingler, Hugo (1921). *Physik und Hypothese. Versuch einer induktiven Wissenschaftslehre.* Berlin / Leipzig.

Döring, Eberhard (1987). *Karl Popper. Einführung in Leben und Werk.* Hamburg.

Duhem, Pierre (1906/1962). *La théorie physique, son objet et sa structure.* Paris, 1906. / *The Aim and Structure of Physical Theory.* Translated by Philip P. Wiener from the second French edition of 1914. New York, 1962.

Düsberg, Klaus Jürgen (1998). "Bemerkungen zur Quantenmechanik." In Keuth 1998, 215–234.

Eccles, John C. (1970). *Facing Reality: Philosophical Adventures by a Brain Scientist.* Berlin / Heidelberg.

Eccles, John C. (1973/1975). *The Understanding of the Brain.* New York, 1973. / *Das Gehirn des Menschen. Sechs Vorlesungen für Hörer aller Fakultäten.* München / Zürich, 1975.

Eccles, John C. (1979). *The Human Mystery.* (The Gifford Lectures, University of Edinburgh, 1977–1978.) Berlin / Heidelberg / New York.

Eccles, John C., and Popper, Karl R. (1977). *The Self and Its Brain: An Argument for Interactionism.* Berlin / Heidelberg / London / New York.

Eells, Ellery (1991). *Probabilistic Causality.* Cambridge, UK.

Eisler, Rudolf (1979). *Kant-Lexikon.* Hildesheim / New York.

Enzyklopädie Philosophie und Wissenschaftstheorie, ed. Jürgen Mittelstraß. Vol. 1, A–G, Mannheim / Wien / Zürich, 1980; vol. 4, Sp–Z, Stuttgart / Weimar, 1996. [EPW]

Feigl, Herbert, and Meehl, Paul E. (1974). "The Determinism-Freedom and Body-Mind Problems." In Schilpp 1974, I, 520–559.

Feyerabend, Paul K. (1962). "Explanation, Reduction, and Empiricism." In H. Feigl and G. Maxwell, eds., *Minnesota Studies in the Philosophy of Science,* vol. 3: *Scientific Explanation, Space and Time,* Minneapolis, 28–97.

Feyerabend, Paul K. (1964). "Realism and Instrumentalism: Comments on the Logic of Factual Support." In Bunge 1964, 280–308.

Feyerabend, Paul K. (1965). "Problems of Empiricism." In Colodny 1965, 145–260.

Feyerabend, Paul K. (1970). "Problems of Empiricism, Part II." In Colodny 1970, 275–353.

Feyerabend, Paul K. (1975). *Against Method.* London.

Feynman, Richard P., Leighton, Robert B., and Sands, Matthew (1965). *The Feynman Lectures on Physics,* vol. 3: *Quantum Mechanics.* Reading, MA.

de Finetti, Bruno (1972). *Probability, Induction and Statistics: The Art of Guessing.* London / New York / Sydney / Toronto.

Fischer, Kurt Rudolf (1991). *Philosophie aus Wien.* Wien.

Fisz, Marek (1973). *Wahrscheinlichkeitsrechnung und mathematische Statistik.* Berlin.

Fleck, Ludwik (1935/1980), *Entstehung und Entwicklung einer wissenschaftlichen Tatsache.* Frankfurt am Main, 1980.

Frede, Dorothea (1997). "Die ungerechten Verfassungen und die ihnen entsprechenden Menschen." In Höffe 1997, 251–270.

Frege, Gottlob (1892/1966). "Sinn und Bedeutung." In *Zeitschrift für Philosophie und philosophische Kritik,* n.s. 100 (1892), 25–50. / "On Sense and Reference." In Peter T. Geach and Max Black, eds., *Translations from the Philosophical Writings of Gottlob Frege,* Oxford, 1966.

Fries, Jakob Friedrich (1807). *Neue oder anthropologische Kritik der Vernunft.* Heidelberg.

Gadamer, Hans-Georg (1934). "Plato und die Dichter." Reprinted in his *Gesammelte Werke*, vol. 5, Tübingen, 1985, 187–211.

Gadamer, Hans-Georg (1942). "Platos Staat der Erziehung." Reprinted in his *Gesammelte Werke*, vol. 5, Tübingen, 1985, 249–262.

Gadamer, Hans-Georg (1960). *Wahrheit und Methode. Grundzüge einer philosophischen Hermeneutik.* Tübingen.

Gadamer, Hans-Georg (1978). "Die Idee des Guten zwischen Plato und Aristoteles." Reprinted in his *Gesammelte Werke*, vol. 7, Tübingen, 1991, 128–227.

Gadamer, Hans-Georg (1983). "Platos Denken in Utopien. Ein Vortrag vor Philologen." Reprinted in his *Gesammelte Werke*, vol. 7, Tübingen, 1991, 270–289.

Gadenne, Volker (1998a). "Bewährung." In Keuth 1998, 125–144.

Gadenne, Volker (1998b). "Bewährung, Wahrheit und Akzeptanz von Theorien." In Gadenne 1998, 89–110.

Gadenne, Volker (1998c). "Spielarten des Duhem-Quine-Problems." *Logos*, n.s. 5, 117–148.

Gadenne, Volker, ed. (1998). *Kritischer Rationalismus und Pragmatismus.* Amsterdam.

Gadenne, Volker, and Wendel, Hans Jürgen, eds. (1996). *Rationalität und Kritik.* Tübingen.

Geier, Manfred (1992). *Der Wiener Kreis: Mit Selbstzeugnissen und Bilddokumenten.* Hamburg.

Geier, Manfred (1994). *Karl Popper.* Hamburg.

Gillies, Donald (1993). *Philosophy of Science in the Twentieth Century: Four Central Themes.* Oxford, UK / Cambridge, MA.

Gillies, Donald (1995). "Poppers's Contribution to the Philosophy of Probability." In O'Hear 1995, 103–120.

Gnedenko, B. W. (1968). *Lehrbuch der Wahrscheinlichkeitsrechnung.* Berlin.

Goodman, Nelson (1955). *Fact, Fiction, Forecast.* Cambridge, MA.

Grünbaum, Adolf (1989). "The Degeneration of Popper's Theory of Demarcation." *Epistemologia*, 12, 235–260.

Günther, Ulrich L. (1984). *Kritischer Rationalismus, Sozialdemokratie und politisches Handeln.* Weinheim.

Gutting, Gary (1980). "Science as Discovery." *Revue Internationale de Philosophie*, 131/2, 26–48.

Habermas, Jürgen (1963/1976). "Analytische Wissenschaftstheorie und Dialektik. Ein Nachtrag zur Kontroverse zwischen Popper und Adorno." In M. Horkheimer, ed., *Zeugnisse. Theodor W. Adorno zum sechzigsten Geburtstag*, Frankfurt am Main, 1963, 473–501. Reprinted in Adorno et al. 1969, 151–191. / "The Analytical Theory of Science and Dialectics: A Postscript to the Controversy Between Popper and Adorno." In Adorno et al. 1976, 131–162.

Habermas, Jürgen (1964/1976). "Gegen einen positivistisch halbierten Rationalismus. Erwiderung eines Pamphlets." *Kölner Zeitschrift für Soziologie und Sozialpsychologie*, 16, 1964, 636–659. Reprinted in Adorno et al. 1969, 235–266. / "A Positivistically Bisected Rationalism: A Reply to a Pamphlet." In Adorno et al. 1976, 198–225.

Habermas, Jürgen (1981/1989). *Theorie des kommunikativen Handelns.* Vol. 1, *Handlungsrationalität und gesellschaftliche Rationalisierung*; vol. 2, *Zur Kritik der funktionalistischen Vernunft.* Frankfurt am Main, 1981. / *The Theory of Communicative Action*, vol. 2: *Lifeworld and System: A Critique of Functionalist Reason.* Translated by Thomas McCarthy. Boston, MA, 1989.

Habermas, Jürgen (1984/2002). *Vorstudien und Ergänzungen zur Theorie des kommunikativen Handelns.* Frankfurt am Main, 1984. / *On the Pragmatics of Social Interaction: Preliminary Studies in the Theory of Communicative Action.* Translated by Barbara Fultner. Cambridge, MA, 2002.

Hacohen, Malachi Haim (2000). *Karl Popper – The Formative Years, 1902–1945: Politics and Philosophy in Interwar Vienna.* Cambridge, UK.

Haller, Rudolf (1993). *Neopositivismus: Eine historische Einführung in die Philosophie des Wiener Kreises.* Darmstadt.

Halmos, Paul R. (1950). *Measure Theory.* New York / Cincinnati / Toronto / London / Melbourne.

Hanson, Norwood Russell (1958). *Patterns of Discovery: An Inquiry into the Conceptual Foundations of Science.* Cambridge, UK.

Harding, Sandra G., ed. (1976). *Can Theories be Refuted? Essays on the Duhem–Quine Thesis.* (Synthese Library, vol. 81.) Dordrecht / Boston.

Helmholtz, Hermann (1867/1962). *Handbuch der physiologischen Optik*, vol. 3. Leipzig, 1867. / *Helmholtz's Treatise on Physiological Optics*, vol. 3. Translated from the third German edition (1910), edited by James P. C. Southall. New York, 1962.

Helmholtz, Hermann (1870). "Über den Ursprung und die Bedeutung der geometrischen Axiome." In Helmholtz 1998, 15–39.

Helmholtz, Hermann (1878). "Die Tatsachen in der Wahrnehmung." In Helmholtz 1998, 147–175.

Helmholtz, Hermann von (1998). *Schriften zur Erkenntnistheorie.* Commentary by Moritz Schlick and Paul Hertz, edited by Ecke Bonk. Wien / New York. Original edition 1921.

Hempel, Carl Gustav (1937). "Karl Popper, Logik der Forschung. Zur Erkenntnistheorie der modernen Naturwissenschaft." *Deutsche Literaturzeitung,* 58, no. 8, col. 309–314.

Hempel, Carl Gustav (1950). "Problems and Changes in the Empiricist Criterion of Meaning." *Revue Internationale de Philosophie,* 4, 41–63.

Hempel, Carl Gustav (1965). *Aspects of Scientific Explanation: And Other Essays in the Philosophy of Science.* New York / London.

Heuß, Alfred (1962). "Hellas." In: G. Mann and A. Heuß, eds., *Propyläen Weltgeschichte*, vol. 3, Berlin / Frankfurt / Wien, 69–400.

Hintikka, Jaakko, and Suppes, Patrick, eds. (1966). *Aspects of Inductive Logic.* Amsterdam.

Hintikka, Jaakko (1985). "True and False Logics of Scientific Discovery." *Communication & Cognition,* 18, 3–14.

Historisches Wörterbuch der Philosophie. Edited by Joachim Ritter and Karlfried Gründer. Vol. 1, A–C, Darmstadt, 1971; . . . vol. 11, U–V, 2001. [HWP]

Höffe, Otfried (1997). "Vier Kapitel einer Wirkungsgeschichte der *Politeia*." In Höffe 1997, 333–361.

Höffe, Otfried, ed. (1997). *Platon, Politeia.* Berlin.

Hoffmeister, Johannes, ed. (1955). *Wörterbuch der philosophischen Begriffe,* 2nd ed, Hamburg.

Horkheimer, Max (1933/1975). "Materialismus und Metaphysik." *Zeitschrift für Sozialforschung,* 2 (1933), 1ff. Reprinted in Horkheimer 1986, 65–94. / English translation in: Horkheimer, *Critical Theory,* translated by Mathew J. O'Connell, New York, 1975.

Horkheimer, Max (1937/1975). "Traditionelle und kritische Theorie." *Zeitschrift für Sozialforschung,* 6 (1937), 245ff. Reprinted in Horkheimer 1986, 12–64. / English translation in Horkheimer, *Critical Theory,* translated by Mathew J. O'Connell, New York, 1975.

Horkheimer, Max (1986). *Traditionelle und kritische Theorie. Vier Aufsätze.* Frankfurt am Main. First edition 1970.

Hospers, John (1946). "On Explanation." *The Journal of Philosophy,* 43, 337–356.

Howson, Colin (1995). "Theories of Probability." *The British Journal for the Philosophy of Science,* 46, 1–32.

Hume, David (1739–40/1978). *A Treatise of Human Nature,* ed. L. A. Selby-Bigge and P. H. Nidditch. Oxford, 2nd ed.

Hume, David (1748/1970). *An Enquiry Concerning Human Understanding.* In *Enquiries Concerning the Human Understanding and Concerning the Principles of Morals,* ed. L. A. Selby-Bigge, 2nd ed. 1902, impression of 1970, Oxford. [EHU]

Hume, David (1779/1990). *Dialogues Concerning Natural Religion,* edited by Martin Bell. London 1990.

Jarvie, Ian (2001). *The Republic of Science: The Emergence of Popper's Social View of Science 1935–1945.* Amsterdam / Atlanta.

Jarvie, Ian, and Pralong, Sandra, eds. (1999). *Popper's Open Society after Fifty Years: The Continuing Relevance of Karl Popper.* London / New York.

Johansson, Ingvar (1975). *A Critique of Karl Popper's Methodology.* Stockholm.

Kant, Immanuel. *The Cambridge Edition of the Works of Immanuel Kant in Translation.* Cambridge, 1992–2002.

Kant's Perpetual Peace: A Philosophical Proposal. Translated by Helen O'Brien, with an introduction by Jessie H. Buckland. London, 1927.

Kant, Immanuel (1953). *Prolegomena to Any Future Metaphysics That Will Be Able to Present Itself as a Science.* A translation from the German based on the original editions, with an introduction and notes by Peter G. Lucas. Manchester, reprinted 1971. [Proleg.]

Kant, Immanuel (1964). *Groundwork of the Metaphysic of Morals.* Translated and analysed by H. J. Paton. New York.

Kant, Immanuel (1997). *Critique of Pure Reason.* Translated and edited by Paul Gyer and Allen W. Wood. Cambridge, UK. [CPR]

Kaufmann, Walter A. (1951/1956). "The Hegel Myth and Its Method." *Philosophical Review,* 60 (1951), 459–486. / "Hegel: Legende und Wirklichkeit." *Zeitschrift für philosophische Forschung,* 10 (1956), 191–226.

Kaufmann, Walter (1965). *Hegel. A Reinterpretation.* New York. Anchor Books edition: New York 1966.

Kelly, K. (1987). "The Logic of Discovery." *Philosophy of Science*, 54, 435–452.

Keuth, Herbert (1974a). "Objective Knowledge out of Ignorance: Popper on Body, Mind, and the Third World." *Theory and Decision*, 5, 391–412.

Keuth, Herbert (1974b). "Deontische Logik und Logik der Normen." In H. Lenk, ed., *Normenlogik: Grundprobleme der deontischen Logik*, Pullach 64–88.

Keuth, Herbert (1976). "Verisimilitude or the Approach to the Whole Truth." *Philosophy of Science*, 43, 311–336.

Keuth, Herbert (1978a). *Realität und Wahrheit: Zur Kritik des kritischen Rationalismus*. Tübingen.

Keuth, Herbert (1978b). "Tarski's Definition of Truth and the Correspondence Theory." *Philosophy of Science*, 45, 420–430.

Keuth, Herbert (1978c). "Methodologische Regeln des kritischen Rationalismus. Eine Kritik." *Zeitschrift für allgemeine Wissenschaftstheorie*, 9, 236–255.

Keuth, Herbert (1989). *Wissenschaft und Werturteil. Zu Werturteilsdiskussion und Positivismusstreit*. Tübingen.

Keuth, Herbert (1993). *Erkenntnis oder Entscheidung. Zur Kritik der kritischen Theorie*. Tübingen.

Keuth, Herbert (1996). "Rationalität und Wahrheit." In V. Gadenne and H. J. Wendel, eds., *Rationalität und Kritik*, Tübingen, 79–97.

Keuth, Herbert, ed. (1998). *Karl Popper. Logik der Forschung*. Berlin.

Keuth, Herbert (2000). *Die Philosophie Karl Poppers*. Tübingen.

Kiesewetter, Hubert (2001). *Karl Popper – Leben und Werk*. Eichstätt.

Kirkham, Richard L. (1992). *Theories of Truth: A Critical Introduction*. Cambridge, MA.

Kneale, William C. (1949). *Probability and Induction*. Oxford.

Kneale, William C. (1974). "The Demarcation of Science." In Schilpp 1974, 205–217.

Kobusch, Theo, and Mojsisch, Burkhard, eds. (1997). *Platon in der abendländischen Geistesgeschichte*. Darmstadt.

Kolmogorov, Andrej. N. (1933/1956). *Grundbegriffe der Wahrscheinlichkeitsrechnung*. Berlin. / *Foundations of the Theory of Probability*, 2nd ed. New York.

Kraft, Victor (1950/1953). *Der Wiener Kreis. Der Ursprung des Neopositivismus. Ein Kapitel der jüngsten Philosophiegeschichte*. Wien, 1950; 3rd ed. 1997. / *The Vienna Circle*. New York, 1953.

Kraft, Victor (1974). "Popper and the Vienna Circle." In Schilpp 1974, I, 185–204.

Kripke, Saul Aaron (1975). "Outline of a Theory of Truth." *The Journal of Philosophy*, 72, 690–716.

Kuhn, Thomas Samuel (1962). *The Structure of Scientific Revolutions*. Chicago.

Kuhn, Thomas Samuel (1970). "Logic of Discovery or Psychology of Research?" In Lakatos and Musgrave 1970, 1–23.

Kuipers, Theo A. F., ed. (1987). *What Is Closer-to-the-Truth? A Parade of Approaches to Truthlikeness*. Amsterdam.

Lakatos, Imre (1970). "Falsification and the Methodology of Scientific Research Programmes." In Lakatos and A. Musgrave 1970, 91–195.

Lakatos, Imre (1976). *Proofs and Refutations: The Logic of Mathematical Discovery*. Edited by J. Worrall and E. Zahar. London.

Lakatos, Imre (1978). *The Methodology of Scientific Research Programmes*. Edited by J. Worrall and G. Currie. Cambridge, UK.

Lakatos, Imre, ed. (1968), *The Problem of Inductive Logic*. (Proceedings of the International Colloquium in the Philosophy of Science, London, 1965, vol. 2.) Amsterdam.

Lakatos, Imre, and Musgrave, Alan, eds. (1968). *Problems in the Philosophy of Science*. (Proceedings of the International Colloquium in the Philosophy of Science, London, 1965, vol. 3.) Amsterdam.

Lakatos, Imre, and Musgrave, Alan, eds. (1970). *Criticism and the Growth of Knowledge*. (Proceedings of the International Colloquium in the Philosophy of Science, London, 1965, vol. 4.) Cambridge, UK.

Leblanc, Hugues (1989). "The Autonomy of Probability Theory (Notes on Kolmogorov, Rényi, and Popper)." *The British Journal for the Philosophy of Science*, 39, 167–181.

Lenin, Wladimir Iljitsch (1970). *Materialismus und Empiriokritizismus. Kritische Bemerkungen über eine reaktionäre Philosophie, Leipzig*. 1st ed. 1909, German ed. 1927.

Levinson, Paul, ed. (1982). *In Pursuit of Truth: Essays on the Philosophy of Karl Popper on the Occasion of His 80th Birthday*. Atlantic Highlands, NJ.

Levinson, Ronald B. (1953). *In Defense of Plato*. Cambridge, MA.

Lewis, David (1973). "Causation." *The Journal of Philosophy*, 70, 556–567.

Lührs, G., Sarrazin, T., Spreer, F., and Tietzel, M., eds. (1975). *Kritischer Rationalismus und Sozialdemokratie*. Berlin / Bonn-Bad Godesberg.

Lutz, Heinrich (1964). "Der politische und religiöse Aufbruch Europas im 16. Jahrhundert." In G. Mann and A. Nitschke, eds., *Propyläen Weltgeschichte*, vol. 7, Berlin / Frankfurt / Wien, 25–132.

Maaß, Otto, ed. (1934). *Platons Staat, Velhagen & Klasings Sammlung lateinischer und griechischer Schulausgaben*. Text, Teil 1–3, Kommentar, Teil 1–3. Bielefeld und Leipzig.

Mach, Ernst (1886/1959). *Die Analyse der Empfindungen und das Verhältnis des Physischen zum Psychischen*. Leipzig, 1886. / *The Analysis of Sensations and the Relation of the Physical to the Psychical*. Translated by C. M. Williams, revised and supplemented from the fifth German edition by S. Waterlow. New York, 1959.

Mach, Ernst (1905). *Erkenntnis und Irrtum. Skizzen zur Psychologie der Forschung*. Leipzig. Reprint of the fifth edition of 1926, Darmstadt 1968.

MacKay, Donald M. (1967). *Freedom of Action in a Mechanistic Universe*. Cambridge, UK.

Magee, Bryan (1973). *Karl Popper*. Glasgow.

Magee, Bryan (1985). *Philosophy and the Real World: An Introduction to Karl Popper*. La Salle, IL. (Revised version of Magee 1973.)

Maxwell, Grover (1974). "Corroboration without Demarcation." In Schilpp 1974, I, 292–321.

Maxwell, Nicholas (1972). "A Critique of Popper's Views on Scientific Method." *Philosophy of Science*, 39, 131–152.

McLaughlin, Robert (1982). "Invention and Induction: Laudan, Simon and the Logic of Discovery." *Philosophy of Science*, 49, 198–211.

Meehl, Paul A. (1970). "Psychological Determinism and Human Rationality: A Psychologist's Reactions to Professor Karl Popper's 'Of Clouds and Clocks.'" In H. Feigl and G. Maxwell, eds., *Minnesota Studies in the Philosophy of Science*, vol. 4: *Analyses of Theories and Methods of Physics and Psychology*, Minneapolis, 310– 372.

Michalos, A. C. (1971). *The Popper–Carnap Controversy*. The Hague.

Miller, David (1994). *Critical Rationalism: A Restatement and Defence*. Chicago / La Salle.

Miller, David (1995). "Propensities and Indeterminism." In O'Hear 1995, 121– 147.

Miller, David (1983). *A Pocket Popper*. London. U.S. ed. 1985.

Miller, David (1997). "Sir Karl Raimund Popper, C.H., F.B.A., 28 July 1902 – 17 September 1994." *Biographical Memoirs of Fellows of the Royal Society, London*, 43, 367–409.

Milne, Peter (1995). "A Bayesian Defence of Popperian Science?" *Analysis*, 55, 213–215.

Mises, Richard von (1928/1981). *Wahrscheinlichkeit, Statistik und Wahrheit*. Wien, 1928. / *Probability, Statistics and Truth*. Dover edition. New York, 1981.

Mises, Richard von (1951). *Positivism: A Study in Human Understanding*. Cambridge, MA. Dover edition: New York, 1968.

Moore, George Edward (1953). *Some Main Problems of Philosophy*, London.

Musgrave, Alan (1988). "Is There a Logic of Scientific Discovery?" *LSE Quarterly*, 2, 205–227.

Musgrave, Alan (1993a). "Popper on Induction." *Philosophy of the Social Sciences*, 23, 516–527.

Musgrave, Alan (1993b). *Common Sense, Science and Scepticism: A Historical Introduction to the Theory of Knowledge*. Cambridge, UK, 1993. / *Alltagswissen, Wissenschaft und Skeptizismus. Eine historische Einführung in die Erkenntnistheorie*. Tübingen, 1993.

Musgrave, Alan (1998). "Explanation, Description and Scientific Realism." In Keuth 1998, 83–102.

Musgrave, Alan (1999). *Essays in Realism and Rationalism*. Amsterdam / Atlanta.

Musgrave, Alan, and Lakatos, Imre, eds. (1970). *Criticism and the Growth of Knowledge*. (Proceedings of the International Colloquium in the Philosophy of Science, London, 1965, vol. 4.) Amsterdam.

Musgrave, Alan, and Currie, Gregory, eds. (1985). *Popper and the Human Sciences*. Dordrecht.

Musgrave, Alan, and Bohnen, Alfred, eds. (1991). *Wege der Vernunft. Festschrift zum siebzigsten Geburtstag von Hans Albert*. Tübingen.

Nau, Heino Heinrich, ed. (1996a). *Der Werturteilsstreit. Die Äußerungen zur Werturteilsdiskussion im Ausschuß des Vereins für Sozialpolitik (1913)*. Marburg.

Nau, Heino Heinrich (1996b), "'Zwei Ökonomien'. Die Vorgeschichte des Werturteilsstreits in der deutschsprachigen Ökonomik." In Nau 1996a, 9–64.

Neurath, Otto (1932/1959). "Protokollsätze." *Erkenntnis* 3, 204–214. / "Protocol Sentences." In Ayer 1959, 199–208.

Neurath, Otto (1935/1983). "Pseudorationalismus der Falsifikation." *Erkenntnis* 5, 353–365 (review of Popper, *Logik der Forschung*). / "Pseudorationalism of 'Falsification.'" In his *Philosophical Papers*, edited and translated by R. S. Cohen and Marie Neurath, Boston, 1983, 121–131.

Nickles, Thomas (1990). "Discovery Logics." *Philosophica*, 45, 7–32.

Niiniluoto, Ilkka (1987). *Truthlikeness*. Dordrecht.

Nilsson, Jonas (2000). *Rationality in Inquiry: On the Revisability of Cognitive Standards*. Stockholm.

Nola, Robert (1987). "The Status of Popper's Theory of Scientific Method." *The British Journal for the Philosophy of Science*, 38, 441–480.

O'Hear, Anthony (1992). *Karl Popper*. London and New York. (First edition 1980.)

O'Hear, Anthony, ed. (1995). *Karl Popper: Philosophy and Problems*. Cambridge, UK.

Osei, Joseph (1994). "Plato's Theory of Change: A Popperian Reconstruction and Its Significance for Traditional and Emerging Democracies." *International Journal for Applied Philosophy*, 8, 39–48.

Passmore, John A. (1960). "Popper's Account of Scientific Method." *Philosophy*, 35, 326–331.

Passmore, John (1967). "Logical Positivism." In *The Encyclopedia of Philosophy*, vol. 5, New York / London, 52–57.

Peirce, Charles Sanders (1960). *Collected Papers of Charles Sanders Peirce*, vols. 5 and 6, ed. Charles Hartshorne and Paul Weiss. Cambridge, MA. [CP]

Pietruska-Madej, Elzbieta (1985). "Should Philosophers of Science Consider Scientific Discovery?" *Ratio*, 27, 7–18.

Plato (1988). *The Laws*. Translated, with notes and an interpretive essay, by Thomas L. Pangle. Chicago / London.

Plato (1990). *Werke* [Works]. Special edition of the *Wissenschaftliche Buchgesellschaft*, Darmstadt. German translation of *The State* [Republic] (vol. 4) by Friedrich Schleiermacher, of *The Laws* (vol. 8) by Klaus Schöpsdau (vol. 8/1) and by Klaus Schöpsdau and Hieronymus Müller (vol. 8/2).

Plato (1993). *Republic*. Translated by Robin Waterfield. Oxford / New York.

Pöggeler, Otto (1997). "Ein Streit um Platon: Heidegger und Gadamer." In Kobusch and Mojsisch 1997, 241–254.

Poincaré, Henri (1902/1952). *La Science et l'Hypothèse*. Paris, 1902. / *Science and Hypothesis*. New York, 1952.

Poincaré, Henri (1905/1958). *La Valeur de la Science*. Paris, 1905. / *The Value of Science*. New York, 1958.

A complete *Bibliography of the Writings of Karl Popper*, up to 1974, compiled by Troels Eggers Hansen, is contained in Schilpp, ed., *The Philosophy of Karl Popper*, 1974 [PKP], vol. 2, 1200–1287. A selected bibliography with publications up to 1984 is contained in Popper, *Ausgangspunkte*, 1984, 335–349. A selected bibliography with publications up to 1998, compiled by Helmut Zenz, is contained in Kiesewetter, *Karl Popper – Leben und Werk*, 2001, 134–168.

Popper, Karl R. (1933/1959). "Ein Kriterium des empirischen Charakters theoretischer Systeme." *Erkenntnis*, 3, 426f. / "A Criterion of the Empirical Character of Theoretical Systems." In Popper (1959) [LSD], 312–314.

Popper, Karl R. (1935/1959). *Logik der Forschung. Zur Erkenntnistheorie der modernen Naturwissenschaft.* Wien, 1935; 2nd ed., Tübingen, 1966 [LdF]. / *The Logic of Scientific Discovery.* New York, 1959 [LSD].

Popper, Karl R. (1938). "A Set of Independent Axioms for Probability." *Mind*, 47, 275–277.

Popper, Karl R. (1940). "What is Dialectic." *Mind*, 49, 403–426. Reprinted in *Conjectures and Refutations* [CR], 1963, 312–335.

Popper, Karl R. (1945). *The Open Society and Its Enemies.* Vol. 1, *The Spell of Plato*; vol. 2, *The High Tide of Prophecy: Hegel, Marx, and the Aftermath.* London, 1945; 4th ed. 1962. [OS]

Die offene Gesellschaft und ihre Feinde. Vol. 1, *Der Zauber Platons*, Bern, 1957; vol. 2, *Falsche Propheten. Hegel, Marx und die Folgen*, Bern, 1958; 7th ed. Tübingen, 1992. [OG]

Popper, Karl R. (1949a). "Naturgesetze und theoretische Systeme." In S. Moser, ed., *Gesetz und Wirklichkeit*, Innsbruck / Wien. Reprinted in Albert 1964, 87–102.

Popper, Karl R. (1949b). "Towards a Rational Theory of Tradition." In *The Rationalist Annual.* Reprinted in Popper 1963, 120–135.

Popper, Karl R. (1953). "Language and the Body-Mind Problem: A Restatement of Interactionism." *Proceedings of the 11th International Congress of Philosophy*, 7. Reprinted in Popper 1963, 293–298.

Popper, Karl R. (1955a). "A Note on the Body-Mind Problem." *Analysis*, n.s., 15. Reprinted in Popper 1963, 299–303.

Popper, Karl R. (1955b). "Two Autonomous Axiom Systems for the Calculus of Probabilities." *The British Journal for the Philosophy of Science*, 6, 51–57.

Popper, Karl R. (1957). *The Poverty of Historicism.* London, 1957. Routledge paperback of the 2nd ed. 1961. [PH]

Das Elend des Historizismus. Tübingen, 1965; 6th ed. 1987. [EH]

Popper, Karl R. (1957a). "The Aim of Science." *Ratio*, 1, no. 1, 24–35. Reprinted in Popper 1972, 191–205.

Popper, Karl R. (1957b). "The Propensity Interpretation of the Calculus of Probability, and the Quantum Theory." In S. Körner, ed., *Observation and Interpretation*, London, 65–70, 88–89.

Popper, Karl R. (1959). "The Propensity Interpretation of Probability." *The British Journal for the Philosophy of Science*, 10, 25–42.

Popper, Karl R. (1963). *Conjectures and Refutations: The Growth of Scientific Knowledge.* London, 5th rev. ed. 1989. [CR]

Popper, Karl R. (1966). *Of Clouds and Clocks: An Approach to the Problem of Rationality and the Freedom of Man.* St. Louis, MO. Reprinted in Popper 1972, 206–255.

Popper, Karl R. (1968a). "Epistemology without a Knowing Subject." In B. van Rootselaar and J. F. Staal, eds., *Proceedings of the Third International Congress for Logic, Methodology and Philosophy of Science*, Amsterdam, 333–373. Reprinted in Popper 1972, 106–152.

Popper, Karl R. (1968b). "On the Theory of the Objective Mind." In *Akten des XVI. Internationalen Kongresses für Philosophie*, Wien. Reprinted in Popper 1972, 153–190.

Popper, Karl R. (1972). *Objective Knowledge: An Evolutionary Approach.* Oxford. [OK]

Popper, Karl R. (1974a). "Intellectual Autobiography." In Schilpp 1974, vol. 1, 3–181. [A]

Popper, Karl R. (1974b). "Replies to My Critics." In Schilpp 1974, vol. 2, 961–1197.

Popper, Karl R. (1979). *Die beiden Grundprobleme der Erkenntnistheorie,* ed. Troels Eggers Hansen. Tübingen. [GPE]

Popper, Karl R. (1981). "The Present Significance of Two Arguments of Henri Poincaré." *Methodology and Science,* 14, 260–264.

Popper, Karl R. (1982). *Quantum Theory and the Schism in Physics.* From the *Postscript to the Logic of Scientific Discovery,* ed. W. W. Bartley III. Totowa, NJ. [QTSP]

Popper, Karl R. (1982). *The Open Universe: An Argument for Indeterminism.* From the *Postscript to the Logic of Scientific Discovery,* ed. W. W. Bartley III. Totowa, NJ. [OU]

Popper, Karl R. (1983). *Realism and the Aim of Science.* From the *Postscript to the Logic of Scientific Discovery,* ed. W. W. Bartley III. London. Reprinted 1994. [RAS]

Popper, Karl R. (1984). *Ausgangspunkte. Meine intellektuelle Entwicklung.* Hamburg; paperback ed. 1994.

Popper, Karl R. (1984/1992). *Auf der Suche nach einer besseren Welt. Vorträge und Aufsätze aus dreißig Jahren.* München, 1984. / *In Search of a Better World: Lectures and Essays from Thirty Years.* London / New York, 1992.

Popper, Karl R. (1990). *A World of Propensities.* Bristol. [WP]

Popper, Karl R. (1994a). *The Myth of the Framework: In Defence of Science and Rationality,* ed. M. A. Notturno. London / New York.

Popper, Karl R. (1994b). *Knowledge and the Body-Mind Problem: In Defence of Interaction,* ed. M. A. Notturno. London / New York. [KPMB]

Popper, Karl R. (1994/1999). *Alles Leben ist Problemlösen. Über Erkenntnis, Geschichte und Politik.* München / Zürich, 1994. / *All Life Is Problem Solving.* Translated by Patrick Camiller. London / New York, 1999. [LP]

Popper, Karl R., and Eccles, John C. (1977). *The Self and Its Brain: An Argument for Interactionism.* Berlin / Heidelberg / London / New York.

Popper, Karl R., and Kreuzer, Franz (1982). *Offene Gesellschaft – offenes Universum. Ein Gespräch über das Lebenswerk des Philosophen.* Wien.

Popper, Karl R., and Lorenz, Konrad (1985). *Die Zukunft ist offen. Das Altenberger Gespräch.* München / Zürich.

Preston, John (1995). "Has Poincaré's Conventionalism Been Refuted? (On Donald Gillies, 'Philosophy of Science in the Twentieth Century')." *Ratio,* 8, 193–200.

Putnam, Hilary (1962). "The Analytic and the Synthetic." In Herbert Feigl and Grover Maxwell, eds., *Minnesota Studies in the Philosophy of Science,* vol. 3: *Scientific Explanation, Space and Time,* Minneapolis, 358–397.

Putnam, Hilary (1974). "The 'Corroboration' of Theories." In Schilpp 1974, [PKP] I, 221–240.

Quine, Willard Van Orman (1961). *From a Logical Point of View: Logico-Philosophical Essays.* 2nd rev. ed. New York.

Quine, Willard Van Orman (1961a). "Two Dogmas of Empiricism." In Quine 1961, 20–46.

Quine, Willard Van Orman (1970). *Philosophy of Logic.* Englewood Cliffs, NJ.

Quine, Willard Van Orman (1974). "On Popper's Negative Methodology." In Schilpp 1974, [PKP] I, 218–220.

Radnitzky, Gerard (1995). *Karl R. Popper.* Sankt Augustin.

Radnitzky, Gerard, and Andersson, Gunnar, eds. (1980). *Fortschritt und Rationalität der Wissenschaft.* Tübingen.

Radnitzky, Gerard, and Andersson, Gunnar, eds. (1981). *Voraussetzungen und Grenzen der Wissenschaft.* Tübingen.

Radnitzky, Gerard, and Bartley, William W. III, eds. (1987). *Evolutionary Epistemology, Theory of Rationality, and the Sociology of Knowledge.* La Salle, IL.

Reichenbach, Hans (1935). "Über Induktion und Wahrscheinlichkeit. Bemerkungen zu Karl Poppers 'Logik der Forschung.'" *Erkenntnis,* 5, 267–284.

Reichenbach, Hans (1951). *The Rise of Scientific Philosophy.* Berkeley / Los Angeles.

Rényi, A. (1971). *Wahrscheinlichkeitsrechnung,* 3rd ed. Berlin.

Ruelland, Jacques G. (1991). *De l'épistémologie à la politique: La philosophie de l'histoire de Karl R. Popper.* Paris.

Russell, Bertrand (1913). "On the Notion of Cause." *Proceedings of the Aristotelian Society,* 13, 126ff. Reprinted in *The Collected Papers of Bertrand Russell,* vol. 6, London / New York, 1992, 190–210.

Russell, Bertrand (1919). *An Introduction to Mathematical Philosophy,* 2nd ed. London / New York.

Russell, Bertrand (1945). *A History of Western Philosophy.* London.

Ryle, Gilbert (1947). "*The Open Society and Its Enemies.* By K. R. Popper." *Mind,* 56, 167–172.

Salamun, Kurt, ed. (1989). *Karl R. Popper und die Philosophie des kritischen Rationalismus. Zum 85. Geburtstag von Karl R. Popper,* Amsterdam / Atlanta, GA.

Salamun, Kurt, ed. (1991). *Moral und Politik aus der Sicht des Kritischen Rationalismus.* Amsterdam / Atlanta, GA.

Savary, Claude (1995). "Discovery and Its Logic: Popper and the 'Friends of Discovery.'" *Philosophy of the Social Sciences,* 25, 318–344.

Schilpp, Paul A., ed. (1949). *Albert Einstein: Philosopher-Scientist.* (The Library of Living Philosophers, vol. 7.) New York.

Schilpp, Paul A., ed. (1974). *The Philosophy of Karl Popper.* (The Library of Living Philosophers, vol. 15.). Books I and II. La Salle, IL. [PKP]

Schlick, Moritz (1925/1985). *Allgemeine Erkenntnislehre,* 2nd ed. Berlin, 1925; paperback edition Frankfurt, 1979. / *General Theory of Knowledge.* Translated by A. Blumberg. La Salle, IL, 1985.

Schlick, Moritz (1930). "Die Wende der Philosophie." *Erkenntnis,* 1, 4–11.

Schlick, Moritz (1931/1979). "Die Kausalität in der gegenwärtigen Physik." *Die Naturwissenschaften,* 19 (1931), 145–162. / "Causality in Contemporary Physics." In *Moritz Schlick: Philosophical Papers,* ed. H. L. Mulder and B. van de Velde-Schlick, vol. 2, Boston, 1979, 176–209.

Schlick, Moritz (1933/1959). "Über das Fundament der Erkenntnis." *Erkenntnis,* 4 (1933/34), 77–99. / "The Foundation of Knowledge." In Ayer 1959, 209–227.

Schroeder-Heister, Peter (1998). "Wahrscheinlichkeit." In Keuth 1998, 185–213.

Schubert, Andreas (1995). *Platon: 'Der Staat'. Ein einführender Kommentar.* Paderborn.

Schurz, Gerhard (1998). "Das Problem der Induktion." In Keuth 1998, 25–40.

Schurz, Gerhard, and Weingartner, Paul (1987). "Verisimilitude Defined by Relevant Consequence-elements." In Kuipers 1987, 47–77.

Seiler, Martin, and Stadler, Friedrich, eds. (1994). *Heinrich Gomperz, Karl Popper und die österreichische Philosophie.* Amsterdam / Atlanta, GA.

Settle, Tom (1989). "Van Rooijen and Mayr versus Popper: Is the Universe Causally Closed?" *The British Journal for the Philosophy of Science,* 40, 389–403.

Settle, Tom (1990). "Swann versus Popper on Induction: An Arbitration." *The British Journal for the Philosophy of Science,* 41, 401–405.

Sextus Empiricus (1955). *Outlines of Pyrrhonism.* With an english translation by the Rev. R. G. Bwy. London / Cambridge, MA.

Sherif, Muzafer, and Sherif, Carolyn W. (1956). *An Outline of Social Psychology,* rev. ed. New York / Evanston, IL.

Shearmur, Jeremy (1996). *The Political Thought of Karl Popper.* London / New York.

Simkin, Colin (1993). *Popper's Views on Natural and Social Science.* Leiden / New York / Köln.

Simon, Herbert A. (1973). "Does Scientific Discovery Have a Logic?" *Philosophy of Science,* 40, 471–480. Reprinted in Keuth 1998, 235–248.

Simon, Herbert A. (1977). *Models of Discovery.* Dordrecht.

Skirbekk, Gunnar (1977). *Wahrheitstheorien. Eine Auswahl aus den Diskussionen über Wahrheit im 20. Jahrhundert.* Frankfurt am Main.

Spinoza, Baruch (1670). *Tractatus theologico-politicus,* anonymously published in Hamburg (really: Amsterdam). *Tractatus Theologico-Politicus,* ed. Gebhardt, 1925, translated by S. Shirley, Leiden, 1991.

Stegmüller, Wolfgang (1971). "Das Problem der Induktion: Humes Herausforderung und moderne Antworten." In H. Lenk, ed., *Neue Aspekte der Wissenschaftstheorie,* Braunschweig, 1971, 13–74.

Stove, David C. (1982). *Popper and After: Four Modern Irrationalists.* Oxford / New York / Toronto / Sydney / Paris / Frankfurt.

Swann, Andrew J. (1988). "Popper on Induction." *The British Journal for the Philosophy of Science,* 39, 367–373.

Tarski, Alfred (1936/1956). "Der Wahrheitsbegriff in den formalisierten Sprachen." *Studia Philosophica,* vol. 1, Leopoli, 1936, 261–405. / "The Concept of Truth in Formalized Languages." In his *Logic, Semantics, Metamathematics: Papers from 1923 to 1938,* Oxford, 1956, 152–278.

Tarski, Alfred (1944). "The Semantic Conception of Truth and the Foundations of Semantics." *Philosophy and Phenomenological Research,* 4, 341–375. Reprinted in *The Philosophy of Language,* 2nd ed., ed. A. P. Martinich, New York, 1990, 48–71.

Teichmann, Jürgen (1983). *Wandel des Weltbildes.* Darmstadt.

Ter Hark, Michel (1993). "Problems and Psychologism: Popper as the Heir to Otto Selz." *Studies in the History and Philosophy of Science,* 24, 585–609.

Thagard, Paul (1988). *Computational Philosophy of Science.* Cambridge, MA.

Tichý, Pavel (1974). "On Popper's Definitions of Verisimilitude." *The British Journal for the Philosophy of Science,* 25, 155–160.

Topitsch, Ernst, ed. (1965). *Logik der Sozialwissenschaften*, Köln / Berlin; Athenäum Taschenbuch: Königstein 1984.

Turney, Peter (1991). "A Note on Popper's Equation of Simplicity with Falsifiability." *The British Journal for the Philosophy of Science*, 42, 105–109.

Ule, Andrej (1994). "Rationality of Science." *Acta Analytica*, 9, 135–144.

Verein, Ernst Mach, ed. (1929/1973). *Wissenschaftliche Weltauffassung: Der Wiener Kreis*. Wien, 1929. / *The Scientific Conception of the World: The Vienna Circle*. Dordrecht, 1973.

Vetter, Hermann (1967). *Wahrscheinlichkeit und logischer Spielraum. Eine Untersuchung zur induktiven Logik*. Tübingen.

Waismann, Friedrich (1930–31). "Logische Analyse des Wahrscheinlichkeitsbegriffs." *Erkenntnis*, 1, 228–248.

Warnock, G. J. (1960). "The Logic of Scientific Discovery. By Karl R. Popper." *Mind*, 69, 99–101.

Watkins, John W. N. (1978). *Freiheit und Entscheidung*. Tübingen.

Watkins, John W. N. (1984/1992). *Science and Scepticism*. Princeton, NJ, 1984. *Wissenschaft und Skeptizismus*. Tübingen, 1992.

Weingartner, Paul, and Schurz, Gerhard. "Verisimilitude Defined by Relevant Consequence-elements." In Kuipers 1987, 47–77.

Wettersten, John R. (1992). *The Roots of Critical Rationalism*. Amsterdam / Atlanta, GA.

Wild, John (1953). *Plato's Modern Enemies and the Theory of Natural Law*. Chicago.

Wild, John (1974). "Popper's Interpretation of Plato." P. A. Schilpp, ed. 1974, [PKP] II, 859–875.

Windelband, Wilhelm (1900). *Platon*. Stuttgart.

Windelband, Wilhelm (1980). *Lehrbuch der Geschichte der Philosophie*, 17th ed. Tübingen. (First edition 1892.)

Wittgenstein, Ludwig (1921/1922). *Logisch-philosophische Abhandlung*. In *Annalen der Naturphilosophie*, 1921. / *Tractatus Logico-Philosophicus*. London, 1922, fourth impression 1949.

Wittgenstein, Ludwig (1953/1960). *Philosophical Investigations*. Translated by G. E. M. Anscombe. Oxford, 1953. / *Philosophische Untersuchungen*. In his *Schriften*, Frankfurt am Main, 1960. [PI]

Zahar, Elie G. (1983). "Logic of Discovery or Psychology of Invention?" *The British Journal for the Philosophy of Science*, 34, 243–261.

Zahar, Elie G. (1989). *Einstein's Revolution: A Study in Heuristic*. La Salle, IL.

Zahar, Elie G. (1995). "The Problem of the Empirical Basis." In A. O'Hear, ed., *Karl Popper: Philosophy and Problems*, Cambridge, UK, 45–74.

Index of Names

Index of Subjects

Bold page numbers indicate that the reference is of special importance.

3 5282 00606 2205